A NEW
DICTIONARY
OF THE
SOCIAL SCIENCES

A NEW DICTIONARY OF THE SOCIAL SCIENCES

Second Edition

Edited by
G. Duncan Mitchell

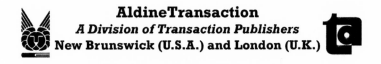

AldineTransaction
A Division of Transaction Publishers
New Brunswick (U.S.A.) and London (U.K.)

First paperback printing 2007
Copyright © 1979 by Routledge and Kegan Paul 1979.

Library of Congress Catalog Number: 2006049795
ISBN: 978-0-202-30878-4
Printed in the United States of America

Library of Congress Cataloging-in-Publication Data

A new dictionary of the social sciences / G. Duncan Mitchell, editor.—2nd.
ed.
    p. cm.

  ISBN 0-202-30878-2 (alk. paper)
   1. Sociology—Dictionaries. 2. Social sciences—Dictionaries.
  I. Mitchell, G. Duncan (Geoffrey Duncan)

HM425.N49 2006
300.3—dc22   2006049795

Preface

A New Dictionary of the Social Sciences, with many entries revised and new ones added, follows the successful career of its predecessor *A Dictionary of Sociology* first published in 1968. That book proved to be a valuable part of the student's equipment; it is confidently hoped that its successor will likewise be as useful.

Some terms are explained quite briefly, others at some length. In sociology it is not possible to be very helpful without discussing various usages *and* the theoretical and other interests which underlie such variations. Thus fairly long entries are given on words such as *authority, consensus, function, role, social stratification* and the like, whereas quite short entries suffice for others like *agnate, eidos* or *mores*. In the choice of words a generous definition of sociology has been employed and some words used by students of cultural and social anthropology, social psychology and political science as well as by sociologists are included.

It remains for me to express my thanks to contributors and to my colleagues in the Department of Sociology in the University of Exeter who have been of assistance, in particular Professor R. A. B. Leaper, Dr J. A. Vincent and Mr Stephen Mennell, and especially my secretary, Miss Rosalind Webber, whose assistance went far beyond typing the manuscript and who helped to reduce the number of errors.

DUNCAN MITCHELL
University of Exeter

Contributors

MARTIN C. ALBROW	Professor of Sociology, University College of Cardiff in the University of Wales
STANISLAV L. ANDRESKI	Professor of Sociology, University of Reading
EDWIN W. ARDENER	Fellow of St John's College and Lecturer in Social Anthropology, University of Oxford
MICHAEL P. BANTON	Professor of Sociology, University of Bristol
DAVID BUTLER	Fellow of Nuffield College, and Lecturer in Politics, University of Oxford
DENNIS CHAPMAN	Research Fellow, University of Liverpool Formerly Assistant Director of the School of Business Studies, Liverpool
PERCY S. COHEN	Professor of Sociology, London School of Economics and Political Science, University of London
DAVID E. C. EVERSLEY	Member of the Senior Research Staff of the Centre for Environmental Studies, London
J. R. FOX	Professor of Anthropology, Rutgers University, New Brunswick, N.J.
ANTHONY GIDDENS	Fellow of King's College and Lecturer in Sociology, University of Cambridge
EUGENE GREBENIK	Formerly Principal of the Civil Service College, Sunningdale
MAX GLUCKMAN (the late)	Sometime Professor of Social Anthropology, University of Manchester
A. H. HALSEY	Professorial Fellow of Nuffield College and Head of the Department of Social and Administrative Studies, University of Oxford
MARGARET HEWITT	Reader in Social Institutions, University of Exeter
S. W. F. HOLLOWAY	Senior Lecturer in Sociology, University of Leicester
ALFRED HOLT	Dean of Social Science, Middlesex Polytechnic
JOHN A. HUGHES	Head of the Department of Sociology, University of Lancaster
JOSEPHINE KLEIN	Psychotherapist
SIR EDMUND LEACH	Sometime Provost of King's College, and Professor of Social Anthropology, University of Cambridge
NIGEL F. LEMON	Head of the Department of Social Sciences, Sunderland Polytechnic
ALASTAIR MACINTYRE	Professor of Philosophy, College of Liberal Arts, University of Boston, Massachusetts, U.S.A.

DONALD G. MACRAE	Professor of Sociology, London School of Economics and Political Science, University of London
GORDON MANLEY	Emeritus Professor of Environmental Studies, University of Lancaster
PETER H. MANN	Reader in Sociological Studies, University of Sheffield
DAVID C. MARSH	Professor of Applied Social Science, University of Nottingham
ERNEST W. MARTIN	Honorary Research Fellow, Department of Sociology, University of Exeter
HERMINIO G. MARTINS	Fellow of St Antony's College and Lecturer in the Sociology of Latin America, University of Oxford
G. DUNCAN MITCHELL	Professor of Sociology and Director of the Institute of Population Studies, University of Exeter
H. D. MUNRO	Lecturer in Sociology, University of Exeter
E. L. PETERS	Professor of Social Anthropology, University of Manchester
BRIDGET A. PYM	Lecturer in Sociological Studies, University of Sheffield
B. H. A. RANSON	Principal Lecturer in Sociology, Lanchester Polytechnic
JOHN A. REX	Professor of Sociology, University of Warwick
ANTHONY H. RICHMOND	Professor of Sociology, York University, Toronto, Canada
B. H. P. RIVETT	Professor of Operational Research, University of Sussex
ROLAND ROBERTSON	Professor of Sociology, University of Pittsburgh, Penn. U.S.A.
WILLIAM H. SCOTT	Professor of Sociology, Monash University, Australia
W. W. SHARROCK	Senior Lecturer in Sociology, University of Manchester
EDWARD A. SHILS	Fellow of Peterhouse College, Cambridge, and Professor of Social Thought, University of Chicago, U.S.A.
LORD SIMEY OF TOXTETH (the late)	Sometime Charles Booth Professor of Social Science, University of Liverpool
WERNER STARK	Professor of Sociology, Fordham University, New York, U.S.A.
DORRIAN A. SWEETSER	Dean of the College of Liberal Arts, Boston University, Massachusetts, U.S.A.
GORDON B. TRASLER	Professor of Psychology, University of Southampton
ROBIN WILLIAMS	Lecturer in Sociology, University of Durham
ROBERT W. WITKIN	Lecturer in Social Psychology, University of Exeter
D. J. A. WOODLAND	Lecturer in Sociology, University of East Anglia

A

abstraction. It is difficult to give a satisfactory definition of *abstraction* since its use often presupposes an oversimple conception of how both thinking and theory construction proceed. Abstraction can be said to take place when we select from the phenomena we study, and whose character we wish to describe, such traits as would form a basis for their classification. The term *abstraction* has two main meanings.

1. It refers to the fact that to describe or explain anything selection is necessary. Every theory, whether in the social or the natural sciences, omits some variables because they are less relevant, or apparently so, to the phenomena to be explained or predicted by the theory. To the extent that knowledge is possessed of the conditions under which the neglected variables are or are not significant, the more powerful is the theory.

2. In the natural sciences abstraction refers to concepts such as a perfect gas or an instantaneous velocity, and in the social sciences to such concepts as a perfectly rational act or a perfectly integrated group. These serve as logical devices or constructs for the analysis and clarification of complex occurrences, and the making of predictions.

Useful discussions of both these aspects can be found in E. Nagel, *The Structure of Science*, 1961, and in L. Gross, *Symposium on Sociological Theory*, 1959.   A.H.

accommodation. The state or process of adjustment to a conflict situation in which overt expressions of hostility are avoided and certain compensatory advantages, economic, social or psychological, are gained by both sides, while leaving the source of conflict unresolved and allowing the structural inequalities giving rise to minority subordination to persist. For example, see Sheila Patterson, *Dark Strangers: A Study of the Absorption of a Recent West Indian Migrant Group in Brixton*, 1964. See ACCULTURATION, ASSIMILATION, CONFLICT.   A.H.R.

acculturation. The process whereby an individual or a group acquires the cultural characteristics of another through direct contact and interaction. From an individual point of view this is a process of social learning similar to that of adult socialization in which linguistic communication plays an essential role. From a social point of view *acculturation* implies the diffusion of particular values, techniques and institutions and their modification under different conditions. It may give rise to *culture conflict* and to adaptation leading to a modification of group identity. G. A. DeVos (ed.), *Response to Change: Society, Culture and Personality*, 1976. See ASSIMILATION, CONFLICT, SOCIALIZATION.   A.H.R.

1

acephalous. Used in relation to societies to describe those that are 'stateless'. In such societies positions of authority within kinship or domestic group provide a means of control together with institutionalized behaviour relating to lineages, tribes and tribal segments. See J. Middleton and D. Tait (eds), *Tribes Without Rulers*, 1958.

achievement role. See ROLE.

action; social action. Action, or behaviour, is a psychological category and has been regarded as the basic unit by many psychologists. In this connection it is usual to speak of the Behaviourists, i.e. those who subscribe to the fundamental propositions of J. B. Watson. Yet a more useful term is that of *social action*, which is used both by social psychologists and sociologists. This is regarded by many as the proper unit of observation in the social sciences. Action is social when the actor behaves in such a manner that his action is intended to influence the actions of one or more other persons. Thus interaction is the context in which the personality develops. (See G. H. Mead, *The Mind, Self and Society*, 1934.) In sociology it was Max Weber who first explicitly used and emphasized social action as the basis for theory. His typology of social action: *Wertrationalität, Zweckrationalität, Traditional* and *Affektuell* was, he held, fundamental for his work, but it was the second category of action, i.e. purposively rational action, that he was mainly concerned with in his analysis of socio-economic systems, for this kind of action, he said, is oriented to a system of discrete individual ends, such that the end, the means and the secondary results are all rationally taken into account and weighed; this was the type of social action associated with Capitalism.

D. Martindale in *The Nature and Types of Sociological Theory*, 1961, considers a number of sociological writers, beginning with Weber, to constitute a school of Social Behaviourists. According to his account they are an impressive collection of people including Thorstein Veblen, Robert MacIver, Karl Mannheim, Florian Znaniecki, Talcott Parsons and R. K. Merton; he associates himself with this school. It is a moot point how far these writers can be usefully so classified, particularly as one important problem, on which there is some disagreement, is how far reliance can be placed on mere observation of external behaviour, without reference to the meaning that action has for the actors in a situation.   G.D.M.

action research. Much social science springs from the desire to alter and improve a social situation, or to help people in need. *Action research* is investigation of a kind oriented to these ends, where the aim is not only to collect information and arrive at a better understanding, but to do something practical as well. Sometimes, the exponents of action research are dubious about the possibility of making detached and scientific studies of human affairs. They may argue, for example, that an investigator cannot but influence the behaviour of the people he is studying, that experimentation is extremely difficult, if not impossible, in the social sciences, that there is the intermediary of the human instrument in measurement, and that all these vitiate the scientific status of social research.

Usually, action research is concerned with social change, with therapy to individuals or a small social group, or has as its object to improve the efficiency of an organization. The theoretical basis of this practice has been set out by Adam Curle in an article in *Human Relations*, vol. II, No. 3, 1949. Action research has been trenchantly criticized by Michael Argyle in *The Scientific Study of Social Behaviour*, 1957, where he argues that the discovery of scientific results is always secondary in action research. He further argues that action research should seek to obtain objective results of two kinds: (1) it should prove that the activity is genuinely effective in increasing output, or in reducing hostility in a group, or in achieving therapy, and (2) it should show the precise conditions under which successful results can be obtained, so that others can do the same.   G.D.M.

adapt; adaptation. Originally, the term is biological in nature and refers to the processes whereby an organism accommodates to its environment. In sociology *adaptation* is used loosely to refer to the manner in which a social system, be it a small group such as the family, or a larger collectivity such as an organization or even a total society, like a tribal society, fits into the physical or social environment. In structural-functionalist theory it has been held that the adaptive system is one of the structural pre-requisites designed to meet a functional problem posed by survival. In any total social system the problem is met by the economic and technological arrangements. See H. Johnson, *Sociology: A Systematic Interpretation*, 1961.   G.D.M.

adelphic polyandry. See POLYANDRY.

adjust; adjustment. A term that is psychological rather than sociological, used by some social psychologists to refer to the process whereby an individual enters into a harmonious or healthy relationship with his environment, physical or social, but occasionally used by some sociologists to refer to a social unit, like a group or organization, accomplishing the same end. The difficulty posed by most discussions, where the term is used, is in coping with the value implications of what is harmonious or healthy, but sometimes in the literature this problem is blandly ignored.

affine; affinity. See KINSHIP.

age-grades; age-sets. The expression 'age-society' in the sense of *age-grade* was used by Heinrich Schurtz in *Alterklassen und Mannerbunde*, 1902, when he suggested that there was a tripartite division in society which reflected the conflict of proximate age groups or generations. He considered the grades of 'the uninitiated', 'the initiated single men' and 'the elders' as potentially universal in human society.

In general, *age-grade* is used to refer to the division of society into a number of sections based upon 'sociological' age. Age-grades form the structural framework through which specific age-sets pass. Different clusters of rights, duties, obligations and privileges are associated with the different statuses in the age-grade divisions of society. Often particular ceremonial or military functions are performed by sets in different grades.

The *age-grade system* is a type of stratification which cuts across the division of societies into tribes, clans and lineages and permits of a high degree of central control within the society.

An *age-set* is a formally organized group of men or women recruited on the basis of 'sociological' age. There are usually public ceremonies when the sets are formed and when the different sets advance through the age-grade structure. Probably the most important of these stages is the initiation ceremony when youths and maidens acquire mature status. In several societies circumcision and clitoridectomy are associated with this *rite de passage*. J. G. Peristiany discusses this in some detail in his book *The Social Institutions of the Kipsigis*, 1939. An interesting variant of the age-set division of society is the form it takes among the Nyakusa of Tanzania where parents and initiated sons live in separate age-villages. This is the subject of a study by M. Wilson in *Good Company: A study of Nyakyusa Age-Villages*, 1951. See INITIATION. B.H.A.R.

agelecism. A term coined by E. Benoit-Smullyan from the Greek word for group in order to characterize the 'synthesis of a positivistic methodology with a particular set of substantive theories'. Chief of these are the sociologistic theories of Émile Durkheim. The origins of agelecism are to be found in the writings of Louis de Bonald and Joseph de Maistre who advanced the notion that the social group precedes the individual and indeed constitutes him, that the group is the source of values and culture, and that social events and changes are not, and cannot be, the effects of purely individual volitions and desires. The term is used in a chapter by E. Benoit-Smullyan entitled 'The Sociologism of Émile Durkheim and his School' in *An Introduction to the History of Sociology*, 1948, edited by H. E. Barnes. G.D.M.

agnate; agnation. In Roman law *agnati* were kinsfolk, men and women, related to each other by descent from a common male ancestor and who were under a single authority in the family. In modern usage the term is restricted to men only without reference to a common familial authority, so that an agnate is one related by descent through males only. Commonly, the preferred term is *patrilineal*. See KINSHIP, PATRILINEAL.

alienation. Broadly speaking, alienation denotes the estrangement of the individual from key aspects of his or her social existence, and in the 1950s and early 1960s, it dominated contemporary literature and sociological thought. (M. Seeman, 'On the Meaning of Alienation', *American Sociological Review*, XXIV, 6, 1959. See also R. Nisbet, *The Quest for Community*, 1953, for an overview of the historical background to the notion of *alienation*.)

Part of the difficulty of providing an adequate analysis of this concept is that the term occurs in such a wide variety of disciplines, including sociology, social and political philosophy, psychoanalysis, existentialist philosophy, and so on. Furthermore, there is the added difficulty that alienation is one of those concepts, which have tended to abound in sociology, used to describe and explain almost any kind of social behaviour and usually succeeding in describing and explaining nothing. Among other things it has been used to

4

explain ethnic prejudice, mental illness, class consciousness, industrial conflict, political apathy and extremism.

It was Marx, following and amending the idealist conception of alienation used by Hegel, who first introduced the concept into sociological theory. For Marx, it is Man's nature to be his own creator by transforming the world outside him in co-operation with others. However, this nature has become alien to man; it is no longer his but belongs to another person or thing. In religion, for example, it is God who is the subject of the historical process holding the initiative and Man in a state of dependence. In economics it is the money that controls men as though they were objects. In short, man has lost control over his own destiny and sees this control vested in other entities. What is proper to man has become alien, an attribute of something else. In capitalism, the social arrangements which formed the context of work alienated the worker in that they failed to provide him with the opportunities for a meaningful and creative existence. The worker is alienated in that he neither receives satisfaction from his work nor receives the full product of his labour. The idea here seems to be that the role-specialization and unequal distribution of authority and rewards, characteristic of industrial production, prevents the worker from exercising his full creative powers endowed by nature. (See K. Marx, *Economic and Philosophic Manuscripts*, 1844, 1959, and D. McLellan, *Karl Marx: His Life and Thought*, 1973.) E. Fromm, *The Sane Society*, 1956, suggests a characterization of *alienation* which is, in a number of respects, close to that of Marx. For Fromm, *alienation* is that condition when man 'does not experience himself as the action bearer of his own powers and richness, but as an impoverished "thing" dependent on powers outside of himself'.

For Marx alienation was as much a structural feature as psychological. However, in the 1950s it began more and more to be regarded as a socio-psychological condition of the individual. This began with Seeman's germinal work noted above. Faced with what he regarded as the vagueness and unclarity of the literature, Seeman isolated the various uses of the term and recast them in a way which would allow them to be operationalized and measured. The first meaning so isolated, 'powerlessness', was that of alienation as a feeling on the part of the individual that he cannot influence the social situations in which he interacts. The second variant, 'meaninglessness', is a feeling that he has no guides for conduct or belief. 'Normlessness' is the individual's feeling that illegitimate means are required to achieve valued goals. 'Isolation' is a feeling of estrangement from the cultural goals of society, and the final variant, 'self-estrangement', an inability to find any self-rewarding activities in life. Each of these Seeman postulates as independent from each other. Each has been measured by means of various attitude scales and allowed the further exploration of the social contexts which can produce alienation. (See, for example, A. G. Neal and M. Seeman, 'Organisations and Powerlessness: A Test of the Mediation Hypothesis', *American Sociological Review*, XXIX, 2, 1962; R. Blauner, *Alienation and Freedom*, 1964, is an analysis of the alienative consequence of different types of work situation. But see also in the more classically Marxian tradition, H. Braverman, *Labor and Monopoly Capital: The Degradation of Work in the Twentieth Century*, 1974.)

These formulations make the term specific to the attitudinal level of social behaviour which, in its turn, is assumed to be associated with certain social structural characteristics. The social conditions held to be productive of feelings of alienation have been seen as, for example, and following the original Marxian idea, the pattern of industrial production. W. Kornhauser sees the decline of semi-autonomous groups within a society, groups such as voluntary associations, local communities, and neighbourhoods, as producing feelings of alienation and, furthermore, making such people more available for the appeals of extremist groups (W. Kornhauser, *The Politics of Mass Society*, 1956). For others the sheer growth in societal scale and the consequent 'depersonalization' of social relations is the main factor producing alienation. Others link the concept with the notion of mass society. (See P. Olsen, *America as a Mass Society*, 1963; S. Giner, *Mass Society*, 1976.)

A number of investigators have concentrated on alienation as it is manifested in limited and specific organizational contexts, arguing that outside such contexts it is rarely clear what the individual is alienated from. This stemmed from a dissatisfaction with uses of the term, noted earlier, which view alienation as a generalized condition affecting the whole of an individual's social perception. Likewise, Dean suggests that alienation is a 'situation-relevant' variable such that the individual can experience different degrees of alienation in different social contexts. (D. Dean, 'Alienation: Its Meaning and Measurement', *American Sociological Review*, XXVI, 5, 1961.)

This attempt to make alienation a more objective, empirically researchable concept free from certain implicit value assumptions, has come under attack, especially from a number of sociologists who consider that sociology can and ought to make value-judgments about the quality of life. (See J. Horton, 'The Dehumanisation of Anomie and Alienation', *British Journal of Sociology*, XV, 4, 1964; L. Feuer, 'What is Alienation? The Career of a Concept', in M. Stein and A. Vidich, *Sociology on Trial*, 1963.) There is no doubt that the attempts, discussed above, to operationalize the concept, have taken it a long way from its original use in Marx, where it is closely tied to a moral and philosophical conception of human nature and, consequently, a category for moral criticism. It was not to be equated simply with attitudes of dissatisfaction with one's life. On the contrary, a person could be satisfied and content, yet to the extent that one was part of a system in which one was treated as an object, a 'thing', having little or no control over one's life and creative powers, then, in Marx's sense of the term, one was still alienated. (See B. Ollman, *Alienation: Marx's Critique of Man in Capitalist Society*, 1971.) See ANOMIE, MASS SOCIETY.   J.A.H.

ambilateral. A term used in respect of those kinship systems where a person is able to choose to which parental kin group he or she will become attached.

anascopic. Adjective used to identify the kind of social theory (e.g., that of George C. Homans) which starts from the individual and looks upward to construct a conception of society. See T. Geiger, ed. P. Trappe, *Arbeiten zur Soziologie: Soziologische Texte*, vol. 7, Neuwied, Berlin, p. 147f. See KATASCOPIC.

6

animism; animatism. The formulation of the theory of *animism* is the work of Sir E. B. Tylor and may be found in his *Primitive Culture*, 1871. The notion was part of a theory of primitive religion which endeavoured to account for the attribution by some peoples of a spiritual existence to animals, plants, and even on occasion to inanimate objects. Tylor argued that early man had a need to explain dreams, hallucinations, sleep and death, and that the need to understand such phenomena led to the belief in the existence of the soul or an indwelling personality. When a man dreamed and saw in his dream a person who was dead, then this was the man's spirit or soul visiting him. Similarly, to dream of oneself in another place was one's own soul parted from the body in sleep.

This idea was modified by some anthropologists, notably R. R. Marett, who in his book *The Threshold of Religion*, 1914, elaborated an idea he had put forward in 1899. This was a theory of *animatism*, a pre-animistic stage in religious development. Marett pointed to the sense of wonder which primitive man was supposed to have, and most especially in regard to unusual natural objects or the unusual behaviour of natural objects like volcanoes, rivers and so forth. To these, he argued, primitive man attributed an 'impersonal power' or 'spiritual force' comparable to the *mana* of the Oceanic peoples, described by Bishop Codrington. Mana is 'a force, altogether distinct from physical power, which acts in all kinds of ways for good or evil, and which is of greatest advantage to possess and control'. Mana enhances the qualities of a thing or a process – crops, children or their growth.

The notion of animism was strongly supported by Herbert Spencer, who held it to be a general phenomenon. Both *animism* and *animatism* have been criticized for being theories that are over-intellectual, the chief critics being Émile Durkheim and Lucien Lévy-Bruhl, both of whom advanced different theories of primitive religion.   G.D.M.

anomie; anomy. The term *anomie* was first used by the French sociologist, Émile Durkheim, to refer to several aspects of social participation where the conditions necessary for man to fulfil himself and to attain happiness were not present. These conditions were that conduct should be governed by norms, that these norms should form an integrated and non-conflicting system, that the individual should be morally involved with other people so that 'the image of the one who completes me becomes inseparable from mine' and so that clear limits were set to the pleasures attainable in life. Any state where there are unclear, conflicting or unintegrated norms, in which the individual had no morally significant relations with others or in which there were no limits set to the attainment of pleasure, was a state of *anomie*.

R. K. Merton uses the term to refer to a state in which socially prescribed goals and the norms governing their attainment are incompatible. Leo Srole has attempted to construct an index of *anomie*. In most attempts to make *anomie* measurable, emphasis is placed on lack of clarity in goals and norms or upon the absence of social ties. All such attempts involve a more restricted use of the concept than Durkheim's which was related to a philosophical conception of human nature. See É. Durkheim, *Division of Labour*, translated 1947; *Suicide*, translated 1951; R. K. Merton, *Social Theory and Social Structure*, 1949, ch. IV.   J.A.R.

anthropology. This is the name given to a cluster of studies of startling diversity imbued with the faith that an integrated science of man in his biological, cultural and social aspects is possible. Taken as a whole, the anthropological range is immense: in time from the first appearances of humans on this planet and, contemporaneously, aspects of *all* societies but more particularly those conventionally classified as tribal and peasant. Anthropology has inherited and maintains European man's post-Renaissance awareness and burgeoning inquiry into the origins and meanings of the variety of peoples, cultures and societies so recently encountered.

The main sectors in terms of which anthropology is presently organized are:

Biological anthropology, which begins with the zoological view of man's status; attempts to trace his origin and development through comparative studies of fossil, recent and living primates; engages in an examination of the nature of racial diversity; examines the effects of various ecological factors on human adaptability and variability, on the growth and decline of populations, etc. The biological anthropologist, although using techniques of his own, is reliant on other disciplines, notably anatomy, archaeology, biochemistry, botany, genetics, geology and palaeontology.

Archaeology, which is the classification of the material remains of human societies on the bases of function, chronology and cultural context as a preliminary to the formulation of explanatory generalizations regarding transformations of societies.

Social anthropology is currently characterized by approaches which, broadly, are associational, semantic and transformational in their emphases.

The associational emphasis abstracts from human activity forms or structures which provide the terms on which people may relate to one another. The principal forms are networks, e.g., of friends (Boissevain); and corporations, e.g., lineages, universities (Smith). A society's associational structures provide the contexts for all kinds of activities (domestic, economic, political, religious, recreational, legal, medical etc.) and are seen as functionally interrelated. Societies may be distinguished by the kinds of corporations and networks they comprise and their modes of interrelationship.

The semantic emphasis seeks to discern the structure of meaning, the inner logic constituting the sense-making core of all those realities which humans create: social situations, myths, novels, theatrical performances, films, rituals and, at a more abstract level of organization, cultures. The view here is that the 'social fact' is a *relation* internal to a system of relations. 'Meaning is found in the system of relations when taken as a whole, rather than in the limited semantic content of single elements considered in isolation' (Arcand). It is not only that this approach allows us to understand the significance of conventional acts, but also the meaning which people attach to innovative technology such as tractors or intra-uterine devices. (See the entry on *Structuralism.*)

The transformational emphasis is essentially historical. The aim is to comprehend the modes whereby societies or, for example, classes are socially reproduced or otherwise transformed over long periods of time. A recent study of this kind challenges a widely held view propounded by Marx, Weber etc. that English society experienced these transitional phases from the eleventh century: feudal/peasant, capitalist/peasant, capitalist/modern (Macfarlane).

These broad channels of anthropological inquiry are supported by a number of contributing disciplines, e.g., demography, linguistics, psychology, etc. See L. Mair, *An Introduction to Social Anthropology*, 2nd edition, 1972; J. Boissevain, *Friends of Friends*, 1974; M. G. Smith, *Corporations and Society*, 1974; B. Arcand, 'Making love is like eating honey or sweet fruit, it causes cavities: an essay on Cuiva symbolism', in E. Schwimmer, ed., *The Yearbook of Symbolic Anthropology I*, 1978; A. Macfarlane, *The Origins of English Individualism*, 1978; J. Honigmann, *Handbook of Social and Cultural Anthropology*, 1973; B. J. Siegel, ed., *Annual Review of Anthropology*; R. Keesing, *Cultural Anthropology*, 1976. See SOCIAL ANTHROPOLOGY, STRUCTURALISM.   H.D.M.

ascribed role. See ROLE.

assimilation. A process of becoming similar or the end state of such a process. In the United States after World War I there was anxiety about the Americanization of immigrants who seemed attached to the cultures of their homelands, so that for American sociologists assimilation came to mean a one-way process whereby American society was to absorb the newcomers without itself undergoing change. This redefinition of the word reflected American concerns and the popularity of organic analogies. Modern writers insist that assimilation is a two-way process, in which both populations undergo change; in many cases it is also a multi-stage process in which clusters of immigrant groups come to resemble one another and later become less distinctive. To analyse assimilation it is necessary to specify the populations that are compared; the elements of their culture or society that are subject to change; and the direction and speed of change on the part of both populations. See ACCOMMODATION, ACCULTURATION, CONFLICT.   M.P.B.

association. The term describes either a process or an entity. The process is of a number of individuals interacting for a specific end or set of purposes. The entity is an organization of individuals who are held together by a recognized set of rules governing their behaviour to one another for a specific end or set of purposes.

Although some associations are large and comprehensive they cannot express the totality of relations which constitute the total life of a community, and thus *association* may be distinguished from *community*. The specificity of aim of an association is seen in F. Tönnies's use of the term *Gesellschaft*, which he contrasts with *Gemeinschaft*. Usually associations are classified according to function, e.g. occupational, religious, recreational, cultural, etc. See COMMUNITY, GEMEINSCHAFT, INSTITUTION.   G.D.M.

attitude. The term is normally used to refer to a learned predisposition evidenced by the behaviour of an individual or group of individuals, to evaluate an object or class of objects in a consistent or characteristic way.

Historically the origin of the term can be traced to two separate sources.

9

The first is its derivation from the Latin *aptus* from which it derived its connotation of 'fitness' or 'suitability'. For example the term was used in this sense by Herbert Spencer when he spoke of the attitude of mind necessary to arrive at correct judgments on disputed issues. This connotation still survives in non-technical usage in such expressions as 'the scientific attitude' or 'an insufficiently critical attitude'. The second source may be traced to the use of the term to describe a posture of the body in painting or sculpture. From this the term became adapted to refer to postures of the body suitable for certain actions and was thus taken up by early experimental psychologists to refer to various forms of muscular and later mental preparedness or set.

While the connotation of fitness or suitability is no longer represented in modern technical usage, the experimental psychological tradition has been developed by behavioural writers who see attitudes primarily in terms of consistency in behaviour. The original behaviourist insistence on the observation of single acts as they were related to single stimuli left little scope to explain the complexities of social behaviour, and attitude thus became used by behavioural theorists as an intervening variable mediating between stimulus and response in order to cope with the extreme complexity of social behaviour. While this behavioural use of the term was similar to that of the earlier experimental psychologists, its use was broadened to allow reference to 'verbal sets to respond' and the term has gradually come to be defined in more subjective terms moving from more restricted usage such as 'attitudes to respond to social stimulation' to speaking of 'radical-conservative attitudes'.

While some writers still remain opposed to a conception of attitudes in any other than strictly behavioural terms, others have been willing to posit intervening variables to mediate observed consistency in behaviour. These variables have conventionally included cognitive components referring to individuals' beliefs about the object or issue in question, affective components referring to his evaluations of the attitude object, and conative components referring to his behavioural intentions with regard to it. These components may be organized in various ways and to varying degrees and are sometimes conceived as constituting subjective representations of values and ideologies. See ATTITUDE RESEARCH, VALUE, IDEOLOGY.   N.F.L.

attitude research. The earliest concern of workers in this field was with measurement; and in particular with the application of mathematical scaling models to behaviour, usually in the form of answers to questionnaire items. The earliest methods were those first developed by Thurstone and his collaborators in the 1920s. These used a group of selected judges who made judgments of a large number of potential attitude items, and these judgments were then used to define the scale values of a more limited set of items which were finally selected for incorporation into the questionnaire. Other methods based upon answers of respondents rather than of judges were the methods of *summative scaling* developed by Likert in the 1930s, and the later method of *cumulative scaling* developed by Guttman during the Second World War, based upon the technique of *scalogram analysis*. More recent research in attitude measurements has concentrated upon the development of alternative methods of data collection many of them based upon unobtrusive observations of everyday behaviour, and on alternative methods of scaling often employing non-metric procedures. For a recent review of research in this area see N. Lemon, *Attitudes and their Measurement*, 1973.

Having established methods for the measurement of attitudes, research then moved on to a concern with attitude change and the more general issue of social influence. Early work was predominantly problem centred and was prompted by interest in the processes of mass communication, perhaps best described in terms of the well-known theme question 'Who says what, to whom, with what effect?' This question formed the basis of the first monograph in the influential Yale Communication and Attitude Change Program. See C. I. Hovland, I. L. Janis and H. H. Kelley, *Communication and Persuasion*, 1953. This programme accumulated a substantial amount of empirical material on such topics as communicator credibility, effect of fear arousing appeals, organization of persuasive arguments, group influences on attitude change, personality and persuasibility, and the effects of active participation in an issue on attitude change. While this programme touched upon nearly all the subsequently central problems of attitude change, its lack of central theoretical focus directed the attention of social psychologists towards the development of theoretical models of attitude change. One of the most influential works in this area was L. Festinger's *A theory of cognitive dissonance*, 1957, which proposed that the fundamental process underlying attitude change was the necessity to preserve consistency between different parts of an individual's belief system. This model, and others of a similar kind, were responsible for a plethora of laboratory and field investigations in the early and mid-1960s which did much to adjudicate between rival formulations and to establish the limits of the underlying principle. Parallel to these activities were others dating back to the end of the war which sought to establish relationships between attitudes and broader personality characteristics. The best-known work in this area is probably that of T. W. Adorno *et al.*, *The Authoritarian Personality*, 1950, which established a relationship between ethnocentric attitudes and deeper personality factors. Research in the attitude change area has been undertaken in a variety of applied settings most typically in areas such as the study of voting behaviour, racial prejudice and discrimination, consumer behaviour and market research, and in studies of the diffusion of innovations. Moreover an attempt to link the more laboratory-based tradition in the study of attitude change to an analysis of the more sociological conception of *représentation sociale* derived from the work of Durkheim is developing on the continent following the work of S. Moscovici in *La psychanalyse, son image et son public*, 1961.

The relationship between verbally expressed attitude and behaviour is however still problematic, and remains of great significance both for measurement and for study of the processes of attitude formation and change. While research has demonstrated a somewhat equivocal relationship between attitude and behaviour it has also shown the importance of considering attitudes to the situation in which behaviour takes place, as well as to the attitude issue, in the prediction of conduct. See ATTITUDE, AUTHORITARIANISM, PREJUDICE, SCALES, SCALOGRAM ANALYSIS.   N.F.L.

authoritarian; authoritarianism. Words in common use, they were brought into the limelight with the publication of *The Authoritarian Personality* (1950), where the concept was decomposed into nine overlapping and loosely related variables: *conventionalism* (rigid adherence to conventional, middle-class values); *authoritarian submission* (submissive, uncritical attitude towards idealized moral authority of the ingroup); *authoritarian aggression* (tendency to be on the lookout for, and to condemn, reject, and punish people who violate conventional values); *anti-intraception* (opposition to the subjective, the imaginative, the tender-minded); *superstition and stereotypy* (the belief in mystical determinants of the individual's fate; the disposition to think in rigid categories); *power and 'toughness'* (preoccupation with the dominance–submission, strong–weak, leader–follower dimension; identification with power figures; overemphasis upon the conventionalized attributes of the ego; exaggerated assertion of strength and toughness); *destructiveness and cynicism* (generalized hostility, vilification of the human); *projectivity* (the disposition to believe that wild and dangerous things go on in the world; the projection outwards of unconscious emotional impulses); *sex* (exaggerated concern with sexual 'goings-on').

It must not be assumed that the concept has the same meaning for different writers, and the merit of each test of *authoritarianism* has to be carefully assessed. See T. W. Adorno *et al.*, *The Authoritarian Personality*, 1950; R. Christie and M. Jahoda (eds.), *Studies in the Scope and Method of 'The Authoritarian Personality'*, 1954. See ATTITUDE RESEARCH. J.K.

authority; legitimation of authority. The performance of authoritative actions, i.e. the exercise of authority, is one of the major forms of power through which the actions of a plurality of individual human actors are placed or maintained in a condition of order or are concerted for the collaborative attainment of a particular goal or general goals.

The major mechanisms of the ordering or concerting of actions are:

(1) *Exchange*;

(2) *Common interests*;

(3) *Solidarity* or *consensus* arising from (a) *mutual affection*, (b) *primordial community*, (c) *community of belief*, and (d) *civil community*; and

(4) *Power-* (a) *influence*, (b) *authority*, and (c) *coercive control*.

Exchange exists when each actor in the relationship reciprocally performs an action which is a service or a good to the other. *Common interests* operate when each actor is motivated to perform the expected action in anticipation of an advantage to be gained from a third party or some other external source. *Solidarity* operates as an instigation of ordered or concerted action when it is believed that advantage will accrue to the collectivity as such or to the other partners as members of the collectivity; the collectivity might be constituted through ties of mutual *affection*, or *primordial* (e.g. kinship, ethnic, or territorial) identity, or on a common possession of *sacred symbols*, or on a common membership in a *civil* community.

The order or the articulation of the actions of a plurality of actors by *power* occurs when the pattern of the actions to be performed issues from an actor or actors other than those whose actions are to be articulated. *Influence* is a form of power which entails (i) the provision of patterns or models through the presentation of concrete exemplary actions or 'ideals'. Influence can also

12

operate (ii) through the provision of cognitive maps (e.g. intelligence-appreciations) and generalized plans (e.g. blueprints of action such as tactical or strategic programmes) which might be incorporated into any of the previously cited mechanisms. *Coercive control* may operate through commands believed to be enforceable by sanctions such as the withholding of rewards (e.g. income) or desired conditions (e.g. physical mobility or physical well-being), or through control over conditions to which the actors must adapt themselves at their own cost.

Authority is that form of power which orders or articulates the actions of other actors through commands which are effective because those who are commanded regard the commands as *legitimate*. Authority differs from coercive control, since the latter elicits conformity with its commands and prescriptions through its capacity to reward or punish. The distinction is an analytical one, since empirically authority and coercive control exist together in many combinations.

Authority is therefore by definition legitimate authority. Its effectiveness in controlling the actions of those towards whom it is directed is affected by the concurrent operation of other mechanisms. Thus (legitimate) authority might be reinforced by the concurrent operation of mechanisms of exchange between the exerciser of authority and the person (or persons) commanded, e.g. the latter might receive a specific payment (wages or salary) in return for the performance of specific actions. The exerciser of authority and the person who is its object might also have *common interests* (although not equally shared) in the attainment of a collective goal such as the winning of a battle or the fulfilment of an economic programme. The exerciser and the object of authority might be linked through *solidarity* which will be served by their collaboration such as the winning of a game or the improvement in the quality of performance of a university; they might also have ties of *personal affection* or of *ethnic identity*, etc. In all these instances, the concurrent operation of the mechanism in question with the exercise of (legitimate) authority might either strengthen or weaken the motivation for conformity with the commands issued by the exerciser of authority and therewith will strengthen or weaken the motivation for the performance of the particular action. It should be emphasized that the different mechanisms might not operate harmoniously. Thus, there might not be common interests between the exerciser and the object of legitimate authority. The exerciser and the object might have no ties or solidarity; they might indeed dislike each other personally or be alien ethnically, etc. They might also be involved in an exchange relationship which is unsatisfactory to the subordinated person in the sense that the reward which he receives is, in accordance with his beliefs, incommensurate with the action which he is expected to perform.

It should also be pointed out that the exercise of coercive control might be harmonious, or in conflict, with the exercise of legitimate authority. The exercise of coercive control in an irregular manner might cause the legitimacy of the authority of the exerciser of coercive control to be questioned and thus make for resistance to it; but at the same time, a substantial attribution of legitimacy might still survive and be effective.

The legitimacy of authority is ultimately a matter of belief concerning the rightfulness of the institutional system through which authority is exercised, concerning the rightfulness of the exerciser's incumbency in the authoritative role within the institutional system, concerning the rightfulness of the command itself or of the mode of its promulgation.

Max Weber classified the modes of the legitimation of authority into *traditional, rational-legal,* and *charismatic.* The *traditional* mode of legitimation consists in the belief that the institutions of authority are continuous with institutions which have existed for a very long time, or that the exerciser of authority has acceded to the authoritative role by a procedure and in accordance with qualifications which have been valid for a very long time, or that the commands which he enunciates are either substantially identical with commands which are believed to have been valid for a very long time or are exercised by him in accordance with a discretionary power which the incumbents, or the predecessors with whom he is legitimately linked, have possessed for a very long time.

The *rational-legal* mode of legitimation rests on the belief that the institutional system of the exerciser of authority, the accession of the incumbent to the authoritative role, and the substance and mode of promulgation of the command (or rule) are in accordance with a more general rule or rules.

The *charismatic* mode of legitimation rests on the belief that the exerciser of authority and the rule or command which he enunciates possess certain sacred properties.

In all three cases the legitimacy of a system of authoritative institutions, the accession of the incumbents, and the substance and mode of promulgation of the rule or command are imputed on the basis of beliefs about some direct or indirect connection with some ultimate legitimating 'power'. That ultimate legitimating 'power' might be the will of God, the founders of the dynasty or society, natural law, the will of the people, etc. In other words, the traditional and the rational-legal modes of legitimation of authority also rest on beliefs about some imputed connection with a sacred, i.e. charismatic, source. They differ from the charismatic mode of legitimation by virtue of their indirect or mediated connection with the sacred source, i.e. charisma, in contrast with the more direct connection of charismatically legitimated authority.

Both rulers and subjects, i.e. the exercisers and the objects of authority, experience a need to believe in the legitimacy of the authority which they exercise or to which they are subject. Rulers experience the need because they see in it a strengthening of their power and also because they have a subjective need to believe that what they are doing is right, i.e. in accordance with some higher law. They need to justify themselves. Their subjects have a similar need to see order in the universe in which they live which will render meaningful, and therewith acceptable, their position; and the deprivations, which are entailed in that subordinate position, by fitting them into a larger pattern. Partly from the cognitive need for order, partly from the need to see meaning in their own position in the world and in their own share of the good and evil things offered by life, they must believe in a pattern in the world's affairs. This is why they wish to see power exercised legitimately rather than illegitimately.

Yet power is often looked upon as illegitimate by those over whom it is exercised. It is regarded as coercive control rather than as legitimate authority. To be legitimate it must be subsumable under a more general pattern or order of meaning. When it obviously fails to conform with that order its claims to legitimacy are refuted.

Power is regarded as coercive control rather than as legitimate authority when it acts unjustly, i.e. contrarily to the highest general rules regarding the distribution of roles, rewards, and facilities. Authority can also lose its legitimacy when its effectiveness in the maintenance of order and in the distribution of roles, rewards, etc., weaken or fail. There is a tendency for effective coercive control to acquire legitimacy, i.e., to have legitimacy attributed to it by those subject to it, when it is effective in maintaining order, even though that order might be injurious to many of those who live under it.

In no society is there a universal attribution of legitimacy to power. The gaps in solidarity (ethnic solidarity and the solidarity of belief) make for a withholding of the attribution of legitimacy; similarly the belief in the existence of divergent interests between the powerful and those over whom their power is exercised can also inhibit the attribution of legitimacy. The failure of the rulers of a regime to establish or maintain the legitimacy of the order which they create or which they are held responsible for having created and maintained renders that order more unstable. The failure to maintain legitimacy heightens the probability of the replacement of the rulers and their regime by another set of rulers and by a new regime. See E. A. Shils, *Center and Periphery: Essays in Macrosociology*, 1975, ch. 1.   E.A.S.

avoidance. In many societies persons or groups who stand in particular relationships avoid each other. As a mode of behaviour, avoidance always expresses respect. Although avoidance involves two parties, and although the prohibitions are binding on both, it is usually the duty of one party specifically to avoid the other, e.g. as when it is the duty of a man to avoid his wife's mother. The extent of avoidance varies from society to society and may include such prohibitions as not eating from the same dish, to not entering the other's village.   B.H.A.R.

avunculate. The special relationship that persists in some societies between a man and his mother's brother.

This term, from the Latin *avunculus* ('mother's brother') is sometimes used to describe the *authority* of the mother's brother over his sister's children in a matrilineal society, and sometimes to describe the *indulgent* relationship that exists between maternal uncle and nephew in many societies, and which includes, for example, privileged joking. Yet again it is used, as in the definition, to indicate *any* specially marked relationship between these relatives.

As examples of its use see A. I. Richards, 'Some Types of Family Structure Amongst the Central Bantu', in A. R. Radcliffe-Brown and D. Forde (eds.), *African Systems of Kinship and Marriage*, 1950.

As a summary of the literature on the subject, and further examples of the variety of usage, see C. Lévi-Strauss, *Structural Anthropology*, ch. 2, 1963, and J. Goody, 'The Mother's Brother and Sister's Son in West Africa', *Journal of the Royal Anthropological Institute*, 89, 1959. See JOKING RELATIONSHIPS, MATRILINEAL.   J.R.F.

B

barbarian; barbarism. A term used colloquially to describe a rude or un-civilized person, originally used to describe a non-Hellene or a non-Roman.

The sociological connotation gained currency as a result of the famous book by Lewis H. Morgan entitled *Ancient Society*, 1877, the sub-title of which is *Researches in the Lines of Human Progress from Savagery through Barbarism to Civilization*. The word *barbarism*, therefore, has been used in a context of social development of the human race as a middle stage. Morgan held that there was convincing evidence that, as he put it, 'savagery preceded barbarism in all the tribes of mankind, as barbarism is known to have preceded civilization'. And he added: 'The history of the human race is one in source, one in experience, one in progress.' Few modern sociologists would be as confident as this. Moreover, the stages of social development were equally clear to him, less so to contemporary sociologists. *Savagery* describes the long formative period of human existence from the earliest times up until the advent of those inventions which ushered in the *barbaric* stage. The latter is marked by four features: the domestication of animals, the discovery of cereals, the use of stone in architecture, and the invention of the method of smelting iron ore. Hunters and gatherers characterize the stage of savagery; the growth of agriculture together with the sedentary manner of life associated with it are features of the barbaric state. Morgan, however, discerned three stages within barbarism. The first of these stages, and the one marking the end of the upper stage of savagery, was notable for the invention of pottery; middle barbarism was the period when the domestication of animals took place in the Eastern hemisphere and the cultivation of land with the help of irrigation in the Western hemisphere. The invention of iron and its use characterized upper barbarism, a period which closed with the growth of the phonetic alphabet. This and the use of writing and the making of metal tools marked the beginnings of civilization.

Various writers made use of Morgan's scheme, altered or improved upon it. Notable among them was Gordon Childe, who in his book *Social Evolution*, 1951, emphasized the technology of food-production as the mark of the change from *savagery* to *barbarism*. Childe questioned Morgan's criterion of writing, as the invention which distinguished *barbarism* from *civilization*, arguing that this would mean the inclusion of the Maya Indians among the civilized even though they had not invented the wheel and relied for cultivation on the primitive slash-and-burn technique.

The fact is that it is by no means as easy as Morgan thought it was to divide up the history of human society into these three stages. Yet the terms have been used by anthropologists. Occasionally, reference is still made to savages, but the term is loosely used to denote members of a non-literate society possessing only a rudimentary technology, and it is used in contrast to *civilized people*. The term *barbarian*, like the term *barbarism,* is little used today.   G.D.M.

Barnard, Chester I (1886–1961). An American businessman who had a keen eye for the nature of organization, he spent most of his working life in the telephone and telegraph industry, finally becoming President of the New Jersey Bell Company. He found time to write a famous work *The Function of the Executive,* 1938. This book and a number of papers of considerable interest on formal social organization have contributed to the literature on occupational roles and the relationship of status systems to the goals of business enterprise.

Becker, Howard (1899–1960). American sociologist who taught at the University of Wisconsin. He believed the essence of sociology to be a consideration of values and advocated what he called 'constructive typologies'. His work drew on that of Max Weber and Leopold v. Wiese. The term 'interpretive sociology' is attributable to him but his later interest lay in analytical studies. He collaborated with H. C. Barnes to edit the large historical reference work *Social Thought from Lore to Science,* 1938, 3rd edition, 1961.

behaviour. See ACTION.

Benedict, Ruth Fulton (1887–1948). American anthropologist and poet. She studied under Boas and Kroeber and in 1922 began a field study of the Serrano Indians of California. Subsequent studies of Indian tribes included the Zuni Pueblo Indians, the Cochiti and the Pima. Her approach was to analyse the characteristic 'culture patterns' of these peoples, a method she described in a paper in 1928, but which was more popularly expressed in her famous work *Patterns of Culture,* 1934. During the Second World War she turned her attention to both Asia and Europe and her examination of Japanese culture published under the title *The Chrysanthemum and the Sword* in 1946 is one of the best known analyses of a value system of a large-scale society; its effect upon public policy in America towards Japan was not inconsiderable. She was a woman of striking appearance, she brought a fresh approach to cultural anthropology and she influenced many others. She taught at Columbia University. Ruth Benedict brought to her work a great depth of perception as well as a sound training in scientific techniques; in her the poet and the social scientist were inseparable.   G.D.M.

bilateral. A term used to describe the transmission of descent or of property rights through both male and female parents, without emphasizing either one or the other lines. The term *bilateral* is used in contradistinction to the term *unilineal*. See KINSHIP.

Bonald, Louis de (1754–1840). French writer who opposed the individualistic ideas of the Enlightenment and who regarded society as a reality in itself having a life of its own.

17

Booth, Charles James (1840–1916). British shipowner, manufacturer, and statistician; his ultimate aim was the improvement of the lot of the common people, but he realized the need for accurate and relevant evidence. Results of his scientific inquiries into statistical aspects of pressing social questions were published in *Life and Labour of the People* (1889–1891), and the more elaborate *Life and Labour of the People in London* (1891–1903). This work aimed to show the 'numerical relations which poverty, misery and depravity bear to regular earnings and comparative comfort, and to describe the general conditions under which each class lives'. Instrumental in the passage of the Old Age Pensions Act, 1908, he wrote several works on the aged poor. See Lord and Lady Simey's *Charles Booth: Social Scientist*, 1960.   G.D.M.

bourgeoisie. *Bourgeoisie* and *Bourgeois* (from the Latin *burgensis*) are late Medieval terms of French origin which refer to the middle class of French citizens, more specifically to the freemen of a burgh. Such people were distinguishable from peasants, on the one hand, and gentlemen, on the other. The terms were used by Karl Marx, who contrasted the Bourgeoisie with the Proletariat. Between these two great classes there was an increasingly antagonistic relationship, which in the last analysis would lead to the destruction of the Bourgeoisie and the establishment of the Dictatorship of the Proletariat. Marx's use has coloured the subsequent use of the term, but there are some variations, for it was not used precisely by him or by those who owe allegiance to his ideas. It may thus refer in a general way to the middle-classes, but more usually to non-Proletarian classes of all kinds, sometimes to non-Socialistic political parties, and commonly to Capitalist society, thus described as Bourgeois society. See PROLETARIAT.   G.D.M.

bride-price. A marriage payment by the kin of a bridegroom to the bride's kin. It is a solemn token of obligation although the exact jural implications may vary from one society to another. Because it was in earlier times thought by Europeans that a wife was being bought, the practice was severely criticized, but today with better understanding of the ritual nature, and often of complexity of marriage payments, the older term has tended to give way to another and it is now customary to call the practice *bride-wealth*. It should be pointed out that where bride-wealth is given as part of the marriage ceremonies there is usually a gift made by the bride's kin to the bridegroom's, although this may be smaller in value. Usually the practice is associated with a patrilineal descent system.   G.D.M.

bride-wealth. See BRIDE-PRICE.

bureaucracy. The term is used both to designate the tasks and procedures of administration as a collective word for a body of administrative officials. Frequently it also indicates inefficiency and an improper exercise of power on the part of officials, and thus has become a term of abuse.

First use of the term (*Bureaucratie*) has been attributed to the economist Vincent de Gournay (1712–59). In the nineteenth century, under conditions of increasing state intervention, it came into regular use among European writers, especially in German as *Bürokratie*, to describe government by officials. In England the term became current in the 1830s during resistance to the centralization of poor relief and public health measures. To Thomas Carlyle it was 'the continental nuisance' (*Latter Day Pamphlets*, iv, 1850). John Stuart Mill wrote in 1860, 'the work of government has been in the hands of governors by profession, which is the essence and meaning of bureaucracy', (*Representative Government*, pp. 40–1.)

Sustained treatment of the concept came in 1895 in Gaetano Mosca's *Elementi di Scienza Politica*, translated in 1939 as *The Ruling Class*, where the author regarded bureaucracy as being so fundamental to the governing of great empires that all political systems could be classified as either feudal or bureaucratic. Robert Michels in *Zur Soziologie des Parteiwesens in der modernen Demokratie*, 1911, translated as *Political Parties*, 1915, extended the concept of bureaucracy from the state to political parties and argued that bureaucracy arose from the administrative necessities involved in running a large organization and reinforced the power of the party oligarchy.

While retaining the term for the staffs of the rulers of pre-industrial empires, Max Weber in *Wirtschaft und Gesellschaft*, 1921, founded the modern sociological study of bureaucracy by freeing the concept from pejorative connotations and emphasizing the indispensability of bureaucracy for the rational attainment of the goals of any organization in industrial society. Within his ideal type, or extended definition, of *bureaucracy* Weber included the following characteristics: fixed areas of official jurisdiction governed by laws and regulations; offices organized on the basis of a clear hierarchy of authority; administration based on written documents and conducted according to procedures for which special training is required; personally free officials appointed on the basis of technical qualifications; appropriation of neither office nor the means of administration by the official who is employed full-time and subject to strict discipline; a career for the official in which promotion is governed by seniority or merit, and a fixed salary (and generally a pension) is paid according to rank. (See *From Max Weber*, edited by H. H. Gerth and C. W. Mills, 1948, pp. 196–244, and M. Weber, *The Theory of Social and Economic Organization*, 1947, pp. 329–41.)

Subsequently sociologists have taken Weber's concept as a starting point but have not been content to be limited by his definition. In particular one stream of writing has emphasized that Weber's ideal type of administrative efficiency entails the features which are responsible for the connotations of inefficiency that the term bureaucracy so frequently possesses. Thus R. K. Merton in his 'Bureaucratic Structure and Personality', 1940, reprinted in *Reader in Bureaucracy*, edited by R. K. Merton and others, 1952, argues that demands on officials to conform to bureaucratic regulations lead to ritualism, defensiveness, rigidity, and difficulties in dealing with the public. This trend culminates in M. Crozier's *The Bureaucratic Phenomenon*, 1964, where the author concentrates on aspects Weber excluded from his ideal type and uses bureaucracy to mean 'an organization that cannot correct its behaviour by learning from its errors' (p. 187).

The identification of bureaucracy with a type of organization rather than with administrative procedures is duplicated in the work of scholars, who, like Mosca, in studying despotic empires have found bureaucracy and the political system so closely associated that they frequently use the term bureaucracy to denote the whole state system. (See for example K. Wittfogel's *Oriental Despotism*, 1954.)

In modern society this has been replicated in both popular and academic usage. *Bureaucracy* has been equated with large organizations and, in so far as the state is both organized on bureaucratic principles and has a symbiotic relationship with large organizations (a condition often referred to as corporatism), it is easy to conceive of modern societies as bureaucracies. 'No sociologist doubts that the dominant type of organization today, whether in the private or public sector, is the *bureaucratic* group.' (Alvin W. Gouldner, *The Dialectic of Ideology and Technology*, 1976, p. 242.) As such bureaucracy is considered to be a phenomenon which transcends the distinctions between capitalist and self-professed socialist societies and has been a prime target for radical protest in the sixties and seventies.

The rapid development and diversification of the phenomena to which the term *bureaucracy* has been attached have resulted in its growing indeterminacy. The author in *Bureaucracy*, 1970, identified seven modern concepts of bureaucracy, namely: as rational organization; as organizational inefficiency; as rule by officials; as public administration; as the organization; as modern society. While the term is unavoidable in referring to a broad set of related problems it can only be used precisely if considerable attention is paid to definition.   M.C.A.

C

capitalism. The term refers to a form of industrial society in which the greater part of economic life has the following characteristics: the concentration and control of the means of economic production (capital) is in the hands of private (i.e. non-governmental) owners; resources and wealth are acquired through the operation of a free market; labour is performed by legally free workers who sell their services on the market; and, the maximization of profit is the goal and stimulus of economic activity.

In what might be termed *classical capitalism* the economic functions of society are served by numerous, highly differentiated and relatively small producers. Each producer, either wholly or in part, owns and controls his enterprise and bears the full risk and benefits of his activity. Control and co-ordination of the many activities and decisions of both producers and consumers are achieved through the operations of the free market in which what is supplied, in what quantities and at what price, are largely determined by demand on the part of consumers and by competition between producers. Essential to such a system is a monetary unit which acts both as a source of wealth and as an accounting medium measuring the profit and loss of the enterprise. (See Max Weber, *The Theory of Social and Economic Organisation*, trans. by A. R. Henderson and Talcott Parsons, 1947.)

The role of government in such an economy, when compared with a socialist type of economy, is secondary, being confined in the main to the removal of restrictions upon the full, unimpeded operation of the system. It is the 'invisible hand' of the free market which ensures that production is adapted to meet human desires. (On the 'market economy' see K. Polanyi, *The Great Transformation*, 1944, and the collection of readings in R. C. Edwards *et al.*, *The Capitalist System*, 1972.)

The nineteenth century saw societies which came closest to this *ideal-type* of classical capitalism, especially in England and the United States. (On this see G. Kay, *Capitalism and Underdevelopment*, 1976.) It was in this period, also, that the term itself came into general use through the writings of the early socialists. A number of writers, however, have suggested that elements of capitalism are to be found before the nineteenth century. Henri Pirenne, for example, suggests that 'all the essential features of capitalism, i.e. individual enterprises, the advancement on credit, commercial profits, speculation, etc., are to be found from the twelfth century on' ('Stages in the Social History of Capitalism', *American Historical Review*, 1914). Henri See, Max Weber, Werner Sombart and others all suggest that capitalistic elements are to be found in most historical societies. However, they concede that it was only in Western Europe during and after the Industrial Revolution that there is found on a societal scale the complex of features known as capitalism.

21

The last fifty years have seen an increased participation by governments in the functioning of the economies of capitalist societies, encouraged partly by a desire to alleviate the worst consequences of periodic depressions to which capitalism has been subject. Along with this increased governmental responsibility there has also been the tendency for capitalist enterprises to increase in scale until the small, individually owned and controlled enterprise is secondary to the large corporations controlled by a group of managers who exercise their control on behalf of the legal owners, the shareholders. (See James Burnham, *The Managerial Revolution*, 1941; J. K. Galbraith, *American Capitalism*, 1956.)

Sociological concern with capitalism has been mainly directed towards its origins and its development. Weber, in *The Protestant Ethic and the Spirit of Capitalism*, translated 1930, saw the origins of capitalism to be, at least in part, due to the rise of ascetic Protestantism in Europe, especially England. He suggested that the Calvinist 'ethic' of asceticism and increasing activity in the world for the glory of God, gave rise to a secular variant which formed the 'spirit of capitalism', the idea that hard work carried its own intrinsic reward. It was this *spirit*, coupled with *rationality*, that was distinctive in nineteenth-century capitalism. Weber's hypothesis goes some way to explain the process of capital formation whereby some of the members of society forego present consumption in favour of further capital investment, a process considered by many to be essential to the beginnings of capitalism. Work, to the ascetic Protestants and their secular descendants of Weber's study, was an activity rewarding in itself and not for the material benefits it might bring. As a result, increases in wealth tended to be channelled into greater productive capacity rather than into increases in consumption.

Sombart also laid great stress upon the *spirit* which inspired the whole epoch of capitalism, a spirit which combined daring and adventure with rationality and calculation. (See Werner Sombart, 'Capitalism', in *The Encyclopaedia of the Social Sciences*, 1930. For a contemporary treatment of the Weberian thesis, see David McClelland, *The Achieving Society*, 1961.)

Probably the best-known writer on capitalism and its development is Karl Marx. Marx argued that the essential feature of capitalism and, indeed, any other type of society, was the social relations of production: the ways in which the means of production were owned and controlled. It was these relationships which formed the basis for the rise of social classes which, in the capitalist system, were the owners and the non-owners of capital, the bourgeoisie and the proletariat respectively. Under the economic laws inherent in the capitalist economy, the bourgeoisie, in order to gain profit, must pay to labour wages less than the full value of its product. Under conditions of rising competition and falling profit margins, characteristic of the later stages of capitalism, the return to labour would become less and less. As a consequence, the proletariat, impelled by their increasing pauperization, would revolt and destroy the system. (See K. Marx, *Capital*, 1976; Horowitz, *Marx and Modern Economics*, 1968; P. Sweezy, *The Theory of Capitalist Development*, 1948; E. Mandel, *Late Capitalism*, 1975.)

To characterize societies which contain elements of capitalism but which fall short of the modal type, or which display other differentiating features, recourse has often been made to terms which contain *capitalism* suitably modified by some qualifying term. For example, Weber distinguishes among other types *booty capitalism*, a system in which wealth was acquired by the financing of wars in the expectation of booty; *colonial capitalism* is a system under which colonies were economically exploited, typically by use of the plantation system. Other writers have distinguished such types as *welfare capitalism*, an economic system in which the state takes an increased responsibility for economic welfare, usually in the form of policies designed to mitigate the worst effects of the malfunctioning of the economy; *managerial capitalism* in which production is concentrated in the hands of large corporations run by managers; *state capitalism*, a system under which the state takes over and exploits the means of production in the interests of the class which controls the state. N. Smelser, in his *Sociology of Economic Life*, 1963, regards this constant creation of sub-types, together with the association of *capitalism* with political ideologies, as contributing towards the unsuitability of the term for rigorous sociological analysis.

On occasions, *capitalism* is used as though it were synonymous with such terms as *laissez faire, the free market, the profit motive, private enterprise*, etc. These usages, however, focus upon one characteristic of capitalism to the exclusion of others, and it is possible to conceive of having any one of them within quite different kinds of economic institutional frames. For example, it is possible to have a free market without the institution of private ownership of production goods. The *profit motive* refers to the character of the motivation behind economic activity and, as Weber points out, is not peculiar to capitalism. The term *laissez faire* refers to an economic philosophy whose cry is for the removal of all restrictions, usually governmental, upon entrepreneurial activity.

In recent years there has been a revival of interest in the particular historical factors which combined to produce the social formation known as capitalism. Especially important here has been the particular role of the peasantry and the transformation of the labour force through the abandonment of legal restraint. According to Marx, for example, the emancipation of the serfs, the destruction of guild restrictions, the separation of freemen from the land and the concentration of the means of production into a few hands were preconditions for the rise of capitalism. (See Barrington-Moore, *The Social Origins of Dictatorship and Democracy*, 1969; Gerschenkron, *Economic Backwardness in Perspective*, 1964; R. Hilton (ed.), *The Transition from Feudalism to Capitalism*, 1976.)

To what extent political and other non-economic aspects of society are to be included within the notion of *capitalism* is a controversial point. Friedman, in *Capitalism and Freedom*, 1963, makes the point that 'economic freedom is also an indispensable means towards the achievement of political freedom', a view endorsed by F. A. von Hayek in *The Road to Serfdom*, 1944. Weber also suggested that democracy in its clearest form can occur only under capitalism. It is a matter of empirical fact that the particular configuration of social characteristics in Western Europe and the United States, which included a capitalistic type of economy, were found together with more or less democratic political systems. (See S. M. Lipset, *Political Man*, 1960.) However, this is not to demonstrate that a capitalistic form of economic organization is a necessary or sufficient guarantee of political freedom. (B. Jessop, 'Capitalism and the State: The Best Possible Political Shell', in B. Smart (ed.), *Power and the State*, 1978; P. Anderson, *Lineages of the Absolutist State*, 1974, provides an excellent and wide ranging analysis of the relationship between modes of production and the rise of different political forms.)   J.A.H.

case study. This is a practice derived from legal studies where a case is an event or set of events involving legal acts from the study of which the student derives both the principles and the practice of the law relevant to the case.

In social work and social administration a case is the object of study in the sense that it requires a full description of the client, family or the administrative situation, so that all relevant matters, affecting the issue or issues of interest may be discerned.

In sociology *case study* method is a holistic treatment of a subject whereby through the detailed examination of one instance information about a class of entities of which this is one may be obtained. The method has been criticized by social statisticians as incapable of providing methodologically sound results of a general nature, but on the other hand it may well be invaluable as a preliminary approach in order to discover the significant variables and provide useful categories which will lead to the formulation of hypotheses which then may be tested by reference to a number of instances. The subjects of case studies are usually families, organizations, social groups and small communities. The case study method is prominent in sociological research. See SOCIAL WORK.   G.D.M.

case-work. See SOCIAL WORK.

caste. See SOCIAL STRATIFICATION.

category. The term was first used by Aristotle in the logical sense that entities are classifiable according to that which may be significantly predicated of them. From Aristotle, Kant adopted the term *category* to denote the elementary concepts of the pure understanding. It is now little used as a term in logic. In non-philosophical contexts, category can be used interchangeably with, and has a similar meaning to, class, type or kind. Its use in sociology parallels that in the natural sciences where, since categories are supposed in general to be mutually exclusive, it is essentially classificatory. Every technical term and concept in the social sciences is a category, because they denote a class of entities of which predications may be made.

On another level, a central problem of the sociology of knowledge has been to give an account of the social causation of man's categories of thought. É. Durkheim and M. Mauss pioneered the attempt to seek for the social conditions which make for man's differential categorizations, and opposed both empiricist and rationalist explanations of man's categories. This French tradition has been continued by such anthropologists as L. Lévy-Bruhl and C. Lévi-Strauss. The main contention of this school is that differential social structures can be defined as the root cause of differential category structures.

The discussion of the source of man's categories has taken a central role in psychology. There are two main schools of thought in the controversy as to whether man's categories are innately or environmentally determined. They are represented by the Gestalt school, who favour at least partial inherent categorical capacities, and the behaviourist school who see man's categories as a purely learned phenomenon. Perhaps a more fruitful view of the problem can be derived from Piaget's work on language in particular and cognition in general; his position is less extreme than the more traditional schools of psychology.   A.H.

cause ; social causation. To say that one event *A* is the cause of a second event *B* may be to assert that the prior occurrence of an event of type *A* is a necessary condition for the occurrence of an event of type *B* ; or that it is a sufficient condition for the occurrence of such an event ; or that it is both necessary and sufficient. To formulate a causal law is thus always to formulate a connection between two classes of event, and thereby to furnish a recipe for producing events of the second kind by producing events of the first kind. Of course we are to the same extent furnished with a recipe for preventing events of the second kind from occurring. Whether or not we are able to make use of such recipes depends not only on the truth of our formulations of causal laws, but also upon the level of technological achievement.

All causal explanation depends not only on our ability to formulate true generalizations about the connections between the events that constitute the causes and the events that constitute the effects, but also on our ability to formulate true generalizations about what would have happened if the particular cause had not operated. We understand the causal effect of a given agency only if we know the truth about certain unfulfilled conditions.

It is sometimes argued that in the social sciences causal explanation has a quite different role from that which it has in the natural sciences. Here a weaker and a stronger contention must be distinguished. The weaker contention is that in the social sciences no causal laws have in fact been established. But if by *causal law* we mean what has been meant so far in this article this contention is plainly false. What critics who advance this contention perhaps mean is that almost all the established generalizations in the social sciences lack convincing theoretical backing. That is, they are distinguishing between mere causal generalizations (All *A*'s as a matter of fact produce *B*'s) and causal laws (All *A*'s *must* produce *B*'s) where the necessity embodied in the law consists in the deducibility of the law from a well-established theory. Yet it is clear that just this kind of backing for our generalizations is frequently supplied in economics, at least, and there seems to be no logical barrier to supplying it elsewhere.

The stronger contention is that not merely *have* no causal laws been established in the social sciences but that no such laws *could* be established. For the nature of human action is such that the regularities to be observed in human behaviour are of a different logical type from the regularities of cause and effect. On this view it is of the essence of human action that it is intentional and rule-guided, and the task of the social scientist is to observe and chart the rules and the concept which inform the intentions by means of which the rules have to be expressed, and which define the way of life of a given society. Underpinning this view is the thesis that *because* human action is intentional and rule-governed, it cannot be causally explained. This thesis is false; it perhaps rests on the mistake of supposing that if two items are such that their descriptions are intentionally and conceptually related, as that of an action and that of its antecedents often are, then these two items cannot stand in an external, contingent causal relationship. But if this were true we could not for example enquire how often injuries and insults actually cause acts of revenge in societies where codes of vendetta prevail and formulate causal generalizations on the basis of observed correlations; which is clearly absurd.

The illusion that causality is unimportant in the social sciences may help to conceal the extent to which key concepts which are not themselves causal presuppose an ability to establish causal truths. So it is with the characteristically sociological notion of function. When it is said that the function of x is to produce y, although in the making of this statement the relationship asserted is not a causal one, the truth of the statement depends upon it being always or mostly true that the bringing about of x is the cause of the occurrence of y.

Finally it is worth remarking that all causal generalizations can be expressed as probability statements; we often contrast the form of a causal law with that of a statement to the effect that if A occurs there is such-and-such a probability that B will occur but of course if the occurrence of A is sufficient condition for the occurrence of B, then if A occurs the certainty that B will occur is a limiting case of such probability.   A.M.

centrality; centrality index. In any social group, considered as a structure of communications between people, it is possible to differentiate among the members according to their centrality. That is to say, each member, according to his or her position in a communication structure, possesses a certain advantage or disadvantage in regard to the number and frequency of communications he or she makes and receives in the group. For a group with a given communication structure, it is possible to calculate the number of communication links between a member and all other members. This may be expressed as a proportion of the total number of such communication links between each member and all other members totalled, whence one has obtained the centrality index of that member. Thus the centrality index of member x is the total number of communication links between group members divided by the number of communication links between x and all other members of the group. It follows that a high centrality index is indicative of a member's favourable position in a communication structure, and *ceteris paribus* such a person having a high centrality index may be said to be in a leadership position, for it is thus possible to estimate quantitatively the degree of influence members of a group may have by virtue of their position in the group. The concept is discussed by J. Klein in *The Study of Groups*, 1956, ch. 4. See GROUP DYNAMICS.   G.D.M.

change. See SOCIAL CHANGE.

character structure. See PERSONALITY.

charisma; routinization of charisma. Charisma, which in Greek means 'divine grace', was used by Ernst Troeltsch and then adopted by Max Weber to

26

designate the ability to lead and inspire by sheer force of personality and conviction without the aid of material incentives or coercion. A charismatic leader, therefore, is one who has no organized 'machine' at his disposal, whose power has not been obtained through institutionalized procedure, and who converts people to his message and secures their obedience by persuasion. The founders of doctrinal communities satisfied these criteria perfectly so long as they had acquired neither an apparatus of coercion nor wealth. Jesus, for example, was a purely charismatic leader. So was John Wesley, Mahomet until he had organized an army, Gandhi before he acquired the backing of the party machine, and Lenin before his return to Russia. The power of the last three remained charismatic, but only partly. The opposite of a charismatic leader is a tyrant who rules through naked force and the fear which he inspires, or a ruler who is obeyed regardless of his personal capabilities and solely in virtue of the office which he holds.

As Weber pointed out, leadership can remain purely charismatic only so long as the number of the followers is small, that is to say at the very beginning of successful movements, because the creation of an administrative machine and the acquisition of funds open possibilities of applying coercion as well as providing remunerative inducements. Moreover the mere duration of the hierarchy inculcates the habits of obedience to the office, which soon acquire a force of inertia independent of the personal qualities of the holder. A transformation of charismatic into institutionalized leadership is usually called its routinization, although 'adulteration' or 'dilution' might be a more illuminating term.

The term 'charisma' becomes superfluous and confusing if it is indiscriminately applied, as commonly happens, to such disparate phenomena as any kind of aura surrounding an office, the supernatural powers attributed to kings and priests, or even simple prestige or status; and the expression 'routinization of charisma' then becomes meaningless.

With the exception of the founders of small sects, leaders can only be partially charismatic. For many of his admirers, de Gaulle had a great deal of charisma, but he also had a police force and the entire apparatus of the state at his disposal to enforce his commands. As the bloody purge in 1934 has shown, Hitler could not rely on his charisma alone, even in his relations with the party stalwarts. Nevertheless, his power over most of the Germans had a very large (though varying) charismatic element, although his power over the conquered nations and his political opponents was based on naked force.

S.L.A.

circulation of elites. See ELITES.

civilization. A term originally derived from the verb *to civilize* from *civis* and *civilitas* describing the acquisition of qualities of politeness and amiability on the part of superiors to inferiors. The Encyclopaedists, however, contrasted civilization not with *barbarism* but with *feudalism*. Consequently, the term has the ring of the Enlightenment about it, for it suggests progress. This use of the term in the late eighteenth century was extended in early sociological writings to a theory of social development. This is clearly seen in Lewis

Morgan's *Ancient Society: Researches in the Lines of Human Progress from Savagery through Barbarism to Civilization.*

A more modern use is to regard human history as being capable of analysis in terms of large units. A. J. Toynbee in *A Study of History*, 1933–1954, points to twenty-one civilizations in the known history of the world, each with its distinctive characteristics, but all sharing certain features or qualities which enable them to be distinguished as members of the same category. Sociologists, like many other people, use the term in a general and vague way as, for instance, in speaking of *modern civilization*, by which is usually meant contemporary urban and industrialized societies. In this respect there is a relationship between *civilization* and *culture*. In the example just given *civilization* tends to be equated with high culture, but sometimes culture is not identified with civilization but instead is contrasted, in the sense that the latter is a more complex social phenomenon, including the organization of material and technological qualities as well as the beliefs, art forms, literature and the body of ideas and values of a people; which more specifically is spoken of as *culture*. An important contribution has been made to the comparative study of civilizations by Alfred Weber, who has analysed civilization as a process. For a synopsis see his *Einführung in die Soziologie*, 1955. His main work, which is an analysis of western civilization as a major historical development, is *Kulturgeschichte als Kultursoziologie*, 1935. An interesting work describing the psychological and sociological processes in the refinement of civilization is N. Elias, *Über den Prozess der Zivilisation*, 1939 (translated *The Civilising Process*, 1978). See BARBARISM, CULTURE, SOCIETY. 	G.D.M.

clan. In modern British anthropological usage, a clan is a named, unilineal descent-group: that is, a body of persons claiming common descent from an ancestor (often mythical) and recruiting the children of either male or female members, but not of both.

The word derives from the Gaelic *clann* meaning children or descendants, and thus refers originally to a cognatic descent-group; anthropologists, however, have usually reserved the term for unilineal groups. An earlier usage favoured the Latin *gens* for unilineal descent-groups of this nature (see L. H. Morgan, *Ancient Society*, 1877), but because this referred, etymologically, to a patrilineal group, American authors tended to use *clan* for matrilineal descent-groups only, reserving *gens* for patrilineal. Often *sib* was used as a generic term for both (see R. H. Lowie, *Primitive Society*, 1920). More recently, G. P. Murdock has suggested that *sib* be used to cover all unilineal groups, while *clan* is reserved for a localized descent-group including the spouses of members (*Social Structure*, 1949). British usage is now standardized in the use of *clan* as the generic term, with *matri-clan* and *patri-clan* denoting the two varieties. Any grouping of clans is a *phratry*.

Classic works on clans include A. L. Kroeber, *Zuni Kin and Clan*, 1917; R. Firth, *We, The Tikopia*, 1936; M. Fortes, *The Dynamics of Clanship amongst the Tallensi*, 1945; E. E. Evans-Pritchard, *The Nuer*, 1940. See LINEAGE, KINSHIP, EXOGAMY, SIB. 	J.R.F.

class. See SOCIAL STRATIFICATION.

class-consciousness. Originally used in a Marxist context where the social system of Capitalism develops to a point where the Proletariat become increasingly aware of their class position *vis à vis* the Bourgeoisie, and hence gain cohesion in the face of their exploitation. Such a consciousness is the prelude to organization and training for the revolutionary conflict which brings about the Dictatorship of the Proletariat.

The term is often used in a loose and general way to indicate a group's self-awareness, and thus can mean a status group's self-identity, through the members sharing a common consumption pattern, in so far as members of the group are frequently aware that their consumption is related to their group membership. See SOCIAL STRATIFICATION.   G.D.M.

classificatory system. A *classificatory* kinship system differs from a *descriptive* one in that certain collateral relatives are addressed or spoken of by terms which also apply to lineal relatives. Thus a man may address his father's brother as *father*, or his father's sister's son may be referred to as *brother*. A small number of kinship terms are thus used for a large number of relatives. The terms *descriptive* and *classificatory* were introduced into analyses of kinship by Lewis Morgan. A famous essay by A. R. Radcliffe-Brown on classificatory kinship systems is to be found in *Structure and Function in Primitive Society*, 1952. Radcliffe-Brown also proffered a structural theory to account for the differences and similarities between kinship systems. See KINSHIP.   G.D.M.

codes; linguistic codes. B. Bernstein has distinguished two patterns of speech which he calls 'elaborated' and 'restricted' codes. These codes represent rules or customs relating to the way people speak both in relation to grammar or the lack of it and syntax. Ways of speaking constitute signals which those who know the code pick-up and others do not. An elaborated code is more explicit and definite, whilst a restricted code leaves the hearer to judge in the light of shared assumptions how to interpret a remark.

Bernstein relates linguistic codes to education pointing out that formal education emphasizes the elaborated code. Those unused to such a code and who rely on a restricted code may be disadvantaged in the educational process. See B. Bernstein, *Class, Codes and Control*, 1971.   G.D.M.

cognate; cognatic. Two persons are *cognates* when they are able to trace their descent from a common ancestor or ancestress regardless of whether the links are through males or females. Thus a *cognatic* kinship system is bilateral, observing no unilineal principle.

Cole, George Douglas Howard (1889–1959). English Labour historian and social theorist who wrote prolifically about all aspects of socialism and working-class life. A product of Balliol College, Oxford, he began his active political career as a member of the Fabian Society, and was described by Maurice Reckitt as having 'a Bolshevik soul in a Fabian muzzle'. This was an inaccurate estimate because the restive Cole was never muzzled. Deeply concerned with social science as a whole, he had long pressed for more attention to sociological subjects at Oxford; and when he was appointed

29

Chichele Professor of Social and Political Theory in 1944 he used his influence to introduce sociology as a permanent part of the university curriculum. His popular books such as *The Life of William Cobbett*, 1924; *The Common People* (with Raymond Postgate), 1938; *Chartist Portraits*, 1941; and his impressive *A History of Socialist Thought* (in four volumes), 1953–1960 are still read, along with much else, even though they can at times be regarded as the hasty forays of a great teacher.   E.W.M.

collective behaviour. Some early social psychological writing was focused on crowd behaviour, for this seemed an important topic. People appeared sometimes to behave quite out of character in crowds, being emotionally swayed or abandoning restraints which were normally noticeable. Gustav Le Bon was one of the earliest writers on the subject (*La Psychologie des foules*, 1895, translated 1896, *The Crowd: a Study of the popular mind*). This kind of study concentrates on the unorganized aspect of collective behaviour, but of course many sociological studies are of organizational behaviour. It may be argued that the two are quite distinct, yet there are some aspects of organized collective behaviour partaking of the characteristics of crowd behaviour, e.g. fashions, financial cycles, morale in organizations and the expression of power in relations between organizations. The theories which aim to explain collective behaviour may be classified into three groups: those which, like Le Bon's, explain crowd behaviour in terms of *contagion*, the rapid communication of moods and the uncritical acceptance of direction; those which describe collective behaviour in terms of *convergence* of people with similar predispositions, ideas and aims; and those which see collective behaviour as being regulated by a social norm which emerges in special situations, known as the *emergent norm* theory. A full discussion of the subject is given by R. H. Turner in *Handbook of Modern Sociology*, 1964, edited by R. E. L. Faris. See SOCIAL ORGANIZATION.   G.D.M.

collective conscience. This term is a translation of an expression used by Émile Durkheim, namely *la conscience collective*, but the difficulty remains of knowing if it should not rather be *consciousness* rather than *conscience*, i.e. should it have a psychological or a moral connotation? Durkheim's definition was that the totality of beliefs and sentiments common to average members of a society form a definite system; it is this system he is referring to when he speaks of *la conscience collective*. A second but related difficulty arises in locating it, for it would appear to be diffused throughout the society. Durkheim on occasion in his *De la division du travail social*, 1893, speaks almost as if there was a social mind in society, and for this reason the concept was not at first much liked in the Anglo-Saxon world, but perhaps we can appreciate its use if we regard it as largely synonymous with the concept *culture*. Thus, like culture, the collective conscience provides the link between one generation and another, it is what is shared in the way of values and sentiments, it is what is upset and shocked by the commission of a crime; it is, says Durkheim, that which defines what a crime is. See DURKHEIM.

                     G.D.M.

colour bar. A colloquial term not having a precise meaning in sociology. It generally implies an institutionalized restriction of access to certain places, amenities, privileges or opportunities according to a socially defined criterion of racial origin. See DISCRIMINATION, PREJUDICE, SEGREGATION, RACE.

community; community centre. Originally the term *community* denoted a collectivity of people who occupied a geographical area; people who were together engaged in economic and political activities and who essentially constituted a self-governing social unit with some common values and experiencing feelings of belonging to one another. Examples are a city, a town, a village or parish, but the idea of community as a goal which people may achieve has become prominent. It arises from the greater mobility of people in modern industrial societies and also the prevalence of mass media of communication. Today industrial concerns spread into many areas and over many countries. Commodities are not restricted in consumption to local areas and there has been a vast increase in communication. *Community*, although less all-inclusive, and slightly more specific in connotation, may be regarded as denoting a community of interests. In modern sociology it remains the case that the term *community* is used in a general and deliberately vague way. For an early attempt to analyse society making use of the concept see R. M. MacIver, *Community: A Sociological Study*, 1917, R. König, *The Community*, 1968 and C. Bell and H. Newby, *Community Studies*, 1971.

The growth of towns and cities and their redevelopment to provide mass housing has led to an awareness of the lack of cohesion and identity of large sections of the population. In answer to this need *community centres* have sometimes been established to provide recreational and cultural activities for people, and to give an opportunity for democratic organization of the residents of an area. They were introduced into the U.S.A. before the First World War, but gained strength in Britain as a result of the work of the Association of Community Centres which has urged the wider development of this kind of provision in connection with new municipal housing estates. Whilst having some cohesive qualities it has to be admitted that community centres can be divisive; they are of course associational in character and therefore limited in the ends pursued. The fact is that they are not communities, but they aim to foster community spirit. To this extent they are contradictory, for in fact a community centre is an association, and only in so far as it is deliberately an association with limited and specified ends can it serve the specific needs of a differentiated urban population. See ASSOCIATION, GEMEINSCHAFT.   G.D.M.

comparative method. The phrase refers to the method of comparing different societies or groups within the same society to show whether and why they are similar or different in certain respects. It was used by eighteenth-century philologists who compared different languages to show from their common characteristics (which also differentiated them from other sets of languages) that they must belong to the same linguistic 'family'. The phrase was subsequently used throughout the nineteenth century to describe the method of discerning similarities in social institutions so as to trace their common origins; however, the method as such was not new having been used by Aristotle in his study of political systems.

Both Montesquieu and Comte, often regarded as the founders of sociology, used or recommended comparison to establish and explain both differences and similarities between societies. Comte suggested the comparison of human with non-human characteristics, to show what was distinctive of the former, and the comparison of societies at the same and at different stages of social development to demonstrate the *laws of coexistence* and the *laws of succession* of social and mental phenomena.

Throughout the nineteenth century there was a strong link between the use of the comparative method and the evolutionist approach, particularly with the growing influence of Darwinism. However, some scholars were not content to establish common origins and to trace the 'natural history' of social phenomena, such as religion and the family, or to 'prove' some theory of the stages of social and mental development; for example, Tylor, like Comte, considered that one of the chief aims of comparison was to discover what he called cultural 'adhesions', or necessary correlations between two or more cultural phenomena, such as a rule of kinship behaviour and a rule of kinship terminology.

But the examples which typify the rather loose and unsystematic procedures of the nineteenth and early twentieth century are to be found in the writings of Sir J. G. Frazer, who used countless illustrations from classical mythology, the Bible and contemporary ethnography to support his theories concerning the characteristics of the human mind and to confirm his hypotheses concerning the origins and development of innumerable customs and beliefs (*The Golden Bough*, 1930–36).

It was J. S. Mill who introduced greater rigour into the discussion by showing that the comparative method was simply an application of the logic of science to ready-made cases, as opposed to experimentally constructed ones; for, as he argued, the scientific method necessarily consists in the comparison of cases which are similar in some respects and dissimilar in others, to show whether certain characteristics are causally connected. However, Mill finally decided that the comparative method did not really accord with the inductive rules of science which he had formulated (*A System of Logic*, Book VI, 1900).

This negative view was challenged by Émile Durkheim. In an early study Durkheim compared the legal systems of different societies at the same and at different levels of development and, using law as an index of the moral character of society, tested his hypothesis that an increase in the division of labour is accompanied by a change in the nature of social integration. Again, in his study of suicide, Durkheim compared the suicide rates both of different societies and of different groups within a society, to show that these rates varied inversely with the degree of social cohesion and with the degree of stability of moral norms; to do this he had also to compare selected indices and determinants of social cohesion and normative stability, and chose types of religious organization, the form of community life, the state of the economy and the polity, and so on. Durkheim concluded, in criticism of Mill, that if comparison was carried out with true precision and control and yielded correlations (rather than invariant causal connections), it could qualify as a quasi-experimental method. Indeed, it has since been argued that Durkheim, particularly in his study of suicide, pioneered the method of *multivariate analysis* in sociology. For example, not content to compare the suicide rates of Protestant and Catholic countries and of Protestant and Catholic groups within any one country, Durkheim compared the two sets of differences to show how far the factor of cohesion, as reflected in religious organization, did operate as an independent determinant of suicide.

A rather different method of comparison to that used by Durkheim is to be found in the work of Max Weber. His method consisted not so much in isolating factors or variables whose operations could be observed in a large number of cases, as in analysing many concrete features of different societies. He did this to show how characteristics, like those of bureaucracy, which are in some respects similar from one case to another are also in other important respects different, in so far as they are affected by other features of the unique historical configuration of which they are a part. Weber's recommendations included the use of *ideal types*; these described the universal characteristics of a social institution or system of beliefs as they would exist in their *pure* form, unaffected by those other elements which make up a unique historical complex. One type of comparison would consist in describing and explaining the variations around a particular ideal type, such as the forms of German and British bureaucracy; another approach would lie in comparing different ideal types, such as those of Protestant and Hindu fatalism, to show how each corresponded to a different system of secular values. Weber demonstrated these correspondences not by establishing statistical correlations but by appealing to a sense of meaningful relationship.

There have been numerous attempts to combine the comparative method with a broad survey of societies in the attempt to establish correlations. Hobhouse, Wheeler and Ginsberg tried in this way to establish a truly empirical scheme of social evolution; they constructed a scale of technological development and then sought to correlate each level on it with particular forms of social life, such as political institutions and moral rules (*The Material C1.lture and Social Institutions of the Simpler Peoples; an Essay in Correlation*, 1915). More recently, Gouldner has made a similar attempt to correlate technological and moral development in his *Notes on Technology and the Moral Order*, 1962. Any defects of such schemes, particularly of the former, lie more in the theoretical assumptions which underlie them, that is, in the idea that societies necessarily develop on all fronts in a well-defined direction, than in the comparative method itself.

Social anthropologists, in their reaction against Frazer and others like him, did tend for a while to equate the comparative method with the worst excesses of the evolutionary approach, accusing the earlier scholars of 'tearing cultural items from their context' and so distorting their meaning. They recommended a *holistic* method and in so far as they did compare societies they did so either to classify them or else to demonstrate the particular similarities and differences between a small number of cases.

In America, the aim of formulating broad generalizations about many societies and testing them statistically by cross-cultural comparison, somewhat in the manner recommended by Tylor, has been sustained far more than in Britain; and for these purposes considerable use has been made of the Human Relations Area Files at Yale. For example, G. P. Murdock in his *Social Structure*, 1949, has asserted the necessary connections between certain property rules, rules of residence and those of kinship behaviour and terminology; while G. C. Homans and D. M. Schneider, in *Marriage, Authority and Final Causes*, 1955, have tried to test their explanation of why one form of marriage preference is commoner than another.

Amongst British anthropologists only S. F. Nadel seemed to sympathize with these aims and methods, though he was fully aware of the difficulties inherent in them. (See *The Foundations of Social Anthropology*, 1949, Ch. IX.) Adopting an intermediate position, I. Schapera has argued for regional comparison in social anthropology, to establish the characteristics of social types. (See 'Some Comments on Comparative Method in Social Anthropology', *American Anthropologist*, LV, 3, 1953, p. 359.) An assumption underlying this argument is that neighbouring societies might share some characteristics, such as those of geography, material culture and language, so that the explanation of differences between them can then be narrowed down to a smaller number of factors. This argument, though persuasive, can be countered by an opposing one: if societies are sufficiently remote from one another, then any similarities between them can be more plausibly attributed to common causes than to mutual influence; for example, any similarities between Japanese and European feudal institutions are more likely to be due to similar political and economic conditions than are similarities between different regions of feudal Europe.

Recently, some sociologists have indicated that different methods of comparison are appropriate to different problems. For example, S. M. Lipset and R. Bendix have compared rates of social mobility in different industrial societies to show that these rates are governed largely by the stage or degree of industrialization; in this they have used methods similar to those of Durkheim, abstracting the relevant variables and establishing measures and objective indices for them, controlling for other influences, adducing statistical correlations, and so on. (See S. M. Lipset and R. Bendix, *Social Mobility in Industrial Society*, 1959.) However, in a recent study of American society, in which Lipset has compared its values and social structure to other societies in Europe and elsewhere, in an attempt to show that values can be independent factors in social causation, the method has been similar to that used by de Tocqueville in the nineteenth century; it consists in making qualitative assessment of relevant historical evidence and interpreting it in terms of its meaningful significance. (See *The First New Nation*, 1963.)

Thus sociologists, who have traditionally opted for comparison in the service of generalization, have come increasingly to accept that a more appropriate method for some purposes is that of comparative history, using certain general ideas about social structure to inform the analysis of a few cases, and to test hypotheses of a very limited range. On the other hand, a British anthropologist, E. R. Leach, has urged his colleagues to seek generalizations by abstracting a small number of variables from their wider context; but he has simultaneously warned them to understand the phenomena in their context before abstracting them. (See *Rethinking Anthropology*, 1961.) In some ways complex societies lend themselves more to the methods of Durkheim, in that their component elements are less tightly integrated than are those of simpler societies, and can therefore be abstracted with less danger of contextual violation; on the other hand, complex societies are less stable, over time, than simpler ones, so that the process of abstracting certain enduring elements for comparison is more difficult and may therefore call for the methods recommended by Weber.

It is clear that the choice of method is governed by the problem investigated. Furthermore, comparison does not in itself yield any particular type of theory or hypothesis, although it may suggest a line of theoretical enquiry, but is a method of testing hypotheses. However deficient it may be in this, it is as Durkheim said the only method available to the sociological disciplines. See ABSTRACTION, METHODOLOGY, FUNCTIONALISM.   P.S.C.

Comte, Auguste Marie François Xavier (1798–1857). French philosopher, moralist and sociologist; he collaborated with Saint Simon from 1817 to 1823, and corresponded with J. S. Mill. He divided *sociology* into social statics and social dynamics. He elaborated the Law of the Three Stages of human thought: theological, metaphysical and positive, which he thought characterized the development both of human knowledge and of society, which correspondingly developed from a military to a legal, and finally to an industrial stage. His view was holistic and organic. The second keystone of his philosophical system was a theorem that the abstract theoretical sciences form a hierarchy, the crown of which is sociology; his synthesis of knowledge was to be the basis of the reorganization of society. Comte believed that social phenomena could be treated scientifically, his method being based on observation, experiment, comparison and history. He viewed the collective facts of history and society as subject to laws and not to individual volition. These ideas were embodied in, *inter alia, Cours de philosophie positive*, 1830–42 (translated by H. Martineau, *The Positive Philosophy of Auguste Comte*, 1853) and *Système de politique positive*, 1851–54.   G.D.M.

concept. In general usage *concept* mainly means notion or idea. It may be defined as the name for the members of a given class of any sort, or as the name for the class itself. More simply, concept is a term referring to a descriptive property or relation.

A concept in sociology is generally regarded as being at a lower level of abstraction than a theory, but a necessary part of any theory, since theories are formed from the concepts employed. Concepts are not, of course, unchanging, and conceptual clarification and redefinition are continuing tasks for the sociologist. A useful discussion of the importance of analysis of concepts in sociology can be found in R. K. Merton, *Social Theory and Social Structure*, revised edition, 1957.

In sociology the prime interest is in the usefulness of concepts for the formation of theories relating to some problem area and the generation of hypotheses for testing. Amongst criteria that have been suggested for the selection of concepts, are precision, empirical anchorage, and usefulness for the formation of theories which have explanatory power for the problem under consideration. The choice and definition of concepts is crucial for the progress of sociology as a science, and the range of disagreement on basic concepts in sociology is still very wide.   A.H.

concrete; the fallacy of misplaced concreteness. *Concrete* is best defined as anything that is specific or individual, as against general or abstract terms, which stress common characteristics or qualities considered apart from their specific setting. *World War II* is concrete whereas *war* is abstract.

A. N. Whitehead in his *Science and the Modern World*, 1925, has called the fallacy of confusing other types of entities with actually existing entities, *the fallacy of misplaced concreteness*. He suggests that this fallacy is pernicious, as it has been responsible for considerable error in philosophical theorizing. It is a fallacy which is inherent in language, for any entity can be the grammatical subject of a sentence and is thus readily treated implicitly if not explicitly as an actual entity.

Talcott Parsons in *The Structure of Social Action*, 1937, uses the fallacy of misplaced concreteness to identify the same error as Whitehead. Parsons has under consideration certain aspects of classical economics and rationalism. The point is that there is no objection to using propositions partially, provided that this is recognized and allowed for. They are then simply abstract formulations on certain aspects of the concrete situation. The fallacy is committed if these propositions are used in any sense as significantly complete representations of the situation in question. Parsons suggested that the rationalist scheme is in breach of the fallacy in that it has underestimated the role of the affective aspects of human behaviour.   A.H.

Condorcet, Antoine Nicolas Caritat, Marquis de (1743–1794). French aristocrat, philosopher, revolutionary and social mathematician; his work covers the whole of the social science field. He collaborated with d'Alembert in the production of *l'Encyclopédie*. His chief work is the *Sketch of an Historical Picture of the Progress of the Human Spirit*, 1795 (translated 1955), which traces the continuous development of mankind through nine epochs; the tenth, beginning with the Revolution, would see the ultimate perfection of humanity, and absolute equality of opportunity. He believed the basis of all progress to be popular education; he advocated state education for children, adults and the handicapped; he wanted co-education, and moral and physical instruction. Also, he favoured civil marriage, divorce, birth control, and the emancipation of women. He saw history's purpose as the discovery and application of the laws of social progress. His influence was widespread; his thought revolutionary; Comte adopted his optimistic historicism.   G.D.M.

conflict; social conflict. The mainstream of nineteenth-century sociological thought underplays the importance of social conflict. From Comte onwards sociologists were concerned to show what institutions were necessary from the point of view of achieving social integration and harmony. Two types of theory were based on opposite assumptions. The Hobbesian tradition posited an initial social state of a war of all against all and this tradition was fortified by the Darwinian notion of a struggle for existence. And Marxists argued that there was a fundamental conflict of interests in society arising from men's differential relations to the means of production and leading to perpetual class struggle.

These disagreements over the role of conflict in social systems continue in contemporary sociology, both in the micro-sociology which studies social roles and relations and in the macro-sociology which studies social and cultural systems.

In the theory of Talcott Parsons, for example, attention is focused on what the author calls 'institutionalized social relations', i.e. social relations in which one actor has expectations of another's action and those expectations are understood and fulfilled. But clearly there are two other possibilities, viz. that in which expectations are not understood and that in which they are understood but not fulfilled. The latter case is the case of conflict at the level of micro-sociology.

Conflict may be of various kinds and it may be limited and regulated. When two individuals compete peacefully for the control of limited resources we speak of *competition* rather than *conflict* and when two individuals with conflicting interests haggle over the terms of an exchange we speak of *bargaining*. Where there is bargaining and free competition at the same time we speak of a *market situation*. But a market situation may break down if there is a restriction on competition and the parties to the market-bargain seek to compel compliance with their own interests by deploying sanctions. In these circumstances the market-situation gives way to a conflict-situation which is resolved on the basis of a balance of power.

Many sociologists, in accounting for the institutions of modern industrial societies, have been inclined to emphasize the integration of social institutions and to posit a mutually sustaining system of such institutions recognizing only the possibility that some institutions rely upon the regulated conflict processes of the market. As against this, 'conflict theory' emphasizes that there may be conflict within an institution and between institutions and that the regulated and peaceful conflict processes of the market may give way to open and non-peaceful conflict.

The main attempt to systematize conflict theory emerges from the writings of Karl Marx. In Marxism the basis of conflict is to be found in the social relations of production. Thus all supporting social institutions support the different 'sides' in this conflict and the unitary concept of a cultural and social system disappears. The political and economic institutions of capitalist society are seen as representing 'the political and economic sway of the bourgeoisie' and as against this there is reference to 'the political economy of the working class'. A conflict between classes in the social relations of production spills over to become a conflict in all spheres and the social system becomes one of 'two great warring camps'.

R. Dahrendorf, on the other hand, has suggested that intra-institutional conflicts occur about authority in all institutions and that there need not necessarily be any overlapping. In particular, he argues that industrial conflict has become institutionalized, i.e. confined within a particular institutional context. Lockwood has drawn attention to the importance of conflict between institutional sub-systems, e.g. there is no necessary harmony between industrial and educational institutions.

L. Coser and M. Gluckman have both argued that orthodox functionalist theory gives insufficient weight to conflict and that it should be revised to take this into account. Both argue that a number of cross-cutting conflicts which ensure that one's ally on one front is one's enemy on another make for social stability. Coser also argues that a looseness of institutional arrangements which permits the terms of some social relations to be fixed after a trial of strength between the parties makes for greater stability than a more rigid structure.

The recognition of regulated conflicts of this kind as a permanent feature of all social structures is now widely accepted in sociology. They do not, however, adequately explain socially disruptive conflicts and in this sphere, the sociology of political revolution, a great deal of theoretical and empirical work remains to be done. Attempts to revise Marxism to give recognition to a greater number of classes by such writers as Karl Mannheim and C. Wright Mills point in this direction. See R. Dahrendorf, *Class and Class Conflict in an Industrial Society*, 1959; L. A. Coser, *The Functions of Social Conflict*, 1956; M. Gluckman, *Custom and Conflict in Africa*, 1955. J.A.R.

conjugal family. See FAMILY.

connubium. *Connubium* (from Lat. *connubium*, marriage) in anthropology refers to the right and obligation of members of a category of men to choose their wives from a prescribed category of women. The two groups are said to have or maintain connubium. Ties established between lineal descent groups on this basis form a *prescriptive alliance*. Such closed systems of marriage may be contrasted with open, or preferential systems where, in theory, choice of a spouse may be made from a much wider range.

In Roman civil law connubium between the parties was a condition of marriage. The law specified the categories so linked. See R. W. Lee, *The Elements of Roman Law* (4th edition), 1956.

Early uses of the term in sociological literature occur in É. Durkheim and M. Mauss, 'De quelques formes primitives de classification', *Année Sociologique*, VI, 1903; see also H. J. Wehrli, *Beitrag zur Ethnologie der Chingpaw*, 1904. H.D.M.

consanguinity. A social relationship based on descent from a common ancestor is described as a consanguinial relationship. Clearly, from the root the connotation is of a blood-tie, but in fact consanguinial relations may not be of this kind. Whilst normally referring to the lineal or collateral relatives of a person, the term may be extended to cover those linked by adoption or by fictional blood-ties, so that some relations are considered consanguine whilst strictly speaking they are nothing of the kind. This difficulty led A. R. Radcliffe-Brown to argue that a better term to use is *kinship* and to differentiate between *kinship* relations (i.e. those based on descent from a common ancestor including fictional ones) from *affinal* relations such as marital relations and those following from marriage. For convenience, however, the term *kinship* sometimes includes affines. See KINSHIP. G.D.M.

consensus. *Consensus* is a variable property of social systems which range from groups of two or more members to whole societies. Consensus exists when the members of these systems are in a state of affirmative agreement about normative and cognitive matters relevant to their action towards one another, towards the central persons or roles in the system, and towards persons, roles, and collectivities outside the system. Consensus is, then, agreement about the rules which should govern their conduct concerning the goals of the system and the allocation of roles and rewards within the system. There is another element present in consensus: this is a solidarity formed by a sense of common identity arising from ties of personal affection, of primordial (ethnic, kinship, or territorial) characteristics, of a shared relationship to sacred things, or of a membership in a common culture or in a common civil community.

Consensus is consensus with respect to the centre of the system, which includes persons, roles, institutions, beliefs, and norms, and which the consensus affirms. The element of solidarity can vary somewhat independently of the cognitive (beliefs) and normative (rules) elements in the consensus. A state of affective solidarity might obtain between sectors of a social system which are in dissensus with respect to particular issues.

The existence of consensus within any social system large or small does not necessarily entail a complete consensus embracing every member and governing every contingency which may arise within the system or in its environment. Thus, there might be more consensus on some issues than on others, and the sectors of the population participating in the consensus might vary so that lines of cleavage which separate the consensual from the dissensual sectors might shift from occasion to occasion. Furthermore, the intensity of the conflict or dissensus on a particular issue (i.e. the absence or suspension, in varying degrees, of consensus on the issue) might vary inversely with respect to the amount and coverage of consensus on other issues which accompanies it and in the strength of the affective element in the solidarity.

Consensus is a necessary component of macro-social order, meaning by 'order' a combination of relatively harmonious collaboration in the execution of agreed or accepted tasks, widespread acceptance of the allocation of rewards, and the relatively or mainly peaceful resolution of conflicts between corporate bodies, strata, and individuals. The importance of consensus to order does not mean that order is possible only on the basis of complete consensus. For one thing, order depends on other factors as well as consensus. But even the fullest consensus is never complete.

What is essential for order is that there should be sufficient consensus about the legitimacy of the central institutional system, about the legitimacy of the mode of access of the incumbents of the major roles of the central institutional system, about the general rules and particular commands which they promulgate, and about the distribution of roles, rewards, and facilities which they influence or for which they are held responsible. If there is a moderate degree of consensus about some of these elements, and especially the first two, conflicts about the last can be contained and partially resolved.

In a narrow and literal sense, consensus can be conceived as the consensus of equals or subordinates in opposition to the central institutional and cultural systems. When we speak of consensus as a factor in the maintenance of social order, we are speaking of consensus between rulers and a substantial and relevant section of the ruled. It is more important for the maintenance of order that the elites of the different spheres and their proximate followings be in a considerable degree of consensus and that the counter-elites and their proximate followings, who are included among the ruled, likewise share in it, though the latter will naturally be less consensual *vis-à-vis* the elites than the various sectors of the elites will be among themselves. Where such a moderate consensus of elites and counter-elites is not present, the working of the central institutional system will be impeded and the hitherto prevailing order will be disrupted.

Complete consensus is impossible. Diverse parochial attachments focused on internally relatively solidary subsystems of classes, ethnic groups, religious affiliations, and local and regional communities, as well as the divergent interests of occupations, professions, and classes, are inevitable in any differentiated society. Likewise, the diverse cultures of generations and of kinship groups continuously generate dispositions which are resistant to complete assimilation into a unitary society-wide consensus. The unequal distributions of authority, income, and deference make for resentment among some of those who are in the lower sectors of the distributions against those in the upper sectors. These separate cultures, divergent interests, and resentments are conducive to the denial of the legitimacy of what is done and enunciated by those in the higher strata who people the central institutional and cultural systems. Thus, even if the latter are fortunate in having a consensus of those strata or groups closer to the centre of society, they are not likely to receive an equal affirmation from the peripheral strata.

Besides this, in practically all large societies, including the mass societies of the present day, the processes of communication from centre to periphery are full of imperfections. Quite apart from the ecological hindrances to the saturation of society by communications from the centre, the unequal distribution of capacities, educational opportunities, resources, and aspirations means that certain sectors of the society, usually those at the lower portions of the distribution of income and deference, are bound to receive less of the central cultural values and beliefs. As a result, they cannot enter as fully into the consensual pattern as those in the upper portions of the distributions.

But all this notwithstanding, all societies normally do enjoy enough consensus concerning the distributions of authority, income, and deference to enable them to continue for very extended periods without civil war and revolution. For one thing, the very fact of effective coercive control tends to have a self-legitimating consequence, so that what often appears to be 'naked power' acquires the aura of legitimacy. If the incumbents of the key roles in the central institutional system are able to persist in their incumbency, with some modicum of effectiveness in maintaining themselves and in implementing their policies, they also succeed in imposing themselves on their societies and therewith in creating some measure of consensus around themselves.

Such consensus is never universally inclusive nor is it ever more than intermittent. Much of the life of any society is lived outside the consensus which focuses on the global distributions of authority, income, and deference. Many of the concerns of most members of any societies are focused on issues which seem not to involve the central institutional system. There are zones of social life which are neither consensual nor dissensual. They are practically irrelevant to the macro-social consensus. Ignorance, indifference, isolation, although they testify to the incomplete inclusiveness of consensus, are very important in the maintenance of order. Hence, order in the society as a whole does not require continuous and universal consensus. Indeed, consensus of the sort under discussion here becomes pertinent only when issues referring to the global distributions emerge.

Nonetheless, even this partial, fluctuating, fragmentary, and intermittent consensus breaks down on occasion. When the central institutional system fails to maintain its normal level of effectiveness, when the elites fail to meet demands which they had previously satisfied, or when new demands cannot be met by the elites, the consensus concerning the legitimacy of their incumbency and their accomplishments undergoes attentuation at crucial points. The counter-elites then find greater support, and their refusal to collaborate within the framework of the previously operative consensus becomes stronger. Revolutions and secessions occur. Old elites are replaced, central institutional systems are remodelled, and then after a time a new consensus is formed to confront the same challenges and obstacles as those which preceded it. See E. A. Shils, *Center and Periphery: Essays in Macrosociology*, 1975, ch. 1. See ELITE. E.A.S.

conspicuous consumption. This term was much used by Thorstein Veblen in his famous book *The Theory of the Leisure Class*, 1899, to describe the wasteful use of expensive articles, ostensibly because they have intrinsic value. Yet the very ostentation signifies a willingness to demonstrate wealth and position by identifying with the leisure class. Conspicuous consumption thus provides for invidious class distinctions because only those who belong to the leisure class can indulge in this behaviour, others can but be envious or else display pale imitations of this behaviour, or more usually be the one *and* do the other. G.D.M.

construct. See CONCEPT.

contract. See SOCIAL CONTRACT.

conurbation. Patrick Geddes in his book *Cities in Evolution*, 1915, coined this word to describe the towns which had grown together in South Lancashire. Today it is a recognized technical term used to describe urban areas formed by the fusion of towns through spreading industry and housing. Although containing open spaces such as parks and playing fields, conurbations are essentially built-up areas in which any agricultural land is only found in enclaves. A special report on the six major conurbations of England and Wales in the 1951 Census analysed Greater London, Tyneside, Merseyside, Manchester, West Yorkshire and the West Midlands, which together contained approximately forty per cent of the total population. By the 1971 Census this figure had dropped to approximately one-third. In United Nations publications the term 'urban agglomeration' is often used, and in the United States the term 'metropolitan area' is used. Census 1951, *Report on Greater London and Five Other Conurbations*, 1956. P.H.M.

Cooley, Charles H. (1864–1929). American social philosopher, sociologist;

41

greatly influenced by Schäffle. Cooley's major works are *Human Nature and the Social Order*, 1902, *Social Organisation*, 1909, *Social Process*, 1918, and *Sociological Theory and Social Research*, 1930. The keystone of his sociology is his organic theory; he viewed society as a whole, composed of differentiated, but 'systematically' related parts, each with a special function. Society is also a psychic entity, with a social mind manifested in organization and institutions. He considered society and the individual to be complements, 'the collective and distributive aspects of the same thing' (1902). He distinguished between *secondary* and *primary groups* which are 'those characterized by intimate face-to-face association and co-operation' (1909). Of the more inclusive groups, class and caste are most important. He developed the concept of *self* as developing in a social context and nurtured by primary groups.   G.D.M.

corporate group. Following Sir Henry Maine, a corporate group may be said to represent the case where there is a perpetuity of an estate, composed of rights over persons, over real, moveable, and incorporeal property, that is shared by an aggregate of persons. Usually corporate groups may be distinguished according to their typical activities and by the kinds of sanctions applied to their members; they may be economic, political, religious and so forth. Clearly, sometimes kinship groups are corporate groups in this sense. The nature of the corporate group was a particular interest of Max Weber, who saw in some of its modern forms the significant elements of modern industrial society. Thus its two chief manifestations are the joint stock company and the political party.

It is difficult to discuss the corporate group with reference to property rights, especially rights over things. Thus the incorporated joint stock company is a group of persons who possess transferable rights to a share in the profits, together with rights of control over the assets, although these latter rights may vary greatly from one case to another. It should be noted that shareholders are not merely owners of tangible property, but that they share in the less tangible, but primarily more important, legal personality of the group. In many cases, of course, ownership has in practice become divorced from control, especially in those instances where the corporate group consists of many members and where an individual's share is small in proportion to the whole.

Although one way of looking at the corporate group is in relation to property, defined as rights over things, another way is to examine it in relation to authority. This was pre-eminently the view of Max Weber in his discussion of the concept *Verband* (translated as 'corporate group'). Weber considered corporate groups as internally differentiated into roles, played by the members, such roles being distinguished by their incorporation of authority to command or their duty of submission to persons playing other roles, themselves incorporating authority.

The subject of corporate groups, their nature, differences in types, and their evolution is one of the principal subjects of sociological investigation. Important contributions to the literature may be found in Max Weber's *Theory of Social and Economic Organisation* (translated by T. Parsons), 1947, and A. A. Berle and G. C. Means, *The Modern Corporation and Private*

Property, revised edition, 1968. See SOCIAL ORGANIZATION, PROPERTY.

G.D.M.

criminology. The study of criminal behaviour. The word seems to have been used for the first time in the writings of the French anthropologist P. Topinard towards the end of the nineteenth century. However, several major studies in penology and the treatment of offenders had been published considerably earlier, notably by Cesare Beccaria (1738–1794) and Jeremy Bentham (1748–1832). An analysis of the geographical distribution of crime in France, conducted by André Guerry, appeared in 1829, and in 1835 the Belgian mathematician Adolphe Quételet published an ambitious study of the social distribution of criminal behaviour in France, Belgium, Luxembourg and Holland, under the title *Sur l'homme et le dévelopment des ses facultés; essai de physique sociale.* In contrast to these investigations, which were essentially concerned with crime as a social phenomenon, the pioneer work of Cesare Lombroso (1835–1909) and his famous pupil Enrico Ferri (1856–1928), the leaders of the Positive School of criminologists, employed the methods of anthropology in the attempt to establish a biological theory of criminality.

Modern criminology has its roots in the disciplines of sociology, psychology, psychiatry and law. It embraces studies of:
1. the nature, forms and incidence of criminal acts, and of their social, temporal and geographical distribution;
2. the physical and psychological characteristics, histories and social origins of criminals (particularly, but not exclusively, of persistent offenders) and of the relations between criminality and other abnormalities of behaviour;
3. the characteristics of victims of crime;
4. non-criminal anti-social behaviour, especially that which is defined as criminal in some countries and not in others, such as homosexual conduct, adultery, prostitution and attempted suicide;
5. the procedures of the police and of the criminal courts, including sentencing practice, social influences upon the decisions of judges and juries, and certain problems of testimony and evidence;
6. methods of punishing, training and treating offenders;
7. the social structure and organization of penal institutions;
8. methods of preventing and controlling crime. (The last four fields of study are commonly grouped under the general name of *penology*.)

Some writers would also include within the purview of criminology the science of criminalistics (i.e. of methods of identifying crimes and detecting offenders) and studies of the origins and development of the criminal law and of public attitudes to crime and criminals.

The methods and strategies of investigation employed in criminology have, for the most part, been borrowed or adapted from one or other of its parent disciplines. (A comprehensive account of contemporary criminological research will be found in *Comparative Criminology*, by Hermann Mannheim, 1965, 2 vols.) *Statistical techniques* are extensively used in the analysis of the incidence of crime. Much basic information about the frequency, nature and geographical distribution of offences, and the age, sex and occupation of offenders, is derived from police records and other official sources. Intensive studies of particular classes of offence or offender, and area studies of the 'ecological' distribution of crimes in urban neighbourhoods, are also important sources of information about the patterns of criminal activity. *Studies of individual criminals* have been carried out by several distinct methods. Psychiatric case-studies, based upon prolonged unstructured interaction between investigator and subject, are mainly used to obtain a longitudinal case-history of the development of the criminal, although there are obvious hazards in retrospective studies of this kind. Psychometric investigations of particular groups of offenders (usually persistent criminals, or individuals convicted of certain categories of crimes) are usually directed to the discovery of individual differences which distinguish criminals from non-criminals or persistent offenders from others. Formal psychological tests, rating scales, objective-behaviour tests, physiological measures, or interview methods may be employed, or a combination of several of these. *Prediction studies* are a comparatively recent development, but promise to become one of the most valuable research strategies of the criminologist. They involve the compilation of 'experience tables', incorporating a wide range of information about a group of criminals and their offences; the subsequent analysis of this heterogeneous array of data in the light of the criminal careers of the sample group (or of their performance in a correctional regime) can yield valuable clues to the determinants of criminal conduct. Rather limited use has been made of *experiments*, although one or two major 'field demonstrations' in the prevention and control of delinquency have been undertaken with rather equivocal results. Controlled experiments in correctional methods have become more common in recent years, usually involving random allocation of offenders between several alternative forms of training or treatment, with careful follow-up evaluation of results. *Sociological* studies of neighbourhoods in which there are high rates of delinquency have thrown light on environmental correlates of delinquency and crime; similar techniques have been used to study the structure and organization of inmate groups in penal institutions. An authoritative review and critique of contemporary criminological writing is contained in G. Nettler, *Explaining Crime* (second edition, 1977). See DELINQUENT, DEVIANCE, PENOLOGY.

G.B.T.

critical sociology. See FRANKFURT SCHOOL.

cross-cousin. Cross-cousins are the children of siblings of opposite sex. Thus an individual's mother's brother's children and his father's sister's children would both be his own cross-cousins.

The term has been used consistently in this way since it was introduced by E. B. Tylor. ('On a method of investigating the development of institutions', *Journal of the Royal Anthropological Institute*, 1889.) It is usual to distinguish the *matrilateral* cross-cousins (mother's brother's children) from the *patrilateral* (father's sister's children). The main issue in the study of the cross-cousin relationship has concerned the interpretation of prescribed or preferential marriage between such cousins which occurs in several societies.

An excellent summary and a provocative theory can be found in C. Lévi-Strauss, *Les Structures Élémentaires de la Parenté*, 1949. This has been attacked in G. Homans and D. Schneider, *Marriage, Authority, and Final Causes*, 1955, and defended in R. Needham, *Structure and Sentiment*, 1962. See KINSHIP, PARALLEL-COUSINS.   J.R.F.

cultural anthropology; culture history. See CULTURE and SOCIAL ANTHROPOLOGY.

culture. *Culture*, in its broadest definition, refers to that part of the total repertoire of human action (and its products), which is socially as opposed to genetically transmitted.

It used to be thought that *culture*, in the sense of a repertoire of learned behaviour socially transmitted, was the exclusive preserve of Man. Much research on Primates recently, however, has shown that social transmission plays a not inconsiderable part in their survival. (See Irven de Vore, *Primate Behavior*, 1965.) This also casts doubt on the 'critical point' theory of the origin of culture in Man. This states that it was a development of the brain which gave rise to the 'capacity for culture'. (See A. L. Kroeber, *Anthropology*, 1923.) However, recent evidence has shown that the early hominid *australopithecus* is known to have made tools. Thus the advent of cultural activities predates the rapid growth of the human brain. (See Sol Tax, ed., *Horizons of Anthropology*, ch. 3, 1964.) This means that cultural and physical evolution developed together and influenced each other.

Most anthropological definitions of *culture* have been modifications of that of E. B. Tylor: 'Culture or Civilization is that complex whole which includes knowledge, belief, art, morals, law, custom, and any other capabilities and habits acquired by man as a member of society.' (*Primitive Culture*, vol. I, 1871.) Several have placed stress on the fact that such behaviour is *learned*, and hence have made the learning process the central aspect of analysis. (See R. Linton, *The Study of Man*, 1936.) Others have seen the ideational aspects of 'social heredity' as crucial, as in the elaborate definition of A. L. Kroeber and Clyde Kluckhohn, '... patterns, explicit and implicit, of and for behaviour, acquired and transmitted by symbols, constituting the distinctive achievement of human groups, including their embodiment in artifacts; the essential core of culture consists of traditional (i.e. historically derived and selected) ideas, and especially their attached values; culture systems may, on the one hand, be considered as products of action, and on the other hand as conditioning elements of further action.' ('Culture; A critical review of concepts and definitions', *Papers of the Peabody Museum of American Archaeology and Ethnology*, vol. 47, no. 1, 1952.) Here artifacts are included as the 'embodiment' of culture, although they are more usually regarded as its products. Sometimes anthropologists distinguish artifacts as *material culture*.

Yet other emphases on the ideational side are present in Robert Redfield's conception of culture as a body of 'shared understandings' (*The Folk Culture of Yucatan*, 1941), while for Malinowski, culture was essentially a response to human needs (*A Scientific Theory of Culture*, 1944).

Most sociologists have used the term explicitly with the ideational meaning, in order to distinguish culture from *society*, or *social structure*, which they consider to be their basic subject matter. Thus, for A. R. Radcliffe-Brown, culture is essentially a set of rules (*A Natural Science of*

Society, 1957). Talcott Parsons and his collaborators in the Theory of Action school regard culture as essentially symbolic and evaluative. 'Cultural objects are symbolic elements of the cultural tradition, ideas or beliefs, expressive symbols or value patterns ...' (*The Social System*, 1951). This view is shared by Pitirim Sorokin (*Society, Culture and Personality*, 1947).

Anthropologists, in contrast to sociologists, have usually taken their whole subject matter as culture, and have not confined its use to ideational aspects of behaviour. Thus the central concept has been that of *custom*, i.e. of traditional and regular ways of doing things. This refers to behaviour alone, while the other concept, *trait*, includes not only behaviour, but also material factors such as house types, weaving patterns, etc. Culture on this model is seen as a cluster of customs or traits. (See John Gillin, *The Ways of Men*, 1948; on traits see, for example, Leslie Spier, 'The Sun Dance of the Plains Indians', *American Museum of Natural History, Anthropological Papers*, 16, no. 7, 1921.) Sociologically inclined British anthropologists have, in some cases, continued to recognize the central importance of custom in regulating behaviour (see M. Gluckman, *Custom and Conflict in Africa*, 1955). By and large, however, British anthropologists have seen culture as either the *content* of social relations (R. Firth, *Elements of Social Organization*, 1951) or have seen structure as one way of looking at culture. These distinctions have been discussed by Gregory Bateson in *Naven*, 1936.

The concentration on items of culture led to several questions. The earliest of these concerned the origin and distribution of traits and customs. Thus, for example, many nineteenth-century writers sought the 'origins' of religion, the state, marriage, etc. (see, for example, H. Spencer, *Principles of Sociology*, 1876). There are two distinct theories in this field. One held that men were everywhere psychologically similar, and that similar problems called forth similar responses. This explained the widespread occurrence of similar customs throughout the world. (See Tylor, *op. cit.*) The other held that man's inventiveness was limited, and that most traits were invented once and then 'diffused' to the other parts of the world. (See W. J. Perry, *The Children of the Sun*, 1923.)

Dissatisfaction with the above 'fragmentary' approaches to culture led to a concentration on *pattern* and *function* in the integration of cultures. Here we must distinguish between Culture, a property of the human race, and *a* culture, which is generally taken to be the distinctive way of life of a particular set of human beings. (Note that a *sub-culture* is generally taken to mean a section of a *National* culture: e.g. The culture of an immigrant group.) The evolutionary and diffusionist approaches had taken the whole field of human culture as their subject matter. Malinowski, however, urged that understanding of specific cultures should be the aim of anthropology (see the article 'Culture', in the *Encyclopaedia of the Social Sciences*). He argued for an analysis of cultures through the 'function' of each element or custom in the total culture. (See his foreword to the third edition of *The Sexual Life of Savages*, 1932.) In America the same concentration on the integration of whole cultures was summed up in Ruth Benedict's *Patterns of Culture*, 1934. This stressed the idea of *cultural relativism*, that is, the principle that a culture can only be understood in its own terms, and that standards from other cultures cannot be applied to it. It also stressed the idea that culture moulded personality, and that ideas of normality and deviance were relative to particular cultures. This idea has since been challenged by, for example, Robert Redfield in *The Primitive World and Its Transformations*, 1953, and from being primarily concerned with cultural *differences* anthropologists have come to be interested in the possibilities of cultural *universals*. (See Clyde Kluckhohn, 'Universal Categories of Culture', in A. L. Kroeber, ed., *Anthropology Today*, 1953.)

The stress on the cultural moulding of personality led to the development of a school of 'culture and personality' which concentrated on the development of the individual. It incorporated much of psychoanalysis (see Freud's *Civilization and Its Discontents*, 1930). It received a stimulus from Margaret Mead (see, e.g. *Sex and Temperament in Three Primitive Societies*, 1935), and from the collaboration of anthropologist and psychiatrist in A. Kardiner and R. Linton, *The Psychological Frontiers of Society*, 1945. For a summary and assessment, see A. F. C. Wallace, *Culture and Personality*, 1961.

There has recently been a revival of interest in the evolution of culture – though not in terms of a search for origins. There are two branches, the 'ecological' represented by the work of Julian Steward (*Theory of Culture Change*, 1955) and the 'technological' as in the work of Leslie White (*The Science of Culture*, 1949). The latter has worked out an approach to cultural evolution which stresses the *autonomy* of culture (see also his *The Evolution of Culture*, 1959). Studies of long-run cultural changes figure in A. L. Kroeber's *Configurations of Culture Growth*, 1944. An influential concept in this sphere has been that of *culture lag*. The central idea here is that various elements in a culture change at different rates, and so integration may be far from perfect. (See W. F. Ogburn, *Social Change*, 1922.)

A pre-occupation stemming originally from the trait approach to culture is that of *culture areas*. Here there is an attempt to mark out geographical areas in which there is a high consistency of traits, and which differ recognizably from neighbouring areas. Thus, for example, in America, the *plains* culture area is distinguished from the *northwest coast*, the *northeastern woodlands*, etc. (See A. L. Kroeber, *Cultural and Natural Areas of Native North America*, 1939.) For South America, see J. Steward and L. C. Faron, *Native Peoples of South America*, 1959; for Africa, G. P. Murdock, *Africa: Its Peoples and their Culture History*, 1959.

A more recent interest has been in the role of language in culture, stemming from the work of Edward Sapir (*Language*, 1921) and Benjamin Lee Whorf (*Language, Thought and Reality*, 1956). For a recent summary see D. H. Hymes (ed.), *Language in Culture and Society*, 1964.

The best discussion of the concept of culture is in Kroeber and Kluckhohn, *op. cit.*, but this is difficult to obtain. There is a lot of discussion in A. L. Kroeber's *Anthropology* (1948 edition), and most text-books on cultural anthropology discuss the term. (See, for example, Melville J. Herskovits, *Cultural Anthropology*, 1955.) There are a number of useful papers in R. Linton (ed.), *The Science of Man in the World Crisis*, 1945; see also C. Kluckhohn, 'The Concept of Culture' in D. Lerner and H. D. Lasswell (eds.), *The Policy Sciences*, 1951. See CIVILIZATION, CUSTOM, DIFFUSION, EVOLUTION, FUNCTION, PERSONALITY, RACE, SOCIAL ANTHROPOLOGY, SUPERORGANIC.   J.R.F.

culture area. See CULTURE.

custom. The term *custom* refers to established modes of thought and action. This general term is used by anthropologists at various levels of abstraction. By its use attention is directed to: the routine acts of daily life: the rules implicit in routine; the cultural patterns discernible in repetitive acts; and the distinctive nature of the whole culture. Let us take these in turn.

M. Fortes, stressing that 'the paramount concern of social and cultural anthropology is with the phenomenon of custom', avers that the researcher's 'main task is to observe and record the minutiae of custom and conduct in their context of social relations' (M. Fortes, 'Graduate Study and Research' in D. G. Mandelbaum, G. W. Lasker and E. M. Albert, 'The Teaching of Anthropology', *American Anthropological Association Memoir 94*, 1963). His emphasis is that of B. Malinowski who wrote of the 'imponderabilia of actual life', those daily routines, those conversational tones, those 'series of phenomena of great importance which cannot possibly be recorded by questioning or computing documents, but have to be observed in their full actuality' (*Argonauts of the Western Pacific*, 1922, p. 18). W. G. Sumner, writing in 1906, regarded the formation of the folkways as due to 'the frequent repetition of petty acts' motivated by interest producing 'habit in the individual and custom in the group' (*Folkways*, 1906, pp. 18 and 19).

Malinowski called for 'the study by direct observation of the rules of custom organically connected' and existing 'in the chain of social transactions' (*Crime and Custom in Savage Society*, 1926, p. 125. Cf. J. Beattie, *Other Cultures*, 1964, pp. 168–70). Sumner, too, emphasized the regulative force of the folkways, calling them mores 'when they include a judgment that they are conducive to societal welfare, and when they exert a coercion on the individual to conform to them'.

F. Bailey emphasizes the distinctive features of a society's 'customary ways of acting and customary ways of believing or thinking'. These features are revealed by analysis, beginning with 'the hypothesis that all the customs are connected with one another and together form a coherent whole'. The anthropologist's task is to find 'a pattern in behaviour of which the people themselves are not aware' (see his article 'Anthropology' in N. Mackenzie, ed., *A Guide to the Social Sciences*, 1966, pp. 59–60). In his *Cultural Anthropology, the Science of Custom*, 1958, F. Keesing writes of a 'particular customary tradition, that is, a *culture*' (p. 25). For R. Benedict 'the fact of first rate importance is the predominant role that custom plays in experience and in belief'. Custom is the lens without which one cannot see at all (*Patterns of Culture*, 1948, pp. 2 and 8).

F. Barth draws attention to the emphasis on unchanging tradition implicit in the concept *custom* and suggests that 'what we empirically observe is not "customs", but "cases" of human behaviour', i.e. cases of *choice*, and that 'our central problem becomes what are the constraints and incentives that canalize choices' (*Models of Social Organization*, Royal Anthropological Institute Occasional Paper No. 23, 1966, p. 1). This approach owes much to R. Firth (see, for example, his article 'Social Organization and Social Change', *Journal of the Royal Anthropological Institute*, 84, 1954). Contemporary studies focus on the symbolic character of customary behaviour. This semiotic emphasis takes as its premise the view that '... the full array of signs and concepts men use to communicate with each other and to interpret themselves and the world around them should be the central object of description and analysis' (D. J. Umiker-Sebok, 'Semiotics of Culture' in *Annual Review of Anthropology,* 1977).   H.D.M.

cybernetics. A branch of natural science concerned with the self-maintenance and self-control of systems, both mechanical and organic, through a feedback process. It also includes the study of communication of information in such systems. This line of enquiry was advanced by the publication of N. Wiener's book *Cybernetics or Control and Communication in the Animal and the Machine,* 1949. It has been described by G. T. Guilbaud in his book *What is Cybernetics?,* 1959. Its possible relationship to sociological research is discussed by D. G. MacRae in 'Cybernetics and Social Science', *British Journal of Sociology,* II, 2, 1951.   G.D.M.

D

Davy, Georges (1883–1976). French sociologist who did much as editor to re-establish the famous publication founded by Durkheim, *L'Année Sociologique*. His contributions to the sociology of law include *La foi jurée*, 1922. Recteur de l'Académie de Rennes 1931–8, he became Doyen de la Faculté des Lettres firstly at Dijon and then in 1950 at Paris.

delicts. In the sociological treatment of legal systems it is necessary to make a distinction other than that between criminal and civil offences, for what is regarded as a civil offence in one society may be a private matter in another, even although it is considered a wrong. A. R. Radcliffe-Brown in an article on 'Primitive Law' in the *Encyclopaedia of the Social Sciences*, 1933, introduced the distinction between the law of *public delicts* and the law of *private delicts*. This allows for a sociological discussion of the different types of sanctions aroused by offences of each type, even when the actual offence may in one society be socially regarded as of a different category from that in another. Murder, for instance, is a public delict in modern Western societies, but among some people it is a private delict. On the other hand, sacrilege or adultery may be vestigial legal relics or not even illegal acts at all, as in Britain, whilst these same offences may be serious public delicts in many simple societies. G.D.M.

delinquent. An adjective commonly used to describe minor criminal acts and infractions of regulations (for example, failure to renew a broadcasting licence) and behaviour which, while not illegal, is generally regarded as anti-social or immoral (such as adultery). It is also applied to individuals in the same sense.

The expression *juvenile delinquent* usually refers to an individual who has been, or is liable to be, brought before a juvenile court, either because he has committed a criminal offence, or for some other reason within the jurisdiction of the court (sometimes described as committing a 'status offence' – for example, being 'beyond the control' of his parents or guardians). See DEVIANCE; SOCIAL DEVIANCE. G.B.T.

demography. This word is defined in the United Nations *Multilingual Demographic Dictionary* (New York, 1958) as 'the scientific study of human populations, primarily with respect to their size, their structure and their development'. The word was probably first used by the Frenchman A. Guillard in his textbook, *Éléments de Statistique Humaine*. W. F. Willcox (*Studies in American Demography*, 1940) quotes a number of different definitions of the word, varying among themselves, some of them more

50

limited than the definition given above. Today the word is generally used to denote the study of phenomena connected with human populations, such as births, marriages, deaths, migration and the factors which influence them. Very occasionally, the term is used by biologists in the study of animal populations.

It is conventional to date the beginning of demography as a science in 1662. In that year John Graunt published his *Natural and Political Observations on the Bills of Mortality*, in which he used the returns of deaths in different parishes of London, to deduce some generalizations about human populations. He showed that the proportions of deaths attributed to certain causes tended to be constant, and attempted to study mortality by constructing a life table (or table of mortality) which follows a group of children born at the same moment of time, until the last of them has died. He was one of the first to recognize the existence of certain statistical regularities in human existence. His work on mortality was followed up by the medical statisticians of the seventeenth and eighteenth centuries who were interested in the study of health, disease and death. Interest in these subjects was probably stimulated by the development of life insurance during that period; moreover, in the conditions then prevailing, the level of mortality was probably the chief determinant of the rate of population growth. The principles underlying the construction of tables of mortality were already understood by Halley in the late seventeenth century even though he lacked adequate data, and methods of constructing such tables were continually improved, until by the middle of the nineteenth century the methods of studying mortality had reached a stage of development which has changed but little since.

Developments in census-taking and vital registration in Europe, during the nineteenth century, led to a considerable improvement in the quality of basic data available to demographers, and stimulated the study of changes in population structure and of reproductivity. Mathematical methods came to be applied culminating in the development of the stable population model by A. J. Lotka in the early years of the present century. In this model, fertility and mortality rates are held constant over time, and it is shown that under these conditions a population tends towards 'stability', in the sense that the proportionate age composition of the population remains the same, and that the population changes at a constant annual 'stable' or 'intrinsic' rate. Whilst stable populations are not normally met with in present conditions, this model of development is useful in setting a norm against which the growth of actual populations can be studied. There is now a whole branch of the subject known as *formal demography* or *demographic analysis*, in which quantitative relations among demographic phenomena are treated in abstraction from their association with other phenomena. See U.N. *Multilingual Demographic Dictionary*.

In societies in which fertility is increasingly being brought under rational human control, demographers have naturally taken an increased interest in this subject, and have given considerable attention to the economic, social and psychological factors which affect individual fertility. (This word is used by demographers to denote actual reproductive performance, as distinct from the physiological capacity to reproduce, which is called fecundity. However, care should be taken as outside demographic literature this distinction is not always adhered to.) The study of fertility clearly means that demographers are interested in social control of reproduction, and in the study of marriage patterns, and it is, indeed, principally in this field that demographers make contact with the other social sciences, such as sociology, economics or social psychology, though the study of mortality also has social aspects. They tend today to be increasingly concerned with attitudes and motivations relating to childbearing and rearing, in order to explain variations in the fertility rate between different societies, or within the same society over different periods. Sometimes the term *population studies* is used to describe these activities, and the word *demography* is reserved for what in this article has been called *formal demography* or *demographic analysis*.

Another aspect of demography deals with attempts to forecast future population movements. The arithmetical techniques used in forecasting are relatively simple and routine, and most of the calculations can now be carried out very quickly on electronic computers. They cannot do more than develop the consequences of certain assumptions on the future course of mortality and fertility, and their correctness will depend on the adequacy of the assumptions, rather than on the methods of construction used.

Recently demographers have become increasingly interested in the study of populations for which only limited or defective information is available. In many developing countries, only rudimentary population and vital statistics exist, and models have been constructed which make it possible to draw valid inferences about these populations from very simple data. The populations of European countries during the era before regular statistics were collected have also been studied, by using information from parochial registers and by the method of family reconstitution. In collaboration with social and local historians, historical demographers have been able to make contributions towards a better understanding of the structure of families and households in the past.

Demography today includes a study of the statistical techniques and relations existing within a population, as well as of the historical and social factors influencing population movements. See H. S. Shryock & J. S. Siegel, *The Methods and Materials of Demography*, 1971 (condensed edition 1976), and T. H. Hollingsworth, *Historical Demography*, 1969.   E.G.

denomination. A term used by sociologists to distinguish a type of religious organization. A *denomination* or church-type of religious organization is contrasted to a sect-type. The word *Church* comes from the Greek word *ecclesia*, which in turn was used by Greek-speaking Christians to designate the reconstituted, Messianic, people of God. Such a local church was always conscious of its representative character, i.e. representative of the whole Church of God. To be sure it often displayed some sect-like qualities, in that it was often persecuted and to that extent represented people who were indifferent, if not hostile, to the prevailing social norms of the Roman world. Since the time of Constantine, when the Church acquired official standing, the connotation has altered somewhat, for its sociologically characteristic feature is an accommodation and association with other institutions. Denominations represent fragments of the Holy Catholic Church, but each displays church-like qual'ties, as distinct from sect-like ones. The membership is open, although there is a ceremony of initiation, tolerance towards other denominations is manifested, usually there is a professional ministry, although lay participation in religious acts of worship is permitted, and sometimes special tasks are given to selected laymen whilst others are retained exclusively by the professional ministry. In any one local denomination there tends to be social compatibility among the members, but in theory and often in fact the denominational congregation is representative of the society at large. See M. Hill, *A Sociology of Religion*, 1973, ch. 4. See SECT. G.D.M.

dependent variable. See VARIABLE.

deprivation. See RELATIVE DEPRIVATION.

derivations. See RESIDUES.

descent. *Descent* is the term used to describe the recognized social connection between a person and his ancestors, where the term *ancestor* denotes the person from whom one is descended. Such descent may be reckoned through the father's family or through the mother's family or through both families. In the first case we speak of *patrilineal descent* and in the second case of *matrilineal descent*. If it is either one or the other we speak generally of *unilineal descent*. Some writers use the terms *agnatic* instead of *patrilineal* and *uterine* instead of *matrilineal*. Where descent is counted through both lines we speak of *bilateral descent*. It should be pointed out that whilst descent is based on biological relationships, some such relationships may be stressed to the exclusion of others. Furthermore, sometimes fictitious biological relationships are assumed, and of course there is also the practice of adoption which may well include a person not biologically related in the descent system. See KINSHIP. G.D.M.

deschooling. A term used to advance the view that education has become too much a part of the economic and social exploitation of society and that our society needs to be deschooled. It is used by I. Illich in his *Deschooling Society*, 1971, and by other writers arguing that the many depend too much on the educated, professional and bureaucratic few.

descriptive systems. See CLASSIFICATORY SYSTEM.

deviance; social deviance. The term 'deviance' is used to refer to behaviour which infringes rules or the expectations of others, and which attracts disapproval or punishment. Until the 1960s the study of deviance was mainly concerned with the nature and origins of deviant behaviour and with the characteristics of people identified as deviants; the emphasis was upon 'social pathology' and the search for solutions to the social problems of crime and delinquency, addiction to drugs, prostitution, vagrancy, sexual deviation, etc. See R. K. Merton and R. A. Nisbet, *Contemporary social problems*, 1961.

A seminal essay by Edwin Lemert (see *Social Pathology*, 1951)

53

distinguished between primary and secondary deviance: roughly, the behaviour through which the individual first drew upon himself the disapproval of others, and the nature and consequences of the societal response to this behaviour. Studies in secondary deviance consider the questions, '(a) how does a person judged to be a deviant react to this designation? (b) how does he adopt the deviant role that may be set aside for him? (c) what changes in his group membership result? (d) to what extent does he realign his self-conception to accord with the deviant role assigned him?' (E. Rubington and M. S. Weinberg, *Deviance – the interactionist perspective*, 1968).

The 'social reactions' approach emphasizes the social definition of deviance; as H. S. Becker pointed out (*Outsiders*, 1963), 'we must recognize that we cannot know whether a given act will be categorized as deviant until the response of others has occurred. Deviance is not a quality that lies in behaviour itself, but in the interaction between the person who commits the act and those who respond to it.' Being identified as belonging to a deviant group or category has (it is argued) profound consequences for the individual, one of which is to place him in a new status.

The assignment of a label ('criminal', 'homosexual', 'prostitute', 'alcoholic', etc.) is the process through which the erring person becomes identified, by others and by himself, as a deviant. A 'label' has much in common with a stereotype; that is, others attribute to the bearer of the label characteristics which are popularly believed to distinguish such people from those not in that category (see E. M. Schur, *Labeling Deviant Behavior*, 1971). Thus one who has been labelled 'alcoholic' is regarded as weak and untrustworthy, whether or not his behaviour has reflected these characteristics; he may in time come to accept this assessment of himself. 'Classes of acts, and particular examples of them, may or may not be thought deviant by any of the various relevant audiences that view them. The difference in definition, in the label applied to the act, makes a difference in what everyone, audiences and actors alike, does subsequently' (Becker, *op. cit.*, p. 130).

Several effects of labelling are described. Practical restrictions upon the person's freedom of action may result. '... labelling places the actor in circumstances which make it harder for him to continue the normal routines of everyday life and thus provoke him to "abnormal" actions (as when a prison record makes it harder to earn a living at a conventional occupation and so disposes its possessor to move into an illegal one' (Becker, *op. cit.*, p. 179). The experience of 'stigmatization' and 'degradation' may also bring about profound changes in the individual's conception of himself and his relations with others. Thus Lemert describes the secondary deviant as 'a person whose life and identity are organized around the facts of deviance' (*Human Deviance, Social Problems, and Social Control*, 1972, p. 63). Schur (*op. cit.*, p. 69 *et seq.*) argues that the labelled individual may be 'engulfed' by a deviant role even though he may persist in perceiving himself as non-deviant.

The 'social reactions perspective' has been criticized for treating deviants as naïve victims of social forces ('most people drift into deviance by specific actions rather than by formed choices of social roles and statuses' – Lemert,

Human Deviance, 1967, p. 51). I. Taylor, P. Walton, J. Young insist that 'In a fully social theory ... the consciousness conventionally allowed deviants in the secondary deviation situation would be seen as explicable – at least in part – in terms of the actors' consciousness of the world in general' (*The New Criminology*, 1973, p. 276). Current controversies in the study of deviance are further debated in the same authors' *Critical Criminology*, 1975. See ANOMIE, CRIMINOLOGY, SOCIAL PATHOLOGY.   G.B.T.

diffusion. The term *diffusion* as used by anthropologists refers to the spread of elements of culture, either singly or in a complex, from local group to local group. It is less frequently used to refer to dissemination within a group.

When we observe that a culture trait occurring in group *A* is similar to a trait in group *B*, can we postulate diffusion and thus an historical connection between the two groups? Or were the traits developed independently? William Robertson (1721–1793) suggested criteria for estimating connection. Two groups, although remote from one another but found to be in similar climates, '... to be in the same state of society and to resemble each other in the degree of their improvement, ... must feel the same wants and exert the same endeavours to supply them ... the same ideas and sentiments will arise in their minds ...' No connection need be assumed. On the other hand, there may be 'arbitrary institutions', not deriving from natural wants. If ' ... a perfect agreement ... should be discovered one might be led to suspect that they were connected by some affinity.' (*History of Scotland*, 1759, I, 273–4).

In estimating such affinity some scholars have limited themselves to accounting for specific resemblances of belief, of modes of social organization, of technology, of art and style. Others, extreme diffusionists, aim to retrace the whole complex dispersion of human culture and to discover origins, believed to be few. Thus Father Wilhelm Schmidt (1868–1954), foremost protagonist of the *kulturhistorische methode*, asserted that the specific task of ethnology is '... not only to understand the conditions existing among the primitive peoples today, but also to recognize in them witnesses and survivals of the oldest development of mankind ... and with their help to construct the objective succession of events and thereby the actual genesis of culture among the different peoples.' (W. Schmidt, *The Culture Historical Method of Ethnology*, trans. S. A. Sieber, 1939, p. 13.) The erudite work of such culture historians is widely questioned. Are the similarities seen in comparing *A* and *B* in 'a perfect agreement'? Or are they analogous, rather than homologous?

For G. E. Smith (1871–1937) and W. J. Perry (1887–1949), taking an extreme position, there was but one *A* whose traits diffused to many societies. The culture of ancient Egypt, a veritable alpha. was deemed to be the radiant source of a world-wide diffusion. 'It can be shown that the first food-producing communities in all parts of the world outside the area of the Ancient East, especially those that could be reached by sea, possessed a culture so similar to that of Egypt in the Pyramid Age that little doubt can exist as to their mode of origin.' W. J. Perry, *The Growth of Civilization*, 2nd edition, revised, London, 1926, p. 76. See R. B. Dixon, *The Building of Cultures*, 1928, and R. H. Lowie, *The History of Ethnological Theory*, 1937.

H.D.M.

Dilthey, Wilhelm (1833–1911). German philosopher; his new methodology for the study of society influenced Max Weber in his notion of *verstehen*. He argued for a sharp division between natural sciences, aiming at external, factual description, and causal-law explanation, and social sciences, concerned with empathic, intuitive understanding of the inner meaning of cultural phenomena. The basis of the latter he held to be an analytical and descriptive psychology able to facilitate, through its systematic knowledge of consciousness, an understanding both of structural (or organic) unity of individual and social life and of its historical development as manifested in cultural systems of art, science and religion; see, for example, *The Life of Schleiermacher*, 1870. He believed *Zeitgeist* determined attitudes of man as he develops through time. See H. A. Hodges, *The Philosophy of Wilhelm Dilthey*, 1952.   G.D.M.

discontinuity; social discontinuity. This term was used by Ruth Benedict in a paper she published in 1938 in *Psychiatry*, vol. 1, and which was reprinted in *Personality in Nature, Society and Culture*, edited by C. Kluckhohn and H. A. Murray, 1949, revised edition 1953. Benedict contrasts continuities and discontinuities in cultural conditioning. Thus societies differ in the manner of instilling a sense of responsibility in their members; some do it regularly and gradually, others display sharp discontinuities, requiring little responsible sense for a number of years and then suddenly requiring a great deal to be shown. Similarly, she pointed to differences in dominant and submissive behaviour and, again, she indicated contrasting sexual roles. In both these cases some societies display sharp variations in cultural conditioning and in some the discontinuity in conditioning is striking. Thus some societies that practise long and elaborate initiation ceremonies may display discontinuities, a boy being extremely submissive towards others before but dominant after the initiation. In our own society the bearing of responsibility may sharply change, and at arbitrary periods in a person's life, from a state where little responsibility is borne to one where a considerable amount is laid on a person. In modern industrial societies there are variations within the society, some of them according to social class membership.   G.D.M.

discrimination; racial discrimination. Colloquially the term *discrimination*, without the prefix *racial*, may be used to mean a simple differentiation between people or situations on the basis of an objective criterion, e.g. age as a qualification for the franchise or measured intelligence and attainment for entry to a University. Furthermore, certain types of discriminatory legislation may be designed to afford special privileges or protection to particular groups who are believed to be less able to defend their rights or interests than others, e.g. factory legislation governing hours and conditions of work for women and young persons. Positive discrimination or affirmative action may be necessary in some cases to overcome past deprivations and provide equal opportunities for certain minorities. See Carnegie Council on Policy Studies in Higher Education, *Making Affirmative Action Work in Higher Education*, 1975.

In sociology the term is used more often to mean the use, by a superordinate group, of its superior power to impose customary or legal restrictions and deprivations upon a subordinate group in order to maintain a situation of privilege and inequality. Such discrimination may be exercised by men against women, by dominant political, national, or religious groups or by one socially defined racial group against another. It may involve a restriction of franchise, enforced residential segregation, differential access to educational or employment opportunities and the imposition of other customary and legal disabilities. In the modern world racial discrimination is still widespread although increasingly resisted by its victims and condemned by liberal opinion. See G. C. Kinloch, *The Dynamics of Race Relations: A Sociological Analysis*, 1974. See COLOUR-BAR, PREJUDICE, SEGREGATION, RACE.

A.H.R.

division of labour. The phrase refers to the division of a work process into a number of parts, each part undertaken by a separate person or group of persons.

The expression *division of labour* was used by Adam Smith in his *Inquiry into the Nature and Causes of the Wealth of Nations*, 1775, where in Chapter 1 he opens his discussion of the improvements of the productive powers of labour by showing that it has depended upon the splitting up of a task into a number of separate parts. This use has been continued in the study of economics. A modern treatment by Georges Friedmann in *Le Travail en Miettes*, 1956, translated under the title *The Anatomy of Work*, 1961, uses the *division of labour* in the sense of specialization.

The specifically sociological use of the term was initiated by Émile Durkheim in his famous thesis *De la division du travail social*, 1893, translated *The Division of Labour*, 1933. In this work Durkheim almost equates it with social differentiation and points to the significance of the growth of this phenomenon for social evolution, as societies characterized by considerable division of labour differ from others in displaying an *organic* cohesion rather than a *mechanical* type of solidarity. The contrast is drawn sharply in Durkheim's thought. Moreover, the significance of social relationships in occupational groups for the development and maintenance of moral ideas is emphasized both in his preface to the second edition of this book, and in his later works.

G.D.M.

divorce. In Western societies and in the United States of America, *divorce* has come to mean the process by which a marriage, recognized as valid, can be revoked in the lifetime of the partners who then revert to single status and are free to remarry. *Divorce* is thus distinguished (a) from *separation*, in which spouses are legally recognized as living in separate households but are not free to remarry since they retain their marital status, and (b) from *nullity*: the legal recognition that a marriage had not in fact been valid.

Not all cultures have so strict a concept of *divorce* and the concepts of *nullity*, *separation* and *divorce* often merge in the practice of some simpler societies. Nevertheless, it is quite clear that the vast majority of societies in all cultures do, in certain prescribed circumstances, allow the absolute dissolution of marital unions within the lifetime of the partners to the original contract and do allow subsequent remarriage.

The circumstances in which a divorce is granted differ a great deal from society to society and from one historical period to another. Among some peoples in eastern central Africa, the wife may divorce a husband who fails to sew her clothes. Until the eleventh century, according to Jewish law, a husband had the right to repudiate his wife at pleasure, whilst the wife had no right to divorce at all. In modern Israel, divorce by mutual consent is recognized by law. Resisted in theory in England, recent legislation in which the concept of the 'matrimonial offence' has been replaced by that of 'the breakdown of marriage' has in practice come very near to accepting mutual consent as the principal ground for divorce.

It is, however, easier to point to the varying circumstances under which a valid marriage may be dissolved than to indicate the extent to which divorce is practised in any particular society. This arises partly through difficulties of precise definition of the concepts of both *marriage* and *divorce* in some societies and also from problems of interpreting crude statistics of divorce even in those societies where the concept is very precisely defined. Observers are less confident than they once were, however, in asserting that there is an insignificant correlation between so-called 'liberal' divorce laws and a high, prevailing divorce rate. More positively, they claim that there is much to suggest that family form and divorce rate are connected in so far as societies in which the nuclear family is set in and supported by some form of composite family structure tend to have fewer divorces than societies such as our own and the United States of America where the independent nuclear family is highly developed.   M.H.

Durkheim, Émile. Émile Durkheim was born near Strasbourg in 1858, graduated at the École Normale, taught Sociology at the University of Bordeaux and then lectured on education and sociology in the Sorbonne from 1902 up till his death in 1917.

He was actively concerned with French politics throughout his life and particularly concerned to discover what values and principles should guide French education when it was placed on a secular basis. In these matters he inherited the collectivist tradition of social thought represented by de Maistre, St Simon and Comte and reacted sharply against the individualist ideas of Herbert Spencer and the English Utilitarians. In his first major work *The Division of Labour* he reacted against the view that modern industrial society could be based simply upon contractual agreements between individuals motivated by self-interest and without any prior consensus. He agreed that the kind of consensus in modern society was different from that in simpler social systems but he saw both of these as types of social solidarity. The primitive form, mechanical solidarity, was based upon the Conscience Collective, the modern form upon the Division of Labour, whose function was not the increase of individual utility or pleasure, but the imposition of a moral order.

The specific task of sociology according to Durkheim was to study not individual but social facts and the two main characteristics of social facts were (a) that they were external to the individual and (b) that they exercised constraint over his conduct. One of the main examples which Durkheim used in his *Rules of Sociological Method* to illustrate what he means by social facts is law and one of the features of law is that it has an existence separable from individual acts of law enforcement, so that it can be studied apart from the individual. But there are some social facts which do not have this obvious embodiment which is separable from study. In these cases the individual's conduct is influenced by a more diffuse 'collective current' and the best that the sociologist can do is to record its effects in the form of a statistical rate.

One of Durkheim's major empirical investigations aimed at doing this. In *Suicide* he studies the variation in the suicide rate between different groups and seeks to explain this in terms of the different collective currents or form of social solidarity to which individuals are subject. Thus the greater frequency of suicides amongst soldiers than civilians and amongst officers than other ranks leads him to posit that this is altruistic suicide in which the individual sees his own life as less important than conformity to group norms. But the greater frequency of suicide amongst Protestants than Roman Catholics is seen as due to a social order in which the individual is required to work out his own salvation. In this case the individual commits egotistic suicide.

There is an obvious relationship between the two forms of social solidarity in *The Division of Labour* and these two forms of suicide. In both books, moreover, Durkheim discussed the pathological case in which there are no social norms to ensure order or in which the norms conflict with one another. This state Durkheim calls *anomie*.

The danger of *anomie* and the importance society accords to preventing it is the mainspring of Durkheim's political writings. In his *Socialism and St. Simon* he sees the whole point of the socialist movement as lying not in a demand for common ownership but as a protest against the suffering of *anomie*. The restoration of a social order whose norms are meaningful to the individual who participates in it should, in Durkheim's view, be the main aim of modern politics. Thus in his *Professional Ethics and Civic Morals* he advocates a form of guild socialism.

As a teacher of education Durkheim was particularly concerned to analyse the nature of the constraint which the norms of society should exercise over the individual. His view of this changed and he came to think more and more, not of a blind external force, but of norms which became internalized. He saw the essence of the power of the norms to lie in their sacredness. In his final work *The Elementary Forms of Religious Life* he suggests that the whole concept of sacredness derived from the individual's experience of the social norms. What men called God was simply Society, which from a subjective point of view had all the characteristics normally attributed to the Deity. To explain this Durkheim used ethnological evidence from the Australian tribes, amongst whom totems had the double characteristic of being regarded as sacred and being the badge or symbol of the clan.

Throughout Durkheim's work a collectivist point of view is emphasized. It is politically collectivist in the sense of being opposed to or asserting the impossibility of individualism. It is methodologically collectivist in holding that social facts cannot be reduced to or analysed in terms of individual behaviour. His emphasis on these points contrasts his sociology sharply with that of Spencer, Weber and Marx, the two first-named because they do seek to analyse social facts in terms of individual action, the last-named because he, unlike Durkheim, sees the object of politics as the liberation of man from limitation and oppression by external social forces.   J.A.R.

dysfunction. See FUNCTION.

dysphoria. See EUPHORIA ; SOCIAL EUPHORIA.

E

ecology; social ecology. The word *ecology* is sometimes used as inter-changeable with *geographic environment* and, consequently, ecological studies are often limited to the study of the direct effect of environment on the material culture of peoples with simple technologies. But ecology is more than a study of man's material adaptation to his physical environment. In botany, plant ecology is not only the study of plants in relation to soils and climate, but of plants in relation to plants and other living organisms in a particular environment. *Social ecology* is likewise concerned not only with the direct response to environment where technology is unsophisticated, but also with the distribution and composition of groups necessary for the exploitation of natural resources, the indirect relationships which spring from these groupings, and the general conceptualization of the cosmos associated with specific habitats. Conceived in these terms, *ecological studies* are extended to include modern urban societies; and such studies are concerned with the social relationship of people in relation to the constraints and permissiveness of urban habitat, and in relation to the environment of industry, its location, the limits it sets to domestic and local relationships, and the different types of social links associated with the various types of industrial technological processes. See E. E. Evans-Pritchard, *The Nuer*, 1940; L. Febvre, *A Geographical Introduction to History*, 1925; C. D. Forde, *Habitat, Economy and Society*, 1934, and 'The Integration of Social Anthropological Studies', *Journal of the Royal Anthropological Institute*, 78, 1948; E. L. Peters, 'Aspects of Status and Rank among Muslims in a Lebanese Village', in *Mediterranean Countrymen*, ed. J. Pitt-Rivers, 1963; and 'Aspects of the Family among the Bedouin of Cyrenaica', in *Comparative Family Systems*, ed. M. F. Nimkoff, 1965; A. Tansley, *What is Ecology?*, 1951. E.L.P.

education. See SOCIOLOGY OF EDUCATION.

egalitarian; egalitarianism. The word refers to a set of prescriptions or assumptions about desirable social relationships between individuals and groups. Egalitarianism, in more or less strong or weak forms, advocates equal treatment for equal cases and seeks to eliminate the use of irrelevant criteria in classifying cases. Examples of egalitarianism in social relationships are universal adult political franchise where race, religion, sex, wealth or educational level are held to be irrelevant criteria or the British National Health Service which, in principle, treats individuals equally according to the criteria of medical need and regards capacity or willingness to pay as irrelevant.

61

Application of egalitarian doctrine varies according to the forms of inequality in different societies. In modern industrial countries the antithesis of equality is usually held to be social stratification. The principle of citizenship (with its claim to equality before the law, universal franchise and basic security against economic, physical and cultural deprivation) may be seen as the champion of equality against the inequalities of social class. For a sociological analysis of equality in modern Britain see T. H. Marshall, *Citizenship and Social Class*, 1949. See also A. H. Halsey, *British Society in the Twentieth Century*, 1978. The classic general statement of egalitarianism is in R. H. Tawney's *Equality*, revised edition, 1951.   A.H.H.

eidos; social eidos. *Eidos* is derived from Gregory Bateson's *Naven*, 1936, a book about a primitive people, and was used to denote the main features and characteristics of a body of ideas prevalent in that society. Charles Madge adapted it and refers to *social eidos* as 'that part of eidos which relates to social institutions and activities'. See his *Society in the Mind: Elements of Social Eidos*, 1964.

elaborated code. See CODES.

elective affinity. The expression *elective affinity* was first used in physical science to refer to the property of a substance whereby it has a tendency to combine with one substance rather than another. J. W. von Goethe employed the term in a different context. Thus in discussing with a correspondent the development of personality he asks 'Who dare estimate the influence of elective affinities?' (Werke, XLIII, p. 153).

The term, as used by Max Weber in his studies in the sociology of religion, denotes a view of society and culture allowing for greater weight being placed on the effects of human thought on social events than most other theories of human society. To begin with the theory holds that ideas are undetermined in their origin, but that only when circumstances are of such a kind as to render them relevant to public and social issues do they become popular and effective in determining social change. Some, like Max Scheler, have held that ideas are like platonic essences, existing in a realm of their own, but that they only become effective through the mediation of a few outstanding men of thought and action, or through an elite which adopts these ideas. (See his *Die Wissensformen und die Gesellschaft*, 1926.) Without being attached to Scheler's metaphysical views, Max Weber believed that the generation of ideas was not necessarily related to social and economic conditions, but was of the nature of an intellectual adventure. Yet he was convinced that for ideas to be influential appropriate social conditions must prevail. Thus a mutual accommodation between the incipient working class movements of the early nineteenth century and the availability of a socialist ideology is an illustration of elective affinity. Other writers who have been concerned with the subject include Karl Marx, Alfred Weber, Karl Mannheim and Alfred von Martin. A general discussion of the theory may be found in W. Stark's *The Sociology of Knowledge*, 1958.   G.D.M.

elite. A minority group (or category) of individuals within a society, who may be socially acknowledged as superior in some sense and who influence or control some or all of the other segments of the society.

The earlier writers on this topic, V. Pareto, G. Mosca and R. Michels, see the elite essentially as a ruling elite or oligarchy. This view amounts to the broad distinction between those who rule and those who are ruled, the minority who have the power and the majority who lack it. Thus Pareto, in his *Mind and Society*, 1935, vol. III, section 2034, differentiates the governing elite, which is the focus of his interest, from the non-governing elite and the non-elite. Mosca, in *The Ruling Class*, 1939, argues the continuous historical division between the ruling class and the class that is ruled. The power division between the elite and the non-elite may be in terms of the total society, as with Pareto and Mosca, or within a particular organization, such as a political party, as discussed by Michels (see his *Political Parties*, 1959, p. 401), 'Who says organization, says oligarchy'. The emphasis in these writers was not only on the discrepancy between the democratic ideology of rule by the majority and the minority rule which actually existed but, more importantly, on the fact that such elitist or oligarchic rule is inevitable within a democracy. As Mosca put it, '... the dominion of an organized minority, obeying a single impulse, over the unorganized majority is inevitable'.

While all writers on elites regard them as minorities, i.e. as numerically much smaller than those they influence or control, some stress their group character, where the elite members in some degree know, interact and co-operate with one another towards certain ends. This cohesive quality of the ruling elite is central in C. Wright Mills's more recent study, *The Power Elite*, 1956. Here the similarity of social background, of attitudes and values, of power skills, the personal and family contact between elite members, and the interchangeability of personnel and family contact between elite members, and the interchangeability of personnel between the top positions of the military, economic and political institutions from which the power elite is recruited, are indicated as the factors fundamental to the cohesion of the elite.

The notion of ruling elite or oligarchy can be contrasted with the Marxian concept of a dominant or ruling class. For while one aspect of the elite is that it must maintain some level of exclusiveness, it must also remain accessible to the influence of the non-elite and recruit new personnel from it in order to retain its power position. In contrast, the Marxian analysis indicates a continuing and increasing inaccessibility or polarization of the dominant and subordinate classes. In addition, elite theory places less emphasis than Marxian class theory on economic power as the sole form of power and allows a variety of bases to the superiority of the ruling elite.

While elite theory began as a criticism of democratic ideology and practice, the ideas of the replaceability of elites and their accessibility to influence by non-elites in a society, have enabled some writers (e.g., J. A. Schumpeter, *Capitalism, Socialism and Democracy*, 1959, and R. Aron, 'Social Structure and the Ruling Class', *British Journal of Sociology*, vol. I, nos. 1 & 2, 1950) to reconcile the ruling elite concept with democracy and to interpret the latter as a political structure of rival elites, such as political parties representing different interests within the society competing for power by winning the electorate's vote, or pressure groups influencing governmental policy. The theme of the accessibility of the elite and the relation of this to *alienation* and extremist mass movements constitutes the basis of W. Kornhauser's thesis, in his book *The Politics of Mass Society*, 1959, and provides a link between elite theory and the theory of *mass society*.

The existence of a ruling elite at the community, as distinct from the societal, level discussed by Pareto and Mosca, has received considerable attention from both American political scientists and sociologists. Broadly, the sociologists (e.g. R. and H. Lynd, *Middletown in Transition*, 1937; A. Hollingshead, *Elmtown's Youth*, 1949; F. Hunter, *Community Power Structure*, 1953, among others) have adopted methods of identifying the power structure of the local community which might be termed *reputational* and *stratificational*, i.e. either a local reputation for being powerful and influential is taken as a criterion for being actually powerful, or the exercise of power by certain key figures of the community is inferred from their interests or their social position. In consequence a power elite has invariably been identified. In contrast, the *pluralist* approach of the political scientists (e.g. N. Polsby, *Community Power and Political Theory*, 1963; R. Dahl, *Who Governs?*, 1961; R. Dahl, 'A critique of the ruling elite model', *American Political Science Review*, 1958) proceeds from the standpoint of actual decisions and initiations of policy within specific issue areas, and has invariably failed to locate a ruling elite, as Polsby says, 'But the evidence indicates that decentralized, fragmented, constrained, reversible and relatively uncoordinated (as among issue areas) decision-making is the rule.' While the findings in both approaches reflect in some degree the methods adopted rather than the social reality itself, the tendency towards a pluralist picture of the decisions-approach results probably from the examination of too few decisions, while the more serious and inherent deficiency of the other method derives from equating the potential for power with its actual realization.

With regard to a power elite at the national level in the U.S.A. and its relation to community power elites, there is a difference of interpretation within the sociological school. Whereas F. Hunter in *Top Leadership: U.S.A.*, 1959, argues for a monolithic power structure at both national and community levels with the former being merely the most important clique of the latter, the power elite of Wright Mills is not dependent on, or recruited from, those at the community level. The latter's interpretation of the American power structure is an internationally oriented, organized top level, i.e. the power elite, a pluralistic stalemated ('balance of competing interests') middle; and a fragmented, passive, powerless mass society constituting the bottom level.

A broader definition of elite, which is not necessarily tied to the notion of political control, refers to any socially visible category of individuals who possess some valued characteristic, such as intellectual ability, high administrative position, military power, or moral authority, and who consequently have high prestige and widespread influence. Here such individuals may or may not manifest some degree of group cohesion, and may simply influence or be imitated by the non-elite rather than directly controlling behaviour politically as implied in the narrower oligarchic sense of elite. Pareto mentions such a view but does not elaborate it. In *Mind and Society*, section 2031, he says: 'So let us make a class of the people who have the highest indices in their branch of activity and to that class give the name of elite.' T. B. Bottomore in his *Elites and Society*, 1964, adopts a definition of elites in this tradition as 'functional, mainly occupational groups, which have high status (for whatever reason) in a society'. Similarly the social anthropologist S. F. Nadel in 'The concept of social elites', *International Social Science Bulletin*, VIII, 3, 1956, particularly stressed the variety of possible elites within a society, their *partially* cohesive and exclusive nature, their normative or standard-setting function, and the generalized character of their superiority even where their criterion of recruitment is quite specific.

This second view of the concept is not only more flexible regarding the degree of cohesion possible in the elite but also stresses the plurality of different elites within a society and the competition and adjustment between them, rather than a single elite–non-elite division of society as in the oligarchic view (W. G. Runciman, *Social Science and Political Theory*, 1963, ch 4). See ALIENATION, MASS SOCIETY, PLURAL SOCIETY, SOCIAL STRATIFICATION.

D.J.A.W.

embourgeoisement. A word used of the British working class to suggest that with the development of the Welfare State and increasing industralization they are becoming more middle-class in their attitudes and behaviour. This is particularly thought to be so in the tertiary sector of employment. Having said this it is difficult to find anyone who has advanced the thesis explicitly, but J. H. Goldthorpe, D. Lockwood, F. Bechhofer and J. Platt criticize the view in *The Affluent Worker*, 3 vols., 1969–71.

empirical; empiricism. A widely used definition of *empirical* in sociology contrasts the term with *theoretical* and *analytical*. Here a field study, which may or may not have an explicit theory, is seen as a different order of inquiry from that which either (a) sets out a conceptual language for analysing social relations, e.g. Talcott Parsons's discussion of social action is largely of this nature, or (b) outlines a theory or explanation of some aspect of social life without testing its truth or falsity. In a conceptual language the concepts are analytical in that they constitute decisions to use words in certain precise ways. The language is thus a structure of stipulative definitions. For example, Weber's distinction between class, as a logical category of people with similar 'life chances', and status group, as a group of people who view themselves as being equivalent in status or prestige, is such an analytical distinction. It is then a further task to see whether such a distinction is useful when dealing with social reality. In this view of *empirical*, therefore, a field study requires an additional procedure, namely to define further these verbally precise concepts in terms of measurement operations, i.e. to 'operationalize' them. A theory, which consists not only of precisely defined concepts, as with a conceptual language, but of propositions asserting relations between the concepts and of deductively related propositions, similarly needs operationalizing and remains 'theoretical' until it is so brought into contact with social reality. This definition of *empirical*, therefore, amounts to a distinction between inquiry, whether a theory as such or simply a conceptual language, which has been operationalized and tested by the social reality, and that which lacks operationalization and whose usefulness or whose validity is therefore still in question.

While this first definition of *empirical* focuses on the specific notion of operationalization as a criterion of testability, a second use of the term has a more general sense, meaning simply inquiry about the world in contrast to analysis which is asserting nothing about the world, namely pure mathematics and symbolic logic. In this view both natural and social science are empirical because they are asserting propositions and introducing theories about social and natural reality, whose validity is testable by experience, i.e. observed facts, whereas logic and mathematics are empty, deductive systems, whose propositions are necessarily true. In the sense that they do not apply specifically to one area of worldly inquiry, mathematics and logic have no content in themselves and it is their very emptiness, the fact that we can make the content of the symbols vary with our particular purpose, that allows them to be so useful to the sciences in explaining the nature of the world. It was to this empty symbolic quality of mathematics in contrast to substantive, empirical inquiry that Bertrand Russell referred when he spoke of a mathematician as being someone who never knew what he was talking about or whether what he said was true. This second use of the term *empirical* parallels the philosopher's distinction between synthetic statements which are about the world and whose validity depends on the world, and analytic statements, which are not about the world and whose validity is established solely by examining the logical structure of the statement.

A further use of *empirical* is central to the related term, *empiricism*. Here an empirical inquiry means one that lacks or has not made explicit the theory guiding its procedures. Such inquiry merely establishes an isolated proposition or empirical generalization, for example, that a greater proportion of manual workers vote Labour than vote Conservative at the General Election. This is not a theory or explanation of the behaviour pattern, but rather the problem to be explained. When this notion of *empirical* is allied to that connected with operationalism (see definition 1), the result is what is generally thought of by more theoretically minded sociologists, as sociological empiricism, i.e. measurable, demonstrable but theoretically unguided sociological generalizations. R. K. Merton speaks of such empiricist sociologists as 'a hardy band who do not hunt too closely the implications of their research but who remain confident and assured that what they report is so'.

Lastly, the term *empirical* is sometimes used loosely to mean a field study rather than library or book research. The contrast here is between primary, first-hand information received directly from the subjects being studied, and secondary or secondhand information. Thus the field of historical sociology would be non-empirical in this sense, since it would rely on written records, while an inquiry into current political attitudes would be empirical in dealing directly with the subjects. See R. K. Merton, *Social Theory and Social Structure*, 1961, chs. 2 and 3.   D.J.A.W.

endogamy. A practice of marrying within a defined group, e.g. a kinship category, a tribe, a social class or a religious denomination. As in the case of *exogamy* the practice may be preferred or prescribed.

environmental studies. This term covers a number of recent developments in several British universities. From the sociological standpoint, studies of the social and economic environment are implied; it is essentially centred on human beings whose welfare is related to housing and sanitation on the one hand, the size, spacing and characteristics of the assemblage of buildings in which they live, the resultant accessibility in respect of sources of goods, ideas and services, both within the urban or rural community, or externally over the country, to the capital or its ports. In some universities such studies are taken care of under the term 'urban geography'. Social psychology may be regarded by many as a function of the man-made environment, including not merely the buildings but also the cultural institutions and even the traditions and customs of the community. Some would deem this to fall within the field of social anthropology.

In many training colleges and schools the term might best be translated as the study of local history, partly through field investigation which commonly takes the form of 'educative walks'; partly, through texts, documents, and population statistics; such studies can easily lead to simple-minded amateur sociology, or to those first stages of comparison which may encourage a student to probe more deeply.

To an architect or town-planner the study of the built environment is implied, with special regard to the efficiency with which its purposes appear to be fulfilled. This implies study of the internal environment and may overlap the domain of environmental physiology. In recent years the reactions of the human body to environment have been widely studied, largely through the need to maintain fitness and energy, both mental and physical, in wartime under stress; allied with this the study of the efficacy of methods of protection, whether through clothing, buildings, heating or air-conditioning, or protection against excess of damaging radiation.

The study of the characteristics and the changes that have taken place and are continuing to take place, and in the external, or outdoor physical environment, makes yet another interpretation of a more fundamental character, involving as it does nothing less than the whole of that Quaternary period in which intelligent modern man has evolved and in which he has developed his techniques, from the use of fire to that of nuclear energy. Essentially this makes a more objective approach which is the domain of the geologist, the ecologist and meteorologist, rather than the social anthropologist, the urban geographer or the sociologist.   G.M.

equilibrium; social equilibrium. *Equilibrium* means a state of balance of a system, implying that there is a normal state with respect to both internal balance and the relationship of the system to its environment.

The concept was diffused to the social sciences from mechanics, although similar notions, such as harmony and adjustment, had long been prominent amoung social analysts. The notion of equilibrium even has relevance to the work of Karl Marx. Marx maintained that capitalist societies were inherently unstable, the instability residing in contradictions, i.e. lack of balance, between the technological spheres of such societies and the system of property ownership. In modern terminology, capitalist societies were regarded as being in a state of unstable equilibrium which, cumulatively, would lead to breakdown and the subsequent establishment of a non-contradictory social order, i.e. a state of stable equilibrium.

Equilibrium is a term used by economists, such as Alfred Marshall, and by sociologists, notably Herbert Spencer (*First Principles*, 1862, ch. 22) during the latter part of the nineteenth century. Its usage at that time was prompted by the desire to systematize the social sciences through the theoretical construction of models of the interrelationships between social phenomena. Another inspirational source was the desire to depict the most efficient or ideal order of things. However, the most influential formulation of the concept of *social equilibrium* has been that advanced by Vilfredo Pareto in his *Trattato di sociologia generale*, 1916, translated *The Mind and Society*, 1935, see vol. 4. Pareto, who was both an economist and a sociologist and who had written a thesis on the equilibrium of elastic solids, said that a social system is in equilibrium if, when 'it is artificially subjected to some modification different from the modification it undergoes normally, a reaction at once takes place tending to restore it to its real, its normal state'. Three converging developments brought the concept of social equilibrium into the core of American sociology in the 1930s and 1940s, firstly, among anthropologists, the shift towards the ahistorical analysis of stable interrelationships in the social structures of primitive societies; secondly, in the upsurge of interest in Pareto's work, notably at Harvard (see L. J. Henderson, *Pareto's General Sociology*, 1935). Finally, cross-fertilization from the work of biologists and physiologists led to a growing interest in the self-regulating properties of biological and social systems, for which the term *homeostatis* was coined.

The most prominent sociological users of the concept of social equilibrium have been the devotees of the theories of Talcott Parsons; see Talcott Parsons and Edward Shils (eds.), *Toward a General Theory of Action*, 1951, pp. 107–9. Seeking to establish a theoretical system of determinate relationships between constitutive variables, Parsons has made the concept central to his work. But at many points in his numerous analyses it is not clear whether he is distinguishing carefully enough between two aspects of the problem of social equilibrium: (a) the positing of a system in equilibrium as a device for articulating relationships of dependency and interdependency between variables; and (b) the imputation of social equilibrium as a description of a real state of affairs, or as an empirical tendency in social life. Although frequently asserting that a concrete social system is never fully equilibrated, one of the keynotes in Parsons's work is the postulate that all social systems tend to approximate a state of equilibrium.

Particularly since the sharp attack of Pitirim Sorokin, in his *Social and Cultural Dynamics*, 1941, pp. 669–93, many sociologists have doubted the applicability of equilibrium to human society, largely because of the fact that societies consist of conscious, acting individuals and not inanimate units making mechanistic responses. In view of this controversy it is all the more important that the following distinctions should be made clear: There are basically two types of social equilibrium – stable and unstable. Stable equilibrium should be sub-divided into static equilibrium and dynamic equilibrium. Static (or stationary) equilibrium refers to a situation in which the system's structure is fixed and unchanging, as is the relationship of the system to its environment. Of course, in a social system there is always activity, but in the case of static equilibrium social activity does not alter, even temporarily, the relationship between the critical variables in the system. Dynamic (or moving) equilibrium involves both activity *and* change. There are changes in the relationship of the system to its environment and there is internal change, but not in the sense of alteration of the basic relationships between the critical variables. There may be temporary changes of the latter kind but because dynamic equilibrium is a stable type of equilibrium there will be a tendency for disequilibrating tendencies to be corrected. Thus there is no overall structural change – change is orderly, involving, for example, increasing specialization in political and economic spheres, but the typical ways of organizing political and economic activities do not change, nor do the basic relationships between the spheres. On the other hand, unstable equilibrium refers to a situation in which a slight disturbance would engender further disturbances without any regulative intervention – leading eventually either to destruction or the establishment of a new kind of balanced structural arrangement of the system. See David Easton, 'Limits of the Equilibrium Model in Social Research', *Behavioral Science*, vol. I (April 1956), also C. E. Russett, *The Concept of Equilibrium in American Social Thought*, 1966.   R.R.

essentialism; methodological essentialism. A term used by Sir K. R. Popper to characterize the Platonic view that it is the task of science to discover and describe the true nature of things, and by 'nature' he means to describe their essences. The essence of a thing has to be revealed to be known. Popper further argues that this pursuit leads to a kind of definition he calls essentialist, and that such definitions are prolix and indeterminate, in short not of much use, if not positively misleading. *Methodological nominalism* is a term used by Popper to describe the view, which he entirely approves of, and which he attributes to all sound scientific enquiry, whereby the object of intellectual activity is to describe the behaviour of an object, noting especially the regularities in its behaviour. Whereas the methodological essentialist may ask 'What is energy?' or 'What is Matter?' the methodological nominalist will ask 'How can the energy of the Sun be made useful?' 'Under what conditions does an atom radiate light?' It is a view which does not emphasize the importance of words and their analysis, but uses words as tools. The kind of definition used by a methodological nominalist will be an operational definition. See K. R. Popper, *The Open Society and Its Enemies*, 1945, ch. 3, and *The Logic of Scientific Discovery*, 1959.   G.D.M.

estates. See SOCIAL STRATIFICATION.

ethnic group. Originally the term *ethnic* was used to indicate belonging to a nation, especially a pagan one. It is now used by sociologists and social and cultural anthropologists to denote membership of a distinct people possessing their own customary ways or culture. The term is thus broader than nationality and permits non-literate peoples to be identified as social aggregates in the same way as more advanced peoples and nations. The Germans, the Jews, the Gypsies are all ethnic groups so also are Congo pygmies and the Trobrianders. It will be observed that the characteristics identifying an ethnic group or aggregate may include a common language, common customs and beliefs and certainly a cultural tradition, but whilst it may be a racial group an ethnic group is not to be confused with such; a nation may consist of several ethnic groups.   G.D.M.

ethnocentrism. A word coined by W. G. Sumner and used in his book *Folkways*, 1906, as a technical term for the 'view of things in which one's own group is the centre of everything, and all others are scaled and rated with reference to it'. Sumner used the term in connection with his distinction between in-groups and out-groups, and associated with it both patriotism and chauvinism.

Ethnocentrism, like several other terms coined by Sumner, has been much used by sociologists and social psychologists, notably in recent years by T. W. Adorno *et al.* in *The Authoritarian Personality*, 1950, where a means of scaling the degree of ethnocentrism is presented. Sumner merely described the phenomenon as leading a people 'to exaggerate and intensify everything in their own folkways which is peculiar and which differentiates them from others'. Consequently, he observed, it therefore strengthens the folkways. Adorno and his associates have shown that it may be regarded as a dimension of the personality and be subject to measurement. See ATTITUDE RESEARCH, PERSONALITY.   G.D.M.

ethnography, ethnology. Ethnography and ethnology are both disciplines concerned with understanding human society. Ethnography refers to the descriptive account of the way of life of a particular society; ethnology to the comparative study of cultural elements in a range of societies. The division is not rigid, and there is considerable overlap also with the subject matter of comparative sociology and social and cultural anthropology. The ethnographic approach is characterized by the depth study of a society through personal contact over a period of a year of more. It normally involves participant observation by an observer who understands the customs and language of the society studied. Early ethnographers were concerned to provide explanations for observed phenomena within the framework of the societies studied, and in this way shared common ground with social anthropologists. One result of this was the publication of *ethnographic monographs* – detailed studies of the characteristic way of life of particular societies. H. Junod's *The Life of a South African Tribe*, 1912–13 was an early example of the application of this approach to the BaThonga, but B. Malinowski's *Argonauts of the Western Pacific*, 1922, analysing the *kula* amoung the Trobrianders, is frequently regarded as the true watershed for the scientific study of non-western cultures.

By contrast to the ethnographers, ethnologists focus upon cultural area groupings, cross-cultural comparisons and evolutionary trends. They are concerned with patterns of association of cultural traits in time and space. The origins of this approach rest with the work of F. Boas in the U.S.A. and Ratzel and Frobenius in Germany. By its very nature, ethnology has depended upon ethnography for its basic data, but in the late nineteenth and early twentieth centuries there was also a significant link with sociology. A. van Gennep's *Les rites de passage*, 1909 (translated by M. Vizedom and G. Caffee as *The Rites of Passage*, 1960) and M. Mauss's 'Essai sur le don',

L'Année Sociologique N.S.1. 1923–4 (translated by I. Cunnison as *The Gift*, 1954) are both examples of this disciplinary integration; but with the increasingly anti-historical stance of sociologists, such studies were not widely pursued during the rest of the twentieth century. What occurred instead was a recognition that there existed much of common interest in the subject matter of ethnography and social anthropology in the U.K., and of ethnology and cultural anthropology in the U.S.A. In the U.S.A. in the mid-twentieth century, the development of ethnology was stimulated by the development of comprehensive data banks such as G. Murdock's *World Ethnographic Sample*. This made the systematic comparison of cultural traits much easier, and with the more recent application of computer analysis, the complexity of analysis of patterns of association has increased. The main problem with this type of work still remains, namely that it is easier to show positive or negative correlations of cultural traits than to develop adequate causal explanations. In Britain, social anthropologists have tended to work with more geographically contiguous societies and have tried to provide explanations for more limited ranges of difference among societies. Whilst G. Murdock's own *Social Structure*, 1949 is a good example of the 'macro' approach, of the 'American School', A. Strathern's 'Descent and alliance in the New Guinea Highlands: some problems of comparison', *Proceedings of the R.A.I.*, 1968 is illustrative of the smaller scale of analysis typical of British scholars.   B.H.A.R.

ethnomethodology. Constructed by analogy with terms like ethnoscience and ethnobotany, the name means 'the study of methods employed by the members of society', the methods being those used to organize and make mutual sense of activities.

Ethnomethodology emphasizes (1) the incarnate character of social phenomena, i.e. sociological terms such as 'culture' or 'organization' refer to the doings and sayings of people and (2) the situated nature of sociological research, i.e. professional sociologists study society from within. It complains that it is typically difficult for researchers to provide detailed correspondence between the doings and sayings that they observe in their researches and the descriptions provided by sociological theories under which such observations are to be brought. It complains also that the idealization of the researcher and theorist as people who look upon society from a vantage point outside of it is analytically inadequate for sociology.

It argues that society is experienced by its inhabitants (including professional sociologists) as the world of everyday life, an utterly familiar, uninteresting, commonplace and taken-for-granted environment. The world of everyday life is one which its inhabitants assume is known in common, and whose inhabitants require of one another that they treat its features as 'natural', 'objective' facts which are given circumstances of inference and action. These attitudes ensure that the world of everyday life is unquestioned and exempt from scrutiny. In so far as professional sociologists share these attitudes, they refrain from studying the world of everyday life as such, typically being more interested in the social structural arrangements which they presume are 'behind' the appearances of daily life. Ethnomethodology claims, therefore, that the world of daily life is a neglected phenomenon and proposes to make it the topic of studies, to determine how it acquires its mundane, commonplace, commonly known character.

Action is to be understood as practical. This is in contrast with prevailing sociological understandings of action as rational or rule-following. Any strict rule-following model, it is argued, will fail because the capacity to act in accordance with a rule requires extensive 'background knowledge' as to how to interpret the role and how to apply it to circumstances. Rational models of action are also deficient. The conditions of rational conduct which they specify, it is argued, are perhaps appropriate to the attitude of scientific investigation but not to conduct of daily life. Rational action is often identified as involving an efficacious combination of means in the realization of ends. Harold Garfinkel conducted a series of informal 'experiments' in which he asked people to adopt the attitudes deemed appropriate to rational action. Adherence to those attitudes did not ensure efficacious conduct but generated disruption, confusion, and disorganization (cf. Garfinkel, 1967, esp. ch. 2).

Action is practical. The actor is subject to the inescapable question 'what next?' He must act, however inauspicious the circumstances of his decision-making may be, according to the requirements of social science models of rationality. Actors do, however, deal with their circumstances, achieve their ends, and manage social organization to a degree they see as adequate for-all-practical-purposes. Decision-making is often able to satisfy the criteria of rationality which are employed in daily life, e.g. that there has been deliberation prior to the decision, that alternatives have been considered and compared, that present experience has been compared with previous experience.

Such practical decision-making involves the actor's use of his common sense knowledge of social structures. He has an assumed grasp upon such things as the typical dispositions and motivations of different social categories, the rules and requirements incumbent upon different social types, and of the specific and local organizations of those social settings in which he is a participant. People in society do sociological reasoning in the sense that they try to work out how the social structures they inhabit are organized and in doing so they use this knowledge of their social setting. Their sociological reasoning is of a practical (not a theoretical) kind used to decide 'what is happening now' and 'what to do about it'.

Ethnomethodologists have made studies of methods of practical sociological reasoning in many different contexts, describing practical decision-making in the conduct of conversations, psychiatric admissions, the award of welfare assistance, the determination of educational fates, the management of sex change, the understanding of the convict code, the relations between adults and children, the working practices of the police, amongst others. Reference: Harold Garfinkel, *Studies in Ethnomethodology*, 1967.   w.w.s.

ethology. A term originally used by J. S. Mill in his famous book *A System of Logic*, 1843, to describe what he called a science of character. In the scheme of the social sciences Mill envisaged the need for a study of the human mind in relation to its environment, which would account for differences in men's characters or what is now called their personalities. The science did develop and is usually known as social psychology; the term ethology as he used it was not adopted by other sociological writers.

In recent years the word *ethology* has acquired a quite different meaning for it usually now refers to a kind of behavioural study of animals emphasizing the non-learned aspects of their behaviour. It is a moot point how far this kind of study can be generalized and applied to human behaviour but some social anthropologists and sociologists have been exploring the possibilities of *human ethology*. See B. M. Foss (ed.), *Social Behaviour of Monkeys*, 1972; R. A. Hinde, *Biological Bases of Human Social Behaviour*, 1974; L. Tiger, *Men in Groups*, 1969. For a review of recent work see V. Reynolds, 'Biosocial Anthropology' in *Man*, vol. XI, no. 3, 1976. See SOCIOBIOLOGY, STRUCTURALISM.   G.D.M.

eufunction. See FUNCTION.

eugenics. The endeavour to develop principles of good breeding is probably as old as man, but its scientific status was established with the publication of Charles Darwin's *Origin of Species*, 1859, and its application to human beings was attempted by Francis Galton a few years later. In his words, the science of eugenics is to study those factors which 'may improve or impair the racial qualities of future generations, either physically or mentally'. This endeavour was thought to be advanced in so far as it was possible to learn more of the laws of heredity, to study the factors underlying human marriages, to examine birth rates and to build up a body of knowledge based on case studies of families. The study of eugenics was later pursued by Karl Pearson, an early English social statistician.

The movement was popular in the pre-war period, but suffered by being associated with racial theories, especially those of Hitler's Germany, and from a tendency to over-emphasize the importance of sound racial stock for human progress. In short, many of the ideas put forward by supporters of eugenics ran counter to egalitarian notions. See K. Pearson, *The Grammar of Science*, 1911.   G.D.M.

euphoria; social euphoria. A term used to denote a state of social well-being. It was used by A. R. Radcliffe-Brown in his discussion of primitive law in the *Encyclopaedia of the Social Sciences*, 1933. Here the distinction is made between a condition of *social dysphoria* which results from the committal of an offence by an individual in society, whereby some strong moral sentiment is outraged, and a state of *social euphoria* which can only be brought about, he argued, if the penal sanction is enforced and the offender punished. Only in this manner, it is maintained, can the community be reconstituted. The theory owes much to Durkheim's analysis of repressive law. See DELICTS.
                                                        G.D.M.

Evans-Pritchard, Sir Edward Evan (1902–1973). British social anthropologist who published a steady stream of articles and books of which the most notable are: *Witchcraft, Oracles and Magic among the Azande*, 1937, *The Nuer*, 1940, *The Sanusi of Cyrenaica*, 1949, *Kinship and Marriage among the Nuer*, 1951, *Nuer Religion*, 1956. Most of his fieldwork was carried out in the

73

southern part of the Sudan among the Azande and the Nuer, but he wrote extensively on general topics. In his Marrett Lecture (see *Social Anthropology*, 1951) he took issue with his predecessor in the chair of Social Anthropology at Oxford, the late A. R. Radcliffe-Brown, arguing that it is improper to regard human societies as subject to scientific inquiry on the basis of regarding them as natural systems. For Evans-Pritchard societies were moral systems and it was pertinent to examine symbols and their meaning to people. In this he helped to direct the interest of social anthropologists into a new direction.

evolution, social evolution. The concept of evolution implies order, change and progress. Applied to organisms it involves the alteration in genetic composition of given populations by such processes as mutation and natural selection. Often the analogy between the development of an organism and the development of human society is made or implied; hence the concept social evolution has been used to refer to certain definite stages through which all societies were believed to pass, in a passage from a simple to a more complex form. Both evolution and social evolution have been used in wider senses, so that just as the concept of evolution has been used by some scholars to refer to *any* change in an organism (not merely change measured in terms of greater complexity), so the concept of social evolution has been used to refer to any incremental change in the social system or its parts (and not simply to the passage of societies through developmental stages). In this latter sense social evolution (gradual change) has been contrasted with social revolution (catastrophic change), although even this distinction has not been rigorously adhered to. In the nineteenth and early twentieth centuries conjectures about unilineal societal development characterized the study of social evolution. More recently, the emphasis has been on more limited patterns of adaptation and change.

While Aristotle was conscious of the process of social change and noted the development and decay of social structures, and Plato considered the possibilities of legislation to bring about changed social conditions, the origins of the concept of social evolution appeared much later. In Thomas Hobbes's *Leviathan, or The Matter, Form and Power of a Common-wealth Ecclesiastical and Civil*, 1651, and in John Locke's book *On Civil Government and Toleration*, the argument that the social organization of 'savage' societies was analogous to that of the ancestors of civilized societies was put forward.

Other scholars of the 'Physiocrat School' writing in the eighteenth century in France developed the theory of stages of societal growth. Montesquieu in *De L'Ésprit des Lois*, 1748, argued that the geographical environment determined the ideal form of any institution for any particular society. David Hume in his book *A Treatise of Human Nature*, 1739, maintained that psychological factors were dominant in the social process. He saw a development from instinct through feeling the emotion to reason.

Saint-Simon in various works argued that there was an evolutionary sequence through which all mankind must pass. He distinguished three stages of mental activity – the conjectural, the miconjectural and the positive. Auguste Comte synthesized the works of many of his predecessors and surveyed a wide range of cultural forms before arguing also that societies pass through three stages. These stages he distinguished as the primitive or theological, the transient or metaphysical and the positive or scientific.

On a mental level Comte felt that the first stage was dominated by beliefs about the power inherent in inanimate objects. During the second stage, he argued, beliefs gradually shifted from the inanimate to the animate and then to notions of essences and forces, whilst the third stage was characterized by logical scientific reasoning. Development in one sphere of society's organization was, he maintained, mirrored in all other aspects. Thus there was a relationship among the material, moral and political conditions of any society. Since he felt that all societies passed through the same stages, he argued that the present organization of 'primitive' societies resembled that of earlier forms of 'civilized' society.

Comte saw society as a social organism possessing a harmony of structure and function. Social progress was, he felt, characterized by increased specialization of functions and a corresponding tendency towards a more perfect adaptation of organs.

Many of Comte's ideas were developed by Herbert Spencer, in his 'Principles of Sociology' (vols. IX and X of *A System of Synthetic Philosophy*, 1862–1896), although he was reluctant to admit any intellectual debt to Comte. Spencer presupposed rather than tried to prove the evolutionary hypothesis. He felt that there was in social life a change from simple to complex forms – from the homogeneous to the heterogeneous and that there was with society an integration of the 'whole' and a differentiation of the parts.

Spencer had developed his own theory of social evolution before the publications of Wallace and Darwin, but he saw in their contribution to biology just the parallel support which he needed. The classic phrase 'survival of the fittest' belongs to him and not to them. Whilst Comte saw society as a social organism, Spencer perceived certain distinctions between the *organic* and *social* and never regarded society as more than analogous to an organism.

Other nineteenth-century scholars were concerned with different aspects of social evolution. For example, Sir Henry Maine in his *Ancient Law*, 1861, argued that societies developed from organizational forms where relationships were based on status to those based upon contract. He also sought to establish the patriarchal family as the primary form of social group. J. J. Bachofen in his book *Das Mütterecht*, 1866, opposed this notion, arguing instead the primacy of the matriarchal family. L. H. Morgan in his *Ancient Society*, 1878, developed Bachofen's notions and established an elaborate sequence of family forms from primordial promiscuity to monogamy through which he thought societies must pass.

E. B. Tylor in his great work, *Primitive Culture*, 1871, linked his observations covering a wide range or different societies to the evolutionary framework. In particular, he sought to establish a sequential development of religious forms; a concern which also motivated Sir James Frazer in *The Golden Bough: A Study in Comparative Religion* (2 vols. 1890, 12 vols. 1911–15), and Émile Durkheim in his *Les Formes Élémentaires de la Vie Religieuse*, 1912 (translated *The Elementary Forms of Religious Life*, 1915). K. Marx and F. Engels in *Das Kommunistische Manifesto*, 1848 (trans. *The*

Manifesto of the Communist Party, 1850) put forward a materialist variant of evolutionary theory when they argued that there would be a transition from capitalist control to rule by the proletariat similar to the earlier development whereby capitalism itself replaced feudalism.

The evolutionary doctrine provided a broad general framework through which the whole progress of human society could be conceptualized. Its rejection in the early twentieth century left a void which only gradually became filled with the structural-functionalist system of analysis. Criticism of this approach during the 1960s and 1970s led to the shift to alternative frames of enquiry (see SYMBOLIC INTERACTIONALISM, PHENOMENOLOGY, ETHNOMETHODOLOGY), but has had significance too for a reconsideration of traditional evolutionary theory and a refinement of some concepts.

At the macro level W. Rostow in *The Stages of Economic Growth: a Non-communist Manifesto*, 1960, identified five stages or categories within which, economically, all societies could be placed. These comprised the traditional society, the preconditions for take-off, the take-off, the drive to maturity and the age of mass-consumption. Such a position has been strongly criticized by those who regard it as highly improbable that the less developed countries will ever follow the pattern of growth of the industrialized world. Andre Gunder Frank argues for example in *Sociology of Development and Underdevelopment of Sociology*, 1971, that the present life style of those in wealthy nations depends on the flow of goods and capital from the less developed areas, whilst P. and A. Erlich in *Population, Resources, Environment: Issues in Human Ecology*, 1970, argue more simply that there are just not enough non-renewable resources to go round should the less developed countries try to emulate the consumption patterns of the wealthy few.

In a less controversial way, the ideas of social evolution have been linked to the growth of social movements. Here the suggestion is that conditions created by earlier movements have created social environments conducive to the development of subsequent ones. In this context, the altered perceptions of the legitimacy of the subordinate social roles played by blacks, women and homosexuals has led respectively to Black Power, Women's Liberation and the Gay Liberation Movements in the U.S.A.

At a different level, P. Berger and T. Luckmann in *The Social Construction of Reality*, 1966, recognize the reciprocal interdependence of individuals and society in creating social reality. These realities are subject to change which may result from incremental shifts in actors' perceptions of themselves and their social worlds, or may result from major alteration or fragmentation of those worlds. Efforts are made to cope with change both at the micro-level of the individual and at the macro-level of society. J. Goody in 'Evolution and Communication: the domestication of the savage mind', *British Journal of Sociology*, vol. 24, No. 1, 1973, illustrates this by a consideration of the significance of literacy, showing that it adds a new dimension to the social action of individuals as well as modifying and extending the total repertoire of cultural knowledge.

In a totally different way, a school of thought spearheaded by B. Skinner seeks to explain social behaviour in terms of the individual's genetic endowment and personal history. In *Beyond Dignity and Freedom*, 1971, he argues that the environment is responsible for the evolution of the species and for the repertoire of behaviour acquired by each member. Skinner rejects explanations of behaviour patterns in terms of the individual's feelings or states of mind, and argues instead that to maximize the achievement of the human organism it is necessary to control behaviour by controlling the environment. Thus he has come a full circle from Comte, for whereas the latter saw progress through the adaptation of the 'organs' of society to the environment, Skinner sees it through the adaptation of the environment to the organism (man). This view has had little significant influence on sociologists. B.H.A.R.

exogamy. A practice of marrying outside a defined group. Such marriages may be preferential or prescriptive. The group may be a kinship group, a tribal segment or a village.

expressive; expressive orientation. It is in small group studies that the adjective *expressive* is mainly used. Thus R. F. Bales in his *Interaction Process Analysis*, 1951, and this author together with T. Parsons and E. A. Shils in *Working Papers in the Theory of Action*, 1952, use the term to denote behaviour of persons in groups in which emotional preferences are expressed, such as liking and disliking, or where friendly or unfriendly remarks are made. This analytical term is used in connection with others such as *adaptive* or *instrumental behaviour*. Some groups are primarily task-oriented as in the case of a work group, a committee or a school class, whilst nevertheless displaying from time to time expressive behaviour. Other groups have mainly an *expressive orientation* as in the case of a group of friends meeting for coffee; the term therefore assists in the analysis of group behaviour as may be seen in J. Klein, *The Study of Groups*, 1956, where the term is extensively used. G.D.M.

external system. In his analysis of *The Human Group*, 1951, G. C. Homans makes use of the concepts of the *external* and *internal systems*. Briefly, he argues that it is useful to consider the structure of a social group as consisting of an *external system*, which is defined as the elements of the system (activities, interactions and sentiments), and their interrelationships in so far as they constitute a means of maintaining the system in its environment. Thus a group of workmen are gathered together in a workshop to work, there is a procedure for carrying out tasks, some division of labour, a reward scheme which satisfies them enough to keep them at work, etc. These various actions, interactions and sentiments combine to constitute the external system. Yet over and above this there is an *internal system*, for there are other actions, interactions and sentiments in addition which develop out of the external system, an elaboration of the system, in fact, and this system reacts back upon the external system to modify it. Thus a work group will engage in social activities, exchange information not relevant to the task, and develop sentiments of personal attachment among the members and so further social organization, of an informal type, develops. See GROUP DYNAMICS, SOCIAL SYSTEM. G.D.M.

77

F

Fabians. The Fabian Society was one of the earliest socialist organizations in England and has been one of the longest lived in the world. Its history has been largely that of a small core of its membership, and indeed could largely be told through the biographies of Sidney Webb (Lord Passfield), Beatrice Potter (Mrs Webb), George Bernard Shaw, G. D. H. Cole and Margaret Postgate (Mrs Cole). The influence of the Fabians as individuals, and on the whole they sought influence, not power, has been very great, but the influence of the Society has often been over-estimated.

The socialism of the Fabians has always been gradualist, not revolutionary; bureaucratic rather than democratic; technical and research based rather than ethical or emotional; elitist rather than popular; Machiavellian more than liberal. Rather strangely the society grew out of a singularly utopian body, the Fellowship of the New Life. Dissidents from the Fellowship formed the Fabian Society in 1883, which Shaw joined in 1884 and Webb the following year. The society was called after Fabius who had commanded Roman armies against the Carthaginians, and who by delay and ruse had kept the armies of the republic in the field during a time of defeat, waging a war of attrition. The Fabians forgot or ignored that it had taken not a Fabius but a Scipio to vanquish Hannibal.

From the beginning the Fabians repudiated Marxism. Webb rightly saw three great tendencies in the advanced capitalist societies of his time (N.B. he had direct knowledge of Imperial Germany and its social legislation), two of which the Marxists ignored or denied. These were (1) the increasing real income of wage workers over time, (2) the growth of administrative or bureaucratic regulation in industry and in local and national government, and (3) the increasing role of monopoly in industry, commerce and finance. Once Mrs Webb became active in the Society they added to these concerns two further elements: (4) a reappraisal of the part played by the Trade Unions and Co-operative Societies in working class life and in the economy, and (5) a solid if limited concern with the conduct of social and economic research to increase the efficacy of their propaganda and the cogency of their programme.

From the first of these points they deduced the possibility of a gradual evolution of socialism within the framework of existing society. From the second they derived a contempt for much of the ordinary activity of politics, and the idea of the permeation of administration and administrators with Fabian ideas. Probably no group of comparable ability has ever so consciously believed in the capacity and ultimate power of bureaucrats and experts. From the third they derived the idea, by way of a formulation of Ricardo's theory of rent which Shaw brilliantly expounded, that socialism in

78

the last resort was a matter of the public control of monopolies and the devotion of monopoly incomes to social purposes. Their appreciation of the growth and significance of working-class economic organizations helped them to the idea that a socialist party should have its foundations in these bodies. Their research interests gave rise to several hundred factual reports (*Fabian Tracts*, etc.) which did much to increase public knowledge of social conditions, but which have proved intellectually barren in as much as they were animated by no scientific and generalizing impulse. But this is not to deny their practical importance.

In 1889 most of these positions were taken up in *Fabian Essays*, a collective, uneven, but still interesting volume. Their elitism was never very clearly expressed publicly, though neither was it concealed. It is accurately but unkindly mirrored in the pages of H. G. Wells, *The New Machiavelli* in which the Webbs appear as Oscar and Altiora Bailey. It finds constant, bitter expression in the pages of Mrs Webb's voluminous diaries. It led the Webbs and Shaw in the end into a curious idolatry of the Russia of Stalin, in which they saw the Russian Communist Party as the equivalent of a group of upper-middle class higher civil servants, and the conduct of Soviet affairs as a rational and scientific bureaucracy.

Down to 1918, however, the extent and fruitfulness of the work of the Fabians was remarkable. They were primary influences in the success of the new London County Council not just as a device of local government but as a force for social reform. They founded the London School of Economics and Political Science in 1895 as the leading scientific centre of teaching and research in the social sciences, without doctrinal affiliation, in Britain. They wrote standard histories of the trade unions and of local government. In their minority report to the Royal Commission on the Poor Laws (1909) they adumbrated half a century of social legislation. They collaborated in the founding of the Labour Party. In 1918 they helped draft the constitution and the programme of the party for the coming generation. Above all, they made social reform serious, practical, widely accepted and factually based. Their total effect has been literally beyond calculation in the domestic affairs of the British people. Since 1918 the Society has been of less importance, but it has remained a source of factual if limited data and of meliorist propaganda.

D.G.M.

facility. A *facility* is anything which is valued as a means to an end. A very general facility in the economic world is money, but other facilities include capital equipment, raw materials and so forth. In society generally all forms of property constitute facilities, in so far as property is transferable. Discussion of the relation of facilities to other rewards may be found in H. M. Johnson's *Sociology: a systematic introduction*, 1961, ch. 3 See PROPERTY.

fact; social fact. The problem of the facts with which the sociologist deals was first clearly raised by Émile Durkheim. Durkheim pointed out that not all facts about human behaviour are necessarily social facts. The fact that thirty per cent of the population have a particular hair-colouring, for example, is merely a fact about a mass of individuals. So also might be the fact that a small percentage of the population are extreme racialists. According to

Durkheim, a fact is social only in so far as it exists externally to the individual and exercises constraint over him.

Unfortunately, such facts are not directly observable and sociologists are often tempted to substitute for a discussion of the forces which do constrain individual behaviour, a discussion of the forces which constrain them and which, they believe, should constrain all men. Durkheim therefore insisted that social facts must be treated 'as things'. This injunction is somewhat misleading since it appears to imply that the constraining social forces can be directly observed. If all that is meant is that such facts must be studied objectively, however, it is acceptable. The problem of theory and method in sociology then becomes one of showing how hypotheses about these external constraining forces can be treated. Such hypotheses will be sociological, i.e. about a social subject matter, provided that they make reference not simply to the biological and psychological constitution of an individual, but to the demands made upon that individual by social norms and other people. É. Durkheim, *Rules of Sociological Method* (translated), 1938, and A. Cuvillier, *Manuel de Sociologie*, 1950.   J.A.R.

false consciousness. A term used by K. Marx indicative of his anti-rationalist view of society. Whilst those who own and control the forces of production, including labour, may have a rational perception of the relationship between their aims and the ways of accomplishing them, those who are subordinate do not. In other words the exploited classes cannot appreciate their true situation. They have a view or set of ideas which act as substitute and preventative; in short they have a false consciousness. Such a false consciousness is manipulated by those who support an ideology in their own interests; sometimes even becoming victims of it themselves.   G.D.M.

family. Although sociologists are convinced that the family is the basic unit of social organization, the term itself remains one of the most loosely defined in their vocabulary. In large measure this arises from a curious reluctance on the part of sociologists, as distinct from anthropologists, to study the institution itself and a perhaps less surprising reluctance on the part of the members of the advanced societies which sociologists study to allow close investigation of a group whose structure and viability so intimately affects their lives. E. W. Burgess and H. J. Locke, in their book *The Family*, 1953, attempted a definition in the following terms: 'The Family is a group of persons united by the ties of marriage, blood, or adoption; constituting a single household, interacting and intercommunicating with each other in their respective social role of husband and wife, mother and father, brother and sister; creating a common culture.' Whatever shortcomings this definition itself may have, it is a good deal preferable to that of Kingsley Davis who defines the *family* as a 'group of persons whose relations to one another are based upon consanguinity and who are therefore kin to one another'. This would be an inadequate definition even of the family in the contemporary West, where *pater* and *genitor* are usually one and the same person; for even here, adoption is a perfectly well-known and recognized basis of family membership. In some simple societies, that bonds of family require social recognition and do not rest merely on the facts of procreation is underlined by the practical requirement that a man should acknowledge himself to be a child's 'father'. In parts of Melanesia, for example, the family to which a child belongs is not determined by the physiological act of birth, but depends on the performance of some social act; in one island, the man who pays the midwife becomes the father of the child, and his wife the mother; in another, the father is the man who plants a leaf of the cycas tree before the door of the house. There are societies in which apparently the physiological role of the male in reproduction is not understood, so that a notion of the biological connection between father and offspring is not part of the cultural ideology. There are other societies in which the connection is understood but little or no significance is attached to it, the husband simply regarding a child born to his wife as his own.

The great drawback of Burgess's definition, however, is that it disguises the very real differences which exist in family structure both between and within particular societies. In fact, his is strictly speaking a definition of the *nuclear family*; a small group composed of husband and wife and immature children which constitutes a unit apart from the rest of the community. Characteristic of modern industrial societies, this particular family form seems to have developed as a consequence of the growth of individualism, reflected in property rights, law and general social ideas of individual happiness and self-fulfilment, and as a corollary of geographical and social mobility. It has also been affected by the increasing state provision for individual misfortune: the individual is now no longer dependent on his family in times of distress. The marked predominance of the relatively autonomous *nuclear family* is a recent phenomenon and appears most fully in the more advanced industrial societies of the West and in the United States of America. Its solidarity depends largely on sexual attraction and companionship between husband and wife and between parents and children. This is usually greater when the *nuclear family* includes young children, but as the children grow up the bonds tend to weaken, first through the influence of peer groups, and later as a result of social and geographical mobility.

Among simpler peoples and in some non-industrial societies, the *nuclear family* is more often incorporated in or subordinated to some larger, composite family structure. N. W. Bell and E. F. Vogel, in their *Modern Introduction to the Family*, 1960, define 'any grouping broader than the *nuclear family* which is related by descent, marriage or adoption' as the *extended family*. More usefully, however, G. P. Murdock in *Social Structure*, 1949, distinguishes between two major forms of composite family. An *extended family*, he states, 'consists of two or more *nuclear families* affiliated through an extension of the parent-child relationship ... i.e. by joining the *nuclear family* of the married adult to that of his parents'. This family form is distinct from the polygamous family which 'consists of two or more *nuclear families* affiliated by plural marriages, i.e. by having one parent in common'.

To make confusion more confounded, however, *extended family* is sometimes used not merely to include but as a synonym for *joint family*. It is more useful to restrict this last term to a form of family which has a number of distinctive characteristics: co-residence, commensality and often joint property and some common family cult. See KINSHIP, MARRIAGE.   M.H.

Ferguson, Adam (1723–1816). Scottish moral philosopher and sociologist. Much influenced by Montesquieu. His best-known book *An Essay on the History of Civil Society*, 1767, was re-published by Edinburgh University Press in 1966. It represents a systematic developmental sociology.

feud. A *feud* is a perpetual state of hostility between two corporate groups, marked by homicide or violence whenever members of the groups meet. Certain pre-requisites are necessary if a feud is to occur. Relationships between feuding groups cannot be of such urgency that hostilities would continuously interfere with the ordinary run of everyday life; they must be of a kind which permit controlled and sporadic outbreaks of hostilities. It follows that feuding groups are highly discrete. As territorial units they are separate, and their economic activities are of a kind which do not require co-operation for productive purposes. Members of groups are concentrated territorially, because dispersal would mean that men could be held to ransom in the territories of other groups. And marriage rules are of a kind which do not compel a wide dispersion of affinal links. This latter condition is best satisfied where parallel cousin marriage is permitted, as among Arabs, for then wives can be recruited from within the vengeance group itself. Demographically, some marriages have perforce to be made outside the vengeance group, but since a significant number can be made within it, the relatively small number of external marriages can be deployed in such a way that affinal alliances are made with only a few groups, leaving others unconnected. Exogamy tends to make for a greater dispersion of linkages, but if this dispersion can be restricted, feud is theoretically impossible; although it is true to say that where exogamy occurs, economic, territorial, political and ritual links tend to militate against feuding relationships.

In societies where discreteness of groups allows the appearance of feud, it is to be seen, essentially, as the competition for the capture of resources of some sort or other, and the outbreak of hostilities marks the calculated efforts of a group to expand its power domain at the expense of another.

Vengeance, as an act of homicide, is part of the feud, but it is to be distinguished from it in that it occurs between closely linked groups, and in this context it can be used to achieve a termination of hostilities, on the basis of a life for a life. See E. Colson, 'Social control and Vengeance in Plateau Tonga Society', in *The Plateau Tonga of Northern Rhodesia*, 1962; E. E. Evans-Pritchard, *The Nuer*, 1940; M. J. L. Hardy, *Blood Feuds and the Payment of Blood Money in the Middle East*, 1903; M. Gluckman, *Custom and Conflict in Africa*, 1955; E. L. Peters, 'Some Structural Aspects of the Feud among the Bedouin of Cyrenaica', *Africa*, 1966.   E.L.P.

feudalism. Sociologists do well to treat the term *feudalism* and its school-book synonym *the feudal system* with some caution, since there was nothing very 'systematic' about feudalism. Though lordship and vassalage were universal features of feudalism, there was everywhere a diversity of practice and custom in every lordship, hence it is impossible, with even the most scrupulous care, to give any brief account of feudalism without conveying the wrong impression.

With this caveat in mind, it is nevertheless generally recognized that developed feudalism was based on a number of principles and relationships, however variously interpreted, one of which we have mentioned already. Fundamentally, the relationship between a vassal and his lord rested on the concept of the fief, which was usually land, although it could be any desirable thing such as an office, revenues in money or kind, the right to collect tolls, etc. To accept the grant of rights and title to a fief was to become the vassal of the benefactor, to whom was given in return pledges of loyalty and service, the faithful performance of which guaranteed the continued right to the fief. The obligations of the vassal were not primarily intended to be economic but political and moral. Hence the obligations of military service and court service – the duty both to help the lord to form a court and to submit to the judgments of the lord's court and none other. In addition to these two sets of obligations there was a third, made up of financial obligations to the lord, of which the most important were *relief* – the sum paid by a vassal's heir for the lord's recognition of his succession to his father's fief; *aid* – money paid on a few occasions determined by custom when a lord was put to unusual expense, for example ransom or the knighting of his eldest son; and the wardship and rights of marriage of a vassal's orphans who were not yet of age to inherit their father's fief.

This third set of obligations served as a practical emphasis of the essential characteristic of developed feudalism, *tenancy*. Although a son might inherit his father's fief, he inherited rights of tenancy, not of ownership. Every holder of a fief was a tenant of one higher than himself; hence one man's lord was another man's vassal. Not until the highest were reached was there any conception of *ownership* and even the most exalted were sometimes seen as owing obedience to something higher than themselves – Providence.

Ideally, feudalism covered Europe with a network of obligations which linked the highest to the lowest through a series of intermediate tenancies, but nowhere was there in practice a fixed gradation of authority. A knight might hold a fief directly from the king; a bishop might hold a fief from an abbot. Hence the model of *the feudal pyramid* gives only the crudest indication of the structure of feudalism.

It has been said of feudalism that in its developed form, 'private law had usurped public law' and it is certainly true that all sorts of services that men ordinarily owe to the public or to one another were translated into a form of *rent* paid for the use of land and defined and enforced by a private contract between the lord and his vassal. Thus the tendency to political centralization, the rise of a professional judiciary, the increasing circulation of money and better communications were all to contribute to its downfall at the end of the thirteenth century.   M.H.

folkways. The term *folkways* was introduced into sociological literature by W. G. Sumner in a book of that title published in 1906.

Classifying social norms in an evolutionary framework, Sumner distinguished *folkways* from *mores* largely in terms of the severity of the sanctions applied to those who offend. Mild ridicule or ostracism follows an infringement of a folkway, severe disapproval an offence against the mores. Folkways, he believed, result from the frequent repetition of acts, i.e. they are habits in the individual and custom in the group. They are unconsciously acquired and those who act in terms of them believe them to be right and true. 'When elements of truth and right are developed into doctrines of welfare, the folkways are raised to another plane.' Thus, do mores emerge from folkways, and in turn laws and institutions emerge from mores.

Sumner believed that 'the life of society consists in making folkways and applying them. The science of society might be construed as the study of them'. Such simple definitions are no longer acceptable to modern sociologists, nor is Sumner's vague and unsatisfactory kind of *ad hoc* classification and analysis but, nevertheless, the terms he introduced have proved to be useful. See CUSTOM, INSTITUTION, MORES, SOCIAL CONTROL.

G.D.M.

formalism; formal school of sociology. A view of sociology which emphasizes the importance of the analysis of the form of a social relationship and the comparative study of cases which differ whilst the form remains constant. Georg Simmel was one of the principal exponents of this view. At the turn of the century he had already carried out studies of such formal relationships as co-operation, competition, sub- and super-ordinate relationships and so forth. He was followed in this endeavour by other German sociologists, notably Alfred Vierkandt and Leopold von Wiese. The influence of these men, known collectively as the Formalists, or the Formal School of Sociology, extended to the United States, where E. A. Ross and Albion Small were interested in Simmel's ideas, and where later Howard Becker introduced v. Wiese's ideas in their joint publication *Systematic Sociology*, 1932. Relevant aspects of Simmel's work are to be found in K. Wolff's translation entitled *The Sociology of Georg Simmel*, 1950. See also N. J. Spykman, *The Social Theory of Georg Simmel*, 1925, and T. Abel, *Systematic Sociology in Germany*, 1929.

G.D.M.

Frankfurt School. A term used to refer collectively to the members of the Institüt für Sozialforschung in Frankfurt established in the days of the Weimar Republic and re-established after World War II in new buildings under its director Theodor Adorno. Originally the ideas of Max Horkheimer (Director from 1930), Herbert Marcuse, Friedrich Pollock, Karl Wittfogel and Leo Lowenthal were published in the *Zeitschrift für Sozialforschung* between 1932 and 1941. The general tenor was philosophical with the ideas of Hegel and Marx applied to epistemology and sociology but with modifications. A recent expositor has declared that critical theory is resistant to summary not least because almost its only unchanging basic thesis is that it is itself changeable. More recent contributions are by J. Habermas and C. Offe. See P. Connerton (ed.), *Critical Sociology*, 1976. See MARXIST SOCIOLOGY, PRAXIS.

G.D.M.

Frazer, Sir James George (1851–1941). British classicist and 'armchair' anthropologist; his interest in anthropology was stimulated by *Primitive Culture*, 1871, by E. B. Tylor; in turn, Frazer greatly influenced anthropologists and allied workers until the decline of classical evolutionism. His major work, *The Golden Bough*, 1900, was a reconstruction of the gradual evolution of human thought and custom through the successive

84

stages of Magic, Science and Religion; science he viewed as a return to the age of magic – but with the correct premisses and techniques to manipulate nature. Religion he understood as 'a propitiation or conciliation of powers superior to man which are believed to direct and control the course of nature and human life'. *Totemism and Exogamy*, 1910, is another important work, which shows the influence of L. H. Morgan. Other works include *Garnered Sheaves*, 1931, and *Anthologia Anthropologica*, 1938–39.   G.D.M.

Frazier, Edward Franklin (1894–1962). American negro sociologist, he was a member of the Chicago school contributing descriptive studies of negro family life in the large cities. His best work is *The Negro family in the United States*, 1939; a later work *Black Bourgeoisie*, 1955, aroused some controversy. He was a popular teacher with a wide experience of educational institutions. He had a tendency to write in a satirical manner.

Friedmann, Georges (1902–1977). French sociologist, author of *Problèmes humaines du machinisme*, 1947; *Òu va le travail humain?*, 1951; *Le Travail en Miettes*, 1956, and other works on the sociology of industry and occupations.

function; functionalism. *Function* has two dominant meanings in sociology. Its Major use is to be seen in the following statement: 'The social function of religion is the maintenance of group solidarity.' Here *function* refers to the diagnosed objective consequence which a social phenomenon has for a wider system of which it is a part. *Manifest functions* are objective consequences for the system which are intended and recognized by the relevant participants; whilst *latent functions* are neither intended nor recognized. (See Robert K. Merton, 'Manifest and Latent Functions', in *Social Theory and Social Structure*, 1949, chapter 1.) In order to distinguish between activities which contribute, on the one hand, to survival of social system patterns and, on the other, to their disturbance, a distinction is made respectively between *eufunctions* and *dysfunctions*. There are thus manifest and latent eufunctions and manifest and latent dysfunctions. Sometimes another possibility is invoked, namely that a set of activities may be of no particular consequence for the state of the system, and therefore, is neither eufunctional nor dysfunctional, as in William J. Goode, *Religion Among the Primitives*, 1951, pp. 1–55.

Function is also sometimes used as it is in mathematics. When it is said that social phenomenon x is a function of phenomenon y it is meant that x varies in proportion, as does y. Although this use must be distinguished from the first, the two are nevertheless related. This is because function as consequence for the state of the system implies that all social phenomena in a system are thought, at least initially, to be relevant to a consideration of its persistence. It is then but a short step to postulating that all phenomena in a system are interrelated and that a change in one area of a social system will have ramifications throughout the system. Thus function as consequence and function as related variation are often closely connected.

Functionalism The antecedents of functional orientations in sociology are illustrated by a dictum of Voltaire, to the effect that if there were no God, it would be necessary for man to invent one; meaning that Voltaire regarded belief in God as functionally indispensable to man. The real impetus to the employment of the term function came with those nineteenth-century sociologists like Auguste Comte and Herbert Spencer who regarded groups of societies or individual societies as being very similar to biological organisms in the way in which they worked. Émile Durkheim in turn argued that any sociological explanation should consist of the discovery, firstly, of a phenomenon's cause and, secondly, of its function; 'We use the word "function" in preference to "end" or "purpose", precisely because social phenomena do not generally exist for the useful results they produce. We must determine whether there is a correspondence between the fact under consideration and the general needs of the social organism, and in what this correspondence consists, without occupying ourselves with whether it has been intentional or not.' (Émile Durkheim, *Les Règles de la méthode sociologique*, 1895, translated *The Rules of Sociological Method*, 1938.)

These earlier functionalist tendencies were mediated to modern sociology through two major developments during the 1920s and 1930s. First, the 1920s witnessed a reorientation among cultural and social anthropologists. This sprang particularly from the work of Bronislaw Malinowski, who was instrumental in establishing an approach which emphasized the importance of analysing primitive societies as sociocultural wholes, accounting for institutions in terms of their relations to other institutions in the same society and their significance in satisfying and meeting the basic needs, notably the biological needs, of individual members. However, Malinowski was less important than A. R. Radcliffe-Brown with respect to the elaboration of the theoretical ramifications of a thoroughly *social* functionalism (cf. *Structure and Function in Primitive Society*, 1952, chs. 9 and 10). Radcliffe-Brown frankly advocated the analogy between social life and organic life; although he tried to avoid Durkheim's emphasis on the 'needs' of the social organism and spoke instead of 'necessary conditions of existence'. This was because he wished to avoid teleological implications, such as the notion of some 'guiding spirit' or mysterious force in social life. However, it should be stressed that Durkheim, probably the most important single influence on modern functionalism, did not adhere to such teleological notions as this, nor was he straightforwardly committed to the biological analogy in the way in which Spencer and Radcliffe-Brown were. Radcliffe-Brown's work involved a distinction between social morphology, the analysis of the network of social relationships constituting social structure, and social physiology, the study of the working and persistence of all interrelated social phenomena in a society.

Secondly, in sociology the same period saw an increasing interest in an abstract conception of social systems, one which did not take as its point of departure concrete, historically isolatable societies. Rather, human societies were regarded as consisting of a series of interlocking social systems. Since Talcott Parsons's *The Structure of Social Action*, 1937, this focus has been increasingly prominent, and it is in Parsons's 'structural-functional' theory that sociological functionalism has attained its most systematic and rigorous formulation. In one of his earliest outlines of this theory, written in 1944, he argued that the significance of the concept of function inhered in its potential for the linking of the structural categories of sociology. Without such a concept the analyst was prone to give a static impression of social systems. A functional approach would produce criteria of the importance of factors and processes and their interrelationships within the system as a 'going concern'. (See Talcott Parsons, 'The Present Position and Prospects of Systematic Theory', in *Essays in Sociological Theory*, revised edition, 1954, ch. 11.)

Parsons has openly described his scheme as being teleological, although his use is more restricted and rather less controversial than older meanings of this term. By teleological he simply means a means–end relationship; either activities or conditions contribute to the maintenance or development of a system, or they are dysfunctional, and thus detract from integration and effectiveness. The principal features of structural-functionalism are as follows: (a) The delineation of boundaries between the social and other relevant systems, notably the cultural, personality and biological systems; (b) An abstract and transhistorical delineation of the major structural units of the social system, and a heavy emphasis upon the normative relationships between these units; (c) An overriding concern with the conditions of stability, integration and maximum effectiveness of the system as abstractly depicted. The functional orientation runs through all these characteristics, one of its most influential aspects being the idea of *functional imperatives*. Deriving in part from experiments on small groups, the term refers to the four basic 'problems' of a social system, problems which all social systems face and which must be adequately coped with if the system is to be adequately maintained. The four functional imperatives are: adaption to other systems and the physical environment; the attainment of system goals; integration; and the maintenance of stability and consistency.

Functional imperatives are similar to, but not identical with, the concepts of *functional requisites* and *functional prerequisites*. The necessary analytic distinctions have not yet been formulated, but generally discussion of requisites and prerequisites refers to the fulfilment of the broadest conditions which are necessary to a system's existence (and which therefore prevent its termination), such as the socialization of new members, a shared system of communication, and methods of assigning individuals to roles. Thus, in comparison, imperatives are narrower in their reference and, being closely confined to the special brand of functional theory termed *structural-functionalism*, are employed mainly in terms of their importance for the analysis of the conditions of system stability and effectiveness, not merely system existence and survival. When the distinction is drawn between prerequisites and requisites, prerequisites refer to the fulfilment of conditions necessary for a system to come into existence, and requisites to the broadest conditions ensuring its survival. (See D. F. Aberle *et al.*, 'The Functional Prerequisites of a Society', *Ethics*, vol. LX, no. 2 (January 1950), pp. 100–11; and Marion J. Levy, Jr., *The Structure of Society*, 1952, ch. 2.)

Particularly since Merton's 'Manifest and Latent Functions' (1949), there have been two major variants of sociological functionalism. Merton helped to precipitate the establishment of a perspective which was less committed to the stability, consensus, and integration foci of structural-functionalism. Thus whilst most sociologists are social functionalists in respect of their concern with systems comprising interdependent parts, and their interest in the unintended social consequences of social action and organization, and also their refusal to reduce the analysis of social life to the psychological level, only structural-functionalists base their work on the highly abstract conception of the normatively integrated system. See Talcott Parsons, 'Recent Trends in Structural–Functional Theory', in Earl W. Count and Gordon T. Bowles (eds.), *Fact and Theory in Social Science*, 1964, ch. 9; P. S. Cohen, *Modern Social Theory*, 1968, ch. 3; H. Strasser, *The Normative Structure of Society*, 1976, ch. 6; and Stephen Mennell, *Sociological Theory: Uses and Unities*, 1974, ch. 6. See SOCIAL SYSTEM.   R.R.

G

Geddes, Sir Patrick (1854–1932). Scottish biologist, he was influenced by members of the Le Play school on a visit to France and slowly began to develop an interest in social problems and the quality of urban life. His interests were wide, covering sociology, economics, social reform, art criticism and civic design. With Victor Branford he founded the Sociology Society of London, largely as a vehicle for his own ideas. He was prominent in the town-planning movement which helped to bring about legislation in 1909. He travelled widely, taught in many universities, but failed to obtain the newly established chair of sociology at London University. He was an enthusiastic polymath, impatient and sometimes tactless, he talked too much and whilst mentally exhilarating he was also exhausting. His endeavour to relate sociological studies to urban development is his abiding achievement. His main works are *Cities in Evolution*, 1915; reissued in 1949, and *Report to the Durbar of Indore* (2 vols.), 1920; the latter is his most important town-planning report.   G.D.M.

Geiger, Theodor (1891–1952). Born in München, Geiger in later life lived and taught in Denmark and visited Canada. He was Professor of Sociology at the University of Aarhus. Influenced by the formalist tradition in German sociology, he later developed a broader interest in macrosociology, both with respect to the sociology of knowledge and social stratification. Among his early writings may be mentioned *Die Masse und ihre Aktion*, 1926, *Führen und Folgen*, 1928, *Allgemeine Soziologie*, 1930. His later works on social stratification and mobility include *Die Soziale Schichtung des deutschen Volkes*, 1932, *Die Klassengesellschaft im Schmelztiegel*, 1949, and *Soziale Umschichtungen in einer Danischen Mittelstadt*, 1951. An article in English on the origins and structure of the Danish intelligentsia appeared in the *British Journal of Sociology*, I, 3, 1950.   G.D.M.

Geisteswissenschaften. A German word used to denote the human or social sciences. It was used in the *Methodenstreit* in contradistinction to the *Naturwissenschaften*, or natural sciences. See METHODOLOGY.

Gemeinschaft. A German term used extensively in sociology, although sometimes translated as 'community', but usually nowadays left untranslated. *Gemeinschaft* and *Gesellschaft* are contrasting types of social order. The contrast was made by F. Tönnies in his book, *Gemeinschaft und Gesellschaft*, first published in 1887, but which ran to several editions. Tönnies also wrote an essay of this title in the *Handwörterbuch der Soziologie* in 1931. In a society characterized by Gemeinschaft relationships there is what he called a 'community of fate'. People share both the benefits and misfortunes of life, although this should not necessarily imply that they do so equally. There is usually a marked involuntary element in such relationships, e.g. as between parent and child, or monarch and subject; there is no instrumental factor, but rather the relationships constitute an end in themselves. *Gesellschaft*, usually translated as 'association', represents relationships that are specific, partial and utilitarian. Thus a contract is indicative of *gesellschaftlische* relationships. The contrast pointed by Tönnies has been made by many nineteenth-century writers preoccupied with the emergence of an industrial civilization; usually there was a tendency to see *Gemeinschaft* relationships as being destroyed by modern social developments; a somewhat similar contrast was made by Sir Henry Maine in distinguishing between societies based on status and those based on contract. Others, like Spencer and Durkheim, also pointed to it. The contrast is not entirely satisfactory for there are elements of *Gemeinschaft* in all *Gesellschaft*-type organizations, but if there are no concrete empirical referents for these terms it must still be added that they have proved most influential in sociological thought. Tönnies's book was translated by C. P. Loomis and published in the U.S.A. under the title *Fundamental Concepts of Sociology*, 1940, and in the United Kingdom under the title *Community and Association*, 1955; the latter includes a translation of the essay in the *Handwörterbuch*. An interesting discussion of these concepts is to be found in a note by T. Parsons in his *Structure of Social Action*, 1937, pp. 686 ff.   G.D.M.

genotype. *Genotype* is a term used to denote the organic structure as it is determined by heredity, precisely the genes. It is used in contrast to the term *phenotype* which denotes the organic structure as determined by genetic factors *and* other factors, which will be environmental.

gens. See CLAN.

Gesellschaft. See GEMEINSCHAFT.

Giddings, Franklin Henry (1855–1931). American sociologist; important for combining psychology with his sociology and his emphasis upon the need for quantitativism. His major works are *Studies in the Theory of Human Society*, 1922, and *The Scientific Study of Human Society*, 1924. The keystone of his sociological system is 'Consciousness of Kind' (later reformulated as 'Pluralistic Behaviour') which unites individual minds which, responding to common stimulation, act upon one another through suggestion, example and imitation to produce a social mind. Giddings's system was a complex and logical scheme; he distinguished between social statics (concerned with structure), social kinetics (concerned with function), and social dynamics (change, development, evolution). Also, he distinguished between ethnic and demotic social compositions (cf. *Gemeinschaft*) and social constitutions or associations for particular ends (cf. *Gesellschaft*). He formulated a law of social change: a community endeavour to perfect its type in compliance with prevailing conceptions of the ideal good. He helped to found the neo-positivist school.   G.D.M.

Ginsberg, Morris (1889–1970). Comparative sociologist, philosopher and social psychologist; first president of the British Sociological Association, successor of L. T. Hobhouse to the Martin White chair of Sociology at the London School of Economics and Political Science and for some years the only occupant of a chair in the subject in Britain. He collaborated with Hobhouse and G. C. Wheeler to publish *The Material Culture and Social Institutions of the Simpler Peoples: An Essay in Correlation* in 1915; author of *The Psychology of Society*, 1921, 9th edition 1964; *Studies in Sociology*, 1932, and many other essays and articles especially on the unity of mankind, and on the idea of progress. He was a careful critic and immensely learned with broad interests; he has been described as possessing a combination of dispassionate intellectual excellence and quiet moral passion. For an appraisal see R. Fletcher (ed.), *The Science of Society and the Unity of Mankind*, 1974.

G.D.M.

group; social group. The American sociologist, Albion Small, in 1905 defined a group as 'any number of people, larger or smaller, between whom such relations are discovered that they must be thought of together'. This definition has come to be seen as too broad a one. Today it is necessary to distinguish an aggregate or category of persons possessing some common features, e.g. the same sex, or the same income, which thus group them in a statistical sense, from a number of persons between whom there are relationships based on interaction. Thus to reinforce the distinction many sociologists use the prefix 'social' for the second use of the term. Very often the expression *social group* is applied to a small face-to-face group of persons, or what C. H. Cooley called a *primary* group. See GROUP DYNAMICS.

G.D.M.

group dynamics. The study of group dynamics, strictly speaking, is the investigation of the manner in which adjustive changes, occurring in a small social group as a whole, are the product of the changes in any part of the group. The term, however, has come to denote the study of small social groups generally. Small group studies gained impetus during World War II, but may originally be said to have been inspired by the writings of C. H. Cooley and Georg Simmel. Cooley distinguished between *primary* and *secondary* groups. The former were defined as face-to-face groups which enjoy feelings of solidarity, groups that are productive of the moral norms operating in adult lives, or groups that reinforce these norms and the stability they produce in human society. Thus the family was regarded by Cooley as the main primary group, but others would include the work group, the club, the college fraternity and so forth. Secondary groups, on the other hand, are the larger aggregates like social classes. Indeed, categories of people rather than social groups proper were included by Cooley, but especially if they are bound by a normative order and display interaction among the members, in which case they constitute an associational kind of secondary group; examples are the trade union, a learned society, the Automobile Association. The study of primary groups is a well-developed feature of sociological investigation; its history has been documented by E. A. Shils in 'The Study of the Primary Group' in *The Policy Sciences*, edited by D. Lerner and H. D. Lasswell, 1951. Simmel's work consists of brilliant essays on aspects of societal relations. He explored the implications of dyadic relationships and compared them with triadic ones, he discussed the nature of superordinate and subordinate relationships, the characteristics of secret societies, and other social phenomena at the micro-sociological level.

Work on small groups gained strength during the last World War, the military organizations of the Allies having come to appreciate the small group as a major factor in maintaining the morale and hence the military efficiency of the soldier. Pioneer work in this field was carried out by S. A. Stouffer in the U.S.A., many of his findings being published in *The American Soldier*, 1949, and by a number of British psychologists employed by the War Office, some of whom later helped to staff the Tavistock Institute of Human Relations in London. Experimental work has been a prominent feature of small group studies. Kurt Lewin's influence has been strong in this respect, and together with R. Lippitt and R. K. White he carried out work with children's groups having different kinds of leadership; this was reported in 1939. Since then more rigorous experimental work has been done to discover the relationship between task performance and communication structures in small groups, notably by H. J. Leavitt in 1951 and by L. S. Christie, R. B. Luce and J. Macy a year later. These studies showed differential degrees of efficiency according to both the nature of the task and the type of communication structure involved. At the same time G. A. Heise and G. A. Miller also added some experimental refinements with consequent theoretical improvements to the subject. These studies are reported and discussed by J. Klein in *The Study of Groups*, 1956. Many other studies have been made, mostly by students of Lewin and many of them at the Center for Group Dynamics at Ann Arbor in Michigan. Two major contributions to the theoretical development of Group Dynamics are those of G. C. Homans, who in his book *The Human Group*, 1950, showed the usefulness of a systematic scheme of thought of a functionalist character by comparing various group studies, and by R. F. Bales, who provided a scheme for the observation and analysis of small group activities in his book entitled *Interaction Process Analysis*, 1951.

The main topics of concern to students of small groups are problems of cohesion, communication, the influence of the group on individual members' perceptions, group morale and leadership. Distinct advances may be claimed in answering some of the fundamental sociological questions about these subjects. Theoretically, in fact, sociology has made considerable strides in this micro-sociological field, although it is uncertain how far generalizations may be extended from small face-to-face groups to larger social organizations. The application of small group theory may be seen in relation to work groups, school classes, therapeutic groups in mental hospitals, and generally in social work. See J. Klein's *Working with Groups*, 1961. For a general short introduction see W. J. H. Sprott, *Human Groups*, 1958, and M. S. Olmsted's *The Small Group*, 1959.   G.D.M.

Gumplowicz, Ludwig (1838–1909). A Polish sociologist, who being both a Jew and a Pole was inclined to be interested in racial, national and social conflict. He was an adherent and modifier of Social Darwinism. He believed that social and cultural evolution was a result of the survival of the fittest in a struggle between (successively) racial groups, states and classes. The ultimate cause of this struggle he held to be the polytenetic nature of the human species and the universal hatred between distinct racial and social groups, but the proximate cause he believed to be the desire for economic improvement. The state evolved when economic exploitation replaced extinction as a policy to be adopted towards subordinated groups. Legal and political institutions were developed by dominant groups to maintain their power. Syngenism and amalgamation are, he believed, secondary factors in social life. Gumplowicz tried to formulate sociological laws as a result of his attempt to define the role of sociology as a scientific subject. His works include *Rasse und Staat*, 1875; *Der Rassenkampf*, 1883; and *Grundriss der Soziologie*, 1885.   G.D.M.

Gurvitch, Georges (1894–1965). Russian sociologist who taught in Russia at the time of the Revolution but left in 1921 to spend three years in Prague before eventually settling in France, where he became a naturalized Frenchman. Whilst retaining a strong Russian accent he lectured at the Sorbonne and later as a professor at Strasbourg University where he succeeded Maurice Halbwachs. He founded the Centre d'Etudes Sociologiques de Paris, becoming its first Director, and in 1948 became Professor of Sociology at the University of Paris and Director of L'Ecole Pratique des Hautes Etudes (6th section). In 1946 he founded the successful journal *Cahiers Internationaux de Sociologie*, to which, from time to time, he contributed articles. From 1960–63 he was the President of the Commission of sociology and demography at the Centre National de la Recherche Scientifique.

His organizing ability and his forceful writing made him a prominent figure in French sociology. He was internationally known for his *Sociology of Law*, 1942, and for his *Traité de Sociologie* (2 vols.), 1958–60. He wrote on a variety of sociological topics. In many ways he was the French Sorokin, learned and erudite, combative, perceiving the role of sociology to be explanatory, for he abhorred the obsession with technical matters related to what he was pleased to call, with marked pejorative overtones, 'testomania' and 'quantophrenia'. He was *par excellence* a philosophical sociologist, standing rather more in the German than the French tradition but, withal, very European and opposed to American empiricism. See his *Sociologie et Dialectique*, 1962. Another interesting work is his *La multiplicité des temps sociaux*, 1958, translated *The Spectrum of Social Time*, 1964.   G.D.M.

H

Halbwachs, Maurice (1877–1945). French sociologist; he was greatly influenced by Durkheim. His work *Les Causes du Suicide*, 1930, differs in important respects from Durkheim's classic: it argues, *inter alia*, that the *anomie* accompanying rapid urbanization is due, indirectly, to individual motivation affecting the degree of adaptation. He was interested in the nature of social classes, which he saw to be revealed in behaviour patterns – the higher the class the greater the approximation to the ideal of the good life within a particular society. (See *L'Évolution des besoins dans les classes ouvrières*, 1933.) He disagreed with Engels's view that the proportion of income spent on rent and clothing is about the same for all classes. In *Les Cadres Sociaux de la mémoire*, 1925, and *La Memoire Collective*, 1950, he presents memory as a product of man's social life; a recollection linked to society through language, spatial-time dimensions, association, etc. Halbwachs also pioneered the development of social morphology in his work of that name (1935).   G.D.M.

hermeneutics. From the Greek word meaning explaining, or making clear. Its use by sociologists is perhaps the most recent development in a long philosophical tradition. Thus the idea that true knowledge of social life can be attained only if human conduct is seen as meaningful action 'whose meaning is accordingly grasped' is discussed as a modern development in sociology by Zygmunt Bauman in his book *Hermeneutics and Social Science: Approaches to Understanding*, 1978. See also W. Outhwaite, *Understanding Social Life, The Method Called Verstehen*, 1975.   G.D.M.

historical sociology. In a sense, all sociological research is historical inasmuch as sociologists' records are of things which have happened or have been observed. The term *historical sociology* is, however, usually applied to the study of social facts which are more than fifty or so years old. Certainly any social facts derived from the nineteenth century are referred to as *historical* whereas the data of a recent General Election are not – a distinction which affords the professional historian a good deal of innocent amusement.

In practice, historical sociology is a particular kind of comparative study of social groups; their composition, their interrelationships and the social conditions which support or undermine them. The social anthropologist examines these things in contemporary simple societies: the *historical sociologist* examines them in the records of societies and cultures prior to his own. 'Ideally', a distinguished professor of sociology once commented, 'we should no doubt prefer that historians should do our work for us, but such work, rubbing our noses hard in the material of social change, is not only

94

salutary in itself and rewarding in the new data which emerges; it cannot but bring us back again to the theoretical problems of social change and social structures which undergo these changes'. See HISTORICISM, SOCIAL HISTORY.

M.H.

historicism. The word *historicism* describes a theory according to which the essence of the phenomena of society and culture consists in their dynamic and developmental character. It must be clearly distinguished from two superficially similar doctrines. *Evolutionism* is a theory of nature rather than of society and culture; it thinks in terms of a natural law of evolution; historicism, on the other hand, lays the emphasis on human reality and human effort. *History*, in spite of the regularities which it evinces, is men's own work, the unfolding of men's original potentialities. Progressivism teaches that men, through their reason, are increasingly successful in mastering their vital problems and in gaining better and better control over nature and even human relationships. Historicism does not see man as mainly a rational animal but rather as endowed with all-round creativity. It uses a much wider definition of culture which comprises also the non-rational elements such as art, and doubts the belief, inherent in progressivism, that human relationships can be improved by conscious intervention.

In its most ambitious representatives historicism became a total philosophy, and saw itself as a modern replacement of medieval organicism. Organicism had maintained that the meaning of an institution, say the state or the church, can best be grasped when the contribution which it makes to the totality of life is identified, as the function of a bodily organ, say the heart or the liver, can best be grasped when the part it plays in the vital process of the body is investigated. Historicism rejected this principle of explication as too static; the organic pattern cannot be transferred from physiology to human studies, but it modelled itself unconsciously on organicism all the same. For the pattern of the physical organism it substituted the pattern of history as a total and inclusive process. What any concrete socio-historical phenomenon means depends on the place it occupies in the totality of history and the contribution it makes to its ongoing process. In this way, the term historicism would appear to describe a specific principle of historical analysis, underlaid by an appropriate general developmental world-view.

The doctrine of historicism had the greatest impact on the study of history itself. It denied that the realities of the past can be properly understood by looking at them from the vantage point of the present; nor was it satisfied with the pure description of historical phenomena which, under the leadership of Leopold von Ranke, historians have usually regarded as the main, if not indeed the only, task of the historian. Historicists such as Ernst Troeltsch, Wilhelm Dilthey, Friedrich Meinecke and Karl Mannheim, taught that the past must be analysed in its own, and not in modern, terms. They asserted the possibility of an *ab intra* knowledge of earlier phases of history, against the insufficient *ab extra* knowledge of those who merely described or judged. Contemporary phenomena, they suggested, always form coherent systems, each of which is dominated by an informing culture-style or indwelling culture-soul (emphases varied), and the historian has only done his work, when he had comprehended, and come to appreciate, this unifying principle. The understanding of it will yield the understanding of all the detail. This attitude is sometimes described as *relativism* and relativism has entered deeply into the meaning of the word *historicism*. When relativist ideas spilled over from the study of history to the discussion of ethics, strong resistances were aroused. A shadow first began to fall on the very word *historicism*. Historicism, it was asserted by its enemies, destroys the foundations of ethical action which must be grounded in abiding, not in changeable, imperatives.

Starting its career in the late eighteenth century, the period of preromanticism, powerfully furthered in the first half of the nineteenth century by the romantic glorification of the past and in the second half by the predominance of evolutionary modes of thought in general, historicism reached the peak of its influence between the two world-wars. But it was also about this time that historicism underwent its first decisive attacks and suffered its first defeats. The word *historicism* then began to contract a definitely pejorative meaning. Vilfredo Pareto, in his *Trattato di Sociologia Generale* (1916–23), tried to prove that the fundamental patterns of human society and culture do not experience any decisive change over the centuries. Human action is always and everywhere controlled by abiding drives characteristic and constitutive of the animal *man*; even the forms of thought are determined by these drives and evince only minor and marginal adjustments, but no deeper developments and above all no decisive advancement. Karl Popper's *The Poverty of Historicism* (1957) brought these and similar criticisms to a wider public. They were successful in fastening the pejorative meaning to the term because the 'spirit of the age', to use a historical concept, had turned away from more dynamic to more static convictions. When the science of physics wrested intellectual leadership from the science of biology, there was a general change of the mental climate, and this made historicism and other kindred doctrines suddenly appear old-fashioned. In so far, however, as philosophies like Logical Positivism overestimate the domination of all reality by the physical-mechanical groundwork of existence, their attack on historicism, which appreciates the autonomy of culture and human life in general in the midst of unchangeable *data*, is less than successful. Historicism may have exaggerated the dynamic character of social phenomena in denying the presence of a (partially) unchanging human nature; its contemners were and are blind in the other eye in not seeing that the difference between different social-cultural periods are in fact real and deep. Thus the term *historicism* appears now to be somewhat ambiguous so far as its undertones and overtones are concerned.

The reduced vogue of historicist modes of thought is, however, due as much to developments within historicism itself as to attacks on it from the outside. It was unavoidable that its principle of derivation should have been applied to its own doctrines. The spread of pan-historical forms of philosophy was soon recognized to be a response to the speeding-up of all, and more particularly all economic and technological, processes since say 1750, the onset of the Industrial Revolution. While the pioneers of historicism were convinced that they had discovered an absolute truth, and the only one that exists, namely that nothing is truly absolute and nothing is eternal except change, even their assertions have been increasingly considered as merely impressions due to a temporary constellation; relativism has been relativized. Besides, historicism has demanded the comprehension of history as a whole, and when the total pattern was envisaged, supra-historical theories unavoidably had to make their appearance. G. W. F. Hegel, for instance, though close to the historicist position, saw history determined by the meta-temporal pattern of thesis, antithesis, and synthesis. A. J. Toynbee considers that there is a recurrence of challenge and response. Dilthey, one of the classics of the historicist movement, who had begun his career by asserting that all phenomena of culture are unique, ended it by presenting a typology according to which the history of philosophy, in the widest sense of the word, is a ding-dong battle between three abiding fundamental attitudes: naturalism, objective idealism and idealism of freedom. In this way, historicism reduced itself to its proper dimensions. Its emphasis on the specific character of culture and society, however, always threatened by an imperialistic pan-scientism, is and remains a contribution of lasting significance. The word is therefore likely to maintain itself in use as a counter-concept to such terms as *mechanicism, perpetualism, absolutism* and the like. w.s.

Hobbes, Thomas (1588–1679). English philosopher; his thought was a reaction against the dysphoria and political unrest of the time. His conception of man essentially was non-sociological – the life of man is 'solitary, poor, nasty, brutish and short', while 'the condition of man ... is a condition of war of everyone against everyone'. Man must, therefore, submit to the great artificial leviathan, the state, which is the product of human reason and social contract; the state must be omnipotent if peace is to be maintained. His sociologically important works are *De Cive*, 1642 – concerned with social relations and proper regulation of society – and *The Leviathan: or the Matter, Form and Power of a Commonwealth, Ecclesiastical and Civil*, 1651. It may be noted that he conceived of the need for synthetic, universal knowledge as the foundation of scientific study of man and society. See COMTE. G.D.M.

Hobhouse, Leonard Trelawney (1864–1929). English social philosopher, sociologist, and editor of the *Sociological Review*. While rejecting extreme theories of social evolution, he himself applied the concept to the development of society and moral life. For Hobhouse, progress comes from man's increasing control over nature – achieved by co-operative interaction. *Principles of Sociology*, sets out his social philosophy; volume one, *The Metaphysical Theory of the State*, 1918, argues that the state is a means, not an end; volume two, *The Rational Good*, 1921, that good is the harmony of mind and environment; volume three, *Elements of Social Justice*, 1921, applies this ethic. *Social Development*, 1924, suggest four criteria for evolution – allowing for retrogression as well as progress: size, efficiency, freedom, and mutuality of service. *The Material Culture and Social Institutions of the Simpler Peoples*, 1951, written in collaboration with M. Ginsberg and C. H. Wheeler, attempts at empirical verification of hypotheses. This work is a comparative study of over 400 societies to show that development of social institutions is correlated with changing economic conditions. G.D.M.

holism. A view of some philosophers, an early and notable example being G. W. F. Hegel, that in order to understand some phenomenon it is necessary to understand it in its entirety, i.e. one must know the whole. This follows from the belief that it is only by a contemplation of an essence that one can fully understand anything. The view has been trenchantly criticized by Lord Russell in his *History of Western Philosophy*, 1946, and in other writings.

The term holism has been ascribed to a sociological approach which argues that it is useful in some instances to think of societies as constituting social systems, with the implication that in studying the whole in this manner one is paying due regard to both the parts and the relationships holding between the parts. Such an approach is a structural approach, and may be said to be of the essence of sociology, or in other words this describes what in fact many sociologists and especially social anthropologists do. See the Introduction to A. R. Radcliffe-Brown's *Structure and Function in Primitive Society*, 1952. It should be noted that if this kind of holism is inadmissible from a methodological standpoint, then it is inconceivable that there can be a natural science of society, for all natural sciences make the assumption that the phenomenon that is studied is systematic in nature. See SOCIAL STRUCTURE.

G.D.M.

homeostasis. A process of *system self-regulation*; involving the maintenance by a system of a stable condition and the return to such a condition following environmental disturbance. See various chapters in Roy R. Grinker (ed.), *Towards a Unified Theory of Human Behaviour*, 1956. See EQUILIBRIUM, SOCIAL SYSTEM.

Horkheimer, Max (1895–1973). German sociologist who spent the years after Hitler came to power in America. Editor of *Zeitschrift für Sozialforschung*, 1933–1939. He returned to become Rector of the University of Frankfurt. Author of *Studien Über Autorität und Familie*, 1935 and (with T. W. Adorno) *Dialektik der Aufklärung*, 1947.

I

ideal type. It might be said that to talk about an ideal type is like talking about wet water, for any type, being an abstraction, is ideal and not real in the sense that a given material object is real: there exists this horse and that, but not a horse in general. The difference between an ideal type and a type pure and simple lies not in the abstractness of connotation but in the definiteness of denotation: whereas the types established by biological systematics have referents which fall under them and nowhere else, this is not the case with ideal types. No horse in general ever lived but there are many horses which satisfy perfectly the specifications of 'horsiness', whilst nothing like a perfectly rational organization has ever been observed. The idea behind the concept of ideal type is that social phenomena, in virtue of their manifold and fluid nature, can be analysed solely in terms of the extreme forms of their characteristics, which can never be observed in their purity. Pareto pointed out that all concepts of physical sciences are idealizations: that no movement without resistance of the medium has ever been observed (but only surmised in case of celestial bodies), that nothing perfectly straight has ever been found, that vectorial analysis assumes movements which never take place, and that social sciences must proceed likewise. As far as social sciences are concerned, the most useful idealizations can be found in the most mature of them, which is not surprising: the concepts of economic theory, such as perfect competition or static equilibrium, provide the best examples of ideal types.

We must distinguish between Weber's imprecise and inconsistent notion and the way in which it can be formulated along the lines he has foreshadowed but in accordance with the standards of contemporary philosophy of science. Weber uses the concept of ideal type in two incompatible senses: in the opening chapter of his essay *The Protestant Ethic and the Spirit of Capitalism* he speaks of the ideal type of Protestant ethics. Now, Protestantism (and therefore Protestant ethics) is not a generic concept (like, for example, the concept of dictatorship), defined by its abstract attributes and denoting an open set, but a proper name of a particular cultural entity (or a *historic individuum*, to use Weber's term) localized in time and space. In contrast, in the methodological introduction to *Wirtschaft und Gesellschaft* Weber treats ideal type as a generic concept, defined by general attributes, and as examples he gives the concepts of rational behaviour and the pure market, where actions are governed solely by the aim of maximizing profits. He mentions Stock Exchange as the nearest approximation of the ideal type of a pure market. Now, pure market can be defined in generic terms, without reference to time and place, and is methodologically analogous to the concepts of physics like 'ideal gas' or 'frictionless pendulum' whereas 'the ideal type' of Calvinist ethics is something entirely different and without an equivalent in the natural sciences.

With the ideal type in the generic sense, that is, in the sense in which 'ideal' is used in physics or 'pure' and 'perfect' in economics, we can see how assertions concerning such a type can be confronted with data despite the non-existence of exemplifications thereof in the empirical world. If an ideal type T is defined in terms of the attributes a, b, and c, the proposition attributing a property d to T can be accepted as correct if we find that the degree of approximation in respect of the attributes a, b, and c corresponds to the degree of approximation in respect of d. Thus, although we know that perfect competition as defined in economic theory can be found nowhere, we can accept the proposition that in a perfectly competitive market marginal cost equals price, if we see that the nearer a market comes to being perfectly competitive, the closer comes the marginal cost to the price.

No equivalent method can be found for validating statements about ideal types in the particularized sense, as in Weber's discussions of Calvinist ethics or the Confucian view of the world, where his *ideal type* is also a proper name for a unique historical individuum. In such usage, *ideal type* can be likened to a caricature, in the non-pejorative sense, of a picture where the most characteristic features are deliberately exaggerated. A good caricature is the most economic method of producing a picture permitting recognition of the individual; but producing such deliberately exaggerated, yet in some sense true, picture descriptions has more affinity with a novelist's art than with anything which could be legitimately called scientific method, not so much because of its intuitive origin (for intuition is the source of all hypotheses) but because it is not clear how such a notion could be logically connected with empirically testable general propositions. It is not even clear what kind of descriptive data would invalidate the applicability of an ideal type to a given case. See Max Weber, *The Methodology of the Social Sciences*, 1949; S. L. Andreski, *Elements of Comparative Sociology*, 1964, ch. 5; R. Fletcher, *The Making of Sociology*, 1971, vol. 2, pp. 426–55.　　　s.l.a.

ideology. The word *ideology* was first used by the French cavalry leader and philosopher Destutt de Tracy (1755–1836) in his *Éléments d'idéologie* (4 vols., Paris, 1801–15). By *ideology* he intended a science of ideas, their truth or error, working through a critical theory of the actual processes of the mind. The word rapidly became generally current, signifying not a science of ideas, but a total system of thought and emotion and attitude to the world, to society and to man. More particularly the term was applied to thoughts and emotions and attitudes in politics – the overtly proclaimed or tacitly accepted *credenda* in terms of which political action was motivated and/or legitimated. Ideology in this sense was often imputed to actors on the political stage as an inference from their deeds and words even though they did not (perhaps could not) formally express it. Ideologies of this kind need not be logically complete or consistent, nor need they accord with fact. Their only unity need be emotional.

More generally, *ideology* is used to mean any conception of the world which of its nature goes beyond what positive science can validate and which carries an emotive tone relevant to social action. Marx and Engels used the word slightly more specifically. In Marxism *ideology* is the term given to any form of thought which has been invaded by the vested interests of a ruling class or the aspiring intentions of subordinate classes. In Marxism ideologies are 'unmasked' or 'evaluated'; that is, behind apparently objective, or disinterested, or noble attitudes a covert, perhaps unconscious class interest is shown to exist.

Karl Mannheim, in *Ideology and Utopia*, 1936, uses the term yet more specifically. To him ideology is all thought distorted by the desire to conserve the present social order or restore the past: ideology is the manifestation of the vested interest or the programme of reaction. It is contrasted with his special usage of the term *Utopia, q.v.*

The study of ideology is a constituent part of the sociologies of religion and politics. It is the central subject matter of the sociology of knowledge. See SOCIOLOGY OF KNOWLEDGE, UTOPIA. G.D.M.

idiographic discipline. Intellectual disciplines may be idiographic or nomothetic. In the former case they are concerned with particular propositions, as is the case in history, in the latter with general propositions, like those of a theoretical science, such as physics, economics or genetics. The distinction was originally made by the German philosopher Wilhelm Windelband, who held that the social sciences may be treated in the same way as the natural sciences but with the exception of history, for history is concerned with the unique and individual aspects of social phenomena. This was the issue in the famous *Methodenstreit* that took place in German intellectual circles at the end of the last century. G.D.M.

incest taboo. This is the prohibition of, or avoidance of, sexual relations with near kin, usually primary relatives (parents, siblings, children).

Writers differ considerably in their definitions of what constitutes 'incest', and hence which sexual relations are in fact 'taboo'. Sometimes it is confined to members of the nuclear family; sometimes it is simply a synonym for forbidden sexual relations with any kin. Sometimes the incest taboo is equated with prohibitions on marriage (*exogamic* prohibitions), although these do not necessarily coincide. Most authorities agree that some form of taboo on sexual relations with some near kin, and particularly primary relatives, is virtually universal, although there are significant exceptions.

The classical psychoanalytic treatment can be found in Sigmund Freud's *Totem and Taboo* (1917), and in his other writings. The attribution of the incest taboo to instinct, fear of inbreeding, socialization, and the positive value of marriage, is discussed in C. Lévi-Strauss, *Les Structures Élémentaires de la Parenté* (1949), and G. P. Murdock, *Social Structure* (1949). See EXOGAMY. J.R.F.

independent variable. See VARIABLE.

individualism. The term is modern, being first employed in the English translation of Tocqueville's *Democracy in America* in 1840. The idea is old, and represents something mainly disapproved of at least until the Protestant Reformation. Durkheim pointed out how in societies where there are comparatively few social roles as a result of a small development of the division of labour, men are bound together in society by their similitudes. All assertion of individuality in unusual forms in such societies is an offence which is probably both immoral and irreligious. The claims of a Socrates are construed as impiety, and the paradox of Platonism is that there would be no place for Socrates in *The Republic*. Higher religions might stress the value of each individual, but they usually condemned extreme manifestations of individuality.

Post-Reformation individualism in religion, although Lutheran in its foundation, rapidly became antinomian. Only the rise of classical political economy in the eighteenth century made individualism respectable (a) by denying the existence of society as a reality exterior to its members; (b) by asserting the advantageous consequences of the economic competition of free individuals; (c) by extolling the development of the division of labour and therefore, if tacitly, of the multiplication of roles and the differences between men. As Durkheim saw it an advanced division of labour means an intensely individualistic society. This development was congruent with the development of doctrines of individual rights in philosophy and law. The result was a view of the ends of society as being concerned with the integrity, independence and defence of the individual; that is, of individualism. Darwinism in the nineteenth century seemed to bring the confirmation of science to the defence of individualist ideology.

Philosophical idealism, sociological realism, and collectivist theories of society and the state have arisen to oppose individualism. The debate continues. See *Individualism* by Steven Lukes, 1973.   D.G.M.

industrial sociology. As a specialized branch of sociology, utilizing both the theoretical concepts of the parent discipline and sophisticated techniques of research, *industrial sociology* has barely reached maturity. It is still somewhat amorphous, and difficult to define briefly. Although much of the classical tradition, and Durkheim and Weber in particular, is relevant to the analysis of industrial institutions, the earlier empirical work was largely uninfluenced by it. Systematic research in the field has developed only in recent decades, and can be said to date from the well-known Hawthorne investigations in the U.S.A. in the early 1930s, whilst in Europe it is almost entirely post-World War II. This late development reflects the traditional predominance of the 'individualist' approach of economics and of psychology, and the similar ideology of the industrial elite and their resistance to the field investigation of inter-group relations in industry.

As research has grown recently, its direction has been influenced both by the need to gain acceptance and by its dependence on external sponsorship. It has therefore been largely problem-oriented, or centred on problems of fairly immediate practical concern. Various aspects of management–employee relations have been studied, but with emphases on joint consultation, patterns of supervisory leadership and the analysis of work groups. Technical change and the demands of technology have also received attention, with particular reference to the impact and handling of change, and to the relations between different levels of technology and various organizational and social factors, including management structure. The structure and functioning of trade unions and management–union relations have also been analysed, although to a lesser extent by sociologists. More recently, the structure and role of occupational groups, and particularly 'white collar' groups, have increasingly been studied.

Although much of the earlier empirical work was limited to the analysis of rather restricted problems, broader concerns are now apparent. The interdependence of social phenomena has increasingly been recognized, and with it the need to study particular problems in terms of their wider social context. Thus the framework of analysis of more and more studies is the social system of the organization, or a major segment thereof, such as the management structure: and, in this connection, organizational analysis, or study of the structure and functioning of organizations, is becoming a dominant concern, with serious endeavours being made to refine, by empirical enquiry, traditional conceptions of bureaucracy. Similarly, more emphasis is now being placed on delineation of the links between structural features of industrial institutions and other important aspects of society, such as the educational system, class structure and community organization. As theoretical horizons have broadened and become more sophisticated, the systematization of empirical findings has also proceeded, and has provided a sounder base both for generalization and for the planning of further original work. A number of general reviews have now appeared, especially in relation to organizational analysis, managerial leadership and occupational groups.

The industrial sociologist's field of study is therefore developing to the point where it may be described as the analysis of industrial institutions and organizations, the relations between them and, in turn, the links between industrial phenomena and the institutions of the wider society. Conceptually, this is correct, but much remains to be done at the empirical level. As regards many of the problems which are, relatively, largely internal to industrial organizations, our systematic knowledge is still fragmentary; in respect of the links between industrial and other institutions it is often sparse. See W. E. Moore, *Industrial Relations and the Social Order*, revised edn. 1957; W. H. Scott *et al.*, *Technical Change and Industrial Relations*, 1956; E. V. Schneider, *Industrial Sociology*, 1957. W.H.S.

inheritance. *Inheritance* denotes the procedures which apply to the transmission of property, either material or immaterial, from person to person at death. In many societies these procedures are patrilineal, matrilineal or bilateral. The practice of testamentary disposition is relatively new and hardly known in simple societies where the norms governing inheritance are usually strict. Inheritance rules therefore tend to indicate the obligations a person has towards others, usually relatives.

The inheritance of physical characteristics, sometimes known as *Darwinian inheritance*, following Darwin's theory of natural selection, presents a somewhat different use of the word. This theory maintains that variations in the form or the function of any species persist only if suited to the environment, i.e. those variations which help the organism to survive are selected for perpetuation. See SUCCESSION. G.D.M.

initiation; initiation rites. Initiation is a ceremonial process by which an

103

individual takes on a new social position. The term is usually applied to the ceremonial activities associated with the *rite de passage* from childhood to adulthood, but may also be extended to refer to the method of entry into secret societies or specialized occupations. The essential characteristics of initiation are the acquisition by the individual of a new set of duties, rights, obligations and privileges, by virtue of his change of status, and the society's recognition of these.

The concept of the initiation rite was developed by A. van Gennep in his *Schema des rites de passage*, where he suggested that life crises fall into three stages – separation, transition and incorporation. In *Les Rites de Passage*, 1908 (translated *Rites of Passage*, 1960) he argues that the notion of separation involves a distinction between the sacred and the profane and between the masculine and the feminine. Transition he interpreted both in a spatial and social sense, whilst by incorporation he referred to re-entry of the individual into the group and to public recognition of his changed status.

Frequently in tribal societies, boys and girls at the time of puberty leave the community for the 'bush' to undergo a period of training for their adult roles. There are often ordeals to be endured and tribal norms to be learned in this period of transition. In Africa, the circumcision of males and the clitoridectomy of females frequently takes place at this time, and tribal markings may be made on the face or back. K. L. Little in *The Mende of Sierra Leone*, 1951, shows that for this tribe these practices are associated with initiation into one of the two great secret societies into which the Mende are divided – the *Poro* for males and the *Sande* (or *Bundu*) for women. Such initiation takes place at about puberty. After initiation individuals may marry. M. Allen in *Male Cults and Secret Initiations in Melanesia*, 1967, distinguishes between *initiation* rites which involve some degree of secrecy and *induction* rites which lack this. He shows that in Melanesia male cults associated with highly developed sex divisions occur most strikingly where locality and corporate group membership are coterminous.

Parallels are not hard to find in western society and the confirmation ceremonies of the Christian Church, or the entry into the Masonic Order, exemplify this. M. Mead in her *Coming of Age in Samoa*, 1953, contrasts problems associated with the change from childhood to adulthood in the U.S.A. and the South Pacific and concludes that public ceremonials of initiation are an important factor in easing the adjustment of individuals to new roles.   B.H.A.R.

instinct. Historically, in the non-human biological sciences, *instinct* was a label for whatever lay at the origin of inborn, unmodifiable behaviour-sequences common to a whole species. With the growing interest in ecology, the description of animal behaviour came to include those aspects of the environment which 'trigger' or 'release' characteristic sequences of behaviour, and it was realized that many species had a range, albeit limited, of alternative ways of responding to attack, threat, sex stimulus, territorial invasion, etc. More systematic study also revealed many conditions in which animals learn to modify their behaviour (N. Tinbergen, *The Study of Instinct*, 1951; C. Schiller, *Instinctive Behaviour*, tr. and ed., 1957; W. H. Thorpe, *Learning and Instinct in Animals*, 1963).

In the human sciences, the search for instincts thus defined led to a dead end. In the early decades of this century, listing instincts was a popular academic pastime. W. McDougall, for instance, listed more than a dozen, each with an accompanying emotion: the parental instinct, the instinct of reproduction, of flight, of repulsion, of curiosity, of pugnacity, of self-abasement and of self-assertion, and so on. This preoccupation with biological constants eventually gave way to the study of perception and learning, processes dependent on environmental as well as constitutional factors, and interest shifted to precise experimental work on the conditions which cause variations in performance. In the 'thirties, the increasing evidence from anthropology, that human nature was vastly more varied and modifiable than had been thought, helped to divert the human sciences into more profitable channels (Ruth Benedict, *Patterns of Culture*, 1934; Margaret Mead, *Sex and Temperament in Three Primitive Societies*, 1935).   J.K.

institution; social institution. In Sociology as in common English usage, this word denotes that which is established, or constituted in society. Phrases such as 'the institution of capital', 'the institution of the family' occur in nineteenth-century translations of Comte. Here the meaning of the word appears to be at its most general, conforming to that given above. A specifically sociological use, however, may be found in Spencer's *First Principles* where he described as institutions the organs that perform societies' functions. Sumner in *Folkways*, 1906, held that an institution consists of a concept (idea, notion, doctrine, interest) and a structure. The *concept* part then dropped from the discussion, and he explained that most institutions grow from folkways into customs, developing into mores and maturing when rules and acts become specified. At this point a structure, i.e. an apparatus or role structure, is established and the institution is complete. Thus an institution is a kind of 'super folkway' – more permanent because rationalized and conscious, whereas the folkways and mores are habitual unreasoned ways of acting. Later he opined that an institution is not one action or norm, but the crystallization of a set of mores – Sumner's examples – marriage, religion, banks – leave the term referring both to abstracts and to concrete organizations. Eventually he relegated marriage to the category of 'imperfect institutions' since, 'it lacks structure or material element of any kind'. In contradistinction the family is an institution – note he wrote of *the* family rather than *a* family.

Later usage is various. All authors agree that an institution is an established way of behaving. But the behaviour to which the term is applied varies among authors, from simple routinized acts to vast complexes of standardized procedures governing relationships between roles in large sections of the social order. In addition to this divergence, some authors consider that an institution, whatever the scope of behaviour referred to, also involves a structure and perhaps a 'material element'. Other writers emphatically reject this suggestion. Thus money, giving notice, collective bargaining, joint stock companies, and the economy may all be referred to as institutions of Western Society. We may now examine in more detail the various usages of the term.

E. Chinoy, *Society*, 1962, noted that there was an increasing measure of agreement that the word *institution* should be used to refer only to patterns of approved or sanctioned behaviour, and that other terms should be used to denote the organizational aspects of such behaviour and the group of persons involved. As examples of the behaviour referred to he gave laws against murder, or conventions governing daily social intercourse, and in subsequent discussion made the word virtually synonymous with the term *norm*. Institutions may thus be divided into folkways, mores, laws, etc. Not all authors, however, follow Chinoy in this manner. More often the term refers to groups of usages governing social relations. To W. Hamilton in *The Encyclopaedia of the Social Sciences* institutions are group procedures, from which deviations by members will be sanctioned with various degrees of severity. Yet they are more complex than mere folkways or mores. He cites the money economy, or democracy, as examples. This usage is common to many authors of elementary texts, e.g. A. W. and H. Gouldner in *Modern Sociology*, who see institutions as standardized ways of solving societies' problems, giving the funeral as an example. In this context institutions of the family refers to aspects of family life such as courtship and marriage.

R. M. MacIver and C. H. Page, *Society*, 1949, differentiated between *institution* and *association*. Institutions are 'established forms or conditions of procedure characteristic of group activity'. The group which performs these standardized actions is termed an *association*. Thus a church is an association, and services are its institutions. One can belong to an association but never to an institution. R. Bierstedt in *The Social Order*, 1957, said that an association unlike an institution has a location, and used the concept of association to distinguish between institutions and folkways. Hamilton (*op. cit.*), however, introduced a structural element at this level, saying that once institutions became formalized they develop personnel with vested interests in the institution's survival. In practice it is difficult to separate behaviour from the groups that perform it, and the materials they employ.

Cooley, *Social Organisation*, 1909, and Davis, *Human Society*, 1948, connoted institutions as vast complexes of norms established by society to deal in a regularized way with what are seen to be its fundamental needs. Davis saw them as sets of folkways, mores and laws interwoven around one or more functions, forming parts of the social structure, set off by the closeness of their organization and the distinctiveness of their functions. There are generally agreed to be five or so of these major complexes such as the family, or the polity; though authors differ as to what these are. In this context, institutions of the family refer to different types of family structure. It is allowed that there is not a one to one correspondence between institutions and societal need. The same need may be served by many institutions, though for some of them this may be only a subsidiary function.

This approach is frequently associated with functionalism, many of whose critics hold that any list of fundamental social requisites is arbitrary. However, with or without subscribing to functionalist theory, analysis of a society or community is often given structure by abstracting and describing in turn each of these complexes of beliefs, practices, roles and, frequently, the 'material element' such as buildings and apparatus. (See R. and H. Lynd, *Middletown*, 1929.) Similarly, anthropological comparisons are frequently not simply of society with society, but are structured around institutional comparison, economy with economy, etc.

Institutions are thus being viewed as the major order units of societies. Pure functionalism envisages them as forming mutually sustaining wholes, but most recent authors have stressed the autonomy of institutions, and even that elements of the same institutions may be oriented to different ends. T. Parsons, *The Social System*, 1951, attempted to explain the limits of institutional cohesion and the disparity in social structures.

Focusing on the structure rather than the behaviour, an organization of individuals such as a hospital, or a public school, may be referred to as an institution. (See B. Wilson on 'Analytical Studies of Social Institutions' in R. Welford's *Society – Problems and Methods of Study*, 1962.) This usage is more common in the literature of Social Administration. Thus, Penal Institutions calls to mind buildings, officers and detainees, while procedures, though implicit, are not the sole or even primary focus of attention.

Most authors acknowledge the existence of the various uses of the word; few are entirely consistent in their own use of it. See H. E. Smith, 'Toward a clarification of the concept of social institution' in *Sociology and Social Research*, 1964. See FOLKWAYS, FUNCTION, SOCIAL SYSTEM, TOTAL INSTITUTION.

B.A.P.

internal system. See EXTERNAL SYSTEM.

interpretative sociology. Just as there are no tools which are good for everything, so there are no descriptions which are good from every point of view. This limitation cannot be circumvented by giving a full description, because such a thing cannot exist; reality is inexhaustible, and nothing can be described completely.

With descriptions which have a practical aim in view the criteria of adequacy are fairly evident; with purely cognitive descriptions the matter is more elusive. One criterion which applies to all descriptions is economy, in view of the fact that reality is inexhaustible but our capacity limited. Economy of expression is partly a matter of stylistic skill, but even more the result of being able to discern what is important and what is not, which means that a good description must be analytic and based on recourse to all relevant theoretical generalizations.

Strictly speaking, all analyses of concrete situations are interpretative; and they can differ only in the degree of sophistication and credibility of their assumptions, and in the extent to which these assumptions have been subjected to scrutiny. Nevertheless, we might retain the term *interpretative sociology* to designate the kind of study which is focused on a concrete case rather than on theory but in which the author formulates new theoretical propositions and uses them for analysing his data in novel ways. See S. L. Andreski, *Elements of Comparative Sociology*, 1964, chs. 1 and 4; and M. R. Cohen, *Reason and Nature*, 1930. W. Outhwaite, *Understanding Social Life: The Method Called Verstehen*, 1975.

S.L.A.

J

joking relationships. A joking relationship involves a particular combination of friendliness and antagonism between individuals or groups in certain social situations. In these situations one individual or group is allowed to mock or ridicule the other without offence being taken. A. R. Radcliffe-Brown in *Structure and Function in Primitive Society*, 1952, distinguished between symmetrical joking relationships, where each party has the right to tease, and asymmetrical relationships where only one party is so privileged.

In many societies joking relationships exist between a man and his wife's or parent's siblings and between a woman and her husband's or parent's siblings. It may also occur between men or women of alternate generations, e.g. grandfather to grandson. Outside the individual relationships of kinship or affinity, joking relationships may exist between groups such as the clans of a tribe, e.g. Tallensi, or between tribes, e.g. as found on the Zambian Copperbelt. In industrial societies joking relationships are frequently found among those working in arduous occupations in confined spaces. Among dockers and miners for example this lessens the risk of accident following abuse, since no offence can be taken for insulting language on the job.

B.H.A.R.

K

katascopic. Adjective used to identify the kind of social theory (e.g. that of Durkheim) which starts from a conception of society and postulates ways in which society influences the individual. See T. Geiger, ed. P. Trappe, *Arbeiten zur Soziologie: Sociologische Texte*, vol. 7, Neuwied, Berlin. p. 147f. See ANASCOPIC.

kindred. See KINSHIP.

kinship. Kinship is social relationship based on real, putative or fictive consanguinity; or on the model of consanguine relations.

Although in anthropology the term *kinship* is often used as a shorthand for 'kinship and marriage', it is usual to distinguish *kinship* (relationship by blood) from *affinity* (relationship by marriage): thus parent and child are *kin*; husband and wife are *affines*. In most societies a child is regarded as the offspring of both parents, and so has relationships of kinship traced through both. Those kin traced through the father are termed *paternal* or *patrilateral*; those traced through the mother, *maternal* or *matrilateral*. The totality of matrilateral and patrilateral kin recognized by a person within a certain degree is sometimes termed his *kindred*. It is also usual to distinguish *lineal* from *collateral* kin. Lineal kin are the direct ancestors and direct descendants of an individual: his parents, grandparents, great-grandparents, etc., and his children, grandchildren, etc. Collaterals are the other descendants of one's lineal kin (parents' siblings, cousins, etc.). Some writers consider a person's siblings and their descendants as lineal, others as collateral kin. Yet another distinction is between primary, secondary and tertiary kin. Primary kin are one's parents and their offspring and one's own offspring (father, mother, brother, sister, son, daughter). Secondary kin are the primary kin of these (father's father, mother's brother, brother's daughter, etc.). Tertiary kin are the primary kin of secondary kin, and so on.

The classic way of defining *consanguinity* is in terms of common *descent* from an ancestor. All the descendants of a common ancestor may be termed a *stock*. Thus an individual is a member of as many stocks as he recognizes ultimate lineal ancestors. Through his parents he is a member of two stocks, through his grandparents of four ... etc. A person is said to be a *cognate* of, or related *cognatically* to, all those people with whom he shares a common ancestor.

For some purposes, however, the descent criterion may be restricted to males, and only those descendants of a common ancestor in the male line will be recognized as kin. These are known as *agnatic* or *patrilineal* kin. If descent is traced through females exclusively for some purposes, then the descendants would be called *uterine* or *matrilineal* kin. These two modes of tracing descent are called *unilineal*; that is, they select one 'line' only, either the male or the female. These principles are not necessarily mutually exclusive within a society. It is possible, for example, for an individual to recognize all cognates as kin for some purposes, but to restrict recognition to agnates for some other purposes. Indeed, almost all kinship systems recognize *bilateral* relationships, i.e. relationships to both maternal and paternal kin. Some societies, such as the Yakö of Nigeria, utilize matrilineal descent for some purposes and patrilineal for others, thus achieving a system of *double unilineal descent*, known usually as *double-descent* for short. See D. Forde, *Yakö Studies*, 1964.

It is also possible to restrict recognition of consanguinity itself in the above fashion, namely, unilineally. This affects the recognition of affinity, which is relative to the definition of consanguinity. Thus, it is possible to claim that a child is related 'by blood' to its mother, but not to its father. In such a case, a child's father would not be a consanguine, but an affine (mother's husband). The opposite case is known in which it is claimed that the father 'creates' the child and not the mother. In this case the mother becomes an affine (father's wife). In these cases relations with patrilateral and matrilateral 'kin' can in fact be relations of affinity within the cultural definition. See E. R. Leach, *Rethinking Anthropology*, 1961, ch. 1.

Among the more important cultural uses of kinship ties are rules of inheritance, succession, group membership and marriage. Inheritance and succession can follow any of the above principles. Also social groups can be recruited on the basis of descent. A group can restrict membership to the children of male members or female members, thus producing patrilineally or matrilineally recruited groups. If these groups claim descent from a common founding ancestor, then they are *descent* groups. A group can of course recruit the children of members of both sexes (i.e. cognatic or bilateral recruitment), but this presents problems in that groups formed on this basis are bound to overlap; a person will be a member of *both* mother's *and* father's groups, for example, whereas with unilineal recruitment he will be a member of *either* mother's *or* father's group.

All these, however, are groups based on descent from ancestors, and they contrast sharply with groups based on the kindred of an individual. The kindred, as we have seen, comprises all the stocks of which an individual is a member up to a certain degree. Many systems set formal limits to this range usually in terms of degrees of cousinship. Thus a kindred can include all cognates up to second cousins, or alternatively phrased, four stocks (the descendants of an individual's four pairs of great-grandparents). These kindreds would overlap and no two persons, except siblings, would be members of the same kindred. Sometimes obligations to a person are divided between different parts of his kindred, the paternal side having one set of responsibilities and the maternal another, and so on. In yet other systems, such as our own, there is no formal limit set to the kindred, and an individual simply recognizes a loosely defined *network* of cognates, not usually beyond the second-cousin range.

Any of the above principles can determine the rules of 'prohibited degrees' of kinship: that is, degrees of relationship within which marriage is forbidden. The Roman Catholic Church, for example, forbids marriage within the second-cousin range. It is usual for restrictions of *exogamy* to apply to descent groups; that is, members of the group, however this is defined, are not allowed to marry each other. At the other end of this scale, it is often the case that certain relatives are *prescribed* as marriage partners, usually cousins of some description, such as *cross-cousins*. In such a system, the distinction between *kinship* and *affinity* often ceases to operate, as all affines may be kin and vice-versa.

It is usual to distinguish between *biological* or *genetic* kinship, and *social* kinship. These contrast most obviously, for example, in the case of adopted children who lack a genetic link with their 'parents', but are socially recognized as 'kin' to them; and vice-versa in the case of a man's unacknowledged illegitimate children. To this end, anthropologists distinguish between the *pater* or 'social father' and the *genitor* or 'biological father' (conversely the *mater* and the *genitrix*; although this is less often needed). Kinship systems, however, usually work on the genetic 'model', even if this is deliberately fabricated. Often relationships between non-kin are assimilated to those of 'real' kinship, as in the case of ritual godparenthood (*compadrazgo*) in Latin America, where, for example, marriage prohibitions are extended to godparents (and their children) as though they were 'real' parents. There are many examples of this process of assimilating non-kin relationships to those of kinship, as with, for example, 'blood-brothers'.

Recent developments in evolutionary theory have underscored the importance of relatedness as a factor in natural selection through the process of *kin selection*. This perspective takes the gene rather than the individual as the unit of selection, and argues that individuals, as carriers of gene replicas, can further selection by 'altruistic' acts that, while they may result in the elimination of the individual lead to the survival of enough gene replicas to ensure that the genes in question survive. Thus, relatives, and particularly close relatives, can be expected under specified evolutionary conditions to act 'nepotistically' towards each other; that is, to favour each other in the struggle for existence over other, less related animals. Since, for example, brothers share 50% of their genes, it would pay an individual to sacrifice himself for three brothers. Other applications of this idea include that of *paternity confidence*. A man's confidence in the paternity of his own children can vary from zero to 100%. Where the confidence is low, then it may pay him to invest his parental efforts in the children of his sister. His relationship to these is less (25% as opposed to 50%), but his certainty of relatedness is 100%. The underlying mechanisms of matrilineal societies may be affected by such considerations, although not consciously, of course. Whatever the details of the mechanism of kin selection, the underlying importance is clear for kinship theory: kinship systems are not arbitrary inventions of the human imagination. In at least some of their aspects they are rooted in biological processes. This, coupled with the fact that kinship groups clearly exist in animals and particularly primates, should lead to a re-evaluation of the basis of human kinship systems.

The systematic study of kinship is relatively recent, although jurists have always been concerned with legitimacy, succession, conjugal rights, degrees of consanguinity, etc. Perhaps J. F. McLennan's *Primitive Marriage*, 1865, marks the beginning of a real comparative study. More influential was L. H. Morgan's *Systems of Consanguinity and Affinity of the Human Family*, 1870. This showed up the importance of *terminology* (the words used to classify kin) as this seemed to vary as systems of kinship and affinity varied. Massive concentration on the relationship between descent, marriage and terminology characterized the study of kinship in the work of W. H. R. Rivers, *Kinship and Social Organisation*, 1914, A. R. Radcliffe-Brown, *Structure and Function in Primitive Society*, 1952, and many others, and continues as a major interest today. Indeed, for some writers *kinship system* means the system of terminology. Still the best outline of the whole topic is Radcliffe-Brown's 'Introduction' to *African Systems of Kinship and Marriage*, 1950. A comparative approach which revives the evolutionary theory of Morgan can be found in G. P. Murdock, *Social Structure*, 1949. The relations between descent and affinity are treated in a brilliant but controversial book by C. Lévi-Strauss, *Les Structures Élémentaires de la Parenté*, 1949. A good historical survey can be found in Sol Tax, 'From Lafitau to Radcliffe-Brown', in F. Eggan., ed., *Social Anthropology of North American Tribes*, 1937. For recent contributions see E. O. Wilson, *Sociobiology: The New Synthesis*, 1975; R. Dawkins, *The Selfish Gene*, 1976; R. Fox, *Biosocial Anthropology*, 1975. See AMBILATERAL, BILATERAL, CLAN, COGNATE, CONSANGUINITY, CROSS-COUSIN, DESCENT, ENDOGAMY, EXOGAMY, FAMILY, INHERITANCE, LINEAGE, MARRIAGE, MATRILINEAL, MOIETY, PARALLEL COUSINS, PATRILINEAL, SIB, SUCCESSION.   J.R.F.

Kluckhohn, Clyde (1905–1960). American anthropologist, educated at the Universities of Wisconsin and Princeton, he was also a Rhodes scholar at Oxford and afterwards studied psychoanalysis in Vienna. Kluckhohn taught at Harvard and together with others exerted a considerable influence in bringing anthropology, sociology and psychology together. His main anthropological monograph was *Navajo Witchcraft*, 1944.

Kroeber, Alfred Louis (1876–1960). American anthropologist; he made important contributions in ethnographic fieldwork as well as in theories of cultural progress, cultural determinism, and philosophy of history. *Handbook of the Indians of California*, 1925, is his major work in ethnology; mainly a 'series of tribal descriptions'. He refined the concept of 'culture-areas', employing quantitatively additional concepts of culture *intensity* and *climax*. He believed that there were three distinct levels of phenomena, inorganic, organic, superorganic; the latter, civilization, initiated by primitive man's introduction of culture; it develops according to laws peculiar to itself, uninfluenced by the organic. *Configurations of Culture Growth*, 1944, attempts to find recurrent patterns of cultural growth in liberal and fine arts, and science, and concludes that the 'highest aesthetic and intellectual achievements in history occurred in temporary bursts of growth, as indicated by the clusterings of geniuses in space and time'. See also his *Anthropology*, 1948.   G.D.M.

L

legitimacy of authority. See AUTHORITY.

Le Play, Pierre Guillaume Frédéric (1806–1882). French engineer and sociologist; disturbed like Comte with contemporary unrest, he wanted peace and order. His detailed investigations of the economic circumstances of about 300 families typical of European industries, localities and conditions led to his major work, *Les Ouvriers Européens*, 1855, which greatly influenced Charles Booth. He propounded the formula *'Lieu, Travaille, Famille'* in the belief that family, the basic unit of social life, was functionally important, *inter alia*, for the subsistence of its members and that the mode of work was influenced by ecology. He viewed social change as cyclical and prosperity as produced when social structure met the needs of daily bread (material things) and essential mores (non-material things). He is important for creating an observational technique applicable to concrete outdoor studies, and for his heuristic formula.   G.D.M.

Lévy-Bruhl, Lucien (1857–1939). French sociologist and ethnologist; the majority of his work was concerned with primitive mentality and he had considerable influence on contemporary psychology. *The Philosophy of Auguste Comte*, 1900, presents a clear guide to Comte and Positivism. Like Durkheim, his contemporary, Lévy-Bruhl demanded a positive moral doctrine as the basis of politics in *Morality and Customs*, 1900. He regarded the thought structure of primitive peoples as determined entirely by collective representations, characterizing it as 'pre-logical'. In *Primitive Mentality*, 1922, he argued that cultural traditions in primitive societies inhibit comprehension of natural causation. Other works include *Mental Functions in Primitive Society*, 1910; *The Mind of the Primitive*, 1927; *The Supernatural and Nature in the Primitive Mentality*, 1935. The primitive society has a different spiritual background from that of modern society. His views engendered many criticisms, not all of them justified.   G.D.M.

lineage. A lineage consists of all descendants in one line of a particular person through a determinate number of generations. Where the living members constitute a recognized social group it may be called a *lineage group*, but sometimes the lineage consists of both the living and the dead. A lineage consisting of all descendants through males of a single ancestor is called a *patri-lineage* or an *agnatic lineage*; one consisting of all descendants through females is known as a *matri-lineage*.

Lineages usually have exclusive common ritual observances, perhaps totemic in nature, and they are usually exogamous. They may have common property rights or offices of a priestly or royal character. A lineage is usually three generations in number, but may be many more, although seldom more than five. See CLAN, DESCENT, KINSHIP.   G.D.M.

Locke, John (1632–1704). English empiricist philosopher; one of the first modern critics of the foundation and limitations of human knowledge. His *Essay Concerning Human Understanding*, 1690, argues that all ideas depend on experience and attempts critically to examine understanding of, *inter alia*, causality, probability, substance, qualities of matters, ideas, words, God and the Universe. Locke's treatises on government stress virtual, mutual contract as the origin of the state; he agreed that a sovereign people may alter the terms of the social contract to meet changing conditions. His view's about property favoured the rising gentry class. *Thoughts on Education*, 1690, propounds a system of formal education, emphasizing self-discipline and the subordination of learning information and grammar by heart to the formation of character; he stressed both mental and physical well-being as important for growth of intelligence.   G.D.M.

Lukács, György, or Georg (1885–1971). Hungarian intellectual and Communist. His best-known work was *Geschichte und Klassen-bewusstein*, 1923, which he publicly renounced in Moscow in 1934 as a departure from orthodoxy. Although not a sociologist he has been of interest to sociologists for what he says about class consciousness.

M

M'Naghten Rules. A set of principles for the guidance of the courts in cases in which the accused has pleaded that he was insane at the time of the act. The Rules are in the form of answers prepared by Her Majesty's judges in 1843 to five questions put to them by the House of Lords following the acquittal of Daniel M'Naghten (also spelt McNaghten, McNaughten, M'Naughten, Macnaughton, McNaughton) on a charge of murder. They require the defence to prove that 'at the time of committing the act, the accused was suffering under such a defect of reason, from disease of the mind, as not to know the nature and quality of the act he was doing, or, if he did know it, that he did not know he was doing what was wrong'. (See 'Daniel M'Naghten's Case' in *Clark and Finnelly's Reports* (Sessions 1843–44).) The questions put to the judges referred specifically to 'crimes committed by persons afflicted with insane delusion in respect of one or more particular subjects or persons' and the judges assumed that 'your lordships' inquiries are confined to those persons who labour under such partial delusions only, and are not in other respects insane'. Although cases of this kind are extremely rare, the M'Naghten Rules have been taken to furnish a test of responsibility for criminal acts of all kinds, and have occasionally been applied in civil cases; but in practice the defence of insanity is generally reserved for cases of murder. The Rules have been strongly criticized on the grounds that they are unduly restrictive, despite the fact that the courts have interpreted them in an elastic fashion. (An account of the application of the M'Naghten Rules in criminal cases will be found in the *Report of the Royal Commission on Capital Punishment* (Cmnd. 8932), 1953, pp. 81–5.) The defence of diminished responsibility, introduced by the Homicide Act of 1957, has partially supplanted that of insanity in cases of murder.   G.B.T.

magic, sorcery and witchcraft. These three phenomena form an interdependent complex of beliefs and practices in many tribal societies. In these societies, more than in industrialized societies, it is believed that misfortunes occur to persons because their moral relations with their fellows have been disturbed. In some tribes it is believed that these disturbances provoke gods or ancestral ghosts to send misfortune. In others, misfortunes are blamed on witches and/or sorcerers. And there are tribes where all these causes of misfortune, and more or others, may be believed in. The most illuminating interpretation of these types of beliefs, and the intellectual system within which they operated, was E. E. Evans-Pritchard's study entitled *Witchcraft, Oracles and Magic among the Azande*, 1937. In this book, which is about a Sudanese tribal people, he shows that to understand the system of beliefs and practices, action had to be approached from the occurrence of a misfortune. This misfortune was interpreted empirically in terms of its agent – sickness, crop-pest, an elephant killing a man, and so forth. But in addition, the Azande were concerned to understand why that particular misfortune had afflicted a particular man, and not another, and at that particular time and place. This particularity of misfortune was ascribed to the evil-doing of a witch or sorcerer. The evil-doer responsible was sought through some form of divination or by means of oracles. Basic Azande oracles were operated by the sufferer putting the names of persons he had cause to believe might wish to harm him to the divinatory device; and since he put the names of those who wished him harm, some enemy was detected. This emphasized the moral elements in these beliefs. For it is hostile motives which set witchcraft or sorcery to work. Evans-Pritchard classified as witchcraft, a belief in an inherent, and often inherited, organic attribute of a person, such as a condition of the intestines. This attribute has a power which can harm others by unobservable means and at a distance. Further, the belief is that a person may have this power, but since he does not feel hostile motives against others, it remains 'cool' and does them no harm. Envy, hatred, malice, greed, anger, are the kinds of vicious feelings that set the power of witchcraft, if one has it, to work. It is believed that a person may have this power and not know it, until his vicious feelings set it to work against others. Evans-Pritchard defined sorcery, in contrast to witchcraft, as the alleged deliberate use of evil magic to harm others. Magic is the employment of substances, rites and spells to achieve aims by means not under sensory observation and control. The sorcerer thus is believed to harm others without assaulting them directly; but again it is vicious and hostile feelings that animate him to do so. Evans-Pritchard then showed that the particular quarrelsome social relationships within which charges of witchcraft and sorcery are made, or from which they were excluded, were set by the general social organization.

Magic is a method of supporting endeavour to control the environment and social relationships by means where the connection of effort with achievement cannot be measured. It is also a principal means of combating witches and sorcerers who interfere with the success of desired achievements.

There has been much fruitful later research on the lines opened by Evans-Pritchard. The distinction between alleged wrongdoers to whom witches and sorcerers can be applied, with basically the meaning and distinction between these terms in English history, is not always applicable to other tribes. But the general intellectual operation of the system, including the way it is insulated against contradicting evidence, and its moral dimension, have been demonstrated to occur in tribe after tribe. The biggest developments in later research have been into the varying incidence of witchcraft accusations in different tribes, and the connection of these variations with variations in social organization. Recent work has also emphasized that accusations of this type have to be analysed within the cycle of development of families, lineages, villages, etc. They are seen as a part of an historical process, involving a whole set of persons, and not only as occurring in dyadic relations.   M.G.

Malinowski, Bronislaw (1884–1942). Polish scientist turned anthropologist. As a young man he was greatly influenced by Frazer's *Golden Bough*. As he was technically an Austrian citizen he was interned on arrival in Australia in 1914, but he persuaded the Australian government to help finance his expedition to the Trobriand Islands. After the war he published a number of works describing the peoples he had lived with and the methods he employed. He became Reader and shortly afterwards Professor of Anthropology in the London School of Economics and Political Science, paid several visits to the U.S.A., and became one of the most outstanding teachers and popularizers of the subject. His functional approach based on an identification of human needs and their institutional expression shaped British social anthropology. Malinowski and A. R. Radcliffe-Brown together may be said to have set the course of development of the subject in Britain and to some extent in the U.S.A. He is particularly well known for his writings about magic, but he did much to stimulate theoretical discussion about institutions, culture and the relationship of psychology to anthropological studies.

His principal works are *Argonauts of the Western Pacific*, 1922; *Crime and Custom in Savage Society*, 1926; *Sex and Repression*, 1927; *Magic, Science and Religion and Other Essays*, 1948. Like the titles of his books, he was rather flamboyant; he was also eccentric, enthusiastic and stimulating. He aroused strong passions and several more staid, and some would say, more scholarly, anthropologists and sociologists have been unable to hide their antipathy. That he will have a prominent position in the history of the subject is not in doubt, but what it will be precisely is still not clear.   G.D.M.

Malthusian theory. 1. The view that there is a tendency for human beings to multiply more rapidly (by a geometric ratio) than subsistence (food, which can only be augmented by an arithmetic ratio). According to the Rev. T. R. Malthus (1766–1834), in the *Essay on the Principle of Population* (1st ed., 1798, 2nd much revised edition 1803) mankind and subsistence are balanced either by positive checks (vice, misery, famine, epidemics, violence) or preventive checks (moral restraint, late marriage and chastity).

2. Generalizations derived from erroneous interpretations of this theory which claim constant danger of over-population in order to justify repressive measures, from the 1834 Poor Law Amendment Act in England to marriage prohibitions in Germany.

Malthus merely claimed a *tendency*: the only actual case of geometric increase (i.e. doubling within a generation) was that of North America. Positive checks operated mainly in primitive societies, preventive ones in civilized states. His *Essay* was originally designed as an answer to utopian theories of perfectibility, hence the Theory is sometimes seen as the expression of pessimism and reaction. He doubted the efficacy of the existing poor laws and indiscriminate charity. He believed in the Wage Fund and thought the remedy for poverty lay with the poor themselves. For a systematic account of Malthus's own theories, see Kingsley Davis, 'Malthus and the Theory of Population', in Lazarsfeld and Rosenberg, eds., *The Language of Social Research*, 1955, pp. 540–53.

Malthus's views made an immediate impact on nineteenth-century thinking. For the *Essay* and its background, see D. V. Glass, ed., *Introduction to Malthus*, London 1953, esp. H. L. Beales, 'The Historical Context of the *Essay* on Population'. It explained the reasons for the large amount of pauperism in early industrial England, and was used to defeat any proposals for social reform. '... the main contribution of his school is that the essence of social policy is that there should be no social policy ...' (Beales, *loc. cit.*). Apart from the 1834 Poor Law, opposition to trade unions and factory legislation was partly based on Malthus, and his view of emigration as a temporary palliative prevented a vigorous overseas settlement policy.

The Malthusian Theory was perpetuated by Samuel Smiles, by the Charity Organization Society (after 1869), and by Darwin who acknowledged his debt to Malthus; Natural Selection and the Survival of the Fittest are developments of basic Malthusian theory.

The Theory also gave rise to the view that mankind could regulate its numbers other than by late marriage; the birth control movement began as *Neo-Malthusianism*. This came to be associated with socialism and social reform, so that its adherents were almost always in conflict with the followers of the Theory proper. It is also related to Eugenics and forms one of the starting points of modern demography. See DEMOGRAPHY, EUGENICS, SOCIAL DARWINISM.   D.E.C.E.

mana. See ANIMISM.

Mannheim, Hermann (1889–1974). Sociologist and criminologist. At one time a magistrate and teacher of law in Berlin and later in 1931 a Judge of the Kammergericht (Criminal Division). He migrated to England in 1934 and held a post in the London School of Economics and Political Science and was mainly responsible for stimulating an interest in criminology with a marked sociological content in his writings on penology.

Mannheim, Karl (1893–1947). Hungarian sociologist who settled in England, and who made major contributions to the sociology of knowledge. *Ideology and Utopia*, 1929 (translated 1936), argues that knowledge, functional in man's adaptation to the environment, varies with the environment; knowledge is class-differentiated since classes present different environments. Knowledge, he declared, is of two types: true knowledge based on scientific criteria; and knowledge relative to classes, e.g. religion, philosophy and traditional knowledge. Sets of ideas serving to promote and defend interests are of two types: those promoting the interests of under-privileged groups and placing their social objectives in the future are termed *utopias*; those defending the interests of privileged groups are *ideologies*. (See also 'Wissenssoziologie' in Vierkandt's *Encyclopaedia of Sociology*, 1931.) His later works turn to the problem of the reconstruction of a war-shattered society; see *Man and Society in an Age of Reconstruction*, 1942; *Diagnosis of Our Time*, 1944; *Freedom, Power and Democratic Planning*, 1951.
                                                                            G.D.M.

marriage. There is no definition which adequately covers all types of human *marriage*. It is an institution of society which can have very different implications in different cultures. Broadly speaking, however, marriage may be defined as 'a socially sanctioned sex relationship involving two or more people of the opposite sex, whose relationship is expected to endure beyond the time required for gestation and the birth of children'. The social sanctions of most cultures would imply a stable relationship, hence *marriage* is not co-extensive with sex life and excludes relationships with prostitutes or any other sexual relationship which is viewed as casual and not sanctioned by custom, law or church.

Biologically, the institution of marriage arises from the facts of human procreation and the rearing of children; from the lengthy period of dependence of children on their parents and the need for prolonged parental care and training. It is the combination of mating with parenthood which, at this level, constitutes human marriage; hence Westermarck's well-known aphorism: 'Marriage is rooted in the family rather than the family in marriage.'

Socially, however, there are added to the sexual and parental ideas of marriage other elements: marriage is given the hallmark of social approval; it becomes a legal contract: it defines the relationship between husband and wife and between parents and children; it has to be concluded in a public and solemn manner, sometimes receiving, as a sacrament, the blessings of religion, and as a rite, the good auspices of magic.

In human societies, marriage appears in a variety of forms: monogamy, polygyny and polyandry; matriarchal and patriarchal unions; households with matrilocal and patrilocal residence. In no culture is marriage a matter of entirely free choice. People related by descent or members of certain classes are often debarred from marrying each other, or else they are expected to marry. The rule prescribing marriage within one's group is called *endogamy*; insistence on marrying outside one's group, *exogamy*. With only very rare exceptions, of which the best known is probably ancient Egypt, there is an almost universal law against marriage between siblings or between parent and child. Beyond the narrow incest group, there are wide differences of 'forbidden degrees' between societies; and within societies the degrees of relationship within which one may not marry can and do change from time to time.

It is important to notice that, even within the framework of these regulations which sanction certain types of marriage whilst prohibiting others, marriage has not until recently in the West and even now only among a limited section in some Eastern countries, been directed towards the sentimental and sexual gratification of the two people most intimately involved. Typically, human marriage has been universally recognized not merely as a relationship which provides for the adequate rearing of legitimate offspring, but also as an institution which establishes legal, moral, social and economic links between the kin groups of the spouses which might or might not be to one or other kin group's advantage. Hence the traditional importance to the approval of the kin group to any marriage of one of its members.

The sociological study of marriage as an institution is far less adequate than either its universality or popularity would seem to warrant. Early studies were largely devoted to hypothetical constructions as to 'original' or 'prior' forms of marriage, usually with a view to establishing Christian monogamous marriage as the end product of social evolution. Analogies with the animal kingdom have been and are still made with particular reference to the mating behaviour of the higher primates, and by the use of peculiar and anomalous aspects of contemporary simple societies as clues, reconstructions have been made of early stages of marital organization which are without existing representative examples. Thus L. H. Morgan, in *Systems of Consanguinity and Affinity in the Human Family*, 1870, and *Ancient Society*, 1877, constructed an evolutionary scheme in which matriliny preceded patriliny and monogamy was the final state. E. Westermarck, refuting Morgan's position in his three-volume *History of Human Marriage*, 1921, argued that man was originally monogamous, relying for proof upon selected examples of monogamy among the anthropoids and the fact that hunting and food-gathering peoples, whom the social evolutionists considered the most primitive economically, were prevailingly monogamous. Briffault, who revived the discussion in *The Mothers*, 1927, postulated matriarchy as prior to patriarchy, and used all three methods of enquiry to produce a scheme less crudely evolutionary than Morgan's but open to the same objections. All these attempts remain at best only elaborate hypotheses which are not refuted on the ground of their irrelevance and the inadequacy of the evolutionary method on which they all fundamentally rest.

More recently, sociologists have tended to concentrate on the pathology of marriage and above all the phenomena of marriage breakdown and divorce. Indeed, so much is this the case, that sociologists tend to appear to be the prophets of doom with regard to marriage in contemporary industrial societies. This myopic interest in marital failure, sometimes tempered with do-it-yourself type studies in marital harmony, is to a large degree a reflection of the greater hazards to which marriage is exposed in advanced industrial societies and of the changed expectations which are entertained of marriage itself. Men and women marry earlier, have smaller families sooner and expect greater personal satisfaction from their marriage than has ever been the case before. Moreover, selection of a marriage partner has become a matter for individual choice rather than family determination. For some, this has made marriage the fulfilment of that Western novelty, romantic idealism; for others, it has become one of the more hazardous speculations of industrial capitalist society. See DIVORCE, FAMILY, KINSHIP.   M.H.

Marx, Karl (1818–1883). Scholar, editor of the *Rheinische Zeitung*, historian, economist and political propagandist, Marx was one of the formative influences of the modern mind. Although a full biography would describe his philosophical views, his social and political thought and also refer to his part in organizing the International, from a sociological point of view interest must be restricted to only a part of his works.

His philosophical outlook was largely influenced by both Hegel and Hegel's materialistic successor Ludwig Feuerbach. Thus Marx put forward a view of history known as economic determinism. He argued that the mode of production (e.g. hand labour or steam power) was fundamental in determining the kind of economy a society possessed, and the kind of cultural and social structure of that society. The economic base was the sub-structure, and the political, religious and artistic features together with social arrangements constituted the super-structure, the latter being conditioned by the former. This basic belief and his ideas about social change (i.e. the dialectical conflict of classes whereby the class structure is progressively simplified into an antagonism of bourgeoisie and proletariat, with the eventual triumph of the latter) were the main sociological features of his thought. The first notion has largely been responsible for the development of studies in economic history: the latter has helped to develop ideas about the class systems of industrial societies – a marked feature of modern sociological research. His close friendship with Friedrich Engels led to their joint publication in 1848 of the *Communist Manifesto*, which appeared in an English translation in 1850. This document contains, in concise form, his views on the class struggle, which is nowhere else very clearly set out. His was a seminal mind for many modern writers. He has influenced more than a few sociologists, but even some of his closest admirers would admit that his methodology was faulty, his historical writing biased and sometimes uninformed, and his sociology naive. Some of his reports about the class struggles in France and the revolutions in 1848 in Prussia and Austria make interesting reading, his economic writings in the famous work *Das Kapital*, 1867–94, are rather dull and tendentious. His occasional papers are polemical and often betray the tetchy and pedantic German scholar that he was. Notwithstanding all this he has exerted a vast influence and, what is probably the criterion of importance in the field of learning, he has led many others to discuss the problems he made his own and he has opened up vast new areas of investigation. Most of the modern social sciences owe their existence in greater or lesser degree to Karl Marx. It is perhaps salutary to recall that he said of himself: '*Je ne suis pas un Marxiste*'.

Some sociologists in recent years in re-examining Marx's writings, especially the early works, have derived inspiration from them. Among these early works may be cited *German Ideology*, published originally in German, 1845–6, but in English in 1938. Both this and selections from various sources translated by T. B. Bottomore and published by him and M. Rubel in their book *Karl Marx: Selected Writings in Sociology and Social Philosophy*, 1956, have helped to stimulate interest in the concept of *alienation*, which has exercised a number of American and British sociologists. T. B. Bottomore has also translated and edited other works. See his *Karl Marx: Early Writings*, 1963. For easy access to Marx's principal works see the subsidized translations published by the Foreign Publishing House of the U.S.S.R. entitled *Marx and Engels: Selected Writings*.

For a sympathetic but trenchant critique of Marx's method, see Sir K. R. Popper's *The Open Society and Its Enemies*, vol. II, 1945; for a discussion of Marx's views in their philosophical context, see J. Plamenatz, *Man and Society*, vol. II, 1963, and for the influence of Marx on Sociology see T. Bottomore, *Marxist Sociology*, 1975.   G.D.M.

Marxist Sociology. Marx did not intend a sociology but a critique of political economy, partly because of its nineteenth-century association with Comte's (*q.v.*) Positivism. Bukharin's *Historical Materialism* (1921) was one of the first to treat it as a system of general sociology. Marxist social theories have drawn extensively from a variety of disparate philosophical and other currents of thought: neo-Kantianism (Austro-Marxists), neo-Hegelianism, phenomenology, existentialism (Sartre), process philosophy (Bloch), logical empiricism (Neurath), Spinozistic rationalism (Althusser), psychoanalysis, structuralism, semiotics, etc. This is reflected in the range of Marxist options concerning the general character of social wholes: equilibrium – maintaining mechanisms (Bukharin), dialectical totalities, 'structures without subject or goals', etc.

The hard core of Marxist social analyses consists in the studies of forms of economic structure and change and of classes, class consciousness and conflicts, tied to specific circumstances according to the principle of historical specificity (Korsch). A notable contribution was Lukács's Weber-influenced contrast between the actual and the potential class consciousness of the proletariat. Since about 1968 with the growth of an academic Marxist community in the English-speaking world, Marxists have contributed to virtually every branch of sociology. In the main their contributions have not been significant in the sociology of the family, small groups, communities, bureaucracies, the military, nationalism, language and symbolism. Distinguished Marxist contributions to the sociology of religion (Kautsky), law (Renner), race relations (O. Cox) have not yet constituted major research traditions. An interesting Marxist school of urban sociology has emerged in recent years (Lefebvre, Castells). The Poulantzas–Miliband debate on the state intimates a possible emergence of a Marxist political sociology. Much work has been done on non- and especially pre-capitalist modes of production (e.g. domestic, colonial, bureaucratic, collectivist) relevant to both historical sociology and the sociology of development typically framed as political economy rather than as sociology proper.

A good deal of the most significant Marxist sociology has dealt with superstructures: Lukács and Goldmann on tragedy and the novel, Hessen and Zilsel on the emergence of modern natural science, Gramsci on intellectuals, the Frankfurt School (*q.v.*) on virtually the whole range of aesthetic experience as well as the 'culture industry', Althusser on ideological state apparatuses, Macherey on literary production, etc. Marxist social thought appears polarized in terms of philosophical orientation and even types of sensibility between the 'scientific' (currently the Althusserian) and the 'humanistic' approaches: for the latter, the categories alienation, reification and 'liberation' play a central role and they stress dialectical reason, praxis and historicity. Both approaches evince a major shift away from historical determinism and evolutionism but remain sharply divided on issues of theory-construction and the status of human agency and consciousness.

Eastern European sociology often good on local sociography draws very extensively on Western, especially American, sociology for concepts and research procedures with little theoretical innovation. Marxist theories and concerns have influenced a great deal of non-Marxist sociology and conversely a good deal of 'Marxist' sociology is radical, critical, feminist or otherwise 'deviant' but often dubiously Marxist. In any case there is no Marxist tenet which is not challenged by some Marxist school or scholar. See T. Bottomore, *Marxist Sociology*, 1975; P. Anderson, *Considerations on Western Marxism*, 1976; T. Bottomore and P. Good (eds.), *The Austro-Marxists*, 1978.   H.M.

mass culture. See MASS SOCIETY.

mass-observation. This was the title chosen for an organization founded in 1937 by Charles Madge and Tom Harrisson. Its aim was to develop the scientific study of human behaviour in Britain, but an unusual feature was the use of large numbers of volunteer 'observers', recruited through publicity in the national press. At one time there were over a thousand of them keeping diaries of their everyday lives and reporting on inquiries into smoking habits, superstitions and bird-watching. The object of Mass-Observation was, ideally, 'observation by everyone of everyone, including themselves'. Perhaps the most important output of the organization was a very large amount of material that was collected on the blitz, rationing, evacuation, political and religious attitudes, propaganda and community activities during the 1939–45 war. The data that has been collected over the years is now found in the Tom Harrisson Mass-Observation Archives in the University of Sussex, much of it the result of reports and studies carried out since the war by full-time observers. The earliest project was a three-year study of the town of Bolton in Lancashire carried out by Tom Harrisson between 1937 and 1940 called *Work Town*, last published in 1977. One of the latest publications, *Living Through the Blitz*, appeared in 1976 shortly after Tom Harrisson's death. See Charles Madge and Tom Harrisson, *Mass-Observation*, 1937; *Mass-Observation 1937–38: the First Year's Work*, 1938; Raymond Firth, 'An Anthropologist's View of Mass-Observation', *Sociological Review*, vol. 31 (old series), April, 1939; W. Albig, *Modern Public Opinion*, 1953. See SOCIAL SURVEY, PARTICIPANT OBSERVATION.   P.H.M.

mass society. A term used to characterize modern Western type societies, most especially the U.S.A. The concept embraces the following features: large-scale industrialization, large urban developments, and the ubiquity of bureaucratic administration. Writers who use this term are often concerned about the relationship of the individual to his society, the degree of freedom an individual enjoys in modern society, how the individual perceives his social environment and how he evaluates it. Broadly speaking, there are two diametrically opposed views. One regards the development of human dignity, and points to evidence of increasing conformity, mediocrity, disillusionment and alienation. The other view denies there is a loss of liberties and stresses the advantages accruing from a weakening of traditional features holding up new developments, and points to a broad and fundamental consensus that contributes to solidarity. There is agreement on the whole that mass society relies on ideological movements, that such movements produce more or less creative and culture-sustaining élites, and that through these elites *mass man*, although unqualified in many respects, is able to participate in important decision-making processes, either by means of party machines, or simply through plebiscites and referenda.

Sociological interests that have made use of this concept are to be found on the borders of political science and psychology. Thus the rise of extreme political movements and their social origins in mass society are a subject for study. (See W. Kornhauser, *The Politics of Mass-Society*, 1960; and P. Olsen (ed.), *America as a Mass Society*, 1963.) But equally, there has been an interest deriving from the study of the social factors conditioning personality types, and especially placing an emphasis on the insecurities and disorientation discernible in the lives of so many people. (See D. Riesman *et al., The Lonely Crowd,* 1950; and E. Fromm, *The Fear of Freedom,* 1943.)

It should be pointed out that frequently there appears to be undue emphasis on social determinism inherent in the use of the term *mass society* as if the associated characteristics are an inevitable consequence, and in this connection it should also be said that the theoretical implications of mass structures are at present little more than guesses; quantitative research into these matters has hardly begun.   G.D.M.

material culture. See CULTURE.

matrilateral. See KINSHIP.

matrilineal. This refers to the tracing of relationship to kin exclusively through females for some social purposes; as a synonym *uterine* is sometimes used.

The word was substituted for the more ambiguous *mother-right (Mutterrecht),* which, like *matriarchy* begged the question of the role of women in societies tracing kinship in this way. In the nineteenth century the study of such systems (often referred to as systems of 'maternal descent(s)') centred on their supposed pre-eminence in early stages of social evolution. J. F. McLennan, *Primitive Marriage,* 1865, and J. J. Bachofen, *Das Mutterrecht,* 1861, started a chain of speculation which persists today in some non-anthropological circles. Evolutionary speculation gave way to functional analysis after a devastating critique by R. H. Lowie ('The Matrilineal Complex', *University of California Publications in American Archaeology and Ethnology,* XVI, 1919), and particularly after Bronislaw Malinowski's *The Sexual Life of Savages,* 1929. (But note that Malinowksi still uses both 'matrilineal' and 'mother-right'.)

The most extended discussion of matrilineal institutions is in D. M. Schneider and K. Gough (eds.), *Matrilineal Kinship,* 1961, which takes up ideas found in A. I. Richards, 'Some types of family structure amongst the central Bantu', in *African Systems of Kinship and Marriage,* A. R. Radcliffe-Brown and D. Forde (eds.), 1950. See DESCENT, KINSHIP, PATRILINEAL.
                                                                                    J.R.F.

Mauss, Marcel (1872–1950). French ethnologist and sociologist, he was Durkheim's literary executor, a relative and close supporter of the master. Mauss wrote essays on the Eskimo, religious observances, the significance of gifts, and on the relationship of sociology to psychology.

Mead, George Herbert (1863–1931). American philosopher, psychologist and historian of ideas. His most influential book was his lectures given in 1927 and 1931 published under the title *Mind, Self and Society.* He held human activity of all kinds to be 'an ongoing social process' and rational minds and selves to be emergents from that process. He taught at the University of Michigan from 1891 to 1893 and thereafter until his death at the University of Chicago. His ideas have been increasingly valuable in the sociological discussion of the relation of the individual to society. G.D.M.

Mead, Margaret (1901–1978). American cultural anthropologist who was for many years Associate Curator of Ethnology at the American Museum of Natural History and an adjunct Professor of Anthropology at Columbia University. Her writings endeavour to relate psychological and cultural factors in societies comparatively. She did much to popularize the subject and render it more relevant to an understanding of contemporary problems, especially the role of women in society. Among her many publications *Coming of Age in Samoa*, 1949, *New Lives for Old*, 1956 and *Male and Female*, 1950 are among the best-known. G.D.M.

methodology One of the uses of this term is to refer to the techniques a particular discipline uses to manipulate data and acquire knowledge. In the main, however, the term is reserved for the more philosophical evaluation of the techniques of investigation current within a discipline. This usage identifies methodology as a branch of epistemology or the theory of knowledge. The classical example of methodology in this sense is J. S. Mill's *System of Logic*, 1898, which sets out to generalize the 'modes of investigating truth and estimating evidence' and which includes discussion of induction and deduction, the idea of a law of nature, causation, experiment, conceptualization and classification, and such like. (A more recent authoritative statement of these issues in the philosophy of science is E. Nagel, *The Structure of Science*, 1961.)

Historically, much of the methodological concern in the social sciences has been directed towards establishing their credentials as sciences. In brief, discussion has centred round the question of to what extent do, or can, the social sciences approximate to the methods and procedures of the natural sciences given the obvious differences in subject matter? To what extent can laws of interaction be discovered when the objects of inquiry are not amenable to experimentation? To what extent can the social sciences be objective? Does the fact that the social sciences deal with human beings necessitate a radical difference in approach from that of the natural sciences? And so forth. As is to be expected, answers to these kind of questions have differed sharply. Some have argued that since social phenomena are essentially 'meaningful' phenomena for social actors they require methods of investigation radically different from those employed by the natural sciences. Max Weber, for instance, argued that for the social scientist to fully 'understand' a pattern of social action, he must imaginatively identify with the social actors involved. However, for Weber, this did not mean that the explanations and findings so derived were not open to evaluation by scientific method. (Max Weber, *The Methodology of the Social Sciences*, translated 1947.)

The prevailing positivistic orthodoxy which typifies most sociological work at the present time accepts the need for the social sciences to use techniques suitable to their subject-matter but holds fast to the idea that they are, nonetheless, sciences in that they accommodate to the logic of science with its commitment to objectivity, the search for causes and law-like regularities, and theoretically inspired empirical investigation. (See, for example, P. Deising, *Patterns of Discovery in the Social Sciences*, 1972, and D. Willer, *Scientific Sociology*, 1967, as well as the classic statement by É. Durkheim, *The Rules of Sociological Method*, 1950.) However, throughout the recent history of the social sciences, especially sociology, there has been a strong anti-Durkheimian resistance to this view. There are signs that it is gaining strength. For an account of this see S. T. Bruyn, *The Human Perspective in Sociology*, 1966. After a series of fundamental critiques of conventional sociological methods, such as the interview and the survey, there is a growing realization that theory and methods are irretrievably intertwined. Particular research methods can no longer be regarded as 'theory-neutral tools' but instead receive their warrants from theories of instrumentation which are derived, in their turn, from domain assumptions about the nature of man and society. (See A. Cicourel, *Method and Measurement in Sociology*, 1964, and D. Phillips, *Knowledge From What?* 1971, and J. A. Hughes, *Sociological Analysis: Methods of Discovery*, 1976.)

There are a number of consequences of this debate which are worth noting. Firstly, it has led to a renewed interest in the social sources of knowledge and its collective validation making methodology, in effect, a branch of the sociology of knowledge (see, for example, P. Filmer *et al., New Directions in Sociological Theory*, 1972, and T. Kuhn, *The Structure of Scientific Revolutions*, 1972). Secondly, there has been a renewed and vigorous interest in language and the common understandings which underpin social action as topics of investigation in their own right rather than simply as hidden resources for 'doing' sociology (J. Douglas (ed.), *Understanding Everyday Life*, 1970). Thirdly, there is growing support for the idea that the social sciences are better viewed as moral disciplines rather than scientific ones (E. Louch, *Explanation and Human Action*, 1964). Fourthly, there are interesting attempts to synthesize the positivistic and humanistic strands in sociological thought. (See especially, R. J. Bernstein, *The Restructuring of Social and Political Theory*, 1976, and A. Giddens, *New Rules of Sociological Method*, 1976). The net result of all this is to bring methodology back into the central place it occupied in the writings of the classical authors such as Marx, Weber and Durkheim. See SOCIOLOGY.

J.A.H.

Mill, John Stuart (1806–1873). English philosopher, economist, social and political reformer. He made important contributions to the methodology of the social sciences and he hoped to generalize procedures of natural science to all experience. His *System of Logic, Ratiocinative and Inductive*, 1842, suggested four 'Methods of Experimental Inquiry', viz., Method of Agreement, Method of Difference, Method of Residues, and Method of Concomitant Variation. Plurality of causes and intermixture of effects hindered induction in the realm of social phenomena; in the absence of experimentation, upon which perfect social sciences would be based, the Method of Inverse Deduction has to be employed. Though conducting no empirical sociological research, he was enthusiastic about the new science due, in part, to the influence of the utopian ideas of Saint-Simon. He was convinced, however, that 'human beings in society have no properties but those which are derived from, and may be resolved into the laws of the nature of individual man'. See R. Fletcher (ed.), *John Stuart Mill*, 1971.

G.D.M.

Millar, John (1735–1801). Scottish lawyer and sociologist. One of the earliest to write on social stratification, his book *On the Origin of the Distinction of Ranks*, 1771, contains a sociology of the family as well as a sociology of occupations and property.

Mills, C. Wright (1916–1962). American political sociologist, who saw sociology as a means of challenging social ideas and prejudices. All sociology for Mills was fundamentally political. He was interested in the centres of power, in social stratification, in the relationship of culture and personality. A large man, he thought in broad and bold terms, intolerant but stimulating, he exaggerated to make his point, and was critical of most other sociologists. His major works include *White Collar*, 1951; *The Power Elite*, 1956; and *The Sociological Imagination*, 1959.

minority. Many sociologists have followed Louis Wirth in regarding this as a political rather than a numerical concept. Thus black people in South Africa may be called a minority even though they constitute more than half the population. This usage has drawbacks: it distracts attention from the presence of minorities within minorities and the overlapping of boundaries between different kinds of boundaries. It is therefore preferable to use 'minority' to designate a category or group that is less than half of a specified population and to differentiate ethnic, linguistic, national, political, racial and religious minorities.

M.B.

miscegenation. This word was coined by two journalists working as the contemporary equivalent of the dirty tricks department of the Democratic Party in connection with the U.S. Presidential election of 1864. Under this title they published a little book suggesting that mating between persons of different stock was to be encouraged since it would produce a superior stock. They implied that this was the policy of the Republican Party. Appropriately, the word is of irregular derivation (it should have been 'miscegeneration'). Use of the word is to be avoided since, apart from its disreputable origins, it reinforces a pre-Darwinian theory of human variation. See Forest G. Wood, *Black Scare*, 1968, pp. 53–7.

M.P.B.

model. Used to assist explanation either by using an analogy showing similarities between the thing to be explained and the phenomenon which is known or better known, i.e. the model, or else by setting out a number of assumptions which are interrelated and limited in scope so as to provide an autonomous sphere for discussion. Models are frequently used in sociology. The very notion of a social system argues the inter-dependencies of the parts of a whole and the comparability with, for example, organic or mechanical systems. See METHODOLOGY, THEORY, SOCIAL THEORY.

G.D.M.

127

moiety organization. The most general meaning of this term is the bisection of a tribe into two complementary social groups.

Some writers would restrict the term moiety to *exogamous* social divisions (see *Notes and Queries in Anthropology*, 6th edition 1951), while others use the term to mean any *dual organization*, exogamous or not. Earlier usage favoured either the simple term 'dual organization' (e.g. see W. H. R. Rivers, *Kinship and Social Organization*, 1914), or simply spoke of two *phratries* (e.g. see L. H. Morgan, *Ancient Society*, 1877). French writers had used *moitié* (e.g. É. Durkheim and M. Mauss, *Primitive Classifications*, 1963 – first published 1903), and this usage, in its English version, became standardized, for example, by A. R. Radcliffe-Brown ('Three Tribes of Western Australia', *Journal of the Royal Anthropological Institute*, 1913) in England, and by E. W. Gifford (*Miwok Moieties*, 1916) in America.

The most extended discussion of moiety organization is in C. Lévi-Strauss, *Les Structures Élémentaires de la Parenté*, 1949. The same author has a provocative discussion in ch. VIII of his *Structural Anthropology*, 1963. For an evolutionary approach, see E. R. Service, *Primitive Social Organization*, 1962. See CLAN.   J.R.F.

Montesquieu, Charles Louis Secondat, Baron de (1689–1755). French aristocrat and philosopher; he made major contributions to early geography and jurisprudence. His work is of importance to the student of the philosophy of history. His *Thoughts on the Causes of the Greatness of the Romans and their Decadence*, 1734, argues that the rise and fall of empires is due to general causes of a moral and physical nature rather than to blind chance. *L'esprit des lois*, 1748, his greatest work, deals with law in general and with governmental forms; he defined natural law as necessary relations derived from nature. Attention is also paid to military arrangements, taxation, manners, customs, tradition, and public opinion, and their dependence on factors such as climate, soil, and geographic conditions; aspects of the economy; religion; Roman, French and feudal law. The work is important sociologically for stressing that rational and naturalistic factors influence human behaviour and institutions.   G.D.M.

mores. *Mores* is a term used to denote behaviour patterns which are not only accepted and traditional, but are prescribed. Breach of mores is punished with greater severity than committing some peccadillo with respect to a folkway. Mores change slowly, they are regarded as of great importance for maintaining social order. The singular *mos* is seldom, if ever, used in sociological literature. The distinction between *folkways* and *mores* was adumbrated by W. G. Sumner in his *Folkways*, 1906. See CUSTOM, FOLKWAYS.
                                                                              G.D.M.

Morgan, Lewis Henry (1818–1857). American lawyer and anthropologist; his theory, based on fieldwork, influenced the work of Engels and Tönnies. He lived with, and was adopted into, the Iroquois tribe; he published *League of the Iroquois*, 1851, the success of which led to further research and to *Systems of Consanguinity and Affinity of the Human Family*, 1869; from this developed *Ancient Society, or Researches in the lines of Human Progress from*

character are open to severe criticism on methodological grounds. The large majority provide insights and interpretations of phenomena without undertaking the systematically controlled and detailed comparative studies that would be required for any scientific proof of the assertions made. A distinction must be made between the psychological and sociological dimensions of national character. D. C. McClelland in *The Achieving Society*, 1961, emphasized the importance of a 'need for achievement' in distinguishing the behaviour of individuals and nations while Richard Lynn, in *Personality and National Character*, 1971, emphasized the underlying importance of different levels of anxiety. Sociologists are more likely to focus on value-orientations and institutional structures. Thus, Talcott Parsons, in *Social Structure and Personality*, 1964, starts with a delineation of what he considers to be the dominant American value system and examines the way in which it is institutionalized in the structure of society. In the American case he emphasizes the importance of instrumental-achievement values. See also Benjamin DeMott, 'Beyond the Dream of Success' in I. Kristol and P. Weaver, *The Americans*, 1976. See PERSONALITY, SOCIALIZATION.   A.H.R.

neighbourhood. This concept may be defined both physically and socially. Physically it refers to a part of a town or city made distinct by boundaries such as main roads, railways, rivers, canals and open spaces and having a certain similarity of housing type within the area. Often a shopping centre with local institutions such as churches, public houses and branch libraries may be the focal points of the neighbourhood. Socially a neighbourhood may be characterized by social similarities of the residents, often especially by similarity of social class or ethnic type. Members of an urban neighbourhood will recognize their neighbourhood as providing certain social amenities at a local level, these being complementary to the amenities of the town or city as a whole. Thus local shops tend to cater for day-to-day shopping, whilst city-centre shops cater for the shopping expedition.

Recognizing the social complexity of rapidly developing cities and the growth of secondary relations ensuing, some social workers and town planners have attempted to create socially conscious local communities by developing *neighbourhood units*, usually of 5,000 population, within towns. Clarence Perry is usually acknowledged to be the originator of this term in 1923, when he suggested the values of a planned local unit with designated local amenities, carefully laid-out road patterns and attention to pedestrian needs. Later community workers added ideas of community centres as focal points for social mixing and *social balance* so as to bring all social classes together in each unit. These latter plans often derived from false analogies with rural villages, overestimated the desire of people for social mixing in urban society, and the neighbourhood concept is now unfashionable with town planners. Clarence A. Perry, *Housing for the Machine Age*, 1939; James Dahir, *The Neighbourhood Unit Plan*, 1947; P. H. Mann, 'The Socially Balanced Neighbourhood Unit', *Town Planning Review*, vol. 29, no. 2, July 1958. See ECOLOGY, TOWN PLANNING, URBAN SOCIOLOGY, ZONING.   P.H.M.

nomads; nomadism. In its common usage the word *nomadism* is used loosely to refer to people who live a tented life and who may or may not wander in search of pastures. Many tribes in various parts of the world move to and from pastures with the changes in the seasons, but the movements of most are so regularized that the term *transhumance* is better applied, for this carries the meaning of movement in fairly fixed directions from watering points in the dry season abode to pastures in the rainy season. Nomads, when they wander, do so within generally defined limits, but their movements within their territories are much more haphazard. The significance in this difference lies not so much in the kind of movement itself, but what this implies. Nomadism occurs where the natural resources are not only scarce, but also insecure from year to year, compelling a move to this area one year, and to another the following year. Its practice requires a very large area to support very small numbers of animals and human beings, and it is only to be found in areas which are marginal for human habitation. The direct limitation of the size of the local group by the paucity and instability of the natural resources gives character to the whole range of social relationships.

It is quite wrong to use the term *nomadism* to apply to any people who live a tented life. Some ethnic groups who live in tents are virtually sedentary, others are tied to towns, markets or oases, and herd animals only as an economic supplement to their agricultural or commercial activities. See F. Barth, *Nomads of South Persia*, 1961; J. Berque, 'Nomads and Nomadism in the Arid Zone', *International Social Science Journal*, vol. XI, no. 4, 1954 (special issue); D. J. Stenning, *Savannah Nomads*, 1959. See TRANSHUMANCE.

E.L.P.

nominalism; methodological nominalism. See ESSENTIALISM; METHODOLOGICAL ESSENTIALISM.

nomothetic disciplines. See IDIOGRAPHIC DISCIPLINES.

norm; social norm. This term is a relative newcomer to the common vocabulary of sociology. M. Sherif in *The Psychology of Social Norms*, 1936, uses it to describe the common standards or ideas which guide members' responses in all established groups.

Social norms are thus general precepts which, being internalized or accepted by individuals, induce conformity in simple actions or in complex ethical judgments, thus increasing group unity.

Early sociologists, such as F. Tönnies and W. G. Sumner, recognized that actions varied in the importance attached to their proper performance and, using severity of sanctions as a basis, classified them as folkways, mores, laws, customs, etc.

Today the word *norm* frequently functions as a generic term for all these, though to call an action a norm or normative is to emphasize that it conforms to community expectations of behaviour. Degree of conformity may vary, but the norm, unlike the ideal, is never far from actual behaviour.

Any type of established group has norms, both peculiar to itself and shared with the wider community. Group norms may contradict each other and sub-sections of groups may employ different norms in the same situation. (See G. C. Homans, *The Human Group*, 1950.)

The term may describe actual rather than expected behaviour. Thus a clustering of responses or attitudes or just what most people do, may be termed the norm without implying constraint.

Following closely from the above in experimental psychology, norm (not social norm) denotes the average test score of a homogeneous population and is used as a standard for comparison. See CUSTOM, FOLKWAYS, MORES, SANCTION.

B.A.P.

normal. Statistically a *normal curve* is a frequency distribution in which mode, mean and median coincide and which is distributed symmetrically about its mean. Thus the bulk of cases cluster around the average value and there are progressively fewer as one reaches extreme values.

In non-statistical terms *normal* means usual or customary. Behaviour of a group member is considered normal when it conforms to, or does not deviate substantially from, the potential behaviour of the other group members in that situation. *Abnormal behaviour* is basically just other than normal, though the phrase often implies maladjustment. Complete agreement is rare on the point at which response becomes abnormal rather than normal. Concepts of the normal (normal behaviour, normal rate of growth) may be formed subjectively or else be operationally defined.

Contemporary sociologists, abandoning the assumption that only Western practices are normal, generally consider that institutions or trends may be normal in one culture, or at one point in time, though abnormal elsewhere, or in other circumstances.

However, the search for universal standards of normality continues. Durkheim in *The Rules of the Sociological Method*, 1920, describes as *normal* any characteristic generalized in a species. Hence crime would be abnormal for individuals, being only a minority activity, but normal for societies since all societies have criminals. Examination of comparative data may reveal whether specific forms of institutions can be considered normal for certain types of society or for society as a genus. See ADJUST, PROBABILITY.   B.A.P.

nuclear family. See FAMILY.

O

Ogburn, William Fielding (1886–1959). American sociologist who held a chair at the University of Chicago. At first an advocate of quantitative methods and applied studies. His best-known work however is *Social Change: with Respect to Culture and Original Nature*, 1922, in which he discusses the factors which explain cultural change, i.e. invention, accumulation, diffusion and adjustment.

open-ended question. This is the type of question used in interview schedules or questionnaires in which the respondent is not restricted in his answer to a choice of predetermined categories, but is allowed a full answer of his own choosing. Rather than checking a pre-set response category, therefore, the answer must be written down in full, by the interviewer in the case of the interview schedule, or by the respondent in the case of the questionnaire. The open-ended question is obviously less simple to categorize for subsequent analysis, but it is useful in cases where the researcher is still at an exploratory stage of enquiry. See P. H. Mann, *Methods of Sociological Enquiry*, 1968. See QUESTIONNAIRE, SOCIAL SURVEY. P.H.M.

operational research. This is concerned with the consequences of decisions in industry, government and in business. For many decisions which are undertaken in these contexts, there is a firm knowledge of what the objectives are, there is a limited range of choice and it is known what will happen if any one of the limited range of choices is taken. Consequently, the task of the decision-maker is merely to carry out the basic arithmetic, no matter in what units the arithmetic is formed, and then to compare the separate decisions against the basic criteria. Operational research is not concerned with these essentially trivial situations. It is concerned with situations in which either the objectives are ill-defined and need to be stated as a result of a logical analysis or, where there is a very large range of choice of alternatives so that it is not possible to survey each one and to retain that particular decision which best meets the criteria or, finally, those decisions where the consequences of any action are not known and where probability enters in. It is with these three main areas that operational research is concerned.

One further point underlines the necessity for the development of a subject such as this. What is at stake in large complex situations are large and complex results. It is no longer possible in these situations for the executive to proceed empirically by trial and error, for what he is faced with so often is trial and catastrophe. Consequently, his basic approach is to build a model of the situation. The model is formed by an understanding of the basic pattern of cause and effect which is obtaining. This will be not so much a rigid deterministic structure but is quite likely to involve probability linkages in which patterns of causes are thought to give rise to patterns of effects. Having, by study and discussion, evolved a hypothetical structure of the decision-making situation, the operational research worker, by observation and the analysis of data, clothes this structure with number. This is the model and it is now possible for the operational research scientist to experiment with the real world situation within the terms of his model.

The basic underlying common factor of all operational research is the craft of model building to represent the consequences of different decisions in executive situations. There are two other basic characteristics. One is the use of mixed teams of scientists. It has been found by experience that scientists from different disciplines working together in a decision-making study each provide a different slant on the problem. This merely reflects the obvious fact that in the real world there are no such things as economic problems or accounting problems or sociological problems or engineering problems or even operational research problems. There are only problems, and the economist, the accountant, the sociologist, the engineer and the operational research worker will all look at them in a different way. The use of the mixed team in operational research ensures that the way in which a problem is approached is indeed inter-disciplinary, with all the fruits that this will yield.

The other characteristic of operational research is the systems-orientation of the studies. By this is meant the realization that it is generally insufficient to accept the first definition of a decision-making problem, for this is often too closely constrained. Decisions have a way of interlocking throughout an organization and the operational research worker seeks to place any particular decision-making problem within the larger context of the organization as a whole.

The operational research worker therefore uses the scientific method to study the consequences of decisions in complex systems of men, money, machines, materials and markets with the object of giving the decision-maker a better understanding of his problems. The method used is the application of science through model construction.   B.H.A.R.

opinion poll. An opinion is a belief or a judgment held by a person which may or may not persist for a lengthy period of time. Opinions have neither the proved property of knowledge nor the unverifiable property of faith. Inherent is the acceptance that other people may hold different opinions.

The desire to assess opinions, to know who holds what opinions and how firmly is the task of the public opinion poll. Usually the method of sampling a population is employed and mostly the organizations carrying out this work rely on single questions. This is because the respondent has to be persuaded to co-operate and so his interest must be maintained without tedium interfering. Very often the question is designed to elicit a choice by the respondent of one of a set of alternative answers. Sometimes, however, open-ended questions are asked but this presents difficulties for the recorder and the analyser of the results.

Opinion polls seek to discover information about political, social, marketing and consumer opinions. Some of the main organizations are the

135

National Opinion Research Center in the U.S.A., the Gallup Poll, BBC Listener Research, and Audits of Great Britain.   G.D.M.

organization. See SOCIAL ORGANIZATION.

P

paradigm. The term *paradigm* has become very widely used indeed in contemporary literature on the philosophy of both natural science and social science, largely as a result of the impact of Thomas Kuhn's seminal work *The Structure of Scientific Revolutions*, 1962, in which it occupies a prominent place. A notion of paradigm was however earlier applied to sociology by Robert K. Merton. He used the term in a prescriptive sense, to codify programmes of research in sociology: a paradigm, for Merton, is an explicitly stated set of concepts and propositions used to guide research investigation within a specific area. Kuhn's usage is quite different from this, and was originally applied to the natural sciences in the context of a contrast with social science. Paradigms in natural science are 'universally recognised scientific achievements that for a time provide model problems and solutions to a community of practitioners' (*The Structure of Scientific Revolutions*, revised edition, p. viii). Research carried out within a paradigm constitutes 'normal science'. The social sciences, in which battles about fundamental issues are still chronic, according to Kuhn are in a pre-paradigmatic state.

Kuhn's use of *paradigm* is notoriously ambiguous: a critic has identified twenty-two distinguishably different senses in which the term was employed in his original work. See Thomas S. Kuhn, *The Structure of Scientific Revolutions*, 2nd edition 1970; Imre Lakatos and Alan Musgrave, *Criticism and the Growth of Knowledge*, 1970; Thomas S. Kuhn, 'Second Thoughts on paradigms' in Frederick Suppe (ed.), *The Structure of Scientific Theories*, 1974.   A.G.

parallel-cousins. These are first cousins whose related parents are of the same sex, e.g. mother's son or daughter and mother's sister's son or daughter. Sometimes the term *ortho-cousin* is used instead. In many primitive societies marriage between parallel cousins is proscribed. See CROSS-COUSINS.
                                                                    G.D.M.

Pareto, Vilfredo Federico Damaso (1848–1923). Italian aristocrat, engineer, political economist and sociologist; his view of society as a system in equilibrium has been greatly influential; also he insisted that sociology should adhere strictly to scientific method, what he called the logico-experimental method. *The Socialist Systems*, 1902, presents a theory of elites. His major sociological work is *Trattato di Sociologia Generale*, 1916 (translated *The Mind and Society*, 1935); this mainly comprises his theory of residues and derivations, which he classifies into diverse groups. Society he sees as determined by physical, external and internal elements; the latter comprise interests, knowledge, residues and derivations and are viewed as equilibrating mechanisms. Most of social life is non-logical. The circulation of elites leads to intermittent periods of rapid and slow social change. See RESIDUES, ELITE.

G.D.M.

Park, Robert Ezra (1864–1944). American journalist, researcher and champion of racial equality, he was educated at Harvard and Heidelberg, his doctoral thesis being on 'Crowds and the Public'. His early days as a journalist created in him a passionate interest in the development of the metropolis and his contact with Simmel in Germany developed his eye for facets of social life and relationships. He became Professor of Sociology at Chicago where he gathered a group of students who became famous for their descriptive studies of city life, delinquent and abnormal forms of social behaviour and small communities. In collaboration with E. W. Burgess and R. D. MacKenzie he wrote a famous work entitled *The City*, 1925. Four years earlier he had published one of the best known textbooks, *An Introduction to the Science of Sociology*. Although he came late to academic work his influence was very great both in stimulating social enquiries and in encouraging a simple and effective style of writing.

G.D.M.

participant observation. A situation where a social research worker becomes as much as possible a member of the group which he is studying and participates fully in the life of the group. The ideal form, where the observer is *wholly* a part of the group and not known by the group members to have any other role, is only attained by using the technique of the spy. In many cases, therefore, the term is used very loosely to describe research carried out by observers, such as anthropologists, who have gone to live for a time in communities and shared their day-to-day lives even though their dual roles are recognized. For original application of this technique see J. J. Hoder and E. C. Lindeman, *Dynamic Social Research*, 1933. See MASS-OBSERVATION, SOCIAL SURVEY.

P.H.M.

patrilateral. See KINSHIP.

patrilineal. This refers to the tracing of relationship to kin exclusively through males for some social purposes: as a synonym, *agnatic* is sometimes used, and a patrilineally related person is therefore an *agnate*.

The origin of the word is obscure but it was probably introduced into anthropology by N. W. Thomas (*Kinship Organization and Group Marriage in Australia*, 1906), and replaced the more ambiguous *father-right, patriarchal* or *paternal descent*. The term is now firmly established throughout the anthropological world, but as late as 1950 it was still being used interchangeably with *father-right* by some authors (see A. R. Radcliffe-Brown and D. Forde, eds., *African Systems of Kinship and Marriage*).

The distribution of patrilineal systems can be found in G. P. Murdock's *Social Structure*, 1949. A good comparative survey exists in I. M. Lewis's 'Problems in Comparative Study of Unilineal Descent', *The Relevance of Models for Social Anthropology*, M. Banton, ed., 1965. See AGNATE, DESCENT, KINSHIP, MATRILINEAL.

J.R.F.

pattern variables. In 1951 Talcott Parsons and E. A. Shils published an essay, 'Values, Motives and Systems of Action' in *Toward a General Theory of Action*, in which reference is made to the *pattern variables*, or types of choices open to purposive human beings; they are dichotomies. As the authors say, one side of a pattern variable must be chosen by an actor 'before the meaning of the situation is determinate for him, and thus before he can act with respect to that situation'. Parsons and Shils originally indicated the existence of five basic pattern variables, each representing polar extremes. *Universalism* and *particularism* are the names of one. In other words, any individual in a situation requiring choice in his relationships with others must ask himself if he is going to act in terms of a universally accepted precept or one particular to the situation in which he finds himself. Is he going to act according to rule or in terms of particular qualities of the person towards whom he is orienting his action? Another set is termed *achievement* and *ascription* (sometimes referred to as *performance* and *quality*) and here a person in deciding how to act focuses his attention on either the achieved aspects of the other person, e.g. his professional qualifications, or else his ascribed qualities, e.g. sex, age, social class. The third set of pattern variables is termed *affectivity* and *affective-neutrality* and represents the difference in choice between a person seeking immediate satisfaction and his postponement or abandonment of it in terms of long range goals, or at least some other goals, perhaps of a moral kind but equally well ones which are merely expediential. Yet another set is known as *specificity* and *diffuseness*, and here the choice takes into account limited and specific factors, e.g. the contrast between a contract entered into, and wider diffuse obligations such as family loyalty. Finally there is another pattern variable, *self-orientation* and *collectivity-orientation*, i.e. is the choice made in terms of the individual's own interests or his perception of the needs of the community?

The point of this scheme of pattern variables is to enable the sociologist to identify the typical choices made, especially of an institutionalized kind, to distinguish as Weber would have said, for example, different types of justice, a rational-legal type from a Kadi-type, or as a modern political scientist has argued, to distinguish between styles of politics (see H. V. Wiseman, *Political Systems*, 1966).

Other writers have sought to elaborate the Parsonian scheme. Thus S. M. Lipset in *The First New Nation*, 1964, has added two more pattern variables: *instrumental* and *consummatory*, indicating a choice between focusing either on means or on ends, and *egalitarian* and *elitist*, where the former stresses respect for persons as such and the latter focuses on position, be it achieved or ascribed.

Pattern variable analysis may be used to identify similarities and differences between cultures, or it may be more restricted in use to refer to aspects of a society, to sub-systems of an institutional kind, such as political systems, or even to particular groups and organizations.   G.D.M.

penology. Strictly, the study of punishment. In its modern usage the term means that branch of criminology which is concerned with the training and treatment of offenders (i.e. 'corrections') and with the control and prevention of crime. Contemporary penology embraces studies of the social structure and organization of correctional institutions, of parole and probation systems, and of methods of dealing with abnormal offenders (e.g. by psychiatric treatment). It also includes studies of police practice and of the sentencing policies of the courts. Prediction techniques are increasingly used to measure the relative effectiveness of such alternative methods of dealing with offenders as fines, conditional discharge, imprisonment, detention, assignment to attendance centres, borstal training, education in approved schools, probation, parole and suspended sentences. Studies of the populations of prisons and borstals are frequently directed to the development and validation of improved methods of classifying inmates and of allocating them to institutions having different regimes or styles of training. Penologists are also concerned to examine the application of new modes of treatment (such as group counselling) within institutions, and to evaluate their effectiveness and their impact upon the organization of the prison. The scope of the discipline extends to studies of public policy in the control of crime, including the deterrent effects of judicial penalties, the development of police liaison schemes, and methods of securing the resettlement and rehabilitation of offenders discharged from penal institutions.

A useful summary of British practice and reflection upon problems in penology is provided by N. D. Walker in *Crime and punishment in Britain* (second edition, 1968). See CRIMINOLOGY.   G.B.T.

personality. A convenient ragbag shorthand way of referring collectively to all the non-environmental elements in an individual's behaviour, without reference to specific psychological processes, taking into account the continuing recognizable identity of the individual in the course of development. The term is best defined by context, as in Kurt Lewin's formula: Behaviour is a function of the interaction of Personality and Environment. That is, individuals will behave differently in what appears objectively the same environment. These differences may be attributable to differences in inborn stimulus-response characteristics and (or, interacting with) differences in the nature and organization of learned responses, which include differences in the way the environment is perceived.

Psychologists have not agreed on one universally most convenient way of decomposing the concept of personality into component processes which, interdependently, constitute the *structure of the personality*. At a very general level there are sub-divisions like perception, learning, affect; Id, Ego, Superego; traits, opinions, attitudes; and so on, useful for different purposes. But such sets of major sub-divisions need meticulous further sub-division, and the interaction of processes at each level also needs experimental and conceptual definition. It is hoped that eventually a set of functionally interrelated concepts will be evolved, ranging from the minutiae of neurology to the organization of total meaningful sequences of behaviour.

Personality-traits. Specific, fairly widespread, predictable reactions to some identifiable condition in an experimental or natural environment. They may be simple and single, as in *ease of conditioning* or complex and interrelated, as in *schizoid traits*.

Personality-types. Categories of people with similar patterns of personality-traits.

Basic Personality Type. Where a group of people living in the same area and socialized in the same way displays the same personality-type in adult life, we may speak of the basic personality type of that culture, as does A. Kardiner, *The Individual and his Society*, 1939, and *The Psychological Frontiers of Society*, 1945; K. Lewin, *A Dynamic Theory of Personality*, 1935. See NATIONAL CHARACTER, SOCIALIZATION.   J.K.

phenomenology. The term *phenomenology* first achieved wide currency in philosophy as a consequence of its use by Hegel in his work *Phenomenology of Mind*, 1807; but the main source of the phenomenological tradition in modern times is to be found in the writings of Edmund Husserl (1859–1938). The dominant concerns of Husserl's phenomenology are expressed in the root of the word itself, derived from the conjunction of the noun form of *phainomai*, to appear, and *logos* or reason. The origins of human reason are to be discovered in the structure of appearance, in the basic ordering of human experience. This emphasis serves to differentiate phenomenology from two other major streams of thought in modern philosophy: analytic philosophy and structuralism. Analytic philosophy gives pride of place to the logical form of language as the channel through which philosophical problems should be approached; structuralists place a stress upon the significance of unconscious principles of the organization of knowledge that are prior to conscious experiences. In contrast to each of these, for phenomenology the act of understanding has primacy of place; the capacity of the human mind to understand meaning is more basic than either formal logic or the modes in which knowledge is articulated or structured.

Three main phases may be discerned in the development of phenomenology in the twentieth century. The first is that of *transcendental phenomenology*, dominated by Husserl's search for the essential foundations of knowledge in experience: an endeavour to formulate a basis for knowledge 'free from presuppositions'. This form of phenomenology has had little influence upon the social sciences, since Husserl's method led him away from society rather than towards it. In order to unearth the essential elements of experience, he held, we have to 'bracket', or 'think away' the everyday world (*Lebenswelt*) of the 'natural attitude', and concentrate upon the inner consciousness of the individual ego.

Although he never abandoned this viewpoint, in his later work (especially in his *Crisis of the European Sciences and Transcendental Phenomenology*, part of which was published posthumously) he came to place more stress upon the direct study of the *Lebenswelt*. This helped initiate a second period in the development of phenomenology, so-called *existential phenomenology* or *existentialism*. The two leading influences here were the early writings of Heidegger (especially *Being and Time*, 1927) and Sartre (*Being and Nothingness*, 1943). Existential phenomenology rejects the search for transcendental categories of knowledge, and instead places the emphasis upon the nature of *being* within the *Lebenswelt*. Existentialism, as practised by Sartre and others, became a modish philosophy in post-War France, and was perceived as much more of a direct challenge to existing forms of social science, particularly by Marxists, than the earlier version of phenomenology had been. Many works have been written either condemning existentialism from a Marxist standpoint, or advocating a creative mixture of the two. In his massive *Critique of Dialectical Reason*, 1960, Sartre came to adopt the latter position, criticizing both his earlier notions and deterministic forms of Marxism.

The third phase in the evolution of phenomenology is that of *hermeneutic phenomenology*, strongly influenced by Heidegger's later works, and prominently represented today by the writings of Hans-Georg Gadamer in Germany and Paul Ricoeur in France. This preserves the idea of the priority of being, but sees language as the all-important medium in which *human-being* is constituted. Language is necessarily intersubjective, and precedes the consciousness of any individual, since it is the very condition of that consciousness. In this version, phenomenology comes much more immediately into contact with the social sciences, since language is recognized as an intrinsically social phenomenon whose characteristics infuse and mould the experiences of the individual. There is a major point of contact here between hermeneutic phenomenology and the philosophy of the later Wittgenstein, which also holds that language is first of all the property of a social community, and that language and the conduct of day-to-day social life are intimately intertwined.

Phenomenology has only relatively recently become an important influence upon the social sciences in the English-speaking world, largely as filtered through the writings of Alfred Schütz (1899–1959). Schütz's major work, *The Phenomenology of the Social World*, was originally published in Austria in 1932, but with the outbreak of the War he emigrated to the United States, and it is there that his ideas have had their greatest impact. Schütz's works do not reflect the concern with problems of anxiety and moral commitment characteristic of Continental existentialism, but in some respects they otherwise share similar perspectives. According to Schütz, orthodox sociology has failed to recognize the significance of the everyday world of common-sense beliefs and practices as the basis of social reality. In studying the ways in which social actors 'typify' actions, and employ 'stocks of knowledge' to create a meaningful social world, we can open a new dimension to sociology. Schütz's version of phenomenology has been taken up and extended by Berger and Luckmann in a series of publications, most notably, *The Social Construction of Reality*, 1966. Schütz's work is also one of the main sources of ethnomethodology, as elaborated by Garfinkel and others. See Edo Pivcevic, *Husserl and Phenomenology*, 1970; Mark Poster, *Existential Marxism in Post-War France*, 1975; R. A. Gorman, *The Dual Vision: Alfred Schütz and the Myth of Phenomenological Social Science*, 1977. See ALFRED SCHÜTZ. A.G.

phenotype. See GENOTYPE.

phratry. See MOIETY ORGANIZATION.

plural society. A term used to denote a society which consists of a variety of communities. This, of course, might be said of almost any society, but the term usually refers particularly to nation-states or confederacies made up of clearly distinct social groups, e.g. Malaysia, Indonesia, India. The major task facing such states is the development of a common will, and usually there is the very minimum to maintain order and provide for self-defence. A discussion of some of these issues is to be found in *Old Societies and New States*, 1963, edited by Clifford Geertz, especially in his own chapter entitled 'Primordial Sentiments and Civil Politics in the New States'. Discussion of pluralist society has a long history, although the term is relatively modern. Thus the issues it brings to mind include discussions on the nature of sovereignty, nationality, the relationship of church and state, and so forth. Among the major contributions to such discussion we may single out for example those of J. N. Figgis, *From Gerson to Grotius*, 1907, and *Churches in the Modern State*, 1913, and H. J. Laski, *Authority in the Modern State*, 1919.

E. A. Shils has used the term *pluralist society* to refer to one in which there is a plurality of centres of power and where there are many areas of privacy together with tendencies for mutual adaptation among the several parts. (See his *Torment of Secrecy*, 1956.)

In recent years there has been a resumption of the discussion among lawyers, which in modern times may be said to have been powerfully stimulated by J. S. Mill's essay *On Liberty*, 1859, and its subsequent critique by J. F. Stephen in his *Liberty, Equality and Fraternity*, 1873. This contemporary development is a debate on the relationship between morals and law. Thus Lord Devlin, in his essay *The Enforcement of Morals*, 1959, argues that the legal system should uphold morality in the interest of maintaining society, a view criticized by H. L. A. Hart in *Law, Liberty and Morality*, 1963. It appears that Lord Devlin firmly believes that common morality is the source of social order, whereas Professor Hart believes that this is not empirically established as yet.

For further discussion of plural society or plural cultures in a criminological context see E. M. Lemert, 'Social Structure, Social Control and Deviation' in M. B. Clinard (ed.), *Anomie and Deviant Behavior*, 1964. For a sociological discussion of the subject of plural society see J. Rex, 'The Plural Society in Sociological Theory', *British Journal of Sociology*, X, 2, 1959. See CONSENSUS.   G.D.M.

political sociology. The systematic study of concrete political phenomena, influencing and influenced by the rest of the social structure and culture, is very old. It is legitimate to regard Aristotle's *Politics* as a work of political sociology. Montesquieu, Ferguson and Tocqueville were all engaged in what today would be called *political sociology*. Of the classical sociologists Weber (cf. his essay *Politics as Vocation*) and Pareto (*The Mind and Society* passim) were pioneers in incorporating a political sociology in the total body of their work. Marxism with its socio-economic explanation of the political, and socially-minded political scientists like Gaetano Mosca in Italy and Graham Wallas in England, advanced essentially sociological theories of political *elites* and of the processes of consensus and dissent. Meanwhile the detailed study of the social groups and interests in voting behaviour was pursued in pre-1914 France by André Siegfried. The phrase *political sociology* to describe this tradition only came into general use after 1945.

Political sociology employs the methods of sociological research, including those of attitude research, to investigate the actual content of political behaviour. It treats political institutions, both formal or constitutional and informal, as parts of the social system, not self-subsistent but implicated in society. It has concentrated attention on *elites* and their membership, on the manifestation and regulation of conflict, or interest groups (which are often not self-aware) and formal pressure groups, on the formation of political opinion. Political sociologists have been especially concerned with political parties as social institutions and with the phenomena of despotic and totalitarian regimes. It is an integral part of sociology which has progressively transformed political science in the direction of a wider attention to empirical reality.   D.G.M.

polyandry. The practice of marriage of one woman to two or more men. The practice is rare and where it occurs is usually a marriage with two or more brothers, whence it is called *adelphic polyandry*, or occasionally *fraternal polyandry*. It has been reported as taking place in parts of Tibet. It may be distinguished from secondary marriage, found in parts of Nigeria, where cohabitation with any one male is exclusive over a period of time although the woman is regarded as still married to other men. Both cases must be distinguished from *wife-sharing* or *wife-lending*, which is much more common, and in all cases is temporary.

polygamy. The practice of marriage between a member of one sex and two or more members of the opposite sex. See POLYANDRY, POLYGYNY.

polygyny. The practice of marriage of one man to two or more women. The practice is not uncommon and is widespread. In many instances the women are sisters, hence the term *sororal polygyny*. In British anthropological circles polygyny is regarded strictly as a sub-class of *polygamy*, but elsewhere there is no very strict distinction between the two terms.

population studies. See DEMOGRAPHY.

positivism. *Positivism* was originally the title of the 'positive philosophy' of Auguste Comte (1798–1857) and as such a doctrine both about the nature of historical development and about the character of sociology, Comte identified three phases in the intellectual history of mankind, distinguished from each other by the nature of the dominant form of enquiry. Earliest of these is theology, next metaphysics and finally sociology. In both the first two phases, since metaphysics is essentially only a secularized version of theology, the search is for first and final causes. With the arrival of a scientific frame of mind, this search is abandoned and replaced by one for efficient causes and for invariant laws. In stressing the criteria of economy and simplicity in our statement of laws Comte anticipated later doctrines which were to claim the name of *positivism*; but, as Sir K. R. Popper has pointed out, he confused the notion of a law with that of a trend. Moreover his belief that the basic laws governing human nature were psychological, inhibited his direct observation of social life. Comte inherited from Saint-Simon not only his systematizing ideal of scientific method, but also the belief that the spread of scientific method provided the basis for a more rational form of social life. The upholding of this new way of life was the task of the Positivist Church which Comte founded, a church which in his ideal society would superintend moral education and secure public rationality. Comte's English disciples included Edward Spenser Beesly, friend and collaborator of Marx in the First International, and Frederick Harrison, both of whom gave important assistance to the trade unions in their struggle for legal recognition.

The term *positivism* has also been used for the quite distinct doctrines of the school of philosophers known as 'logical positivists' or 'logical empiricists'. The central tenet of this school is the thesis that the meaning of a statement is, or is given by, the method of its verification. Consequently unverifiable (or unfalsifiable) statements were held to be meaningless, the statements of traditional metaphysics and theology being included in this class. The assertions of logic and mathematics are, on this view, empty of factual content, but meaningful, being tautologies. In the philosophy of science there is a natural link between the verificationalism of the logical positivists and the operationalism of Bridgman; both tend to treat theories as more or less elaborate devices for deriving predictions from data and to be suspicious of the multiplication of theoretical entities. But individual philosophers of this school such as Carnap, Hempel and Ayer have in fact developed in a variety of philosophical directions.

Talcott Parsons in *The Structure of Social Action*, 1937, calls *positivistic* any social theory which involves 'the view that positive science constitutes man's sole possible cognitive relation to external (nonego) reality, man as actor, that is'. By this he means any system in which it is assumed that human action can be adequately characterized without regard to the agent's own standpoint. He takes utilitarianism to be the prime, although not the only, example of such a system; and the break which he makes with the key positions of utilitarianism, its individualism, its means–ends view of human action, its thesis that the ends of action are simply given, he takes to be also a break with positivism. This break he also discerns in earlier writers in the social sciences, sometimes carried through in a partial way, sometimes as above all with Weber much more thoroughly.

The core of meaning that is present in all the varied uses of *positivism* can be seen as twofold. Positivism always involves taking natural science (rather than, for example, history) as the paradigm of human knowledge, and it always involves taking a particular view of the nature of science. But even on this latter topic so-called positivists have held such different views that the term is scarcely ever illuminating without further explanation.   A.M.

poverty; poverty line. The use of the concept of *poverty* and theories concerning the origins of poverty have been of the greatest importance in the development of sociological ideas, particularly in the nineteenth century. The notion that it was laziness that led to poverty had a profound influence on social theory, since it was thought that any direct attempt to alleviate poverty would encourage idleness and discourage thrift, and that a cure of this kind would be worse than the disease. Such thinkers as Bentham, as a philosopher, or Thomas Chalmers, as a theologian and social theorist, assumed, according to what appeared to be commonsense at the time, that it was quite impossible for this reason to attempt to lessen the wide disparity which then existed in the distribution of the nation's income.

Nevertheless, the existence of the poor, and a multitude of the very poor at that, was a heavy and sometimes a crushing burden on the social conscience of Victorian England. Charles Booth, a successful Liverpool merchant and shipowner, became entangled in controversy with the Social Democratic Federation in the 1870s, objecting strenuously to the statement that a quarter of the population was living in poverty. Booth carried out a careful survey of conditions in London in the 1880s, and his confidence in capitalist enterprise was shaken when he found that the proportion was substantially higher, namely a third. To arrive at this result he adopted what would now be called an operational definition of poverty, which was found to be convincing by public opinion, thus making the calculation of the proportion in poverty possible by providing a basis in the *poverty line*. Booth's Poverty Survey has been repeated on many subsequent occasions by Rowntree, Bowley and others. This kind of investigation has been one of the main sources of *scientific* sociology in the twentieth century. See BOOTH.   S. of T.

praxis. A Greek word meaning action. Used by Marxist-oriented sociologists in the context of an epistemological argument to advance what they call critical sociology, itself oriented to changing society. One of the earliest philosophers to use the term was A. Cieszkowski in his *Prolegomena zur Historiosophie*, 1838, where he dilates on the consequences of Hegelian philosophy in order to urge a post-theoretical *praxis* in which the highest conceivable synthesis of being and thought may be attained and issue in practical social life. Although Marx himself may not have been aware of this book he certainly made much of the idea and in recent years through the influence of the Frankfurt School the term has been much in evidence. See D. McLellan, *The Young Hegelians and Karl Marx*, 1969 and T. Bottomore, *Marxist Sociology*. See ACTION RESEARCH, MARXIST SOCIOLOGY.   A.G.

prejudice. A popular usage of *prejudice* refers simply to hostility between ethnic and racial groups within a society, without specifying whether the hostile relationship is one solely of unfavourable attitudes, or of both unfavourable attitudes and actions, e.g. 'The whites of the southern United States are prejudiced against the Negroes.'

A more precise definition limits prejudice specifically to an unfavourable (or favourable) *attitude* towards a group which may, or may not, lead to overt hostile (or friendly) action, e.g. '... prejudice is an attitude that predisposes a person to think, perceive, feel and act in favourable or unfavourable ways towards a group or its individual members.' There is no simple, direct connection between prejudiced attitude and prejudiced act, and examining their relationship is only one segment of the broader problem of the relation of attitudes to actions in general.

An even narrower definition restricts the term to an attitude which is not justified by reality. The prejudiced group may lack, or may distort, information with the result that its attitude does not 'fit' the actual situation or the actual attributes of the group which is the object of the prejudice. In the two definitions above, prejudice need not be irrational in this sense. For

146

example, white workers might express hostile attitudes and actions towards coloured workers who, by accepting lower wages, were, in fact, preventing them from obtaining employment. Such hostility would not be prejudice in this narrowest sense, but rather would be rationally based. The essence of this third 'irrational' use of the term prejudice is nicely expressed as 'being down on something you're not up on' in G. W. Allport's *The Nature of Prejudice*, 1958.

The social psychological treatment of prejudice, whether as attitude or more narrowly as irrational attitude, has invariably been confined to the unfavourable rather than the favourable meaning of the term, i.e. with ethnic and racial prejudice, and it is broadly of two kinds. Firstly, there is the approach which stresses, as the principal cause of prejudiced attitudes, the nature of the personality, which is seen as either (a) being unbalanced or disturbed in some way (e.g. N. W. Ackerman, M. Jahoda, *Anti-Semitism and Emotional Disorder*, 1950); or (b) having developed into a certain personality type (e.g. T. W. Adorno *et al.*, *The Authoritarian Personality*, 1950). Secondly, there is the view, best exemplified by M. and C. W. Sherif in *An Outline of Social Psychology*, 1956, which sees prejudiced attitudes as part of the normal process of internalizing group norms and values. Such attitudes are simply learned, like any other attitudes, in the course of being a group member and are not necessarily manifestations of abnormality. M. and C. W. Sherif say '... it must be emphasized that typically the formation of prejudiced attitudes is not the product of "distorted" personality development. Prejudiced attitudes are formed through the same processes as other attitudes derived from group norms. The main problem in attitude formation towards out-groups is that of (the) internalization of group norms,' (*op. cit.*, p. 661; B. Bettelheim and M. Janowitz, *Dynamics of Prejudice*, 1950). See also, P. Secord and C. Backman, *Social Psychology*, 1976. See ATTITUDE, ETHNOCENTRISM, RACE, STEREOTYPE.   D.J.A.W.

primary group. See GROUP; SOCIAL GROUP.

probability. *Probability* is the study of inferences under conditions of uncertainty. If a particular event can happen in a number of different ways, the probability of a particular outcome is a positive number lying between 0 and 1 which is associated with this outcome. Thus, the throw of a die may result in the uppermost face showing one of six different numbers; each of these would have associated with it a positive fraction, denoting its probability, and the six probabilities would add to unity. There are different views about the meaning of the probability: some writers regard it as measuring the relative degree of rational belief in the particular outcome; others would regard it as a limit to which the proportionate frequency of the particular outcome tends, in a large number of trials. The modern mathematical theory of probability, in common with other branches of mathematics, is axiomatic in character, and regards the probability of an event, as undefined, concerning itself mainly with relations between probabilities, and the calculation of probabilities of fairly complex events, from those of more elementary events.

In the social sciences, it is common to use proportionate frequencies as approximations to the probability of an event; thus the proportion of survivors from a large number of births to a particular age is normally taken as the probability of surviving to that age.   E.G.

probation. Probation is a method of dealing with offenders against the law, and has been defined in Great Britain as 'the submission of an offender while at liberty to a specified period of supervision by a social caseworker who is an officer of the court: during this period the offender remains liable, if not of good conduct, to be otherwise dealt with by the Court' (Report of the Departmental Committee on the Probation Service, 1962, Cmnd 1650). In some countries probation is a form of suspended sentence in that the offender is put on probation in lieu of, say, serving a term of imprisonment and if he breaks the probation order he then serves the term of imprisonment. In Britain, however, and some other countries the Court makes a probation order instead of sentencing the offender, but in all cases the basic principle is that of giving an offender the chance of rehabilitating himself under the supervision of a Probation Officer whose duty is to assist, advise and befriend. This practice grew up in England and the United States of America in the early nineteenth century when the idea of supervision by a person nominated by the court was added to the long-established principle of binding over an offender to be of good behaviour. It was embodied in legislation later in the century, for example, in New Zealand in 1886 and in England in 1887. Since then most countries have developed statutory systems of probation as an enlightened and constructive method of dealing with offenders instead of imprisonment.

In England and Wales the probation service is the responsibility of the Home Office and administered locally by Probation Committees, and in recent years the functions of probation officers have been widened considerably. For example, they provide reports to assist the Courts to come to decisions about sentencing offenders, and they have become responsible for the aftercare and parole of discharged prisoners and for certain welfare functions in prisons. The probation service has also been given the responsibility for providing alternatives to imprisonment, for example, the organizing of community service and the running of bail hostels.   D.C.M.

professions; professionalism. The term *professions* denotes service occupations that apply a systematic body of knowledge to problems which are highly relevant to central values of the society. (See D. Rueschemeyer, *Canadian Review of Sociology*, 1964.)

In their classic study, *The Professions*, 1933, A. M. Carr-Saunders and P. A. Wilson claim that 'the typical profession exhibits a complex of characteristics, and that other vocations approach this condition more or less closely, owing to the possession of some of these characteristics fully or partially developed'. This complex of characteristics is professionalism. Many writers have attempted to list the elements of professionalism. Abraham Flexner in *School and Society*, 1915, stressed individual responsibility, practical application of an intellectual technique, a tendency towards self-organization, and increasingly altruistic motivation. Morris Cogan, after surveying numerous attempts to define the term *profession*, concludes that 'a

148

profession is a vocation whose practice is founded upon an understanding of the theoretical structure of some department of learning or science and upon the abilities accompanying such understanding. This understanding and these abilities are applied to the vital practical affairs of man. The profession ... considers its first ethical imperative to be altruistic service to the client.' (*Harvard Educational Review*, 1953). Geoffrey Millerson has analysed the characteristics enumerated by 21 commentators and lists the following as most frequently mentioned: (1) a profession involves a skill based on theoretical knowledge, (2) the skill requires training and education, (3) the professional must demonstrate competence by passing a test, (4) integrity is maintained by adherence to a code of conduct, (5) the service is for the public good, (6) the profession is organized, (*The Qualifying Associations*, 1964). It has been argued that the term profession should be reserved for those occupations which possess these characteristics, i.e. have achieved professionalism. Therefore those occupations which are held to resemble professions but which are not yet fully professionalized, like social workers, pharmacists and nurses, are termed 'quasi', 'semi', 'marginal', and 'minor' professions. Originally the term profession denoted certain vocations, law, medicine and divinity, which in pre-industrial Europe were the only occupations that gave people without unearned income the opportunity to make a living which did not entail commerce or manual work. Hence officers in the army and navy were also included. S.H.

proletariat. Originally this term referred to the lowest social class in Ancient Rome, but it was used later to refer pejoratively to low-class persons anywhere until Marx precisely used it to refer to industrial workers, both rural and urban, who had to work to live because they owned no capital, but only their labour. Proles engage in industrial work of a manual kind, they tend to be in a near state of poverty. Some social classes or elements of them are forced into proletarian status from time to time, such as white-collar workers and also smallholders or peasants who lose their ownership of land to become firstly tenants and then employees of larger farmers and landowners. Thus the Proletariat is the class which stands in contrast to the Bourgeoisie, which is a class owning capital and with which the Proletariat is in mortal conflict. See BOURGEOISIE. G.D.M.

property; corporate property. The term *property* is usually closely associated with the term *ownership*, but this suggests that property consists of a right or rights by a person over things or persons (legally respectively *jus in rem* and *jus in personam*). Whilst this is the slightly older connotation there is a more recent one which suggests that property consists of those things, material or otherwise, over which persons have rights. Essentially, property is transferable either by inheritance or sale or gift.

Private property in the sense of an exclusive right to the enjoyment and disposal of things in some absolute and unrestricted sense is usually only approximated to and may be said to be more of an idea than a reality.

Corporate property is a term used by sociologists, and indeed by others, to denote instances of shared rights. Thus many simple societies display complicated shared rights over land and other material objects, sometimes also of immaterial objects like magical spells and ritual knowledge. However, the term usually refers to the vesting of ownership in a body of people considered as a single entity, having corporate personality in law. A modern mutation of this is the joint stock company which in fact is a capital fund owned by a number of stock-holders. The development of this phenomenon has been described by A. A. Berle and G. C. Means in their book *The Modern Corporation and Private Property*, revised edition, 1968. For an historical account of ideas of property see R. Schlatter, *Private Property*, 1951. See CORPORATE GROUP, FACILITY.   G.D.M.

psephology. *Psephology* is a word used to describe the study of elections. It first appeared in print in 1952 and is derived from ψῆφος, the pebble which Athenians dropped in an urn to vote. Because of the popularization of opinion polls and electoral speculation, the word has sometimes been employed narrowly to refer to election forecasting, but this journalistic application in fact covers only a small part of the work of psephologists.

The systematic study of all aspects of elections is essentially a mid-twentieth-century development. Three distinct national styles have emerged although each now draws increasingly on the others; the French, inspired by Andre Siegfried, have focused on electoral geography, drawing maps to show correlations between demographic data and voting behaviour; the Americans, led first by Paul Lazarsfeld, have pioneered a more sociological approach, using sample surveys to discover who votes how and what characteristics and attitudes are associated with support for particular parties; the British, influenced by the Nuffield College series of election studies, have found their prime inspiration in history, seeking to record and explain what politicians do at the national and local level in their efforts to influence votes.

Properly speaking, there is no clear distinction between *psephology* and political sociology or political history. In democratic countries elections are an integral part of the whole political process and there can be little point in studying them in isolation. Electoral problems can, however, be divided between law and practice. In Britain at least, electoral law has been concerned with five main issues, (a) the franchise (who is entitled to vote?), (b) registration (how shall the listing of electors be administered?), (c) corrupt practices (what are the permissible limits to vote-gathering, either through the expenditure of money or other pressures?), (d) electoral systems (how shall votes in the country be related to seats in Parliament?), (e) redistribution (what boundaries shall constituencies have?). But, despite pressure for minor amendments, the legal framework under which elections are conducted in Britain is now generally accepted and excites little interest. On the other hand, the electoral process is the subject of increasing academic and practical attention with studies concentrating both on the nature and efficacy of the parties' efforts at persuasion and on the way in which electors perceive political events and personalities and translate their perceptions into voting behaviour. See the Nuffield College series after each election published since 1945 entitled *The British General Election of 19—*; A. Campbell *et al.*, *The American Voter*, 1960, abridged version, 1965; S. Rokkan, UNESCO (ed.), *An International Guide to Election Statistics*, 1969; R. Rose (ed.), *Electoral Behaviour*, 1974.   D.B.

150

puberty rites. See INITIATION.

public opinion. See ATTITUDE RESEARCH.

Q

questionnaire. A form of data collection instrument utilizing a common set of questions about a particular research area. It is normally used in the context of survey research. It is usual to employ questionnaires with literate respondents when they are required to write answers to the questions, but the same frame may be used with illiterates if interviewers note their responses. In the latter case responses should be recorded in the first person.

There are great difficulties in trying to convey common meanings across heterogeneous populations as given expressions do not necessarily provoke common responses. The ideal is that each question should convey the same meaning, the true meaning, the intended meaning to all respondents. Except in 'control' situations, questions should always be posed in the same order with the same wording.

Standardized questionnaires differ in the degree to which questions are structured. In an *open-ended questionnaire* the respondent is free to answer the question as he wishes. In a *closed-ended questionnaire* the respondent must select from a number of responses. These may vary from the *yes/no* responses of a simple questionnaire to a selection of answers from the *multiple-choice* or *cafeteria* type of questionnaire.

Whilst the open-ended questionnaire allows for a fuller response it is more difficult to code the replies than with the closed-ended questionnaire. The latter channels responses into predetermined categories. Both types of questionnaires suffer from the difficulty of being sure that different respondents will code their similar feelings in the same way. Mailed questionnaires enable a larger sample of any population to be reached more cheaply than is possible with a team of interviews, but the problem of non-respondents is always acute. 				B.H.A.R.

Quételet, Lambert Adolphe Jacques (1796–1874). Belgian social statistician who was interested in the application of mathematics to social phenomena, he emphasized regularity in social events and introduced the concept of the 'average man'. His major work, *On Man and the Development of his Faculties: An Essay on Social Physics*, 1835, contains a survey of many statistical researches on the development of both physical and intellectual qualities of man and concludes that the normal curve of distribution commonly holds in social events. His ideas were further developed in *Anthropometry: the Measurement of the different Faculties of Man*, 1871. The importance of his work lies in demonstrating that statistics can be employed instrumentally to understand social phenomena. His argument that the perfection of a science can be judged by the ease with which it can be approached by calculation has been influential. 				G.D.M.

R

race. A word introduced into English in the sixteenth century, and initially used to designate a category of persons whose similar characteristics could be attributed to common descent. From about 1800, largely because of the influence of the French comparative anatomist Cuvier, the word was increasingly used to designate a permanent zoological type and often equated with a species. In *The Origin of Species*, 1859, Charles Darwin demonstrated that there were no permanent types in nature; he recognized 'geographical races or sub-species' as 'local forms completely fixed and isolated', but it was only with the establishment of population genetics that the underlying mechanisms were revealed. If the word race is used in modern biology it designates a subspecies, a local form which is an adaptation to a particular environment produced by natural selection. All these three uses of the word can still be noticed, but in very recent times a fourth has appeared. Legislation is enacted against discrimination on grounds of a person's racial group; official forms, as in connection with a census, may record a person's race. Unlike the previous uses of the word this one does not convey any explanation of the causes of physical variation. In sociology the use of 'race' entails many difficulties since the popular understanding of race often echoes the pre-Darwinian sense of race as type and is incompatible with an approach from population genetics. In general, beliefs about race are used by relatively powerful groups to exclude or demarcate others, whereas ethnic groups are based upon voluntary identification. See M. Banton and J. Harwood, *The Race Concept*, 1975.   M.P.B.

Radcliffe-Brown, Arthur Reginald (1881–1955). English social anthropologist, who studied under W. H. R. Rivers at Cambridge, where he became a Fellow of Trinity College. His early fieldwork was carried out in the Andaman Islands from 1906 to 1908, and in Australia from 1910 to 1912. He was less notable for his field studies, able and original though they were, than for his teaching, his organization of research programmes and his remarkable ability to inspire others. Together with Malinowski, he may be said to have been responsible for the rise of British Social Anthropology. His influence was not confined to England for he held teaching posts in Australia, South Africa, China, Egypt and the United States of America, where from 1931 to 1937 he taught at the University of Chicago and did much to shape the thought of a rising generation of anthropologists. In 1937 he accepted the Chair of Social Anthropology at Oxford University and after his retirement continued to teach at Rhodes University and at the University of Manchester.

Radcliffe-Brown's writings were not numerous, for he was reluctant to publish unless he could make definitive statements. His articles on kinship systems, on social structure and function, on totemism, and on law, have been particularly important contributions. His chief interest was in synchronic studies of primitive peoples. Much influenced by the thought of Montesquieu, Comte and Durkheim, he was an exponent of what he called 'comparative sociology'. By this he meant the discernment of the structural principles governing human relationships derived from the comparative study of social systems. This is seen most clearly in the lengthy essay which serves to introduce the studies of kinship, which he edited with C. D. Forde under the title *African Systems of Kinship and Marriage*, 1950. Other publications include his first monograph *The Andaman Islanders*, 1922, *Structure and Function in Primitive Society*, 1952, and the posthumously published book, *A Natural Science of Society*, 1957, which represents his methodological views as recorded by students in his Chicago seminar. Those who heard him lecture will recall the rare quality of clarity, and simplicity of exposition he displayed. See FUNCTION; FUNCTIONALISM.   G.D.M.

radical rationalistic positivism. See POSITIVISM.

rationality. The term denotes thought and action which are conscious in accord with the rules of logic and empirical knowledge, where objectives are coherent, mutually consistent and achieved by the most appropriate means.

The conviction that rationality, or reason, is the distinctive characteristic of human beings has made it a central theme in Western philosophy for over two thousand years. In so far as this has led to an over-estimation of the place and power of reason in human society, it has been criticized as the doctrine of *rationalism*.

In British sociology L. T. Hobhouse incorporated the notion of *rationality* in its widest sense into his theory of human development as an organic principle which harmonized all aspects of individual and social life (see *Development and Purpose*, 1913).

Max Weber, especially in *Wirtschaft und Gesellschaft*, 1921, has been responsible for the most extensive use of the term in sociology. He classifies all action into four types: purposively rational ('zweckrational'), action where means are correctly chosen to obtain ends; value rational ('wertrational'), where action is in accord with conscious value standards; affectual; and traditional; the last two types being regarded as deviations from rational action. (See M. Weber, *The Theory of Social and Economic Organization*, 1947, p. 115.) In addition Weber applies the concept to institutionalized aspects of society and contrasts authority based on belief in the exceptional qualities of an individual (charismatic), *op. cit.*, p. 328. The subjection of social life to precise regulation, the extension of exact calculation in the economy, and the application of scientific methods to production Weber terms rationalization and regards as the most important trend in Western society, though at the same time he holds that these features, which he calls formally rational, frequently conflict with material rationality, or the satisfaction of human needs.

Weber's use of the concept of rationality involves taking elements normally comprised within it, e.g. use of logic, adjustment of means to ends, conscious espousal of values, and designating each one rational irrespective of its relation to the others. This enables him to emphasize the possible conflict of these elements (something which the broad meaning of rationality minimizes), but the consequent great variety and frequency of the use of the concept leaves it uncertain whether it retains any constant meaning. Fortunately it is always clear in what particular sense Weber is using the term so that subsequent sociologists have been able to benefit from his substantive points while remaining unaffected by this uncertainty. (See A. Eisen, 'The meanings and confusions of Weberian "rationality" ', *British Journal of Sociology*, XXIX, 1, 1978.)

Two uses of the concept of rationality have been of recent major interest to sociologists. Methodologists have argued for the necessity of explaining human action by setting it in the context of the actor's reasons, motives, and experience, and have termed this 'the assumption of rationality' (see Q. Gibson, *The Logic of Social Enquiry*, 1960, ch. XIV).

H. A. Simon in *Administrative Behaviour*, 1947, employs the term in contexts where the actor's objectives, available means, and the limitations on his action may be precisely specified. The investigator's aim is to determine what is rational, that is how efficient achievement of the actor's objectives may be maximized. This approach, adapted from economics for the study of administration, thus lays down strict conditions for the use of the concept. The sociologist falls prey to rationalism, if in adopting this concept of rationality, he assumes that these conditions for its use, i.e. actors possessing precise objectives, etc., are automatically fulfilled in the situations he is studying.

Social theorists of the Frankfurt School have denied the claims to rationality of modern organizational forms arguing instead that they reflect domination and alienation. 'The apparatus defeats its own purpose if its purpose is to create a humane existence on the basis of a humanized nature. And if this is not its purpose, its rationality is even more suspect' (Herbert Marcuse, *One Dimensional Man*, 1964, 1968 ed. p. 121). Recently Jürgen Habermas has attempted to specify the nature of a truly rational society by arguing that only full and free communication between equals produces rational thought. Rationality is thus made dependent upon the form of an ideal society rather than being viewed as the driving force towards that end. See J. Habermas, *Toward a Rational Society*, 1971; *Knowledge and Human Interests*, 1972; *Theory and Practice*, 1974. See ACTION, AUTHORITY.

M.C.A.

realism; social realism. *Social realism*, or perhaps more accurately *sociological realism*, is a view about the nature of sociological thought. Is society an entity in itself or is it merely so many individual persons? The nominalist would hold the latter view, the realist would say that it is meaningful to speak of society as having a reality *sui generis*.

Social realism is a very old view, and its classic statement is to be found in Plato's *Dialogues* where the Athenian Laws (i.e. society) press their claims upon Socrates, an individual, indicating that the individual is completely dependent upon the whole of which he is a part. To be sure there are other elements in Platonic thought about the relation of the individual to society, but social realism is one element. *Social realism* is an idea which has had a long history. In modern sociological literature there are tendencies towards it prominent in the thought of Durkheim and also in that of Radcliffe-Brown. The former's social realism appears in all his various works, but especially in *Les formes élémentaires de la vie religieuse*, 1912, whereby he focused attention on the common value system, symbolically revered in the religious cultus. Although he toyed with the notion of a group mind he cannot be said to have been a social realist in the substantialist sense, but he did emphasize the debt the individual owes to his society. Radcliffe-Brown held an organicist view of society which enabled him to speak of society as a social system and to point to various structures of relationships and functional factors; all of which points to the view that to discern the significance of the part one must see its place in the larger whole, a whole that possesses some reality. It is doubtful if any sociologist is an unqualified *realist*, but it is difficult to see how a person can claim to be a sociologist without holding the view in some form, however, qualified. For a discussion of the subject see W. Stark, *The Fundamental Forms of Social Thought*, 1962. See AGELICISM, HOLISM.

G.D.M.

recidivist, recidivism. Recidivists are repeated offenders who neither learn to avoid detection nor are deterred from committing further offences either by conviction or the sentence they receive; recidivism is the practice of such criminal behaviour

Redfield, Robert (1897–1958). American anthropologist, he was educated at Chicago and became Professor of Anthropology there. His outlook was a broad one and he did much to bring anthropology and sociology together. Redfield wrote a number of monographs on Mexican and Guatemalan communities. A notable study was his book *The Folk Culture of Yucatan*, 1941, which contained a theory of social change. He was an urbane and generous scholar as may be seen in his reflective study *The Little Community*, 1955, and in *Peasant Society and Culture* which he published a year later.

reductionism. 'Reductionism' is usually taken to apply to any doctrine that seeks to explain a higher-order phenomenon in terms of a lower-order one. Such a doctrine can be held in various forms, and applied in many different areas of intellectual endeavour. One form of reductionism is the notion that the laws of all other sciences can be in principle reduced to, or expressed in terms of, the laws of micro-physics; another is the thesis that all mental faculties can be expressed as events in or states of the brain. In sociology, the most important form of reductionism is probably that which asserts that all terms which refer to groups or collectivities (e.g. state, bureaucracy, industrial firm, etc.) can be in principle expressed as descriptions of the behaviour of individual actors. This view has come to be known as 'methodological individualism'; its leading advocates have included Max Weber and Sir Karl Popper. Neither author denies that collective concepts may be legitimately used in the social sciences; but they insist that these are merely 'shorthand descriptions' of a multiplicity of individual actions. See Arthur Koestler and J. R. Smythies, *Beyond Reductionism*, 1969; John O'Neill (ed.), *Modes of Individualism and Collectivism*, 1973. A.G.

156

reference group. The term *reference group* was introduced into the literature on small groups by Muzafer Sherif in his textbook *An Outline of Social Psychology*, 1948, where he uses it in contrast to the term *membership group*. Whilst the latter obviously refers to a group a person belongs to, the former is one which affects his behaviour. Of course, the two may coincide and it is usually the case that a person's membership groups are also his reference groups. But the distinction is made in order to indicate the fact that the norms and standards governing a person's behaviour may be those of a group he would like to have membership in, but which he cannot easily join. This is clearly often the case with socially mobile people. The term is frequently used in discussions of attitude formation, adaptations and the like.   G.D.M.

relative deprivation. This concept was introduced by S. A. Stouffer *et al.* in *The American Soldier*, 1949, but was later formalized by R. K. Merton in *Social Theory and Social Structure*, 1961, and extended to a theory of reference group behaviour. Individuals see themselves as deprived (or privileged, hence 'relative gratification') by comparing their own situation with that of other groups and categories of persons. The extent to which they will see themselves as deprived will vary according to the category or group selected as the basis of comparison.

Stouffer found in two sections of the American army that non-commissioned officers in the Military Police, who had completed only part of their high school education, had a considerably more favourable view to their promotion chances in their section of the army than their counterparts of similar educational level in the Air Corps had of their promotion chances, even though the actual opportunities for promotion were much worse in the Military Police. This is explained, in terms of relative deprivation, by the Military Police non-commissioned officer feeling more highly rewarded (i.e. less relatively deprived) in comparing his promotion with the 83 per cent of those with identical education in his section who had remained privates, as against the Air Corps non-commissioned officer comparing his rank with only 53 per cent of those of his educational level who similarly had not been promoted.

Merton classifies Stouffer's use of the concept into (a) those cases where the individual takes as a base of comparison the individuals with whom he interacts or the groups of which he is a member, and those where this is not the case, i.e. out-groups or non-membership groups; and (b) membership and non-membership groups of similar and those of different social status from that of the given individual. It is particularly in its discussion of non-membership groups as a source of values and attitudes, a notion thus derived from Stouffer's concept of relative deprivation, that reference group theory constitutes an important contribution to sociology. S. A. Stouffer, *Social Research to Test Ideas*, 1962, ch. 2. See REFERENCE GROUP.   D.J.A.W.

residues. V. F. D. Pareto, economist and sociologist, in his famous treatise on general sociology, paid particular attention to what he called 'non-logical theories'. These were explanations of phenomena, religious and philosophical in nature, other than those proffered by natural science. Such explanations, he maintained, have two elements, a relatively permanent element which he called the *residue* and a relatively variable element which he called the *derivation*. Residues display human sentiments or states of mind, and these are to be found generally in human society, ancient or modern, primitive or advanced. The residues are, however, masked or disguised in varying forms, superficially often very different, but behind all derivations the residues remain and may be revealed by sociological enquiry.

Pareto distinguished six classes of residues; the first two being the most important. They are the *instinct for combining* similars or opposites; the *persistence of aggregates* which denotes the propensity to conserve the things combined from generation to generation; the need to express sentiments by means of external acts, a feature of religion; sentiments concerned with social life and cohesion, e.g. sentiments of loyalty and patriotism, self-sacrifice and propriety; individualistic sentiments related to the integrity of the individual and his property; and sentiments related to sexual appetites.

Derivations, or justification for the residues, fall into four classes. They are assertions, appeals to authority, the justification of sentiment itself, and verbal proofs. Both *residues* and *derivations* play a large part in Pareto's social analyses, especially in his analysis of class structures and the circulation of elites, which enabled him to account for political and social changes. See Pareto's *Mind and Society* (the English translation of the *Trattato di sociologia generale*), 1935, and also S. E. Finer's *Vilfredo Pareto: Sociological Writings*, 1966. See PARETO, ELITE.   G.D.M.

respondent. The term is used to denote a person who replies to a questionnaire or who gives answers to questions by an interviewer using an interview schedule; it is a term commonly used in social survey work and is interchangeable with the term *informant*.

restricted code. See CODES.

ritual, rites of passage. Ritual, like a poem, is a concentrated, focused marshalling of symbols redolent with arrays of meaning. Like myth, ritual through metaphor and metonymy makes statements about and allows the exploration of major relational systems in the socio-cultural context of experience.

Transfers of power or of goods, assertions of legitimacy, the establishment of new bonds or alliances or the breaking of old ones, the progression through personal or societal developmental phases are commonly marked by rituals which assemble, juxtapose and examine polysemic symbols, thereby connecting the focal activity with the society's major paradigms. The troubled mind, disturbed relations between people and nature, between individuals or groups may be rectified by constructions of order through ritual.

This view of ritual as primarily a mode of carefully constructed communication is frequently extended to everyday life. Mundane reality is fabricated moment by moment through our ritualistic presentations to one another of the appropriately related symbols of speech, clothing, gestures, furnishings, etc.

The term *rites de passage* (called transition rituals by J. Beattie in *Other*

Cultures, 1964, p. 211) was put forward by the Flemish anthropologist, Arnold van Gennep, writing in 1909 (translated *The Rites of Passage*, 1960). He adduced evidence for the universal occurrence of ritual sequences whenever a passage from one state to another occurred in a simple society, whether in the status change of an individual, or in the transformations of nature or in the affairs of a community. See J. LaFontaine, ed., *The Interpretation of Ritual*, 1972; V. Turner, *The Ritual Process*, 1969; M. Vizedom, *Rites and Relationships: rites of passage and contemporary anthropology*, 1976.   H.D.M.

role, social role; role-taking; role conflict. A *social role* is the expected behaviour associated with a *social position*. A position is simply the label or the means of identifying a particular social role, and often in the literature on the subject the two terms are used interchangeably. Thus the position of 'doctor' identifies a particular body of expected behaviour or the role of doctor. To define a social position is to state the essential or minimal features of the expected behaviour or role. Strictly speaking, however, to define a social position completely, i.e. sociologically as opposed to logically, is to indicate *all* its role prescriptions. In this sense the terms *positions* and *role* are only analytically separable.

Role is a relational term. One plays a role *vis-à-vis* another person's role which is attached to a *counter position*, e.g. the doctor plays his role as doctor in relation to the patient's role. The relational aspect of the role concept centres on the notion of *role-taking*, which is discussed below.

The expectations that the role partner in the counter position has of ego's role are usually referred to as ego's *role obligations* or duties, and the expectations that ego has of his role partner are ego's *rights*. The expectations between the focal position of ego and another counter position are said to constitute a *role sector*. The expectations between a focal position and a number of different counter positions make up what R. K. Merton in his *Social Theory and Social Structure*, 1957, has called the *role set*, e.g. the local doctor will have role relations with patients, with the doctors of the local hospital, and with his fellow doctors as a member of his professional association, and so on.

It will be seen that the role concept is one at the individual level, the level of interaction. It is individuals, not organizations, institutions or sub-systems, who play roles and occupy positions. The term *role*, unfortunately, is sometimes used in a sense quite different from that being discussed here to mean the part played by a social sub-system, organization or institution within a larger social system, or more narrowly, as its function or positive contribution to the larger system.

Role as the expected behaviour of a position, is, at least in the more recent role literature, distinguished from ego's actual behaviour in that position. T. M. Newcomb in *Social Psychology*, 1951, thus refers to the actual behaviour as distinct from the role itself, as the *role behaviour*, while T. R. Sarbin in 'Role Theory' (ch. 6 in G. Lindzey, *Handbook of Social Psychology*. vol. I, 1959) uses the term *role enactment*. While actual behaviour obviously bears some similarity to the role prescriptions of the position, there are also discrepancies between them, which are of fundamental interest to the role analyst and which may stem from a variety of factors, such as the clarity and specificity of the role prescriptions themselves, how ego interprets the prescriptions, and his ability to carry them out.

An additional distinction to that between role and role behaviour, which is usually ignored in the role literature, can also be made. The expected role behaviour is not necessarily identical with the ideal role behaviour. As a patient I may observe the doctor to actually *perform* certain behaviours, I may *expect* him to do certain things, and lastly, I may think he *should* behave in this way rather than that as a doctor. Thus there may be differences between these three dimensions which could constitute a legitimate focus of empirical enquiry. Hence ideal role can be differentiated from expected role but the two seem often to be used synonymously, cf. Newcomb's discussion.

In the empirical investigation of the role concept both expected ways of behaving and expected qualities or attributes of the role player have been the focus of attention (cf. Sarbin, *op. cit.*, 1959, and N. Gross, W. Mason, A. W. McEachern, *Explorations in Role Analysis*, 1958). It may perhaps be observed that the more roles are defined in terms of attributes rather than behaviourally, the more difficult it becomes to maintain a distinction between the role concept and that of *the self*.

Role-taking. When social interaction is conceptualized in role terms a further concept is utilized, that of *role-taking*. Interaction could conceivably be discussed in purely external, behavioural terms, i.e. ego does something or says something to alter and the latter is observed subsequently to do or say something else. In this way interaction could be seen either as a chronological sequence of behaviours or the behaviour of alter might be seen as a simple or direct response to that of ego. In role analysis, however, the intervening concept of role-taking is introduced and the notion of response between actors made both more precise and more subjective. Role-taking, or taking the role of the other, means that ego responds by placing himself mentally or imaginatively in the role of the other person in order to regulate his own behaviour, not necessarily in the direction of conformity, in view of alter's expectations. Thus the initiation of a piece of behaviour by one actor and the reactions to it by other actors, i.e. *inter*-action, can be discussed by the sociologist in terms of such role-taking. Interaction conceived in role terms is, therefore, essentially social in M. Weber's sense, since the actors are adjusting their behaviour in terms of their conceptions of their own roles and those of others.

Role-taking is not only a property of adult interaction, it also underlies the socialization process, the *learning* of social roles. The idea of role-taking is fundamental, for example, to the work of the social psychologist G. H. Mead (see A. Strauss, *The Social Psychology of George Herbert Mead*, 1962). Mead's discussion centres on the relation between role and the social self, more particularly on how the child becomes a social being by playing roles and taking the roles of other figures. The term *self* has been employed more in the role literature than *personality*, and as used by Mead and later experimentally by Sarbin, may be viewed as *subjective personality* or what ego thinks he is as a person, how he sees himself. A crucial stage for Mead in the development of the child's social self is that between the nature of role-taking at the earlier 'play' stage and that at the later 'game' stage. In the former the younger child takes the roles of other figures, teacher, mother, policeman and so on, and acts these other roles singly or individually. In the latter the older child can place himself in the roles of a number of other positions *simultaneously*. For example in playing a team game it is through being able to imagine the roles of *all* the other players that he is able to play the game. Mead here refers rather misleadingly to the other roles constituting a *generalized other* for ego, but a more appropriate expression would be an organized other. Underlying Mead's discussion of role-taking is an idea similar to Piaget's notion of egocentricity in the very young child. For if the child at the game stage can mentally organize a *number* of other roles, he also sees those roles as something distinct from his own self and his own role, whereas the younger child with singular role-taking does not make such a distinction. In his own mind he really *is* the policeman, the teacher, the cowboy, etc. The simultaneous organization of other roles by ego is thus crucial to the emergence of his own self-awareness.

Sarbin has developed Mead's role-taking theme by introducing the idea of people varying in ability or aptitude to take the role of other positions (see, for example, T. R. Sarbin, D. S. Jones, 'An Experimental analysis of Role Behaviour' in E. Maccoby, T. Newcomb, E. Hartley, *Readings in Social Psychology*). A further analytical refinement in role-taking is found in R. Turner's article 'Role taking, Role standpoint, and Reference group behaviour', *American Journal of Sociology*, LXVI, 4, 1956, where he distinguishes between role-taking in which we actually adopt the standpoint of the other person's role (cf. Mead's play stage) and that where we do not identify in this way. Secondly, *reflexive role-taking*, where we place ourselves in the other's role in order to see how we appear to the other person, is distinguished from non-reflexive role-taking, where we are not concerned with this evaluation of our self and role by the other person.

Role Conflict. This may be experienced by ego at two levels, firstly, within his own body of roles, and secondly between his own roles and those of other actors.

In the former, for example, if there is a discrepancy between ego's perception of his role and his perception of his actual role behaviour, this could have harmful effects on his self-image. Thus if ego sees a great difference between how he should act as a husband and how he actually does behave, he may become neurotic or cynical about himself as a person. Another form of conflict within ego's own body of roles occurs when he perceives some incompatibility between performing certain prescriptions of one of his roles and carrying out those of another of his roles, e.g. as employee bringing home work from the office to improve his chance of promotion and as husband spending after-office hours with his wife; or wanting to vote, as a responsible citizen, for one political party from intellectual conviction and feeling compelled, as a son, to support another party from loyalty to the family's traditional way of voting. W. Burchard in his article 'Role conflicts of Military Chaplains', *American Sociological Review*, XIX, 5, 1954, examined this form of conflict between the military chaplain's roles as religious leader and military officer.

Conflict may arise at a second level when the way ego perceives his role differs from the definition of his role by the occupants in counter positions. It is this form of role conflict, the lack of consensus on a given role by different role occupants, that is discussed by Gross and his colleagues, *op. cit.*, 1958. While the sociologist has typically used role as the unit of the social structure, he has been much less concerned empirically with the content, limits and conflicts of social roles as defined by their occupants and has in consequence overstressed the coherence of the social structure, the degree to which the actors agree on the role prescriptions and the extent to which the role prescriptions constitute an integrated pattern. The greater the lack of role consensus, i.e. dissensus, the greater the potentiality for conflict between occupants of positions. Gross's work represents a major attempt to measure how the actor actually defines his role and the extent of consensus in such role definitions between different role occupants. The study is concerned with the role of the school superintendent and discusses both *intraposition consensus*, agreement on role definition among occupants of the same type of position, e.g. among the school superintendents, and *interposition consensus*, agreement on role definition between occupants of counter positions, e.g. between school superintendent and school board member.

If the actor perceives role dissensus between himself and the occupants of counter positions, a further problem arises as to how he will resolve this conflict. Gross proposes a theory of role conflict resolution in which the individual chooses, avoids or compromises between conflicting expectations of other actors in terms of (a) how legitimate he perceives these expectations to be, (b) how strong he perceives the sanctions against his non-conformity to these expectations to be, and (c) whether he gives priority to the sanctions or the legitimacy of the expectations, or compromises between the two. Using the theory, Gross correctly predicted the mode of conflict resolution in 91 per cent of the cases of role conflict reported by the school superintendents. See M. Banton, *Roles*, 1965; W. J. Goode, 'A Theory of Role Strain', *American Sociological Review*, XXV, 4, 1960; B. Biddle and E. J. Thomas (eds.), *Role Theory: Concepts and Research*, 1966; R. Dahrendorf, 'On the History, Significance and Limits of the Category of Social Role' in *Essays in the Theory of Society*, 1968. See CONSENSUS, REFERENCE GROUP, SELF, SOCIAL STRUCTURE. D.J.A.W.

role-handicap. A term introduced into sociological literature by H. D. Kirk (see his *Shared Fate: A Theory of Adoption and Mental Health*, 1964) to point the contrasts between people in certain kinds of situations, where the culture provides in the one case for behavioural expectations, and in the other case it does not do so, or does so inadequately. Thus, for example, adopting parents are role-handicapped as compared with natural parents in some instances, such as the death of a child, for natural parents will receive the support of understanding and sympathy of family and friends readily and firmly, whereas there is no great likelihood that an equivalent degree of support would be forthcoming to help adoptive parents, whose grief may be no less. Again, the situation of people facing disaster is different if the disaster occurs during war-time, when the populace is prepared for hardships, than it is in peace-time, when they are less prepared psychologically, and we may say that the latter represents a case of role-handicap. See RELATIVE DEPRIVATION, ROLE. G.D.M.

Ross, Edward Alsworth (1886–1951). American social psychologist and sociologist, he was a prolific writer who produced twenty-eight books and numerous articles. He was one of the first to write on social psychology. Ross was a man of strong views and independent character; he resigned from the staff of Stanford University on a public issue connected with the treatment of coloured workers employed by the Southern Pacific Railroad, a company having some connections with the University. Ross belonged to that early tradition of American sociology which was moral and prophetic in outlook.

S

sacrifice. W. Robertson Smith and E. E. Evans-Pritchard, in their writings on *sacrifice*, represent what appears to be two fundamentally opposed views. The former placed overwhelming emphasis on the commensality of the sacrificial meal; the latter relegates this meal to a place of peripheral significance, and he argues that *sacrifice* (which, like Robertson Smith, he sees as central to religion) must be understood in terms of the relationship between man and something which lies right outside his society. Both scholars, in fact, include religious beliefs and their social concomitants in their analyses. Neither attempt to pass off sacrifice as magic: when a person sacrifices for rain it is not expected that the act will, of itself, magically precipitate a cloud-burst, since what is implied by a failure of the rains is that the relationship between God and his people has been disturbed, and this is made manifest by some disruption in the natural order of man's relationship to man and to nature. But since a disturbance in a mystical relationship has occurred it has social consequences, and since sacrifice is concerned with the restoration of mystical relationships, it is concerned with the relationships between human beings as well. When, therefore, a sacrifice takes place, it does something to social relationships, in the sense that participants gather together for a specific purpose. A life, in animal or symbolic form, is offered as a surrogate for an individual or a group, but in either case it is the concern of the group of participants, for an individual has no more freedom to wantonly offer a surrogate life than he has to end his own in suicide or to withdraw his membership by departure. Life belongs to a social group. The symbolically charged commensal meal demonstrates the rights of control a group exercises over its life. Ultimately, however, since all life comes from God, He must be included in the covenanted restoration and revitalization of the unity between man and man. In this way the unity of the social group is made effective, for the bond thus established is conceptually indissoluble. See E. E. Evans-Pritchard, *Nuer Religion*, 1956; G. B. Gray, *Sacrifice in the Old Testament*, 1925; H. Hubert and M. Mauss, *Sacrifice: Its Nature and Function* (trans.) 1964; A. Loisy, *Essai Historique sur le Sacrifice*, 1920; W. Robertson Smith, *The Religion of the Semites*, 1927.   E.L.P.

Saint-Simon, Claude Henri de Rouvroy, Comte de (1760–1825). French aristocrat, founder of socialism in France and writer, he suggested much that was later adopted by Auguste Comte. Their joint work, *Plan of the Scientific Works Necessary for the Re-organisation of Society*, 1822, gives a clear formulation of the purpose of sociology and states the law of the three stages of social development. His associations with medical scientists led him to entertain an organic theory of human society which proved to be a seminal idea in the nineteenth century. His interest in industrial development and social re-organization is manifest in his work *L'Industrie*, 1817, *L'Organisateur*, 1819, *Du Système Industriel*, 1821 and *Catéchisme des Industriels*, 1923. But his most important book is *Le Nouveau Christianisme*, 1825, which is concerned with the cause of the poor and the role of religion in alieviating poverty. It was this book that led to his break with Comte. He believed passionately in progress, seeing it to depend on the advancement of science, the protection of the industrial class, and the maintenance of industrial organization.

He experienced wealth and poverty, a spell in prison and a broken marriage, and he once attempted suicide but only succeeded in wounding himself in one eye. Nevertheless, he abounded in ideas and enthusiasm. After his death some of his disciples, the Saint-Simonians, developed his ideas into a system of socialism but it was a variety quite different from its contemporary form.   G.D.M.

sampling. *Sampling* is the term used to denote the collection of information and the drawing of inferences about a *population* or *universe* from an examination of only part thereof, the *sample*. This method is widely used in social research, where it may be impracticable or prohibitively expensive to obtain information from every member of a population. By investigating only a section of the population specially skilled interviewers or enumerators could be used, and more attention given to the organization of the enquiry, so that the quality of the information collected may be higher than in a full-scale survey.

When a sample only is studied, there is always a chance that it may not be representative of the population from which it is drawn. But, provided the sample is selected by a probability method, in which each item of the population has a determinate chance of being selected, it is possible to assess quantitatively the risk of drawing a wrong conclusion. A sample so selected is called a *random sample*, one in which each item has an equal chance of selection is called a *simple random sample*. In the selection of such samples no latitude is left to the interviewer or investigator; he is presented with a list of persons selected and is not permitted to interview anyone else. Should it not be possible to make contact with the persons selected for the sample, or should they refuse to give the information, even after several recalls, the substitution of others is not normally permitted or, if permitted, definite procedures for selecting the substitutes are laid down. Such random or *probability sampling* is thus expensive in money and effort, compared with the method of *quota sampling*, still used by some market research agencies, where the selection of the sample is left to the interviewer, subject to certain constraints designed to bring about the resemblance of the sample to the population in certain known respects. Though cheaper, it is impossible to assess the reliability of such a sample, and it must be emphasized that resemblance between sample and population in respect of one characteristic does not guarantee resemblance in respect of the characteristic sampled for. For this reason, quota sampling is not now used in serious sociological research.

When a probability sample is selected it may be selected in a single process, or in several stages (multi-stage sampling). In each case, it is useful to have a *sampling frame*, i.e. a list of all the units in a population arranged in some order. If all the items are numbered, a single stage simple random sample may be selected with the help of a table of *random sampling numbers*, i.e. a set of numbers in which all digits and combinations of digits appear with roughly equal frequency. The items corresponding to the numbers in the table will be selected for the sample. Where the list exists and is not numbered, *quasi-random sampling* is sometimes used, every nth item of the population being selected. This method must, however, be used with some care, for if there is a periodicity in the list with respect to the characteristic sampled for, randomness may be disturbed.

If it is known that a population may be divided into sub-groups or *strata* which vary between themselves with respect to the characteristic sampled for, it can be shown that an increase in accuracy may be obtained by taking a separate sample in each stratum. This method is known as *stratified random sampling* and different sampling fractions may be used in different strata. Another single-stage method of sample selection is *cluster sampling*. A population may be clustered, e.g. a group of individuals may live in a block of flats, and in this case, the inquiry may be conducted more efficiently by taking a sample of the clusters and investigating every individual in the cluster. Though the accuracy of the sample is reduced by this method, so also is the cost of collecting the information, as the interviewer will not have to spend so much time travelling from respondent to respondent, and the loss in accuracy may be more than made good by increasing the number of units investigated.

However, in most large-scale inquiries, and almost always when a population which is widely scattered is studied, some form of *multi-stage sampling* is used. In this method, a sample of first-stage units is selected and within these a further sample is chosen. Thus, the first-stage units may be local authorities or schools, and the second stage units may be households or schoolchildren. Here, again, the cost of collecting the information is reduced, as travelling time is reduced. More than two stages may be used in the sampling process, and the first stage units are sometimes selected with probability proportionate to their size. Multi-stage sampling may be combined with stratification, and very complex designs are sometimes used, depending both on the nature of the problem and on the sampling frame that is available.

To show how the degree of reliability of a sample may be assessed, we need to introduce the concept of the *sampling distribution*. Suppose we have a population of N items, of which a certain proportion p possess a given characteristic, say they own a private car. Out of this population a number of different samples of size n can be drawn, this number is very large, when n is small in relation to N. In each of these samples there will be a certain proportion of persons, who are car owners, and the frequency distribution of these proportions is called the sampling distribution of p, and the standard deviation of the distribution is called the *standard error* of p. It may be shown that for large values of n, say $n \quad 30$, this distribution will tend towards the normal or Gaussian form, and that the standard error of p will be

$$\sqrt{p\left(\frac{(1-p)}{n}\right)\left(1-\frac{n}{N}\right)}.$$ Thus, in 95 per cent of all *samples* the

proportion of car owners will lie in the range

$$p \pm 1.96 \sqrt{p\left(\frac{(1-p)}{n}\right)\left(1-\frac{n}{N}\right)}.$$

The larger the value of the sample size n, the smaller the standard error. A little study of the formula will show that the sample size n is much more important in determining the size of the standard error, than the *sampling fraction* n/N, which shows the proportion of the sample to the total population. At first sight this leads to the surprising result that a sample of, say, 2,500 individuals has much the same reliability, whether it comes from a population of 100,000 individuals or one million. It is always the aim of an efficient sampling method to give maximum reliability at minimum cost, but it will be clear that any sampling design must achieve a compromise.

Sampling has been used for a considerable period of time, but properly controlled methods of sampling in social research only date from the beginning of this century. In England and Wales, Professor A. L. Bowley was one of the first investigators to use sampling methods in his five towns survey before the first world war. Since that time sampling methods have been applied in many branches of social investigation, in public opinion surveys, the assessment of social mobility, the study of performances in intelligence tests and similar fields. Recently, sampling has been used by official statisticians, the Family Census taken on behalf of the Royal Commission on Population in 1946 was taken by means of a 10 per cent sample, and the Census of Population in Great Britain in 1966 was taken on a sample basis. In the United States census of population, important supplementary information has been obtained on a sample basis, and a continuous survey of the Labour Force by means of samples is being undertaken. Indeed, it is likely that sampling will increasingly supplant full-scale investigations, and that the latter will in future take place only when they are required for administrative purposes. See A. Stuart, *Basic Ideas of Scientific Sampling*, 1962; W. G. Cochran, *Sampling Techniques* (2nd edition), 1963.   E.G.

sanction; social sanction. A *sanction* is a means of enforcing a rule or law and may be positive or negative, i.e. it may take the form of a reward or a punishment. As applied to a group or society the prefix *social* is commonly used. This itself reflects the use of the term in conjunction with discussion of social order and control, for it has been sociological practice, since W. G. Sumner's *Folkways*, 1906, to classify social norms in terms of the kinds of sanctions imposed, or at least in terms of the severity of negative sanctions imposed to secure conformity. A. R. Radcliffe-Brown in a famous article on the term *sanction* in the *Encyclopaedia of the Social Sciences*, 1934, distinguished between *diffused* and *organized* sanctions. This does justice to the means of social control other than those incorporated in legal enactments and, moreover, also points to the importance of positive sanctions, i.e. signs of approval spontaneously displayed in social situations.   G.D.M.

savage. See BARBARIAN; BARBARISM.

scales; scalogram analysis. While there is considerable difference both in the type and the method of scale construction, they all require, in principle, that an individual responds with expressions of approval or disapproval, agreement or disagreement, to a set of carefully standardized statements or items. The pattern of responses provides a way of inferring the respondent's attitude concerning the subject to which the scale items refer and also allows him to be assigned a score which represents his position along a quantitative scale.

In principle, the construction of a scale requires the selection of a set of items such that the acceptance or the rejection of one implies a different degree of favourability or unfavourability in attitude. For example, if we wish to measure attitudes towards war, then a scale to measure these attitudes might include the following items: 'The benefits of war outweigh its attendant evils', 'Compulsory military training in all countries should be reduced but not eliminated', 'It is difficult to imagine any situation in which we should be justified in sanctioning or participating in another war'. (Items selected from D. D. Droba, *A Scale for Measuring Attitude Toward War*, 1930.) Obviously, any respondent who endorses the first item is at the pro-war end of the continuum, whereas one who endorses the last item is towards the anti-war end of the continuum; the respondent who endorses the second item is in an intermediate position. The scale could be refined further by the inclusion of items signifying finer grades of opinion with respect to war. It should be pointed out that scaling techniques need not be confined to the scaling of attitudes but, as Guttman points out, to 'any problem involving the assigning of numerical values to qualitative observations in an attempt to evolve a single rank ordering'. See Louis Guttman, 'The Basis for Scalogram Analysis', in S. A. Stouffer *et al., Studies in Social Psychology in World War II*, vol. 4 (*Measurement and Prediction*), 1950.

Scalogram analysis is a technique for determining the scalability of a particular set of items or observations. The term derives from the parallelogram pattern of responses which data constituting a 'perfect scale' assume. See S. A. Stouffer, 'An Overview of Scaling and Scale Theory', in S. A. Stouffer *et al., op. cit.* See ATTITUDE.   J.A.H.

Schäffle, Albert (1831–1903). German economist and sociologist; he was influenced by Comte and Spencer. *Bau und Leben des Sozialen Körpers*, 1875–78, argues that the structure, life and organization of social bodies is analogous to that of biological bodies; he employed biological analogies, some of them doubtful, in the belief that this alone enables systematic classifications of social relations and social functions to be carried out. He regarded societies as the ultimate and most complex equilibrium of forces in the world; thus he made an important contribution to the beginnings of analysis in terms of a system. He emphasized the holistic approach to the study of the social organism. This work also deals with social psychology, political economy and political science. His posthumously published *Outline of Sociology*, 1906, abandoned biological analogies. G.D.M.

Scheler, Max (1874–1928). German philosopher and sociologist, his thought was largely influenced by phenomenological method. His main contributions were in the fields of social psychology and ethics. Among his early work were essays, later translated into English under the titles *The Nature of Sympathy* (translated 1954), and *Ressentiment* (translated 1961). His later work was an attempt to establish a basis for objectivist values in an age given over to relativism and subjectivism. His later works are *Schriften zur Soziologie und Weltanschauungslehre*, 1923–4, and *Probleme einer Soziologie des Wissens*, 1924; a work published two years later further develops his thought: *Die Wissenformen und die Gessellschaft*. A product of the Imperial German academic world, he was deeply committed to the intellectual life, independently minded and oblivious of fashions. His value to sociologists lies in his insights into human behaviour and his willingness to tackle the fundamental philosophical problems of our age. G.D.M.

Schütz, Alfred (1899–1959). Austrian soldier and social scientist who emigrated in 1938 to France and then to the U.S.A. where he made contact with the New School for Social Research in New York, but he became a full-time business manager. In 1941 he joined the editorial board of *Philosophy and Phenomenological Research*. Only one book of his was published in his lifetime, *Der Sinnhafte Aufbau der sozialen Welt*, 1932, translated *The Phenomenology of the Social World*, 1967. However, three volumes of *Collected Papers* have appeared since 1962. His importance lay in his attempt to provide a basis for phenomenological sociology, that is, a sociology without philosophical presuppositions. His contributions to sociological thought focus on the structure and functioning of consciousness and the structure and functioning of the social world as a set of mental constructs. The question he addressed himself to was: What is the social reality with which sociologists concern themselves?' He argued that sociologists should examine commonsense beliefs and actions. Like Max Weber he was an exponent of what Howard Becker called 'interpretive sociology' and hence he was critical of positivism. He tried to apply his ideas to the realms of literary criticism, musical appreciation, politics and the sociology of knowledge. See H. E. Wagner (ed.), *Alfred Schütz on Phenomenology and Social Relations*, 1970. See PHENOMENOLOGY. G.D.M.

scientific method. See METHODOLOGY.

sect. The distinguishing features of a sect-type of religious organization have been adumbrated by Ernst Troeltsch, but were foreshadowed in the distinction made by David Hume between two kinds of 'false religion', namely those displaying superstition and those displaying enthusiasm (see his *Essays, Moral and Political*, 3rd edition, 1748). Troeltsch in his famous book *Die Soziallehren der christlischen Kirchen und Gruppen*, 1911, translated by Olive Wyon, *The Social Teaching of the Christian Churches*, 1931, contrasts the Sect-type with the Church-type. Whereas the Church-type is a conservative type of religious organization lending stability to the society, a sect is a comparatively small group aspiring to individual inward perfection, often drawing its members from the lower classes or associating itself with those elements of the lower classes opposed to both state and society.

The essential qualities of the sect are that it is a voluntary association whose members have to prove themselves qualified by some claim of personal merit such as having had a conversion experience, or having a knowledge of doctrine, or being recommended by another member or members of good standing. A sect emphasizes exclusiveness, regarding the membership as consisting of the elect or at least a gathered remnant, possessing enlightenment; its members all aim to achieve personal perfection. A sect is at best indifferent and at worst hostile to the society within which it exists. It may practise expulsion of those who do not conform to its standards and rules, and usually does excommunicate marginal members from time to time; thus emphasizing its own purity.

Troeltsch points out that sects are regarded by Churches as having fallen away from the true church, usually as a result of having exaggerated some aspect of the true religion, if not actually having falsified it by extensive qualifications. Sects, however, usually regard themselves as the exponents of the true and primitive religion which the established church or other denominations have corrupted.

It has been noted by some writers, such as H. R. Niebuhr in his book *The Social Sources of Denominationalism*, 1929, that a sect-type of organization scarcely survives the first generation, but changes into a denomination and acquires church-type characteristics. However, Bryan Wilson has argued, in an article 'An Analysis of Sect Development', *American Sociological Review*, vol. 24, no. 1, 1959, that some sects do in fact retain their sect-type qualities for a long time, and in the process of arguing his case he distinguishes a number of sub-types of sects: the *conversionist*, which seeks to alter men; the *adventist*, which seeks to change the world; the *introversionist*, which endeavours to replace worldly values by higher inner personal values; and the *gnostic*, which more or less accepts the standards of society but seeks to achieve social goals by mystical means. (See B. R. Wilson, *Sects and society: A sociological study of three religious groups in Britain*, 1961.) See DENOMINATION, SOCIOLOGY OF RELIGION.   G.D.M.

secularization. Secularization and alienation are terms regularly used by those who contribute to the sociology of religion in the West. On examination, neither is used consistently and, certainly as regards secularization, not infrequently use betrays a partial if not superficial familiarity with the nature and practice of religion itself. *Secularization* (or 'the secularization process') is the term popularly used to depict a situation in which the beliefs and sanctions of religion become – or are in process of becoming – increasingly discounted in society as guides to conduct or to decision-making.

In the literature, these trends are commonly demonstrated by reference to the statistics of Church attendance and the use of the rites of the Church. For example, many pages have been covered with detailed tables illustrating the fact that, in England, many fewer people attend Church on Sundays than was the case thirty, forty, fifty, certainly a hundred years ago. Again, complicated statistics are produced to show that fewer people are now baptised, confirmed (where this is the practice of a Church) and married under the aegis of ecclesiastical institutions. Less attention is paid to the use of religious rites for the disposal of the dead which continue to be widely used, even by those who would not claim to be 'religious'.

Straightforward statistical studies of this kind are reinforced by religious 'sociography' (cf. SOCIOLOGY OF RELIGION) and the general implication is that in advanced, urbanized and industrialized societies, ecclesiastical institutions have declined in social significance since increasingly large sections of the public are no longer associated with their practices and observances.

Before setting out the principal reasons offered for these statistical trends, it is useful to consider the relevance of the particular statistics adduced to establish them. First, it is well to be wary of equating Church attendance with religious commitment. The reason for this is that religious groups vary markedly in the emphasis placed on frequency of attendance and on the importance of their members attending particular religious rituals. It would astonish those of the Protestant tradition if their less frequent use of the sacrament of Holy Communion were assumed to be an indication of less commitment to Christianity than that of their Roman Catholic brethren, on whom weekly attendance at Mass is a matter of regular discipline. Second, it is essential to understand that figures of communicants in any denomination are only the crudest guide to its official membership. Some regularly extend an 'open invitation' to communicate at their Holy Table, irrespective of baptismal status or formal Church membership. In either case, it is perhaps not unduly cynical to remark that the validity of statistics of Church attendance depend a good deal on the manner in which they are collected and the conscientiousness of those who, in the individual places of worship, are responsible for collecting them. It has not been altogether unknown for clergy to inflate figures of attendance for political purposes.

Again, it is all too easy to assume that 'membership' of particular religious groups can be readily established by reference to the statistics of religious initiation. In the Church of England, for example, baptism alone establishes the right to vote for, and serve on, the consultative bodies of the Church yet the rite of confirmation is required to admit an individual to the sacrament of Holy Communion. Unlike the Roman Catholic Church, the Church of England has never held that baptism established denominational status with regard to the availability of sacraments.

Finally, one may well ask what indication do statistics of the use of religious rites give of their significance for those who avail themselves of them? How true is it that the traditional 'white wedding' was and is of social rather than sacramental significance for those who insist on having one? Is the continuing religious context of the burial of the dead anything more than a superstitious anxiety 'to leave no stone unturned'?

In the nature of the case, such questions are fundamentally unanswerable and indicate the need for a cautious approach to statistical evidence of religious practice not merely in contemporary society but in previous generations for whom it has been confidently and often erroneously claimed that religion was of profoundly more significance, often disregarding the fact that religious 'adherence' was often compulsory in the 'Ages of Faith'.

Fortunately, the examination of the *secularization* of society is not confined to the fascinated scrutiny of available statistics. Comte, for example, analysing the relationship between thought processes and social development argued that the extension of human knowledge freed man from the need to appeal to supernatural forces for the explanation and justification of the human predicament. 'Man come of age' was to become, during nineteenth and twentieth centuries, the proud claim of those who increasingly understood and were able to control the environment in which they lived. 'Providential' explanations of plague and pestilence gave way to their clinical treatment. The success of the application of human reason to the elucidation of issues previously thought to be beyond the comprehension of man inevitably undermined his belief in his dependence on God as the guide and adjudicator of his activity. Truly, 'the hammer of the geologist had cracked the Rock of Ages'.

The question still remains, however, as to how and why, in the nineteenth and twentieth centuries, it was acceptable to ask questions for which earlier inquirers would have been put to the stake. An intelligent appraisal of Weber's work on Protestantism leads some to argue that the more 'reasonable' approach of Protestantism itself contributed to an increasing reluctance in Europe to accept 'traditional' explanations and sanctions. More frequently, it is argued that first urbanization and then industrialization positively required for their success rational rather than Providential solutions for the problems they themselves created. Certainly religious adherence has always been more precarious in towns than villages.

A great deal more work remains to be done in this field, for much is claimed for statements, which, on examination, are more statements of opinion than of fact. And if more work is required in this field, more work is also needed to trace the reaction of religious institutions to the social environment in which they now find themselves, an environment in which it is entirely possible for a man to travel from the cradle to the grave protected from the normal vicissitudes of life by the acts of man rather than the intervention of God.

All too aware of the implications of this reality for their own credibility, religious institutions have sought to make their public 'image' more consonant with institutions which owe nothing to the concept of God. National assemblies elected by local synods and councils have gradually replaced older, authoritarian, systems of Church Government. 'Consultation' rather than 'direction' has become the key-note of decision-making of Churches looking for members familiar with the procedures of political democracy. Increasingly, a distinction is made by Church leaders themselves between the conduct to be looked for in non-believers and in members of their own communions. Churches have themselves accepted the 'secular' society as a credible alternative to a society dominated by the worship and acceptance of God. *Secularization* has gone a good deal farther than merely diminishing the numbers of those who 'belong' to the Church: it has affected the constitution and the judgments of the Church itself. See D. Martin, *A General Theory of Secularization*, 1978.   M.H.

segregation. Literally a separation of individuals or groups for social purposes.

In some cases, such separation is voluntary and preferred by all those concerned. Thus religious groups wishing to preserve their characteristic form of worship, to educate their children in the same faith and to minimize the possibility of inter-marriage, may prefer to segregate themselves for residential, educational, recreational or religious purposes and with varying degrees of strictness. Sociologically speaking, the function of such voluntary separation is to preserve cultural autonomy and to reduce the occasions for overt conflict with members of another social group. It may nevertheless give rise to covert conflict and tension. The situation in the U.S.A. is discussed by Will Herberg in *Protestant, Catholic, Jew*, 1955.

More often, segregation, in housing, schools, recreation, employment, etc., is involuntary and enforced by a dominant group upon a subordinate one, particularly where the differences are defined in racial terms. Such segregation then becomes a form of racial discrimination. In its most extreme form, as in South Africa, *apartheid* involves legally enforced segregation in almost every sphere of life with serious consequences for individual and political freedom as shown by Heribert Adams in *South Africa: Sociological Perspectives*, 1971. In other countries ethnic residential segregation may be partly voluntary and partly maintained by discriminatory practices in the real estate market. In the United States, Albert Simkus, *American Sociological Review*, vol. 32, no. 1, 1978, showed that residential segregation by occupation and race in ten urban areas diminished very little between 1960 and 1970. In Britain residential segregation of racial and immigrant minorities is also high; see R. I. Woods, *The Stochastic Analysis of Immigrant Distributions*, 1975. See COLOUR-BAR, DISCRIMINATION, PREJUDICE, RACE.

A.H.R.

self. Normally used to define an intervening variable which serves to describe and integrate the psychological characteristics of an individual. These characteristics are inferred on the basis of the individual's statements describing his own personality as he perceives it himself.

As the term is used by some social psychologists it has a meaning virtually synonymous with *self-image*. Some writers, such as G. Murphy in *Personality: a biosocial approach to origins and structure*, 1947, view the self simply as the person's conception of himself as a totality, but say nothing about the way in which this conception is achieved. Others with a more sociological orientation such as G. H. Mead in *Mind, Self and Society*, 1934, regard the self as predominantly social, and claim that the individual through implicitly taking the role of *the other* forms a conception of the self which is based upon others' responses to himself.

As the term is used by the more psychoanalytically-orientated psychologists it has acquired the connotation of an acting agent which is responsible for varying amounts of the individual's behaviour. For example H. S. Sullivan in *The Interpersonal Theory of Psychiatry*, on the one hand, reduces self to the *self system*, a set of techniques for dealing with anxiety. Alfred Adler, on the other hand, in *Theory and Practice of Individual Psychology*, 1934, has evolved a theory of the self as a highly personalized subjective system, with a characteristic life-style which the self seeks actively to enhance. See PERSONALITY, ROLE.

N.F.L.

sib. This has two distinct usages in modern anthropology. The British usage confines *sib* to an ego-centred group of cognates within a certain degree; it is thus synonymous with some meanings of *kindred*. In the terminology of some American writers, however, sib means any unilineal descent-group.

The word is from the Anglo-Saxon *sib* (German *Sippe*), and amongst the Teutons referred to a defined range of kin within the general body of an individual's kinfolk. The sib had various responsibilities towards the individual who was its focus. British writers have tended to use the word, if at all, to refer to this Teutonic grouping. American writers, however, largely following R. H. Lowie's *Primitive Society*, 1920, have often used sib to mean a unilineal descent-group, and this usage was reinforced by G. P. Murdock's *Social Structure*, 1949.

An account of the Teutonic sib can be found in B. S. Phillpotts's *Kindred and Clan*, 1913, and a summary of its main features in A. R. Radcliffe-Brown's introduction to *African Systems of Kinship and Marriage* (A. R. Radcliffe-Brown and D. Forde, eds., 1950). The American usage (not by any means universal amongst American anthropologists) can be found in Murdock, *op. cit.* See CLAN, KINSHIP, LINEAGE. J.R.F.

Simmel, Georg (1858–1918). German philosopher and sociologist; he made important contributions by his emphasis upon interaction in the field of microsociology and group dynamics, in the study of types of social process and in the conceptual analysis of society. *Philosophie des Geldes*, 1900, examines the effects of a money economy upon society and social life, and of the relationship between rationality of science and capitalism. Sociology should study the forms rather than the content of social life and discover social laws of society; the latter comprise reciprocal relations between individuals. *Soziologie*, 1908, examines the nature of reciprocal relations, dyads, tryads, the role of the stranger, modern city life, personality, subordination and authority, and 'the endless variety of the forms of social life'. G.D.M.

situs. A term used to denote a differentiation in Society not obviously evaluated in terms of superiority or inferiority. Distinctions of sex, clan membership and occupations of equal esteem are examples. See E. Benoit-Smullyan article, *American Sociological Review*, 1944.

Small, Albion Woodbury (1854–1926). American sociologist; he founded the *American Journal of Sociology*; he was not a very original thinker but he did much to advance sociology in America. *Introduction to the Study of Society*, 1894, his first introductory textbook, proposed social structure and function as a subject for sociology. *General Sociology*, 1905, presents a theory of social interests and their conflicts; interests pervade individual and group life and fall into categories of health, wealth, sociability, knowledge, beauty and rightness. Society is viewed as the product of countless attempts by individuals to resolve and satisfy interests. In the process of association the primary pattern is conflict of interests; but conflict resolved into co-operation among individuals by socialization. Other works include *The Meaning of the Social Sciences*, 1910, and *Origins of Sociology*, 1924. G.D.M.

Smith, Adam (1723–1790). Scottish political economist whose famous book *On the Nature and Causes of the Wealth of Nations*, 1776, contains not only a significant discussion of the division of labour in society but also a sociology of economic development and the growth of towns and cities. *The Theory of Moral Sentiments*, 1759, is a moral philosophy encapsulating an embryonic social psychology.

social administration. The term *social administration* refers either to the work of those who administer the social services or to the discipline of study concerned with the analysis of social policy, its implementation through social action and its effectiveness in dealing with social problems. As an academic study it was established in Britain early in the twentieth century as an essential subject in the first training courses for social workers. At that stage it was confined essentially to knowledge of social legislation such as the Poor Law and to an understanding of the ways in which the social services could be used to help persons living in poverty.

The development of more extensive social policies, the growth of elaborate social service organizations with intricate administrative systems, and the rapid increase in the body of knowledge about social conditions and human needs widened considerably the scope of the subject. Whilst the basis of its subject matter is still the study of the social services they must be examined within the social, economic and political systems of the society in which they exist. Hence use is made of the knowledge and methods of the social sciences to identify and measure social and individual needs, but the main concern of Social Administration is the analysis of social policy within a society and on a comparative basis between societies, the organizational and administrative processes involved in translating policy into action and its effectiveness in meeting individual and social needs.

It is of course an essential subject of study for those who intend to enter the profession of social work, but it is no longer purely vocational in its aims. It has developed into a systematic discipline designed to add to the growth of knowledge about particular aspects of societies. See R. M. Titmuss, *Essays on the Welfare State*, 1958, 3rd edition 1976; David C. Marsh (ed.), *An introduction to the study of Social Administration*, 1965, also journals such as *Social and Economic Administration*, 1967, et seq. (now *Social Policy and Administration*).   D.C.M.

social anthropology. Social anthropology is a discipline whose relations with sociology have always been close. The fact that it has always included the study of non-Western societies gives it a special academic emphasis. The extent to which this emphasis has been accompanied by findings of explicit general relevance to all societies, including our own, has varied from time to time. At present, the subject is in one of its relatively universalistic conditions, and frequently overlaps the interests of sociologists.

In the nineteenth century the scope of general anthropology was particularly broad: the 'study of man', as a physical and social being, from a generally historical perspective. Its theoretical development was linked closely to the evolutionary assumptions of palaeontology. The modern 'primitive' societies formed, in that context, evidence for the supposed social organization of early man. Within general anthropology, social anthropology served to give social flesh to the arid archaeological record. L. Morgan, Sir E. B. Tylor, Sir J. G. Frazer and other anthropologists of the early period broke out of this mould. Social and physical anthropology began their effectual separation. Later the collection of data among living populations inevitably raised questions as to the adequacy of the historical preoccupations of the 'armchair' theorists.

The years from 1900 to 1920 were critical in the transition to the modern subject of social anthropology. In Britain B. Malinowski (Polish-born) and A. R. Radcliffe-Brown received their training; in the United States F. Boas and his students were making their mark. The new subject saw itself as studying other societies empirically, by first-hand contact, and for their own sakes; not, that is, as an exercise in historical reconstruction. The French school of sociology associated with É. Durkheim was influential in providing some theoretical backing for this approach. Malinowski, looking back on the period of change, attributed a particular importance to the year 1910 and soon after. It is interesting to see that he lists as important events: ethnographical surveys by C. G. and B. Z. Seligman, R. Thurnwald, E. Westermarck, Sir B. Spencer, and W. H. R. Rivers, together with works on religion and ritual by É. Durkheim, A. Van Gennap and L. Lévy-Bruhl. Radcliffe-Brown's work on the Andaman Islands and Malinowski's own early research fell into the same period, followed by the latter's prolonged fieldwork in the Trobriand Islands during the First World War. For American anthropology F. Boas, A. L. Kroeber and others had already made important contributions.

The subsequent rapid establishment of modern social anthropology between 1920 and 1940 now appears remarkable. By the end of the period the majority of British social anthropologists had been trained by Malinowski, or were associated with Radcliffe-Brown. For British social anthropology a style was set which has always given it a slightly different flavour from the 'cultural anthropology' of the United States. Malinowski explicitly used the label *functionalist* for his own theoretical approach, which he even called a 'school'. Radcliffe-Brown's ideas, although similar, were differently expounded. The *functionalist* problem was to justify the study of 'primitive' societies once historical reconstructions had been rejected. Explanation consisted in the demonstration that all parts of a society interlocked. Malinowski generally termed the parts *institutions*, and saw each of these as rooted in basic *bodily needs*. For Radcliffe-Brown the *organic* was located elsewhere; as an analogy for the nature of the social whole itself, which was stated to resemble an organism. The key term, for him, was more often *structure* than *function*, and he came to favour a taxonomic view of the anthropological task: to compare and classify such 'structures'.

This *high functionalism* of the inter-War years raised many problems. It is now clear that it defined itself theoretically less by what it positively was, and more by what it rejected: badly founded historical speculation (evolutionist, diffusionist), premature sweeping worldwide comparisons, and the ranking of societies as inferior or superior. Its positive statements rested upon a new, sounder ethnographic practice, and the assertion of a universal standard for judging the rationality of social systems. The stress on observation, however, combined with the justified rejection of speculative analyses, tended

176

occasionally to diminish attention to more intellectual and symbolic aspects of society. An outstanding corrective to this tendency was Evans-Pritchard's study of Azande witchcraft.

Malinowski died in 1942, and Radcliffe-Brown retired soon after the War. There followed a 20-year period of apparent consensus for which the term *structural-functionalism* is commonly used. Malinowski's theory of needs was tacitly abandoned. His emphasis on fieldwork was retained, while there was a continuation and development of the interest in formal aspects of social organization once more associated with Radcliffe-Brown. The linguistic and psychological interests of Malinowski found new successors. The period was marked by a rapid growth in the numbers of professional social anthropologists, and the establishment in Britain of an *Association of Social Anthropologists* in 1946, alongside the older *Royal Anthropological Institute*. Research funds from Colonial Development and Welfare sources were relatively plentiful and British studies reflected this by certain common pragmatic emphases of the time: *jural* − land tenure, inheritance; *juridical* − court systems, dispute solving; *political* − traditional systems of authority and power. These emphases also coloured the dominant approaches to kinship, later grouped as *descent theory*. The view of descent systems as describing corporate groups with jural, juridical and political functions, was embodied characteristically in studies of African lineage systems. The 'structural' aspect of structural-functionalism was largely typified by this particular vision of traditional societies. It is noteworthy that the economic study of such societies was frequently treated separately as *economic anthropology*. The contributions to this subfield were substantial, and the economic studies were influenced by the prevailing 'structural' views of society. Nevertheless, many analyses of the period could and did dispense with detailed economic analysis.

The location of the main *structural-functionalist* consensus in these areas of social anthropology is highlighted by the rather muted controversies of the period. These throw light on deviations from the consensus. There was, for example, Sir E. E. Evans-Pritchard's insistence on the restoration of an historical dimension to social anthropology, and his classification of the subject as a humanity rather than a science. His work and that of his students, in the field of religion, although not controversially presented, was not uncommonly perceived as slightly idiosyncratic. Sir Edmund Leach's attacks on descent theory, and his demonstration of its inadequacy as a general theory of kinship systems, led him to differ with both Fortes and Gluckman. In economic anthropology the main debates were on the nature of 'primitive economics' − whether they were *sui generis* or part of general economics. Largely missing from the structural-functional period was a concern with large questions, such as the philosophical implications of the treatment of humanity as a scientific 'other'.

American *cultural anthropology* during the same period was distinguished from *social anthropology* mainly by a different scope and history. Its field practice was not greatly different, but it retained its links with history, archaeology, art, and linguistics, in part because of the academic organization of Amerindian studies, its original main base. The thirties saw also the influence of psychology through the 'patterns of culture' school associated with Margaret Mead, Ruth Benedict and others. The studies of national character and of 'basic personality' of the wartime and post-War years led to a spate of interest, which soon declined. G. Bateson, a theoretician associated with the group, prefigured in his *Naven*, 1936, several modern interests in social anthropology. During the post-War years there was a consensus parallel to that in British social anthropology, with a characteristic stress in the American case on *componential analysis* and *ethnoscientific* studies. The formal methods dealt with areas of cultural terminology (kinship, colours, medical terms, and the like). This work had important influence on later studies of cognitive categories in social anthropology.

By the 1960s, internal criticism of both British and American traditions had begun to converge. It was then caught up with the increasing vogue for the *structuralism* of C. Lévi-Strauss, a movement which made innovation fashionable. It is of interest that the term *structure* as used by Lévi-Strauss did not derive directly from its use by Radcliffe-Brown and others but from a conscious analogy with structural linguistics (*Anth. Str.*, 1958). Although the early work of Lévi-Strauss dated from the 1940s and many of the critics of the consensus period had already been influenced by him (Leach, 1961), the 'structuralist' influence rose to its height mainly by 1970. The nature of *structuralism* as a theoretical phenomenon has been variously described. There is no doubt that most of the liveliest critics of social anthropology were for a time involved with or reacting to the new movement. At its simplest, structuralism provided a mode of analysis of the symbolic aspects of society (mainly myth, but also totemic and other systems of classification). At its most complex it made statements about the universality of modes of structuring thought. Among these, the principle of binary opposition was the most commonly resorted to, but various other analogies from linguistic usage were proposed. When the innovating wave had died down by about 1975, social anthropology had taken on a more universalistic appearance. Its claims as an academic discipline had been much widened. Philosophical and linguistic problems had become a central part of the subject. The methodological aspects were relatively disappointing, and a strong reaction against structuralism became apparent. In the same period marxist influence also came to the fore, mainly in association with French anthropologists (Godelier, Meillassoux, Terray), and some form of 'structural-marxism' became accepted in some quarters as the solution to the various difficulties of both structural-functionalism and structuralism. Nevertheless, the practice of fieldwork, and the empirical concomitants of the newer outlook, cannot yet be said to have been radically changed. For a time *transactionalism*, an approach associated with the name of Frederik Barth, appeared to advocate a new kind of approach to human behaviour. See G. Lienhardt, *Social Anthropology*, 1964; Lucy Mair, *An Introduction to Social Anthropology*, 2nd edition 1972; Paul Bohannan, *Social Anthropology*, 1963; R. M. Keesing, *Cultural Anthropology*, 1976. See ANTHROPOLOGY.   E.W.A.

social behaviourism. See ACTION.

social change. This is at once the most difficult and most fascinating problem in sociology. Modern sociology began with attempts by Auguste Comte and other nineteenth-century writers to explain the causes and the course of social change which was dramatically expressed in the French political and the English industrial revolutions. Nineteenth-century sociology was dominated by the search for a theory of social change, or social dynamics, which would reveal the 'laws of motion' of societies. The rise of capitalist society and the social upheavals which accompanied it, including urban growth, industrialism and mobility of men and ideas, imparted a powerful stimulus to the sociological analysis of change.

Most of the resulting theories had an evolutionary character. The most influential of them was put forward by Karl Marx. Marx's theory of history held that the 'mode of production', i.e. the technology of production and the social relations of production generated by it, was the fundamental element in society, the 'substructure', on which all other institutions, political, religious and familial, are 'superstructure'. As technology advances so opportunities arise for the use of new modes of production and therefore for new classes to wrest economic and political power from existing ruling classes. Thus according to Marx 'the history of all hitherto existing societies is the history of class struggle'. Another great nineteenth-century sociologist, Herbert Spencer, saw the evolution of society from small-scale simplicity of structure and function to large-scale and powerful differentiation. He gave sociology in general, and the study of social change in particular, much of its terminology and he advanced his theory of super-organic evolution before Darwin's *Origin of Species* appeared in 1859. The American social anthropologist Lewis Morgan (*Ancient Society*, 1877) also produced a developmental theory of cultural evolution through three 'ethnical periods' – savagery, barbarism and civilization.

Marx's theory was the point of departure for Max Weber's work on social change – the genesis of capitalism. Weber's theory was that the development of the Western bourgeoisie was necessarily preceded by Calvinism and other puritan religious movements as creators of indispensable psychological-conditions. He accepted the Marxist theory of an emerging bourgeoisie seizing favourable opportunities for capital accumulation, the creation of a propertyless proletariat and the exploitation of a new technology permitting factory production. But he held that these 'material' conditions though necessary were not sufficient. They existed elsewhere whereas Calvinism or its equivalent social counterpart did not. Weber's method was to use history as a kind of natural laboratory for testing a hypothesis. In *The Protestant Ethic and the Spirit of Capitalism*, originally published in 1904 and translated in 1930, he showed the affinity between the ethic of Protestantism and the capitalistic organization of economic enterprise. Then, in his comparative study of the world religions, he sought to establish the non-existence of indigenous capitalism without the ascetic spirit of Protestantism.

In the early twentieth century attempts at large-scale theorizing about social change fell out of favour in sociology and efforts were concentrated more on the detailed study of particular societies, communities and institutions using increasingly exact methods of observation, survey and measurement. More recently the older and still valid problems of economic growth and social development have been tackled afresh, stimulated by the spread of industrialism into the 'underdeveloped' world. There is now no one theory of social change but a complex debate betwen Marxist, Marxisante, and liberal or pluralist theories. Though sociologists now agree, from a variety of ideological standpoints, that change is the normal condition of society everywhere, the fundamental dispute between materialist and idealist theories remains. Two influential books on theories of social change are A. Gouldner, *The Coming Crisis of Western Sociology*, 1971, and D. Bell, *The Coming of Post-Industrial Society*, 1973.   A.H.H.

social class. See SOCIAL STRATIFICATION.

social cohesion. *Social cohesion* (or cohesiveness) has no generally agreed-upon meaning, and is often used informally, usually in reference to situations in which individuals are bound to one another by common social and cultural commitments.

Cohesiveness is most frequently employed as a property of small groups; involving, firstly, the attractions which a group has for its members, and, secondly, the forces which induce individuals to remain group members. The uses of *cohesion* and *cohesiveness* in small group analysis are surveyed in Dorwin Cartwright and Alvin Zander (eds.), *Group Dynamics*, 1960, ch. 3.

A less restricted use of *social cohesion* derives from the work of Émile Durkheim in his books *De la division du travail social*, 1893, (translated *The Division of Labour*, 1933) and *Le Suicide*, 1897 (translated *Suicide*, 1951). For Durkheim the degree of social cohesion was a property of groups, organizations and societies, one which affected a wide variety of behaviour, such as the committing of suicide. Some sociologists thus invoke the term in reference to large and small groups manifesting three main characteristics: individual commitments to common norms and values; interdependence arising from shared interest; and individual identification with the group.

A persuasive redefinition is advanced by Amitai Etzioni. He defines *cohesion* as 'a positive expressive relationship between two or more actors' (*A Comparative Analysis of Complex Organisations*, 1961, ch. 8). This deliberately avoids the term group, since cohesion *itself* is often taken as a defining characteristic of groups. It also does not imply shared values or goals, but only common norms specifying the conditions of the relationships in question.   R.R.

social contract. In the history of political philosophy the expression *social contract* has occurred repeatedly. Johannes Althusius in his *Politica Methodice Digesta*, 1603, argued that society was to be explained in terms of a basic social contract amongst citizens for society, or sociability, he said, is natural to mankind. Hence to speak of *contract* is merely to use a quasi-legal expression to describe what is really fundamental to human nature. In this sense he spoke of the relations of man to man. However, Althusius also described the relations between government and people as a contract, from which it may be incidentally concluded that there is no single sovereign but that government is delegated by the sovereign people. Richard Hooker, in his *Laws of Ecclesiastical Polity*, 1594, arguing that man is naturally sociable, did not see the necessity for a social contract theory for this was to introduce an artificial element. In this respect he differed from Thomas Hobbes, whose theory of the natural rights of man led him to postulate a social contract, for, he said, originally men gave up their natural rights, freely handing them over to a sovereign; this they had done absolutely, without limit and irrevocably. He argued that if men pursued their natural rights they would destroy each other and that the firm hand of the sovereign was a pre-requisite for peace and prosperity. Hobbes thus combined the two social contracts of Althusius. This line of thought was taken up critically by a number of European writers, most famous of them being John Locke who, in his essay *On Civil Government*, 1690, discussed the nature of the social contract in relation to property. Some years earlier a German scholar, Samuel Pufendorf, in his *De Jure Naturae et Gentium*, 1672, expounded the theory of natural law and in the process developed ideas about property and social contract, but it was Locke to whom the credit goes for the natural right theory of property which laid the basis for the 1688 Revolution and the beginning of modern political thought. The essence of Locke's theory of property is that man has a right to that part of nature with which he has mixed his labour, provided there is an abundance of that which is natural. But, as he put it, 'no man's labour could subdue or appropriate all, nor could this enjoyment consume more than a small part; so that it was impossible for any man, this way, to entrench upon the right of another or acquire to himself a property to the prejudice of his neighbour, who would still have room for as good and as large a possession (after the other had taken out his) as before it was appropriated' (*Of Property*, Bk. II, ch. V). If modern property rights were created by men, they are valid only because there is a general agreement to respect such rights and this is in the nature of the social contract.

The general ideas of social contract, as they were formulated in the sixteenth and seventeenth centuries, came under criticism in the eighteenth century in the writings of David Hume, who countered Locke's teaching by asserting that government wherever it was found owed its origin not to contract but to conquest and usurpation. But he hastened to add that government survived because of the 'common sentiment' of the people, for people will acquiesce in government provided it is not too tyrannical; the common sentiment, however, is not the same as a social contract. (See his *Inquiry concerning Human Understanding*, 1748, and his *Inquiry concerning Principles of Morals*, 1751.) Social contract theory received a great fillip as a result of the success of J. J. Rousseau's *Le contrat social*, 1762, in which he argued that men as a result of their compact in giving up their natural liberty gain a civil and moral liberty. Sovereignty resides in the community for there is in every man's will an element which stands for the good of the whole. These elements constitute the general will and it is this which is sovereign in a free society permitting the pursuit of those inalienable rights of man – life, liberty and the pursuit of happiness; ideas which, through their influence on Thomas Jefferson, have helped to shape the American nation.

Nineteenth-century individualistic philosophy, especially as displayed in the writings of Herbert Spencer, tended to rest on a belief in the desirability of freedom for men to enter into relationships to their mutual benefit. Government was desirable only in so far as it enforced legal contracts freely entered into. Jurists like Sir Henry Maine argued that social progress represented a movement from societies where *status* was prominent to ones where *contract* was prominent, but the contract they speak of is *legal contract*. It was Durkheim who pointed to the non-contractual elements in contracts, and showed that prior to the establishment of such contractual arrangements there is a set of common values, itself the basis of social order and stability. (See his *Division of Labour*, 1893.)

It is thus necessary to distinguish between *social* and *legal contract*, but it is also possible to see in the works of both Spencer and Durkheim on the one hand, and the earlier political philosophers on the other hand, a common problem – the problem of how the social order is maintained.   G.D.M.

social control. The term *social control* broadly indicates an aspect of sociological discussion concerned with the maintenance of order and stability. It may be used in the narrower sense of denoting the various specialized means employed to maintain order, such as 'Codes, Courts and Constables', or it may be used to categorize discussion of social institutions and their interrelations in so far as they contribute specifically to social stability, e.g. legal, religious and political institutions. Social control is one of the fundamental subjects of sociological discussion and arises in all arguments about the nature and causes of both stability and change. Among social anthropologists the discussion has centred of late around a comparison of simple societies, some of which display formal means of social control, whilst others betray an almost complete absence of them. See E. E. Evans-Pritchard and M. Fortes, eds, *African Political Systems*, 1940. A general discussion of social control may be found in T. B. Bottomore's *Sociology: A Guide to Problems and Literature*, 1972, Part IV.   G.D.M.

social Darwinism. This expression came into use in the early years of the twentieth century to designate doctrines claiming to apply to society the principles established in Charles Darwin's work, *On the Origin of Species by Means of Natural Selection; or, The Preservation of Favoured Races in the Struggle for Life*, of 1859. The key element is that of variations transmitted by heredity which are subject to processes of selection. For Darwin, fitness was a question of leaving more offspring to transmit particular qualities. In social Darwinism the process was seen as *the survival of the fittest* but it was often based on a circular argument: the fittest were those who survived; how did one know they were the fittest? Because they had survived! There was much evidence to suggest that selection operated on humans but it was more difficult to determine the social unit corresponding to the Darwinian species. The first response was to conceive of individuals competing with one another (intra-social selection); this was for a time reflected in writings by T. H. Huxley, Herbert Spencer and Benjamin Kidd. Another view was that societies struggle with one another for survival (inter-social selection); this was exemplified first by Walter Bagehot in *Physics and Politics*, 1873, by Ludwig Gumplowicz in *Der Rassenkampf* and by the anthrop-sociological school of O. Ammon and G. V. de Lapouge. Social Darwinism reinforced the element of ruthlessness in the imperialism of the period before World War I; it was used to justify selective immigration quotas in the U.S.A. after that war; and it reappeared in Sir Arthur Keith's argument of 1931 that prejudice serves an evolutionary function in separating inter-breeding populations.

More recently scholars have begun to doubt whether social Darwinism constituted a coherent school of thought. Some sociologists, like William Graham Sumner, wrote along social Darwinist lines at one period of their careers and not at others. In the early years of the twentieth century the only groups exemplifying a distinctly social Darwinism approach were those forming the Eugenics movement. However, if social Darwinism is to be identified by a style of argument it is relevant to note the presence of that style in the works of some contemporary popular ethologists like Konrad Lorenz and Robert Ardrey. See R. J. Halliday, 'Social Darwinism: A Definition', *Victorian Studies*, 1971, 14, 389–405. M.P.B.

social distance. One of the early studies in measuring prejudiced attitudes was by E. S. Bogardus and it was he who made use of the concept of *social distance*, i.e. attitudes of like or dislike towards other groups on the part of an individual. Bogardus asked a series of questions of his 1,725 American informants about forty different nationalities. Each question represents a category of 'distance'. Thus informants were asked if they would admit a person of a given nationality to close kinship by marriage, or to membership of a club, or as a street neighbour, or give him employment in the same kind of occupation, etc. His social distance scale produced remarkably consistent results in America, both geographically and over a period of time. One curious feature of the American scene is the lowly place the Turks occupy in the American view, but it would seem that at that time there was a general distaste for foreigners. See ATTITUDE, STEREOTYPE. G.D.M.

social ecology. See ECOLOGY.

social engineering. It has been supposed by some sociologists that the study of the social sciences can be made the basis of *applied* as well as theoretical work. The implication of this is that a technology can be developed, for the purpose of improving human societies, by combining value-judgments as to desirable kinds of social life with sociological theories concerning patterns of social organization and trends of social development. The American sociologist, L. F. Ward, for instance, thought that a *social telesis* could be formulated which would make it possible to develop a means of promoting the common weal by harnessing the energies of sociologists and others to the administrative agencies of governments particularly those concerned with planning.

It is, of course, a moot point whether or not it is possible to arrive at an understanding of the course of the events which occur in any society in the abstract, without attempting to deal with the problem of why they take place, in terms of the aspirations of individuals and the objectives which men attempt to attain by common action in groups, parties and associations. Human beings lead lives that are shaped at least as much by reason and obligation as by social influence, and unless this is taken into account, the study of human society becomes highly unreal. Furthermore, it is an artificial process to study the growth of values otherwise than in the context of the life of an actual society or societies. It is arguable, therefore, that the fundamental nature of social processes makes it impossible to establish a technology that can be separated from social philosophy on the one hand and sociology on the other.   s. of t.

social evolution. See EVOLUTION.

social history. In Britain, *social history* long ago ceased to be a description of manners and customs, although traces still survive as, for example, in a war-time best seller's reference to 'the history of people with the politics left out'. It has not become the history of men and women in their social relationships and groupings. As such, the subject derived from the economic historians' desire to seek explanations of the causes and consequences of economic change in fields outside their own province. For a time, it seemed likely that economic and social history would develop a division of labour in their related interests and yet retain their early unity of outlook. That hope has been falsified in recent years as the economic historians who work in the modern period have become 'fishermen for quantitative data with nets manufactured by economists'.

After a somewhat faltering start in the 1950s, *social history* has in recent years won a place in British universities as a subject respectable and respected in its own right. Moreover, sociologists who earlier dismissed *social history* as an unnecessary distraction from their 'real' work of studying contemporary society, now accept the fact not merely that sociology cannot be restricted to the study of the present but that it is impossible to comprehend the present in isolation from the past.   M.H.

social mobility. In modern industrial societies there is a hierarchical arrangement of statuses in which advantages in wealth, power and esteem increase as the hierarchy is ascended. Unlike the situation in caste, estate, and earlier class systems, movement from status to status can be achieved by means which are in the control of the person.

The social system can be presented as a process in which adaptation to social and economic change takes place by changes in the rewards offered to different occupations. These rewards attract persons from less valued positions to more valued positions. The process takes place symbolically through changes in the reputation of occupations, and the classic study by D. V. Glass, *Social Mobility in Britain*, 1954, used the Social Grading of Occupations by J. Hall and D. Caradog Jones as the basis of its analysis. This approach has been followed in the *Oxford Studies in Social Mobility* using *The Social Grading of Occupations* by John A. Goldthorpe and Keith Hope. In that the esteem in which occupations are held is associated with the name of the occupation, this revaluation is often accompanied by a change of designation.

Many occupations require a certain standard of education for entry or for the performance of the work and role; in such cases, mobility can only take place between generations. This had led to many investigations into the processes of social selection in higher secondary education, as determinants of social mobility.

Within broad occupation groups there are rankings which correspond to the extent of power and responsibility and are differentially rewarded.

184

Positions are achieved by competition, modified by patronage and nepotism. In bureaucratic organizations the rules governing mobility tend to be well defined, and age is in many cases an important factor. Many bureaucracies have no provision for downward mobility.

Robert K. Merton in *Social Theory and Social Structure*, 1957, has drawn attention to the existence of structural barriers to social mobility, an issue of considerable importance where status can be influenced by religion, colour or ethnic origin. See BUREAUCRACY, SOCIAL STRATIFICATION.   D.C.

social order. See SOCIAL COHESION.

social organization. This term means the interdependence of parts, which is an essential characteristic of all enduring collective entities: groups, communities, and societies. These interdependent parts are given different names by different sociologists. Usually they consist of some or all of the following: tasks and other activities; relationships among roles; values, norms, and beliefs; subgroups within a larger unit; and (in societies) institutions.

The term also has two minor uses: (a) to refer to the particular kind of organization under study (e.g. the social organization of a factory), and (b) casually, as a synonym for social structure or a related term.

The word *organization* by itself refers to a type of group, usually a bureaucracy.

Early sociologists and social philosophers used the term with reference to societies; later usage applies it to groups of all sizes. Auguste Comte defined social organization as 'general social agreement', and argued, with polemical intent, that government is powerless without its support. '... the principle which lies at the heart of every scheme of social organization [is] the necessary participation of the collective political *régime* in the universal consensus of the social body.' (See *The Positive Philosophy of Auguste Comte*, trans. 1893, 3rd edition, p. 65.) Herbert Spencer, in *The Principles of Sociology*, vol. I, 1882, used *social organization* to refer to the interrelations (integration and differentiation) of the economic, political and other divisions of society. Émile Durkheim, in *Le Suicide*, 1897 (translated *Suicide*, 1951), used the term to refer almost exclusively to social integration and individual regulation through consensus about morals and values. Charles H. Cooley, in *Social Organization*, 1909, pioneered the later interest in the social organization of primary groups with his view of social organization as the 'differentiated unity of mental or social life'. According to Cooley's analysis, mind and one's conception of self are shaped through social interaction, and social organization is nothing more than the shared activities and understanding which social interaction requires.

Currently, *social organization* is used to refer to the interdependence of parts in groups of all sizes, from cliques of workers, to hospitals and factories, to societies. Talcott Parsons, in 'General Theory in Sociology' (in *Sociology Today*, edited by Robert K. Merton *et al.*, 1959), starts with the idea that 'all social systems are organized in the sense that they are structurally differentiated ...' George C. Homans, in *The Human Group*, 1950, refers in passing to social organization but prefers the phrase *social system*; the interrelated parts of social systems are activities, interaction, and sentiment, and he proposes a series of hypotheses about how they are related. Leonard Broom and Philip Selznick, in *Sociology: A Text with Adapted Readings*, 3rd edition, 1963, devote an entire chapter to the subject. They define *social organization* as 'the patterened relations of individuals and groups' and identify it as one of the two basic sources of order in social life, the other being norms and values. They discuss social organization on three levels of analysis: in interpersonal relations, in associations and communities, and in societies. The subject is further dealt with in a general way in their chapters on primary groups, associations, the family, religion, education, minorities, and crime and delinquency.

Today, few sociologists study social organization in a comprehensive way. Those who do often use the other terms; thus Parsons and Homans prefer to speak of *social systems*. The term is so broad as to be synonymous with much of the subject matter of sociology, and research has moved on to detailed study of aspects of social organization. For example, we have studies of why certain technical innovations were adopted in the British textile industry, the degree of unity in the power structure of certain American communities, how new members of California cults are recruited, or the effects of the extended family on occupational mobility in Kentucky. However, the necessity for social organization if any group is to survive and be effective is so universally recognized in sociology that reference to it, implicit or explicit, is to be found in almost all sociological research and all sociological theory. See BUREAUCRACY, COMMUNITY, SOCIAL STRUCTURE, SOCIAL SYSTEM.   D.A.S.

social pathology. Pathology is the study of the basis of disordered function. Medically this means it is the study of the processes and causes of disease, and just as it is difficult sometimes to say precisely what disease is and correspondingly difficult to say what health is, so the sociologist who borrows this term and refers to *social pathology* experiences the difficulty of knowing what the normal and desirable state of social life is, deviations from which may be described as pathological. Most people would agree that crime and delinquency, alcoholism and drug-addiction, vagrancy and illegitimacy are pathological aspects of modern social life, but it may be recalled that E. M. Lemert's book on *Social Pathology*, 1951, included a chapter on 'Radicalism and Radicals' and that in some European countries the behaviour of conscientious objectors would be considered suitable for inclusion under this rubric. In any case it is a term borrowed from the biological sciences, like many others in the sociologist's vocabulary, and it presupposes for its use a functionalist outlook. Usually, the expression is used very loosely to mean deviant behaviour, it is unusual for it to bear much weight of meaning. When functionalists wish to indicate pathological aspects of human society they usually speak of *dysfunctions*. See DEVIANCE; SOCIAL DEVIANCE, and FUNCTION.
                                                                                    G.D.M.

social philosophy. This branch of philosophy is closely related to sociology on the one hand and ethics on the other. It has often been difficult to distinguish clearly between them.

There are essentially two aspects: firstly, there is a philosophy of the social

186

sciences in the same sense that there is a philosophy or methodology of the natural sciences, that is a rigorous examination of the concepts and procedures used in sociology. A detailed philosophical scrutiny is possibly more applicable to sociology than the natural sciences, because of the serious disagreements which exist on both methodological and substantive questions, and a general lack of terminological exactitude. An up-to-date treatment of the methodological problems of the social sciences can be found in E. Nagel, *The Structure of Science*, 1961.

Secondly, whereas sociology is concerned with the study of values as facts, social philosophy is concerned with the discussion of values, that is, with the interpretation and estimation of social phenomena in terms of ethical principles. A good example of such social philosophy is provided by S. I. Benn and R. S. Peters in *Social Principles and the Democratic State*, 1959, which sets out to argue from philosophical presuppositions to the recommendation of a modified utilitarianism. See also M. Ginsberg, *Essays in Sociology and Social Philosophy* (3 vols.), 1956, 1961.   A.H.

social policy. The term *social policy* is not used technically, but rather merely describes the policies of governments in respect to a range of social services. Thus matters pertaining to health, education, housing, social insurance and national assistance are to be included under this description.

The social sciences have, of course, in Britain for long been oriented to discussion of such policies, although in the U.S.A. they have been conceived usually in very broad and general terms as related to social policy. Thus in 1951 two American social scientists, D. Lerner and H. D. Lasswell, edited a review of the social sciences in relation to broad matters of public and social policy entitled *The Policy Sciences: Recent Developments in Scope and Method*. This work aimed to stress the importance of the social sciences for clarifying the assumptions behind social thought, to disentangling values from facts and for arriving at suitable methods for thinking about issues and testing ideas: above all for converting general principles into specific indices of action.

In Britain there has been a development of thought in recent decades about specific aspects of the Welfare State. Attempts have been made to determine trends in social thought, to examine the implications of present policies for future policy-making, and to discern the wider issues involved in pursuing given policies and their effects upon social thought. The notion of poverty and the view of pauperism has clearly altered since the Poor Law Amendment Act of 1834 as the institutional structure of Britain has altered, and it is in tracing these changes in social institutions and in social thought that we may see the development of a specialized academic tradition. A concise and clear contribution to this field may be found in T. H. Marshall's *Social Policy*, 1965, where it is suggested that the task of social policy is to determine the order of priority of claims against the national product. See also journals like *Social Policy, Social and Economic Administration*, 1967 *et seq.*, now *Social Policy and Administration*. See SOCIAL ADMINISTRATION.   G.D.M.

social position. The term *social position* is in many cases synonymous with terms like *social status* or *social role*, but this is because there is a general lack of precision in the use of these terms in sociological literature. A. R. Radcliffe-Brown preferred to speak of *social position* because he wanted to emphasize the point in a social structure occupied by a person. Thus in a structure of kin relationships there are the positions of father, mother, son and daughter, and by virtue of these positions and the norms associated with them the occupants behave in more or less determinate ways. Radcliffe-Brown distinguished *social position* from *social role* by arguing that a social structure is rather different from a social organization and that in the latter, such as a school, there are elements which are similar to social positions, e.g. headmaster, assistant masters, pupils, etc., but whose behaviour is more properly regarded as an arrangement of activities, and for these elements the appropriate term to use in describing them is *role*, for they together constitute a system of roles. This is to make a distinction between an institutionalized structure and an organization; other structures, for example, are those involving husbands and wives, professional men and their clients, kings and their subjects. It has to be admitted, however, that this kind of precision is frequently lacking in general sociological works, and Radcliffe-Brown's usage has but a limited acceptance. See his *Structure and Function in Primitive Society*, 1952. See ROLE, SOCIAL STRUCTURE.   G.D.M.

social psychology. The study of individuals in interaction and in relation to their social environment.

The family provides the earliest environment, and so *family-relationships* are one field of study in social psychology. *Socialization* covers child-rearing techniques such as feeding, toilet-training and the management of emotions, as well as the acquisition of language, and co-operation and conflict. Each of these areas forms also a separate field of study, developmentally in terms of preparation for adult life, and in the circumstances of adult behaviour, and conceptually. Linguistics is currently coming into prominence. The study of socialization leads to comparative work in *culture and personality*, of preliterate societies, of other historical epochs, of contemporary literate cultures, and as between social classes.

Socialization fits the child for the *roles* of adult life: expected ways of behaving in frequently recurring situations, in family-life, occupational life, community and associational life. The concept of role is fundamental to analysis in social-psychological terms, because it defines the individual's behaviour in terms of the social environment which is currently relevant to the problem in question. *Small-group theory* and the *theory of large complex organizations* single out those social environments which have formal boundaries and formally-defined role-structures. Multiple-group-membership and rapid changes in society have encouraged the study of role-conflicts. An important concept here is that of the reference-group, by which others regulate their behaviour.

Roles are governed by norms defining proper behaviour. Hence an interest in social pressures to conform – in perception, and in various kinds of performance. An important applied field is industrial social psychology. The experimentally-created small group provides a major methodological tool for the study of social pressures.

Socialization and later social pressures create similar configurations of attitudes in various sets of people. The concept of *attitude* is a difficult one to handle in terms of individual psychology, and attitudes are best thought of in terms of regular and general responses to questionnaires and interviews. The methodology of *attitude-research* provides a highly refined and intellectually stimulating discipline, but on the whole the results of attitude-surveys have not yet contributed much to the detailed understanding of social behaviour, or to the development of social or psychological theory. The studies indicate the distribution of responses to questions about social concerns like minority-groups, other social classes, other nationalities, proposed legislative actions, and so on, or they predict behaviour and preferences in the near future in such matters as voting or the demand for consumer-goods. This field of study as yet appertains only marginally to social psychology, because the focus of interest has been mainly on the percentage-distribution of simple responses in large populations. More work is needed on the relation between traits in the individuals who compose the populations, and on the social relationships of the individual, which are likely to have shaped these responses and to have been shaped by them.

Conventionally psychology is mainly concerned with the individual's biological equipment and the effects of later experiences (e.g. learning, brain injury) upon processes which are biologically given. Sociology is mainly concerned with aggregates of individuals (e.g. social classes) and with social forces which are relatively unalterable by single individuals (e.g. the distribution of educational opportunity, or the growth of towns). Social psychology is not clearly distinguishable from either. The student who wishes to understand the non-payment of hire-purchased goods, alcoholism, the drift of the population in Britain from North to South, the problems of old age, unofficial strikes or reading backwardness, will need to draw on material and concepts from many different sources. Currently these are organized into different social sciences, but a trend towards a more unified approach is perceptible, though some are still preoccupied with the logic of a strict delimitation of boundaries.

These issues are discussed in G. Lindzey, ed., *Handbook of Social Psychology*, 1954; E. E. Maccoby, T. M. Newcomb and E. L. Hartley, eds, *Readings in Social Psychology*, 1958; D. Krech, R. Crutchfield and E. Ballachy, *Individual in Society*, 1962; P. E. Secord and C. W. Backman, *Social Psychology*, 1972. See ATTITUDE RESEARCH.   J.K.

social reform. The relationships between sociology and social reform are complicated and obscure. Some theorists, who have played a prominent part in the shaping of social thought, such as Sydney and Beatrice Webb and G. D. H. Cole, would not be thought by some to have been sociologists, whilst many others have considered their work to be too 'pure' to have any direct connection with social reform. At the same time, there can be no doubt that many social and political philosophers have influenced the shaping of social doctrine and the course of social history.

There is, for instance, the overwhelming influence of Marx to be reckoned with, whose importance is to be found more in the stimulus he gave to the foundation and working of social movements than to the explanations he had to offer of the organization of actual societies, or of the internal strains or conflicts existing within them. His contribution to social reform was therefore made as a philosopher or social theorist rather than as a scientist. The same may be said of many other people from Auguste Comte to Sir Charles Loch, whose overt intention was to base ideas for action on the 'facts' of a situation, but who only succeeded in producing doctrinaire views as to what should be done. Nevertheless, expressions of these kinds of opinions have been exceedingly influential, and whilst Marx is still regarded by many as having provided textbooks of social reform, Loch established the stimulus to much theorizing by social workers and administrators about what needs to be done in matters of individual and family behaviour.

The growth of an attitude of mind or school of thought which seeks to bring the value judgments of political and social philosophers on the quality of social living into a direct and mutually supportive relationship with the scientific study of societies as they are, has proved to be much slower than might have been expected a hundred years ago. Capital punishment, for instance, still tends to be examined from either the moral point of view as an expedient that is fundamentally wrong, or from the scientific (or quasi-scientific) point of view as providing a deterrent to murder which cannot be abandoned. The more complex view, that hanging cheapens human life and therefore provokes murder, with the consequence that its abolition encourages a more moral attitude, as is thought to have happened in the countries which have abolished it, is too subtle an argument for the common man to understand in existing circumstances in this country.

Perhaps the best example which can be quoted of the relationship between fact and value in matters of social reform is the seminal work done in this regard in Charles Booth's poverty survey. From the sociological point of view, Booth's most important achievement was, by an elaborate analysis of the economic institutions of his times, to show that the bulk of poverty was the outcome of the malfunctioning of the economic system, and not of the immorality and vice of the individual, such as laziness or drunkenness. There was also the whole problem of the disparity between a family's needs and its income, which established the chief characteristics of the economic cycle of working class family life. Specific economic institutions, such as the port transport industry, were at fault, in so far as they led to casual employment of workers at low rates of wages, and thus to equally low standards of social behaviour.

This analysis, backed by the moral assumptions of Victorian middle-class life, led to strong demands for social reform, which were ultimately successful. Similar kinds of survey work have been continued in other fields, as, for instance (in the United States), in regard to the psychological characteristics of so-called races, and race relations. Gunnar Myrdal's well-known enquiry, carried out in the 1940s, based as it was on the work of many other social scientists that had been completed during the century, made the value-judgments implied in it explicit. His book, *An American Dilemma*, 1944, showed that if Negroes were oppressed, even though their genetic inheritance could not be shown to be inferior to that of the white man, severe frustrations would be set up, and tensions would be likely to lead to explosions, as has happened since in several parts of the world. Social reform in matters of race relations was therefore given the greatest support by Myrdal's work.

The future will show how far this kind of work has been accepted by social scientists generally, or whether they will determine that the scientific aspects of their work will prevent it from being influenced by values. If it is agreed that sociology must be *value-free*, as some suppose that Max Weber demanded, its connection with social reform will become tenuous. The issue is still in the balance. See SOCIAL ENGINEERING.   s. of T.

social science. The term Social Science is often loosely applied to any kind of study which is concerned with man and society but in the strict sense it refers to the application of scientific methods to the study of the intricate and complex network of human relationships and the forms of organization designed to enable peoples to live together in societies.

In the middle of the nineteenth century the term gained currency in Britain when a diverse group of people tried to encourage the application of scientific methods to the study of social phenomena by forming, in 1857, the National Association for the Promotion of Social Science. It achieved some success but had little effect on developing a systematic discipline of study, though it did serve as a model for the formation in 1865 of the American Social Science Association which became much more effective and influential than the relatively short-lived British Association.

Later in the century in France and England some of the founders of the new discipline of sociology hoped that it would become the social science embracing history, economics and political science. This conception of an all-embracing social science was not, however, generally accepted by scholars in other disciplines and it was not until the twentieth century that the term appeared to have a specific meaning in Britain.

In the first decade of the twentieth century social science acquired a restrictive meaning in Britain when it was used as a descriptive label for courses of study designed for the training of social workers. At the same time, however, the terms Social Study or Social Studies were also applied to courses of this kind with the result that Social Science, Social Study and Social Studies become synonymous. These training courses all relied to a considerable extent on the disciplines of economics, history, law and philosophy (and later psychology and sociology) for their basic sources of knowledge but gradually there were developed in addition specialized fields of study in social administration and the techniques of social work.

The confusion caused by using the umbrella term Social Science for these courses was avoided in the United States of America by the adoption of the term Social Work for those disciplines of study which were essential for the education and training of social workers and applying the generic term the Social Sciences to the disciplines of, for example, economics, psychology and sociology.

Until the middle of the twentieth century there was a tendency in Britain (though not to the same extent in America) to regard those disciplines of study concerned with man and society such as economics, anthropology, psychology, sociology and politics as distinct and separate from each other, but it is now recognized that the scientific study of human relationships and that complex organization society must be the concern not of a Social Science but the Social Sciences. The rapid growth of knowledge and the higher degree of specialization in the longer established disciplines, the development of new disciplines like Social Administration and of more refined theories and specialized techniques of Social Work have transformed in a relatively short time the earlier concepts of social science. But just as the scientific revolution gave rise to an array of highly specialized natural and physical sciences which we conveniently label 'science' so too we can now speak of a group of disciplines whose interests are in man and society which may be conveniently referred to as social science. See SOCIOLOGY, SOCIAL WORK.

D.C.M.

social statistics. This term may be used in two different senses. It may refer to the application of statistical methods to social problems; alternatively it may be used for the actual numerical data which have been collected that have a bearing on these problems.

The history of the word *statistics* is traced briefly in G. U. Yule and M. G. Kendall's treatise *An Introduction to the Theory of Statistics*; it is stated there that 'the words "statist" "statistics" "statistical" appear to be all derived from the Latin *status* in the sense acquired in mediaeval Latin of a political *state*'. At first statistics described the circumstances and instititions of a state verbally, but during the nineteenth century the term gradually acquired a narrow significance, 'the exposition of the characteristics of a state by numerical methods'. Later still it came to be applied to the actual numerical data, which described these characteristics, was extended to numerical data in other sciences and finally was used for the methods employed in analysing such data and drawing inferences from them.

The science of *statistics* must thus be distinguished from *statistics* in the sense of data. Taking the latter meaning first, it is by no means easy to delimit the field of social statistics. Perhaps the most appropriate definition would be that 'social statistics consist of quantitative data, dealing with topics which are of interest to sociologists'. There will obviously be some overlap with other statistics. Statistics of marriages and family composition will interest the demographer, statistics of income distribution the economist, statistics of health and disease the medical man. Yet, in a sense all these are 'social statistics' just as much as statistics of crime, education, housing and so on, which are normally regarded as lying in this field.

However, the meaning described above is secondary, and less important. In its more important connotation social statistics may be regarded as 'the method of collecting, analysing and interpreting numerical information about social aggregates'. This method, of course, has much in common with other branches of statistics, with its application to phenomena studied in other sciences. But there are also some distinctive features. In the first place the collection of numerical information about social aggregates presents its own difficulties. Such information cannot always be obtained by direct observation, but must usually be elicited from respondents by means of questionnaires and in surveys. The design and working of questionnaires so as to elicit maximum response and present minimum ambiguity thus becomes a matter of interest to the social statistician. Similarly, he will be concerned with problems of interviewing and with dealing with a situation, in which some respondents refuse to provide the information that they have been asked for. This problem of refusals becomes particularly important, when information is collected, not from the whole of an aggregate, but only from a sub-group by *sample*. In the third place, social statisticians are often interested in the analysis of data, which can be *ordered* but not measured, e.g. the classification of housing conditions into good, fair, indifferent and poor, and methods have been devised for dealing with this type of information.

A great many social enquiries today proceed by means of the sampling method, and the design and analysis of sample surveys has become an increasingly important part of the social statistician's work. This problem is treated in greater detail in the article on sampling.   E.G.

social status. This is the position occupied by a person, family, or kinship group in a social system relative to others. This determines rights, duties and other behaviours, including the nature and extent of the relationships with persons of other statuses.

Social status has a hierarchical distribution in which a few persons occupy the highest positions. The simplest theoretical model of the status system would be a distribution in which position was determined competitively by the possession of abilities relative to the demand for abilities in the society. The institution of private property, inheritance, differential taxation, and social services all modify the form of the distribution of statuses.

The child is placed in society by its family and kinship group. They determine its education, its initial endowment of wealth and the esteem of the family in which it was born is transmitted to the child. This may include elements of class, caste, or estate. From this position the child may lose, maintain, or improve its status by its achievements in competition with others.

Social status is determined by education, income, possessions, and the social valuation of occupation and of other activities in society. All modern societies have a number of honours systems which introduce the element of social worth in a system which is primarily based on economic competition. The process of status determination operates through the invidious comparison of the style of life determined by the factors given above. Attempts are made to achieve high status by some persons who concentrate their resources upon the purchase of certain visible items of the style of life of a higher group: these are popularly called *status symbols*.

Although social status can be considered as a continuous variable, there is a tendency for the population to group itself into fairly distinct clusters around incomes corresponding to broad occupation groups. The thesis that the working class was adopting the life style of the middle class 'embourgeoisement' has been examined by John A. Goldthorpe, D. Lockwood, F. Bechhofer and J. Platt in their *The Affluent Worker* studies and a new scale of social grading of occupations has been constructed by John A. Goldthorpe and Keith Hope as a part of the *Oxford Studies in Social Mobility*.

American studies of communities such as *The Status System of a Modern Community*, 1942 (Yankee City Series) by W. Lloyd Warner and Paul S. Lunt have concentrated on showing how similarities in education, income, property and occupation lead to the formation of groups with a high degree of interaction and of consensus in values, attitudes and tastes. This

193

phenomenon is made use of in research into the markets for consumer goods.
See SOCIAL MOBILITY, SOCIAL STRATIFICATION, SOCIAL STRUCTURE. D.C.

social stratification. To define but not delude, to use words which have at least
two permissible meanings, to express concepts which already have particular
overtones for the majority of their readers; these are the perennial problems
of the academic sociologist. Few concepts exemplify them more clearly than
that of *social stratification* and associated terms like *social class*.

Social stratification is one manifestation of the sociologist's general interest
in the basic principles of social organization. It is a particular kind of social
differentiation and necessarily conveys the notion of hierarchical ranking, a
ranking which produces strata into one of which all members of the society
under investigation fall and within which all are equal but between which
there are recognized and sanctioned differences which place one higher, or
lower, than another in the admitted social order. Thus the American
sociologist, Talcott Parsons, defines social stratification as 'the differential
ranking of the human individuals who compose a given social system and
their treatment as superior and inferior relative to one another in certain
socially important respects'.

Immediately it is important to note two things. First, that although in
theory social strata are made up of individuals and families, individuals or
individual families may not in fact always fit in to the conceptual framework
of the stratification system of their society. Second, that hierarchical ranking
is not necessarily invidious ranking. (So pervasive has been the influence of
Marx, not merely in the nineteenth- but in the twentieth-century discussion
of social stratification, that it is with some difficulty that sociologists show the
same detached view in their own studies in this field as they do, for example,
in the sociological study of family and kinship.) Both *caste systems* and
systems of estates, two forms of social stratification in which the differences
between strata are very marked and elaborately institutionalized, illustrate
these points.

Castes A pure caste system is rooted in the religious order and may be
thought of as a hierarchy of hereditary, endogamous, occupational groups
with positions fixed and mobility barred by ritual distances between each
caste. Empirically, the classical Hindu system of India approximated most
closely to pure caste. The system existed for some 3,000 years and continues
today despite many attempts to get rid of some of its restrictions. It is
essentially connected with Hinduism. In theory all Hindus belong to one of
four main groups, denoted by a colour, these were originally in order of
precedence the Kshatriyas (a warrior group), the Brahmans (a priestly group),
the Vaishyas (trading and manufacturing people) and the Sudras (servants
and slaves). These are all mentioned in the Hindu writings of the sixth
century B.C.Later the Brahmans replaced the Kshatriyas in the prime position.
Outside these four main castes there are over fifty million so-called
'outcastes', but of course these too are part of the caste system, sharing the
dominant beliefs about ritual pollution; they are among the least privileged
and their occupations are among the least esteemed, e.g. those of the tanner
or the washerman. There are many castes and especially sub-castes. In the
1901 Census, which tried to establish the order of ranks, 2,378 main castes

194

were identified, but the Ahir caste alone was found to have 1,700 sub-castes. These sub-castes are further closed by the essential rule of endogamy, i.e. prescribed marriages within the group. Membership of a caste, or more precisely a sub-caste, is hereditary and ascribed. Ascribed membership and endogamy together with compulsory monopoly of an occupation or narrow range of occupations produces a tightly-knit local community with exclusive social and religious practices. Between castes the only permitted form of social mobility within the lifetime of an individual is by *hypergamy*, by which a woman may, under rigidly controlled circumstances, move up into her husband's caste on marriage.

Unfamiliar and unacceptable though such a system must appear to the eye of a Western observer, any overtones of invidious ranking of castes are in the eye of the beholder. For its members, a caste system is a coherent and comprehensive system of allocating ritualistic functions on the basis of a ritualistic social order to which all subscribe.

It is precisely on this score that to apply the concept of caste to the social stratification of slave-states of North America is both inaccurate and misleading. Here the deep and entrenched social divisions between the white and coloured populations, although, as in contemporary South Africa, given the veneer of religious sanction, arise not from allocation of differential functions in a ritual order but from allocation of menial tasks to men of distinct colour. Essentially, the caste system is a functional system related to commonly accepted norms in the light of which social stratification is a manifestation of the purposive order of society. Although a caste or sub-caste is not organized deliberately, there may be a sub-caste council or *panchayat*, which punishes those who offend against the ritual rules.

Estates Whilst the strata of castes are an interpretation of the laws of religious ritual, the strata of systems of estates are defined by the laws of man in societies for whose ruler divine authority is commonly claimed. Hence in the estate system it is not necessary to know a man's place in a ritual order but rather to know the man-made, though divinely inspired, law by which he lives. Complicated though these laws invariably were, their universal characteristic was that they defined not merely the rights but the duties of members of estates and thus provided a clear system of social order based on responsibilities enforceable either in the courts or by military strength.

In theory at least, this system of rights and duties usually extended throughout the population, hence, unlike the caste system, estates have no 'outcastes': all could exert some claim on the established social order. (It is in respect of their possession of human rights that serfs are commonly distinguished from slaves who, being legally the chattels of their masters – 'property with life in it' – have none. In practice, however, this was a distinction without a difference in some manifestations of serfdom such as, for example, serfdom in the Black Soil regions of Imperial Russia.) Like caste systems, estates had institutionalized barriers to social mobility, but whilst the barriers in the caste system rest on ritual impurity, the barriers of systems of estates are legal and, being man made, can be modified in particular circumstances. This distinction between these two systems of social stratification may be illustrated both negatively and positively. Recruitment into the Church, for example, was not limited to any one section of the community nor was attainment to high office. Promotion within the Church was indeed an explicitly sanctioned means of social mobility, albeit technically limited in social significance since, in a celibate church, mobility only affected one individual for his own lifetime. In the secular sphere, however, the king might ennoble a distinguished servant just as he also had the power to grant legal immunity from the normal operation of feudal laws to whole cities. In both of these circumstances, changes of social position were essentially inherited.

Estate systems have a long history. They emerged in the ancient Roman Empire, and persisted in Europe until very recent times. The Medieval position in England, whilst not very clear, may help to illustrate an estate system, for whilst the King, Lords and Commons comprised the main estate divisions there was a less clearly defined division into Clergy, Nobility and Commons. As far as participation in government was concerned the clergy were partially incorporated into the nobility through the spiritual peers. The position in France was more rigid, and the system of estates of Clergy, Nobles and Third Estate remained until 1789. When they sat as an instrument of government it was separately as parts of the States-General. In their development there was some differentiation within estates. Thus the descendants of the original nobility were *noblesse de l'épee*, owing their privileges to their warrior background. Later additions to the nobility were as a result of service, a *noblesse de robe*. It should be noted that the nobility are ranked. Originally a count was an administrative official, whilst a duke was a military leader, hence dukes rank before counts. In some parts of Europe, e.g. Sweden, there were four estates. Thus down till 1866 there were in that country Nobles, Clergy, Citizens and Peasants.

Social Classes   Since both in caste and estate systems social position is normally ascribed, it follows that both will be undermined by pressures tending to promote the value of individual merit and its regular reward. Hence both disintegrate under the impact of capitalism and of industrial capitalism above all which, requiring both specialization of function and efficiency of performance, emphasize the desirability of promoting individual merit with the result that, according to Karl Marx, social classes emerge between which there are no legal or supra-natural barriers to mobility. Classes, he argues, are defined in terms of their relationship to the instruments of production and the distribution of wealth. Essential to Marx's thesis are the twin ideas of class-conflict and class-consciousness, both of which arise from the invidious comparisons that can be made between class membership and power. (See the *Communist Manifesto*, 1848.) Space does not allow for a full discussion of Marx's writings on social class. It is only possible to draw the reader's attention to the irrefutable fact that his historical prediction of the increasing polarization of society has not become an observable reality. Some forty years ago, A. M. Carr-Saunders and D. Caradog Jones, in *Social Structure of England and Wales*, 1927, commented that if social classes were indeed based on economic differences, then the redistribution of wealth and the levelling out of incomes which had been achieved in the past generation might lead one to reject the notion of class as purely arbitrary. One might also add that, if conflict and consciousness are necessary characteristics of systems of social class, then the apparent absence of both in the mid-twentieth century only makes one more doubtful of the usefulness of Marxist class theory as a tool of contemporary social analysis.

To query the usefulness of the concept of class in contemporary society is not, of course, to imply the disappearance of social distinctions and social differentiation (if some societies are today more egalitarian than they have been in the past, nevertheless within them, some are more equal than others), rather it is to point to the greater importance of the differential status of particular groups as opposed to large social classes. There is no evidence of the emergence of a society in which social differences are unknown but it has become increasingly clear that social status, which in contemporary Britain is emphatically associated with occupation, is the effective key to contemporary social stratification. Thus if castes are rooted in a ritual institution and estates in the institution of law, social classes must be seen to spring from the economy. It was Max Weber's achievement, following his reflections on Marx's ideas, to see that *classes* are not social groups but aggregates of people possessing the same life-chances. (See 'Class, Status and Party' in *From Max Weber: Essays in Sociology*, 1947, edited by H. Gerth and C. W. Mills.) Nevertheless social groups can be identified which are relatively endogamous and whose members display a similar style of life. These *status groups*, as Weber called them, maintain distinctiveness, but largely today as a result of occupational connections. As the path to so many occupations is through the educational system we should see this modern development in social stratification as rooted in both social institutions, i.e. economy and education.

It was largely as a result of T. H. Marshall's famous essay, *Citizenship and Social Class*, 1946, that the development of civic, political and social rights came to be more clearly related to the changes in the system of social stratification in Britain. If the need for formally free labour was an essential of early Capitalism, political rights followed from the success of the rising Bourgeoisie, which Capitalism produced, demanding their place in the sun. Social rights, which we see reflected in the social services and in greater and better educational provision, have followed as a result of the rapid expansion in industrial societies of white collar occupations and the extension of skilled and technological work. But the modern type of socially stratified industrial society has failed to rid itself of the endogamous element. This is because the unit of the stratified system is the family and because social status is a non-financial reward. An element in such a reward must be the advantage given to the children in the family. It may be argued, although not all would agree, that this kind of society depends upon differential status advantages for the adequate supply of professional people, whose training is long and demanding, and whose standards of professional conduct are of an order requiring the special and additional socializing process this implies.

The literature on social stratification is immense. A very good survey of it up until 1952 was carried out for UNESCO by D. G. MacRae, 'Social Stratification: A Trend Report and Bibliography', *Current Sociology*, II, 1953–4. Other works to be mentioned are J. Littlejohn, *Social Stratification*, 1972, and R. Bendix and S. M. Lipset, *Class, Status and Power*, 1953. On *caste* see A. Hocart, *Caste: A Comparative Study*, 1950; on *slavery* and *serfdom* see the classic work by I. Ingram, *A History of Slavery and Serfdom*, 1895, H. Maynard, *The Russian Peasant and Other Studies*, 1942, G. Myrdal,

An American Dilemma, 1944. A simple introduction to the subject is *Stratification* by R. K. and H. M. Kelsall, 1974; a collection of interesting and varied essays is *The Social Analysis of Class Structure*, 1974, by F. Parkin. See SOCIAL MOBILITY, SOCIAL STATUS. M.H. and G.D.M.

social structure. Within the field of anthropology the concept is central to the structural-functional approach of British social anthropology, whereas the American cultural anthropologists have utilized primarily the concepts of *culture process* and *culture history*. (See F. Eggan, 'Social anthropology and the method of controlled comparison', *American Anthropologist*, LVI, 1, 1954.) In social anthropology the term is often used interchangeably with *social organization* (see M. Fortes, 'The structure of unilineal descent groups', *American Anthropologist*, LV, 1, 1953, p. 21), and has been employed particularly in the analysis of the kinship, political and legal institutions of primitive societies. R. Firth is an exception, for in his *Elements of Social Organization*, 1956, and his *Social Change in Tikopia*, 1959, he explicitly distinguishes between the two terms. Although regarding both terms as heuristic devices rather than as precise concepts, he sees *social organization* as concerned with the choices and decisions involved in actual social relations ('the working arrangements of society'), while *social structure* refers to the more fundamental social relations which give a society its basic form and which set limits to the courses of action organizationally possible. Fortes, in his article 'Time and social structure: an Ashanti case study' (Fortes (ed.), *Social Structure*, 1949), sees the term as applying to any ordered arrangement of 'distinguishable wholes', i.e. institution, group, situation, process, social position, but E. E. Evans-Pritchard in *The Nuer*, 1940, restricts the term to the relationships between groups, while E. R. Leach in *Political Systems of Highland Burma*, 1954, revised edition 1964, focuses the concept on the set of ideas about the distribution of power between persons and groups.

The emergence of the concept in British social anthropology since the writings of A. R. Radcliffe-Brown may be viewed broadly as having had three purposes. Firstly, there had been the attempt to distinguish explanation and description in terms of *culture* from that in terms of *social relations*. This distinction constitutes the core difference in approach between American cultural anthropology and British social anthropology. Within social anthropology itself a second purpose has been to isolate from the *content* of social relations some formal, underlying (structural) *principles*. Thirdly, again within social anthropology, the concept is distinguished from that of *social function*, i.e. the forms from the effects of social relations.

In contrast to B. Malinowski, who in *A Scientific Theory of Culture*, 1961, adopted a very generalized view of culture, including within this concept material culture, values and norms, together with actual behaviour, Radcliffe-Brown differentiates the culture of a society from its social system and social structure. In *A Natural Science of Society*, 1957, he sees the culture of a society as its standardized modes of behaviour, thinking and feeling, while its social structure 'consists of the sum total of all the social relationships of all individuals at a given moment in time'. Seen thus the social structure is the non-processual aspect of the social system. It constitutes the static state of the social system, the system at any one point in time. Radcliffe-Brown further insists that culture can only be studied scientifically *via* the social structure, i.e. when cultural modes are conceptually recast as social relations, then a science of social systems and social structures becomes possible, but a science of culture as such is not possible. The cultural anthropologists of the U.S.A. have largely adopted a view of culture similar in inclusiveness to that of Malinowski and in consequence have, in contrast to Radcliffe-Brown, given priority to the cultural rather than the structural frame of reference. For example, G. Murdock, in his article on 'British Social Anthropology' in *American Anthropologist*, LIII, 3, 1951, insists on culture as the proper object of study for anthropologists and complains that through its exclusively social structural approach to the data of preliterate societies, British anthropology has neglected, among other things, the important problems of cultural change, the transmission of culture between generations and the diffusion of culture geographically. Similarly, R. Lowie, in 'Ethnography, cultural and social anthropology', *American Anthropologist*, LIV, 4, 1953, regards the analysis of social structure as but one aspect of the study of culture. Contemporary British social anthropologists, following Radcliffe-Brown's line of thought, acknowledge the inseparability of culture and social structure but give priority to social structure as the basic frame of reference rather than *vice versa*. Hence Fortes says '… social structure is not an aspect of culture but the entire culture of a given people handled in a special frame of theory', and he stresses this view that the structural approach allows the investigator to speak of different levels of structure while the cultural approach is committed to treating each culture trait or process as of equal importance with every other.

The current use of *social structure* in British social anthropology in terms of a body of principles underlying social relations, rather than their actual content, stems from Radcliffe-Brown's concept of *structural form* ('… the general or normal form of [the] relationship, abstracted from the variations of particular instances, though taking account of these variations') rather than from his own use of the term *social structure* as defined above. To Radcliffe-Brown the social structure was an empirical reality existing at a single moment of time, while the structural form was an abstraction from reality by the investigator and implied a period rather than a moment of time. Modern social anthropologists such as Fortes, Evans-Pritchard, Firth and S. F. Nadel, use the term social structure essentially in this sense to identify the structural principles underlying any particular body of social relations. 'What is really important, however, is not merely the determination of the "parts" and their interrelations but the elucidation of the principles which govern structural arrangement and the forces for which these stand … When we describe structure we are already dealing with general principles far removed from the complicated skein of behaviour, feelings, beliefs, etc., that constitute the tissue of actual social life'. (cf. Fortes, *op. cit.*, 1949). Fortes disagrees with Radcliffe-Brown that structure can be a genuine empirical property of social relationships and argues that it is always an abstraction of the investigator. Hence he considers Radcliffe-Brown's distinction between *social structure* and *structural form* to be invalid. Leach sees *social structure* as the anthropologist's logical construction or model, and is supported in this view by C. Lévi-Strauss ('Social Structure' in S. Tax (ed.), *Anthropology Today:*

Selections, 1962, p. 322). The most systematic anthropological analysis of the concept, S. F. Nadel's *The Theory of Social Structure*, 1957, dissents, however, from this interpretation since the coherence of the social structure is not seen to include the logical coherence and predictive power of a model as typically conceived in natural science. Nadel's work is important on this issue since it reminds us that it may not be possible to speak of *the* social structure if this is a derivative from the matrix of roles within the society. Rather a society has a multiplicity of social structures since a role matrix may lack coherence through roles being either logically or factually unconnected with one another. He identifies two formal principles in which the coherence of a role system inheres, (1) command over action, (2) command over resources and benefits. An attempt to operationalize Nadel's two criteria is that of M. Freilich in 'Toward a model of social structure', *Journal of the Royal Anthropological Institute*, 95, 1965.

In distinguishing the concept from *social function* Radcliffe-Brown moves from structure viewed from the standpoint of the total society, *the* social structure, to the notion of sub-structure or particular set of social relations, so that *a* social structure is said to have a function if it contributes to the maintenance of the structural continuity of the total system (see 'On the concept of function in social science' in his *Structure and Function in Primitive Society*, 1952).

Compared with anthropology, the concept in the field of sociology has had more currency but has also been frequently used with very little precision. Sometimes the phrase *a social structure* is used to mean simply a social regularity, to indicate that the behaviour is repetitive and non-random. In this sense *social structure* and *social system* are contrasted with the notion of *aggregate*. A further usage and perhaps the most common at the level of total society amounts to a blanket term for the broad arrangement of elements or units (sub-systems, types of organization, institutions, etc.) within the society, sometimes with a statistical emphasis, e.g. D. C. Marsh, *The Changing Social Structure of England and Wales*, 1871–1961, 1966. When the concept is used at a level other than the societal, when speaking of *a* social structure rather than *the* social structure, it also shows strong similarity with the social psychologist's concept of *group structure* as applied to small, artificial, laboratory groups. (See D. Cartwright and A. Zander, *Group Dynamics*, 2nd edition 1960, ch. 34.)

As in anthropology, it is a core concept of the structural-functional approach. It is typically viewed as the interrelation of social positions and roles. (See T. Parsons, *The Social System*, 1951; R. K. Merton, *Social Theory and Social Structure*, 1961; H. M. Johnson, *Sociology*, 1962.) Interaction within the social system is conceptualized more specifically in terms of actors occupying positions (or statuses) in which they play roles *vis-à-vis* other positions. In Parsons's discussion *social system* is a wider concept than *social structure* and includes the functional aspect of the system, the positive and negative consequences of sub-structure for the total system, in addition to its structural aspect. Parsons's view of the relation of *structure* and *process* is essentially similar to that of Radcliffe-Brown. The initial social reality is a 'dynamic process', but in order to describe and explain this reality, the investigator has to 'freeze' some parts of it, and these then constitute the structure. In this sense Parsons sees the social structure as only relatively more static than the processual or functional aspect of the system. He further conceptualizes the institutions of the society as complexes of such positions and roles. While Parsons distinguishes between changes *within* the structure of the social system and changes *of* the social structure, he has been criticized for placing too great an emphasis on structural integration and continuity. (See D. Lockwood, 'Some remarks on *The Social System*', *British Journal of Sociology*, VII, 2, 1956, and R. Dahrendorf, 'Out of Utopia: toward a reorientation of sociological analysis', *American Journal of Sociology*, LXIII, 1, 1958. For a similar criticism of the social anthropologists see E. Vogt, 'On the concepts of structure and function in cultural anthropology', *American Anthropologist*, LXII, 1, 1960.) Functionalist sociologists have tended to assume the structural integration of a society and its sub-systems rather than regarding this as problematical. (See A. Gouldner, 'Reciprocity and autonomy in functional theory' in L. Gross (ed.), *Symposium on Sociological Theory*, 1959, and D. Wrong, 'The oversocialised conception of Man', *American Sociological Review*, XXVI, 2, 1961.) N. Gross *et al.*, in *Explorations in Role Analysis*, 1958, similarly have indicated that *role consensus* or agreement in role definition among a set of role occupants is an empirical and not an *a priori* question, so that by extension the integration of the total social structure becomes problematical too. Merton had utilized the concept particularly in his discussion of deviancy arising from *anomie* or normlessness. *Anomie* is seen as the resultant of a hiatus between culture structure (goals) and the social structure (means). He has, however, been criticized for oversimplifying the problem of deviancy by adopting, like Parsons, a 'value consensus' view of the social structure. (See E. M. Lemert, 'Social Structure, Social Control and Deviation' in M. B. Clinard (ed.), *Anomie and Deviant Behaviour*, 1964; J. Beattie, *Other Cultures*, 1964, ch. 4; M. Levy, *The Structure of Society*, 1952.) See CULTURE, FUNCTION, SOCIAL ANTHROPOLOGY, SOCIAL SYSTEM, STRUCTURALISM.   D.J.A.W.

social survey. The *social survey* is a systematic collection of facts about people living in a specific geographic, cultural, or administrative area.

Social surveys are usually for dealing with many related aspects of a social problem. They provide the data for administration, rather than for the development of sociological theory, and although they often contain illustrative or descriptive material, they are generally quantitative, and the history of the social survey is intimately bound up with the development of statistics.

The early ancestors of the social survey are the Doomsday Book, Stow's *Survey of London*, Camden's *Britannia*, the essays of seventeenth- and eighteenth-century demographers, Arthur Young's reports to the Board of Agriculture, and the two Statistical Accounts of Scotland.

The modern social survey is the product of the intellectual response of the urban middle classes to the social conditions of town life in the nineteenth century. After 1801 the decennial census, itself a social survey, provided a framework into which members of philosophical societies could fit studies of poverty, literacy and health. The establishment of the Manchester Statistical Society in 1833, and the London (now the Royal) Statistical Society shortly after, created centres for the discussion of problems and the development of techniques. T. S. Ashton in his *Economic and Social Investigations in Manchester, 1833–1933*, 1934, traces the influence of the work of the Manchester Society on research in the fields of poverty, education, industrial and social conditions. Statistical societies had an important influence on government policy resulting in the publication in 1842 of Edwin Chadwick's *Report on the Sanitary Condition of the Labouring Population of Great Britain*, the first of a long series of Social Surveys undertaken by the State.

From the mid-century the National Association for the Promotion of Social Science stimulated interest in the production of monographs dealing with more narrowly defined topics. At the same time there were many descriptive and even fictional studies made by writers associated with Charles Dickens. The most notable work of the period was *London Labour and the London Poor* by Henry Mayhew, 1859, one of the founders of *Punch*.

In the modern period three kinds of Social Survey can be differentiated. The Poverty Survey originating in the work of Booth, Rowntree and Bowley, the Ecological Survey developed by Ratzel, Redus, Le Play and Geddes and the Functional Study of the City in which the work of Sherwell, the Chicago School, the Lynds, Warner and Lunt and others have been important.

Charles Booth's survey *Life and Labour of the People*, 1897, contained an account of the population of London classified by income, an account of social domestic and religious conditions as well an many remarkable descriptive accounts of such matters as 'The Jewish Community'. This latter essay written by Beatrice Potter, later Mrs Webb, has interesting theoretical implications and was based on observations made as a 'participant observer'. In 1899 B. Seebohm Rowntree published his survey of York, *Poverty: a Study of Town Life*. This work was influential because it was based on direct interviews, it *measured* poverty, it analysed the relationship between income and expenditure through life, and it became the datum for other surveys made by him at intervals during fifty years. A. L. Bowley published *Livelihood and Poverty* in 1915; he employed the technique of sampling, used in the biological sciences, enabling reliable results to be achieved with great economy of time and effort. Through his teaching, Bowley created a whole generation of social surveyors in academic, administrative and commercial fields.

Patrick Geddes, a biologist turned sociologist, took Le Play's concept of Folk, Work and Place as a basis for city and regional surveys for town planning purposes, and did many planning surveys in India. This influence has continued in human geography and in town and country planning, and through his friend and disciple, Lewis Mumford.

Although there was a vast production of surveys in the U.S.A. on the traditional model, the analytical studies of the Chicago School led by Robert E. Park made a distinctive contribution. These studies have a strong ecological basis, but developed into studies of social relations around specific functions. Arthur Sherwell's *Life in West London*, 1899, a neglected work, was an isolated precursor of the Chicago School.

Unconnected in time and personnel with the Chicago School and using the analytical framework of social anthropology, Robert S. and Helen M. Lynd published a descriptive study *Middletown* in 1929 and followed this in 1937 with *Middletown in Transition*. From this developed what should be more correctly called the *sociological survey*, the study of the social processes of a city or region of which the Yankee City series is a remarkable and pioneering work. This began with the publication in 1941 of *The Social Life of a Modern Community* by W. Lloyd Warner and P. S. Lunt. The field methods of social anthropology were used by N. Dennis, F. Henriques and C. Slaughter in *Coal is Our Life*, 1956.

The Social Survey is widely employed in consumer market research, and the Office of Population Census and Surveys in Britain makes studies of the whole range of social, economic and administrative problems. See SAMPLING, SOCIAL STATISTICS, TOWN PLANNING, URBAN SOCIOLOGY.   D.C.

social system. A *social system* basically consists of two or more individuals interacting directly or indirectly in a bounded situation. There may be physical or territorial boundaries, but the fundamental sociological point of reference is that the individuals are oriented, in a wide sense, to a common focus or interrelated foci. Thus it is appropriate to regard such diverse sets of relationships as small groups, political parties and whole societies as social systems. Social systems are 'open' systems, exchanging information with, and frequently acting with reference to, other systems.

Modern conceptions of the term can be traced to the leading social analysts of the nineteenth century, notably Auguste Comte, Karl Marx, Herbert Spencer and Émile Durkheim; each of whom elaborated in some form or other conceptions of the major units of social systems (mainly societies) and the relationships between such units – even though the expression *social system* was not a key one. Thus in Marx's theory the major units or components of the capitalist societies with which he was principally concerned were socio-economic classes, and the major relationships between classes involved economic and political power. The most influential conceptualizations of the term have been those of Talcott Parsons, stemming from his *The Structure of Social Action*, 1937, and finding recent expression in 'An Outline of the Social System', in Talcott Parsons *et al.* (eds.), *Theories of Society*, vol. I, 1961, ch. 2. Parsons's devotion to this issue has two main aspects. First, what is called the problem of social order; i.e. the nature of the forces giving rise to relatively stable forms of social interaction and organization, and promoting orderly change. Parsons took Thomas Hobbes's *Leviathan*, 1651, as his point of departure in this part of his analysis. Hobbes had maintained that man's fundamental motivation was the craving for power and that men were always basically in conflict with each other. Thus order could only consist in strong government. To counter this Parsons invoked the work of Max Weber and, in particular, Durkheim, who had placed considerable emphasis on the functions of normative factors in social life, such as ideals and values. Factors of this kind came to constitute the mainspring in Parsons's delineation of a social system. Thus in his major theoretical work, *The Social System*, 1951, he defines a social system as consisting in 'a plurality of individual actors interacting with each other in a situation which has at least a physical or environmental aspect, actors who are motivated in terms of a tendency to the "optimization of gratification" and whose relations to their situations, including each other, is defined and mediated in terms of a system of culturally structured and shared symbols' (pp. 5–6). The major units of a social system are said to be collectivities and roles (i.e. not individuals as such); and the major patterns or relationships linking these units are values (ends or broad guides to action) and norms (rules governing role performance in the context of system values). Parsons's second major interest has been to make sociology more scientific and systematic, by developing abstract conceptions of the social system; one of his points being that even though Weber placed much emphasis upon normative factors as guiding action, there was in Weber's sociology no elaboration of a theoretically integrated total system of action. (See Parsons's 'Introduction' to Max Weber's *The Theory of Social and Economic Organisation*, trans. A. M. Henderson and Talcott Parsons, 1947.) Hence the attempt to combine in one framework both a conception of actors in social situations and an overall, highly abstract, 'outside' view of the major factors involved in a social system as a going concern.

Various points in Parsons's formulation have been criticized. Notably, objections have been made to the emphasis upon normative regulation, and it has been alleged that Parsons neglects social conflict under the pressure of his systematic perspective; i.e. preoccupation with systemness and analytical elegance blinds the sociologist to dissensus in real life and spurs him to stress integrative phenomena in his analyses. (See Ralf Dahrendorf, 'Out of Utopia: Toward a Reorientation of Sociological Analysis', *American Journal of Sociology*, vol. LXIV, no. 2, 1958, pp. 115–27.) However, it is widely agreed that sociologists should operate with some clearly defined conception of what constitutes a social system. Thus, for many sociologists the term *social system* is not by any means restricted to those situations where there is thought to be binding normative regulation; but in order to qualify as 'social' a system must involve a common focus, or set of foci, of orientations and a shared mode of communication among a majority of actors. Thus on this basis there can be a system of conflict.

It is also generally recognized that for many purposes it is *analytically* necessary to distinguish social from cultural and personality systems – although the term social system is sometimes, for convenience, used to encompass all three. Whilst *personality system* refers to those aspects of the human personality which affect the individual's social functioning and *cultural system* covers actual beliefs, concrete systems of values and symbolic means of communication, *social system* in this context refers to forms and modes of interaction and organization, such as the authority structure of an organization or the division of functions in a family. Although long recognized by sociologists and anthropologists, these distinctions have been made particularly significant in the work of Pitirim Sorokin: see his *Society, Culture and Personality*, 1947, esp. pp. 63–4.   R.R.

social telesis. See WARD, L. F.

social work. Social work is a term used to describe a variety of organized methods of helping people in some need which they cannot meet unaided. Organized methods were developed in the nineteenth century in Great Britain and the United States of America when concern for people's spiritual and material welfare was focused on the economic conditions of the poor. This concern for the improvement of material conditions was later extended to the promotion of mental and emotional well-being.

The organization of social work has tended to be related to specific needs or problems, for example, poverty, delinquency, and mental or physical disablement, and at first the impetus to provide help on a systematic basis came from voluntary associations. By the end of the nineteenth century social surveys had demonstrated the need for governmental action to deal with major social and economic problems. The growth of the social services and of the body of knowledge in the social sciences enabled social work to concern itself not only with material needs but with the psychological and social problems of individuals and groups in society.

Social work methods fall into three main categories: social casework which is concerned with individuals and their families; social group work in which association with others is the primary therapeutic agent; and community work in which the focus is on the development and utilization of neighbourhood and community resources. The boundaries between these three methods are not distinct and in all social work great emphasis is placed on enabling people to use their own resources and those already existing in the community in order to help themselves.

The practice of social work has become increasingly professionalized and in the 1960s there was a dramatic increase in the number of professional courses run by Universities and other educational institutions in the United Kingdom. The emphasis of these courses has been on generic training rather than as in the past on separate specialisms. This movement away from narrowly defined specialisms has been accentuated since 1971 by the growth of social service departments in local authorities in England and Wales, social service boards in Northern Ireland, and social work departments in Scotland whose objectives are to provide comprehensive social work services not defined by specific needs. Furthermore there is now a statutory body, the Central Council for Education and Training in Social Work, which was established in 1971, and is responsible for approving courses and the granting of professional qualifications throughout the United Kingdom for all forms of social work, including probation. See the publications of the C.C.E.T.S.W. See SOCIAL ADMINISTRATION, SOCIAL SCIENCE, PROBATION.   D.C.M.

socialization. The shaping of human behaviour both mental and physical through experience in social situations. Socialization subsumes all the processes of enculturation, communication and learning, through which the individual human organism develops a social nature and is able to participate in social life. Some of these processes operate continuously throughout life to shape and reshape attitudes, for example the media and information services, while others operate at specific stages in the life cycle, for example the processes by which a society communicates to the elderly or the sick what behaviour is expected of them, that is to say what their roles consist of.

Although socialization into different roles (chiefly occupational) has been studied by social scientists in respect of a large number of organizations, the greatest attention has been reserved for socialization in childhood as it takes place in the home, the community and the school. Early socialization is thought by most social scientists to be critical in determining the social identity of the child and his later participation in social life. Differences in socialization practices occurring in different social classes have been explored together with their effects. Specific child rearing practices have been invoked to explain such phenomena as achievement motivation, authoritarianism, educational failure, individualization and so forth. Of particular interest to social scientists has been the acquisition of morality, that is the development of internalized standards and values. Durkheim and Freud, for whom moral duty, feeling, commitment and passion were central to the problem of the acquisition of morality, emphasized the importance of relationships with parents and parent figures in the socialization process whereby cultural values become constitutive of the human personality. Theorists such as G. H. Mead and Jean Piaget, on the other hand, who are primarily concerned with the intellectual aspects of moral socialization, i.e. with moral reasoning and judgment, emphasize the importance of relationships with peers as the means whereby individuals develop a principled, self-reliant and co-operative response to social life. See D. A. Goslin, *Handbook of Socialisation, Theory and Research*, 1969; U. Bronfenbrenner, *Two Worlds of Childhood*; P. Secord and C. Backman, *Social Psychology*, 1972; S. Freud, *New Introductory Lectures in Psychoanalysis*, 1933; J. Piaget, *The Moral Judgement of the Child*, 1932.   R.W.W.

societal; societal system. A term originally used by A. G. Keller and limited in its current use largely to some American sociologists. Keller wanted an adjectival term corresponding to *society*. In his use it refers to the organizational features of social life. (See his *Societal Evolution*, rev. ed. 1931.) Keller also used the expression *societal system*, but this has no very clear meaning apart from a general reference to topics relating to government, social class structure, law and other institutionalized aspects of modern human society.

society. The term *society* is one of the vaguest and most general in the sociologist's vocabulary. It may denote anything from a primitive non-literate people to a modern industrial nation-state, or from the most general reference to humankind to a relatively small organized group of people.

Social anthropologists have been accustomed to thinking of a non-literate people as constituting a society in the sense that they reproduce themselves, share a body of customs, maintain social order through the application of sanctions, and are located territorially. More recently the notion of such a people as constituting a *social system* has tended to replace the idea of them being a *society*. The use of the term *society* has been extended to become coterminous with nation and even with a larger conglomerate stretching over a substantial period of time – a *civilization*.

There have, of course, been many attempts to classify societies. The nineteenth-century sociologists tended to make a sharp distinction between the relatively simple, undifferentiated society and the modern complex industrial type; thus the distinction between *primitive* and *modern societies*, or between *non-literate* and *literate societies*. Durkheim contrasted what he called *segmental* and *organic* structures, the former being societies where the parts are so many replicas of each other, the latter displaying complex differentiation with organic-type relationships between the parts. A more recent kind of classification has been between *open* and *closed societies*, a distinction which gained currency with the emergence of totalitarian democracies, where the government is supported by mass opinion, in its turn manipulated through the control of information and the careful indoctrination of the populace by mass media of communication, educational institutions and the use of plebiscites and controlled elections. Thus a *closed society* is one illustrated by the totalitarian type, but also by the traditional simple society which resists change, whereas an *open society* is one which admits changes in institutional structures especially those arising through free critical discussion.

Society, used in the sense of *Gesellschaft* or an association of people with limited ends, who in their pursuit make certain organizational arrangements, is another practice, but is not limited merely to sociologists. In this sense, we may speak of the Society for the Propagation of the Gospel.

The total world of human beings, who cannot exist independently of each other, and who in their interactions develop edifices of culture, is also referred to as *human society*. This use of the term, loose, vague and extremely general, is nevertheless indicative of the nature of man. Thus even when considering the first use of this term we are bound to recall that human society, as also separate human societies, demands a system of recruitment, values and their transmission from one generation to another, some means of enforcement and discipline, and withal a facility for inspiring individual members to an extent that they are willing to subordinate their individual and sectional interests, even at times their existence, to the wider interests of maintaining that which is essentially human, namely their social world. For this reason the term *society* cannot be separately considered apart from others such as *culture, personality* and *religion*.   G.D.M.

sociobiology. The attempt to explain human behaviour in terms of the needs and drives of the organism and culture in terms of biological evolution. For an exposition see E. O. Wilson, *Sociobiology: the new synthesis*, 1975; for a critique, see Marshall Sahlins, *The Use and Abuse of Biology*, 1977.

sociogram. See SOCIOMETRY.

sociography. A word used chiefly by Ferdinand Tönnies, the German sociologist who carried out several surveys of north Germany, mainly concerned with the description of criminal activities and their distribution. He also wrote a description of the great strike in the port of Hamburg between 1896 and 1897 in which he traced the influence of various power groups. Tönnies placed great emphasis on the proper use of statistics and his use of the term *sociography* covers descriptive sociological studies using statistics. He himself obtained the term from the Dutch ethnologist, S. R. Steinmetz, who used it in *Geloof en Misdaad*, 1913, to refer to descriptions of the living conditions of civilized peoples, but it was Tönnies who is associated chiefly with its use. He preferred this term to that of *social statistics* as the latter term was customarily restricted to census data. Today the word *sociography*, whilst not in very common use, refers to descriptive studies of both a qualitative and a quantitative kind.   G.D.M.

sociology. The word was first employed in French by Auguste Comte and in English almost simultaneously by an anonymous writer on Comte in *Blackwood's Magazine*, and by John Stuart Mill in Book VI of his *Logic* (1843). By it is intended the fact and the programme of a science of society, comparable to the sciences of nature in its rigour, its methods, its systematic interconnectedness and its freedom from emotion and ethical or aesthetic valuation. Investigations and theories that may be properly thought of as sociological ante-date Comte. In Britain the first systematic theory of society as a whole is to be found in Adam Ferguson's *History of Civil Society*, published in Edinburgh in 1767. Early systematic investigations of the modern kind begin with the volumes of Sir John Sinclair's *Statistical Account of Scotland* in the 1790s and Sir Frederick Morton Eden's *The State of the Poor*, 1797.

The concept (and fact) of sociological rigour have had a long development. In Comte they are merely an aspiration. Today the techniques of empirical investigation and their quantification meets most claims of strict rigour. Comparative and theoretical sociology are as rigorous as the data and the state of the advancing discipline allow. On the whole the methods of the subject do not permit of experiment but only of observation and comparison. In comparison the canons of Mill's *Logic* are still dominant, in particular the method of concomitant variation. (Both the methods of difference and agreement are also employed.) Sociological theories have often, perhaps usually, been elaborated beyond the facts available. They are to be judged by the test of their fruitfulness in yielding hypotheses, their power to explain and co-ordinate diverse and recalcitrant data, their economy in so doing, and their degree of internal logical coherence. Today there exists no dominant body of sociological theory, but most sociologists are discriminatingly eclectic. It is certainly true that there is a theoretical convergence of ideas in sociology, and that even theories differently expressed in the past are being found to be complementary in practice.

Contemporary theory derives historically from three main sequences of thought. Comte (1795–1857) stressed developmental tendencies in society dominated by the conceptions which men held of the world and their place in it. The sequence of stages (metaphysical, theological and positive) is one of stages of thought, each a criticism of the previous one, each correlated with specific religious and political structures. L. T. Hobhouse (1864–1929) carried this analysis furthest in his *Morals in Evolution* (3rd edition), 1915, and *Social Development*, 1924. The major light thrown by this tradition has been on the mechanisms of law and moral institutions in pre-industrial societies and in refining the methods of sociological comparison.

The sequence which culminated in France in the work of Durkheim (1858–1917) owes its positivist bias to Comte, but its analysis is largely based on Herbert Spencer (*Principles of Sociology*, 3 vols., 1876–96) who first established working usages of the terms *structure, function* and *social institution*. Durkheim's stress on functional questions, the unique nature of *social facts* exterior to and constraining individuals, the independence of sociology from psychology, the rigorous use of variation as a clue to function, and his concepts of types of social solidarity, has been perhaps the greatest single source of influence on the thought and practice of sociology and social anthropology.

Karl Marx (1818–1883) and Max Weber (1864–1920) are related less by sequence than by the criticism of Marx by Weber. Weber was a diffuse, suggestive and fragmentary writer. His sociology has proved rich in concepts of high generality which are yet of exploratory value, and to him we owe the clear analysis of how a specific kind of logical model, the *ideal type*, can be employed in sociological explanation; the definition of what in behaviour is specifically social, i.e. social action; the clarification of the main types of social action in terms of their rational component; the sociological analysis of *bureaucracy*, etc. His studies of the sociology of religion employ the method of difference and introduced a new complexity and realism to the role of religion in economic life and the fruitful concepts of *charisma* as a precipitant in specific religious and political situations, and of *disenchantment* as the social concomitant of increasing rationality in social relations. He had perhaps the richest mind in sociology to date, but the logical power and exemplary investigation of Durkheim (cf. his *Suicide*, 1897, and *Elementary Forms of the Religious Life*, 1912) have perhaps left a deeper mark on the subject.

If we add to these names those of G. Simmel (1858–1918) and V. Pareto (1848–1923) we have mentioned nearly all the main influences on modern sociological conceptions which are still at work. This does not mean that sociological theory is over: new concepts, for example that of the *social role*, have been added; much excellent theoretical criticism goes forward; new systems are devised; but the legacy of thought has been so great that sociology has not had to be theoretically very creative for nearly two generations. What has happened is that the discipline has been institutionalized. It is now practised in all industrial and many developing nations, including all those officially Marxist with the possible exceptions of Albania and China. The decisive example in this has been American. The quantity and quality of American sociology has in fact dominated the sociology of the period since 1930. By 1900 many American universities taught and researched in the field, Chicago having taken the lead in the 1890s and holding it until about 1930. Sociology first became a profession in America: today it is an international one with something over 12,000 practitioners throughout the world.

The word *sociology* has changed in significance. It is used adjectively as a more grandiose word for 'social'; more legitimately and most frequently it is employed to describe any social investigation or research employing rigorous and controlled methods of inquiry; sometimes it refers to social philosophy or to *social diagnostics* or meditation on and appraisal of the leading social characteristics, trends and problems of our time; it is sometimes (see below) a synonym for social work or social administration. Centrally, however, and as a medium of education and research it continues to mean the dispassionate attempt to elaborate an explanatory science of society in all its variety and detail.

As such it has given birth to a number of specialisms created by the growth of knowledge and the obvious advantages of the division of scholarly labour.

Among these are the sociologies of knowledge, of religion, of art, etc.; the special sociologies of forms of social life such as rural, urban, industrial and political sociology; and the specific sociologies such as linguistic, criminological and legal sociology. Social anthropology is essentially the sociology of pre-literate societies, but its particular methods are becoming incorporated in all sociology, applicable in all societies. In addition sociology has profoundly affected the public organization and professional life of charity so that social work is sometimes treated as an integral part of sociology. The methods of sociological investigation are employed to provide data in local and national administration. They provide facts and theories for the practice of management. They are essential to commerce in the conduct of market research. As a consequence there is a tendency to regard the major justification of sociology as its utility, and to regard such activities, legitimate in themselves, as the true justification of the discipline. In fact they are, and will remain, parasitic on its major concerns.

These may be summarized as being: (a) the study of social structure; (b) the study of social composition, i.e. the nature, proportions and diversities of the various groups, categories and classes in societies; (c) the constructing of accurate descriptive inventories of the social life of society; (d) the study of culture and life-style in society; (e) the elaboration and testing of methods of research both qualitative and statistical. These are, of course, all inter-connected, and in total comprise the enterprise of sociology at this point of time. Their influence is widely permeating other areas of knowledge, in particular, perhaps, history, classics and oriental studies. They raise new problems for philosophy. It is not too much to say that sociology has become one of the major forms of our self-awareness in the twentieth century.

D.G.M.

sociology of education. This is a branch of sociology which analyses the institutions and organizations of education. Among the founding fathers of sociology Weber sketched a 'sociological typology of pedagogical ends and means' (see H. H. Gerth and C. W. Mills, *From Max Weber: Essays in Sociology*, 1947) and Durkheim expounded a functional view in his *Education and Sociology* (translated by S. D. Fox, 1956) and his *The Evolution of Educational Thought* (trans. 1977). But the development of sociological studies has flourished mostly since World War II.

At its most general level the sociology of education is concerned with the functional relationships between education and the other great institutional orders of society – the economy, the polity, religion and kinship. Such studies are necessarily comparative. Within this broader context however a particular system of education or even a school or class may be treated as a self-contained system of social relationships and studied by application of theories of social organization. Such an educational system or subsystem or individual school or college will have a formal constitution which defines its aims, the distribution of roles and resources within it, the disciplines, powers and the content and method of teaching. Formal constitutions however neither exhaustively define nor completely describe the actual relationships of an organization. In any school or college there will also be informal or unconscious value assumptions and patterns of power, influence and

210

communication. Schools, like any other social organization, are instruments in the pursuit of ends, but within them there always develop spontaneous loyalties, friendships, habits of work and routines of communication which may support or oppose but in any case will modify and elaborate the functioning of the school as a social system. The classic study along these lines is W. Waller, *The Sociology of Teaching*, 1932.

The process of education is thought of sociologically as the formal transmission of culture, with its elements of preservation, dissemination and innovation. In simple societies this process is not formalized except in *rites de passage* but in industrial societies education as it takes on disseminating and innovating functions is elaborately organized so as to meet the requirements of society for basic moral education, literacy and numeracy, for specialized training related to the demands of the economy, for skilled workers, scientists and professional people, and for additions to knowledge through research.

Very broadly and with many national variations, educational development in industrial or industrializing societies goes through three overlapping stages: first universal primary education is established as in Europe by the end of the nineteenth century; second universal secondary education is developed as in the United States of America between the wars; and third, given the secondary school base, a mass system of higher education begins to emerge. Many 'underdeveloped' countries are now passing through the first stage. The second and third stages typically generate pressures towards modifying the previously separate and selective organization of secondary schools so that each stage of education is comprehensively linked to the succeeding one.

Within the context of expansion sociologists are interested in the selective function of education. This theme runs through many studies of school organization and the relation between schools and social structure, especially social class, family and neighbourhood. The interaction of these social forces with the internal organization of the school are explored in order to unravel the social determinants of educability. Data from many countries show that social class and its correlates have a systematic effect on educability and educational selection so that, for example in Britain, the chances of achieving a university degree are six times better for a middle class than for a working class child. The social determinants of academic success remain powerful notwithstanding the widespread tendency towards formal equality of opportunity in modern educational systems. The theoretical notion of meritocracy, i.e. rule by persons identified and educated according to natural talent, has to be understood within this context.

Since 1960 the sociology of education has attracted new theoretical attention from Marxist, ethnomethodological, and Weberian writers. The older functionalist orthodoxy has been comprehensively challenged and the relation between educational and social policy has been debated as educational systems continue to expand. Christopher Jencks's book *Inequality: A Re-assessment of the Effect of Family and Schooling in America*, 1972 and R. Boudon, *Education, Opportunity and Social Inequality*, 1974, are two influential books in this respect. The most up-to-date general review of the field and a collection of readings illustrative of the major developments in

211

the 1960s and 1970s is J. Karabel and A. H. Halsey, *Power and Ideology in Education*, 1977.   A.H.H.

sociology of knowledge. The idea that our knowledge is in some measure a social product is comparatively recent. The importance of economic and other interests in shaping human belief was, it is true, often though sporadically recognized. Direct reflection on the influence of social structure on knowledge is a product of the experience of exotic societies and of a new style of reflection on our records of the past, in particular on the history of Greece and Rome. Such books as Father Couplet's *Confucius Sinarum Philosophus* (1687) and the long polemic of Reformation and Counter-Reformation produced the scepticism of which the masterpiece is Bayle's *Dictionnaire historique et critique* (1697). But universal doubt does not lead to a sociology of knowledge. A decisive step was Vico's *New Science* (1725) in which heroic literature is shown to be the thought mode of a specific kind of society. Of subsequent writers Herder alone did much to go beyond Vico, but G. F. Creuzer's *Symbolik und Mythologie* (1810) signalled the still continuing advance of classical scholars into the field.

Marxism raised the problem of a sociology of knowledge in specific form and offered a solution to it. According to Marx and Engels all knowledge has been distorted, directed and conditioned by the interests, conscious and unconscious, of conflicting exploited and exploiting classes. This distortion can be studied in past societies, but will cease in the future when a classless society has been established in which, as there will be no conflict of interests, so social passion and desire will not intrude upon an objective impartial appreciation of the phenomenal world. The explanatory power of Marxism should not be underestimated – cf. F. Antal's *Florentine Painting*, 1947, or the literary criticism of G. Lukács – even today. But it is ultimately untenable as a total sociology of knowledge because it is part of a system indefensible in the light of contemporary sociological information, untrue in important respects, neglectful of great areas of society and history and methodologically questionable.

In France Émile Durkheim approached the problem in a new way. In *The Elementary Forms of the Religious Life*, 1912, and the essays translated as *Sociology and Philosophy* in 1953 he argued that the basic categories of our perception and ordering of experience (space, direction, time, causality, etc.) derive from our social structure, are part of that structure, and support and sustain it as a viable mode of social life. It is quite clear that in great measure this is true for simple societies. But the uneven development of historic complex societies and the rise of alternative ways of approaching experience (such as natural science) make the theory inadequate as a complete solution of the problem. M. Granet's *La Pensée chinoise* remains the chief monument of the Durkheim school.

Through Neo-Kantianism Ernst Cassirer in the *Philosophie der Symbolischen Formen* (1923–9), and in *Essay on Man* (1945), might seem to have revived a Comtean solution. Comte's three stages of social evolution had been stages of forms of thought of which the last, positivist, stage is alone objective. But what Cassirer is doing is to assign a validity to each form of thinking and knowledge and, while this illuminates in detail many ways of thought, it yields no sociological light, for it is unconnected with any theory of social structure. His data, however, must be accounted for in any adequate sociology of knowledge. Its sociological utility for archaic society can be verified in H. Frankfort *et al.*, *The Intellectual Adventure of Early Man*, 1947.

The most elaborate attempt to deal with the foundations of the sociology of knowledge will be found in Karl Mannheim's *Ideology and Utopia*, 1936, and *Essays on the Sociology of Knowledge*, 1952. Mannheim directly faced the problem of the sociology of knowledge with great philosophical learning and methodological ingenuity, but a certain poverty of social facts. If knowledge is a social product, how can objective knowledge be possible? If it is impossible we are abandoned to nihilism. To avoid this Mannheim offers the idea that intellectuals, alienated from society by being intellectuals, stand apart from social structure and can be free of the burden of society in return for assuming the graver burden of responsibility, alienation, objectivity, and criticism. To most sociologists the subject remains of absorbing interest, the problems it raises are unsolved.

See ALIENATION, HISTORICISM. D.G.M.

sociology of law. The study of the *sociology of law* is well known in continental Europe, rather less so in the U.S.A., and Britain. In many instances the exponents of this subject have themselves been lawyers but there have been one or two notable exceptions, such as Émile Durkheim, but his classification of law, sociological though it be, is also over-simple. Durkheim's aim was to relate a type of law (retributive) to a type of society (primitive) and to contrast it with another kind of law (restitutive) associated with modern industrial (or organic) society. Max Weber, himself trained in law and economics, sought to analyse social systems relating law to other aspects of society. His *Wirtschaft und Gesellschaft* includes a lengthy and important treatise on the nature of rationality in law and administration (translated *Law in Economy and Society*, 1954). There have been numerous European contributors to the subject, one of the most outstanding being the Austrian scholar E. Ehrlich whose treatise, originally published in 1913, was translated into English under the title *Fundamental Principles of the Sociology of Law* in 1936, another is Georges Gurvitch's *Sociology of Law*, 1942. All these writers see law and legal systems as part of society, as social institutions related to other institutions and changing with them; they see law as one means of social control and hence endeavour to relate it to a moral order, to a body of customs and ideas about society. Clearly, the sociology of law is itself related to jurisprudence, but it is not the same. The study of systems of law may well be a necessary preliminary to the sociology of law, but the latter is wider in scope for it seeks to perceive the relationship of systems of law to other social sub-systems like the economy, the nature and distribution of authority, and the structure of kinship and family relationships. In Britain some social anthropologists have examined the system of law and courts in relatively simple societies and sought to determine their relationships to other aspects of the social system, notable instances being Max Gluckman's *The Judicial Process among the Barotse*, 1955 and his *Politics, Law and Ritual in Tribal Society*, 1965, but the attention of sociologists has hardly been turned to the

213

sociology of law in modern societies. In the U.S.A. there are signs of a growing interest in the subject but this has stemmed mainly from the work of jurists even though some, like David Riesman, have claims to being social scientists as well. A number of sociologists and lawyers have collaborated to produce an interesting and suggestive work entitled *Society and the Law: New Meanings for an Old Profession*, 1962, by F. J. Davis *et al.*   G.D.M.

sociology of occupations. The term refers not to a clearly delineated field of sociological enquiry, but to a heterogeneous range of studies dealing with the problem of how the occupational structure and particular occupations articulate with other segments of society like the family, the economy, the educational system, the political system, and the system of social stratification. Investigations centre upon the following themes (1) the division of labour, its causes and consequences, (2) the function and meaning of work and related phenomena such as leisure, unemployment and retirement, (3) the study of specific occupations as diverse as the hobo, the prostitute, the dockworker, the clerk, the architect, and the physician. Research has concentrated on such topics as the amount and method of remuneration, recruitment and training, career patterns, conflicts inherent in the role, the relation between personality and occupation, interpersonal relations at work, the public image of the occupation, and the distribution of power and prestige within the occupation.

Man, Work and Society, 1962, edited by Sigmund Nosow and William H. Form, a collection of readings, and two useful textbooks: Edward Gross, *Work and Society*, 1958, and Theodore Caplow, *The Sociology of Work*, 1954, give a good survey of the field. See DIVISION OF LABOUR, INDUSTRIAL SOCIOLOGY, PROFESSIONS.   S.H.

sociology of religion. The early sociological studies of religion had three distinctive methodological characteristics: they were evolutionist, positivist and psychological. These features may be illustrated from the work of Comte, Tylor and Spencer. In Comte's sociology, one of the fundamental conceptions is the so-called *law of three stages* according to which human thought has passed historically and necessarily, from the theological through the metaphysical to the positive stage. Comte treats theological thinking as intellectual error, which is dispersed by the rise of modern science. He traces within the theological stage, a development from animism to monotheism; and he explains religious belief in psychological terms by reference to the perceptions and thought processes of early man.

The work of Sir E. B. Tylor, *Primitive Culture*, 1871, and Herbert Spencer, *Principles of Sociology*, vol. III, 1896, was more rigorous and shows more clearly the features we have mentioned above. Both thinkers were concerned to explain, in the first place, the origin of religion. They believed that the soul was the principal feature of religious belief and set out to give an account in rationalist terms of how such an idea might have originated in the mind of primitive man. According to this, man obtained his idea of the soul from a misinterpretation of dreams and death. As with Comte, their explanation of religious phenomena is in terms of psychological dispositions, intellectual errors, and the conditions of social life. Other nineteenth-century social scientists, notably Karl Marx and Sir J. G. Frazer, approached the study of religion in a similar way.

An alternative approach to the study of religion was formulated by Émile Durkheim in *Les formes élémentaires de la vie réligieuse*, 1912, although it had been propounded earlier by Fustel de Coulanges, at one time Durkheim's teacher. Durkheim argued that in all societies, a distinction is made between the *sacred* and the *profane*. Religion, he stated, is 'a unified system of beliefs and practices relative to sacred things, that is things set apart and forbidden; beliefs and practices which unite into a single community called a Church all those who adhere to them.' In Durkheim's theory, the collective aspects of religion are emphasized: the function of religious rituals is to affirm the moral superiority of the society over its individual members and thus to maintain the solidarity of the society. 'The god of the clan can be nothing but the clan itself.'

Durkheim's emphasis on ritual as against belief was to prompt later anthropologists to undertake functionalist investigations of religion and the work of Malinowski in *Magic, Science and Religion and Other Essays*, 1948, and of A. R. Radcliffe-Brown in *The Andaman Islanders*, 1922, has shown how religion works in simple communities to maintain social cohesion and to control individual conduct.

In the study of civilized societies, Durkheim's theory has proved less helpful, for here religion is as frequently divisive as it is unifying. That is to say, while it unites particular groups it may provoke conflict between groups in the larger society. Moreover, in civilized societies, and especially in modern societies, beliefs and doctrines have more importance than ritual. It was this change of emphasis which fascinated L. T. Hobhouse and led him to examine the influence of intellectual development on social institutions and he gives particular attention to the development of moral ideas. Hence, in discussing religion in his major work, *Morals in Evolution*, 1907, he is entirely concerned with the moral codes of the major religions and especially of Christianity. The codes are examined as doctrines and analysed in a largely philosophical way. Their relation to social behaviour is considered in very general terms.

Max Weber, also profoundly impressed by the social implications of religious beliefs, differed from Hobhouse in his treatment of them in important respects. In the first place, it is not based on any evolutionary scheme. Secondly, it is largely concerned with a single major aspect of religious ethics, namely with their connection with the economic order, which he examines from two points of view. First, the influence of particular religious doctrines upon economic behaviour; second, the relations between the position of groups in the economic order and types of religious beliefs. Moreover, Weber is less concerned with ethical doctrines as expounded by theologians than with these doctrines in their popular form as the guide to everyday behaviour. Weber's best-known work, *The Protestant Ethic and the Spirit of Capitalism*, which was the starting point for his studies of religion, aims to show the part played in the origin and development of modern capitalism by Calvinist ethics.

Since the work of Weber and Durkheim, few theoretical contributions have been made to the sociological study of religion. Weber's influence has stimulated two principal and related lines of inquiry, one concerned with the characteristics, doctrines and social significance of religious sects, and the other with the connection between social classes and religious sects. An important early contribution came from his friend, Ernst Troeltsch, whose *The Social Teachings of the Christian Churches*, 1912, is a more detailed account than Weber's of the social ethics of different Christian churches and sects. In the same field of concern with sectarian movements is H. R. Niebuhr's *The Social Sources of Denominationalism*, 1929. More recently, there have been detailed empirical studies of particular sects in terms of their relations with and responses to the social milieu in which they exist. In England, Bryan Wilson's *Sects and Society*, 1961, was a substantial addition to and corrective of earlier work. In France, the work of H. Desroche has dealt in particular with the relation of religious sects and socialist political groups. There have also been valuable studies of sects in developing countries, especially in the continent of Africa, which on the one hand provide vivid – sometimes horrific – illustrations of the way in which religion can operate as an essential element in the establishment of social identity and, on the other, demonstrate how inadequate is the view that religion is the 'opiate' of the socially deprived and politically oppressed.

The second line of inquiry has also dealt with the issues Weber formulated. First there has been a continuing debate on the significance of the Protestant ethic in the origin and growth of modern Capitalism. Second, there has been more intensive and exact study of the differences between social classes in religious belief and observance.

In America where, contrary to the European trend, religious belief and practice have tended to increase rather than decline and where church attendance is high, with little noticeable differences between the social classes, W. Herberg, *Catholic, Protestant and Jew*, 1955, and N. J. Demareth, *Social Class in American Protestantism*, 1965, have attempted on the one hand to apply Durkheimian notions of social solidarity and on the other to expand Weberian hypotheses on the social foundations of sect allegiance.

In connection with similar studies, there has also gradually emerged a very useful sociography of religion. It is particularly advanced in France, where G. le Bras has inspired many descriptive and quantitative studies, the best known in this country probably being F. Boulard's *Premiers itinéraires en sociologie réligieuse*, 1954. This kind of study has been pursued in a wider context, that of the process of secularization, which it is generally agreed, has been taking place in Western societies over the past century.

Nearly all the studies referred to above have shared in common the major premise that religion was about God(s) and could best be studied in terms of the activities of institutionalized religious groups. In 1965, the publication of Harvey Cox, *The Secular City*, sparked off a lively discussion which continues to this day as to whether such 'traditional' assumptions are adequate to the study of religion in human society. Religion, it is claimed, has been 'transformed' in modern society: is no longer the exclusive property of ecclesiastical institutions; and, it would appear, can persist quite happily, innocent of any concept of 'God'. Thus 'religion' is to be found not only in the Churches but in the community action group, the political party or the social services. Curiously enough, it does not appear to have occurred to those who advance this novel view that a concept of religion which would include both Marxists and Baptists can only appear both bizarre and offensive to members of both groups.   M.H.

sociology of science. An aspect of the sociology of knowledge in which the nature of scientific and technological ideas, concepts and theories is related to other kinds of ideas of a philosophical kind and more especially to social institutions and organizations or even to characteristics of persons.

A considerable discussion has taken place on the manner in which science and technology are related to the need for man and his society to adapt to a physical environment. It follows that the sociology of science bears upon a number of institutional aspects of society, e.g. the economy, education, religion and politics.

An early consideration was A. Comte's classification of the sciences including what he called at first *social physics* and later *sociology*. The present vogue for sociology of science developed out of the growth of history of science, largely a post-war phenomenon. Prominent among the contributions by historians was Sir Herbert Butterfield's *The Origins of Modern Science 1300–1800*, 1949. Contemporary studies refer to the communication structures in the scientific world, the way in which new ways of thinking develop and the social problems created by innovation. Thus a more sociological start to the history of science was given in 1962 when Thomas Kuhn published *The Structure of Scientific Revolutions* in which he argues that what he calls 'normal science' presupposes a conceptual and instrumental framework or *paradigm* accepted by the whole scientific community. But, he points out, the consequential mode of scientific practice brings inevitable 'crises' which cannot be resolved within this framework and science only returns to a normal state when the community accepts a new conceptual structure which may again determine its search for new facts and better theories.

The position taken by Kuhn is shared by Sir Karl Popper whose *Logic of Scientific Discovery*, 1959, also stresses the role of revolutions. But they differ in their evaluation of the role of criticism in the development of science. This was the subject of a symposium in London in 1965 which resulted in a report edited by I. Lakatos and A. Musgrave, *Criticism and the Growth of Knowledge*, 1970. See also M. J. Mulkay, *The Social Process of Innovation: a study in the Sociology of Science*, 1972, and L. Sklair, *Organised Knowledge*, 1973.   G.D.M.

sociometry. A term coined by Jacob L. Moreno, an Austrian psychiatrist who emigrated to the United States of America. As a refugee camp administrator after the First World War, he was interested to develop techniques for releasing spontaneity in people in distressed circumstances by allowing them to group themselves according to their own choices. In America he further developed this as a small group therapeutic and research technique. The practice of *sociometry* consists of the administration of a questionnaire in which the subject chooses five other people in rank order of their attractiveness as associates, either generally or in relation to some specific activity. It was later extended to cover negative choices. The results are

217

plotted on paper in diagrammatic form, hence the term *sociogram*. This technique, whilst simple, is only suitable for small groups but, within this limitation, it has been found very useful. Moreno himself does not appear to have used it much in small group experimental investigations, and indeed his theoretical approach seems to be so vague and general, not to say bizarre, that this is not surprising, but a wide variety of other people engaged in research have made good use of it, including Helen H. Jennings, who used it in detailed studies of women in correctional institutions in America; see her *Leadership and Isolation*, 1943.

Sociometry has aroused considerable interest because, once it has been decided what is implied in inter-personal choices recorded in this manner, it is possible to present the results quantitatively. Thus measurements may be made of, say, the incidence of group coherence, which is the number of reciprocated choices multiplied by q, divided by the number of unreciprocated choices multiplied by p, where p/q is the chance ratio of reciprocated to unreciprocated choices.

Moreno's original exposition is found in his book *Who Shall Survive?*, 1934, and in the journal he founded, called *Sociometry*, see vols. 1, 6, 9 and 13. The best critical exposition and appraisal is that of G. Lindzey and E. F. Borgatta in the former's *Handbook of Social Psychology*, vol. I, 1954, ch. 11.

G.D.M.

Sombart, Werner (1863–1941). German historian and sociologist. His *Der Moderne Kapitalismus*, 1902, and *Der Bourgeois*, 1913, are important contributions to the study of modern society at the pre-World War I stage of its development.

sorcery. See MAGIC.

Sorokin, Pitirim Alexandrovich (1889–1968). Russian sociologist much influenced by war and revolution and their aftermath. He wrote a lengthy essay on hunger which was smuggled out of the Soviet Union when he left in 1922 during the great famine, subsequently to be posthumously published in 1975 under the title *Hunger as a factor in human affairs*. Emigrating to America, he taught first at the University of Minnesota and then at Harvard.

Sorokin's interests were wide and he wrote on sociological aspects of art, knowledge, politics and social stratification. Of his principal works *The Sociology of Revolution*, 1925; *Social Mobility*, 1927–41 and *Contemporary Sociological Theories*, 1928 are a typical selection, but his major work was *Social and Cultural Dynamics*, 1937–41 in which he displays comparative sociological analysis in the grand manner. The titles of the four volumes are illustrative: I. Fluctuation of forms of Art; II. Fluctuation of Systems of Truth, Ethics and Law; III. Fluctuation of Social Relationships, War and Revolution; IV. Basic Problems: Principles and Methods.

Sorokin was not just a speculative sociologist. He carried out detailed empirical studies to discern the signs of the times and toward the end of his life sought for solutions to world problems. In 1954 he wrote *The Ways and Power of Love: Types, Factors and Techniques of Moral Transformation*, and on retirement from Harvard founded and carried on the work of his Harvard

Research Center in Creative Altruism. His independence of mind, his breadth of knowledge and his devotion to the responsibilities of scholarship were well-known; he could be scathing about quackery as witness his *Fads and Foibles in Modern Sociology* (1955).   G.D.M.

sororal polygyny. See POLYGYNY.

Spencer, Herbert (1820–1903). British engineer and editor, philosopher and sociologist. Spencer was self-taught and consequently his learning was highly selective. He was one of the first exponents of evolutionary theory. His *First Principles* was published in 1860 and provided an outline of universal knowledge, but already he had written a paper on the 'Development Hypothesis' in 1852, seven years before Darwin's *Origin of Species*, in which he outlined a theory of organic evolution and came close to perceiving that the key to evolution might lie in the struggle for survival. The year 1887 was memorable for Spencer, for in that year he arrived at his universal law pertaining to physical, organic and social development whereby 'the transformation of the homogeneous into the heterogeneous is that in which progress essentially exists'. His *Principles of Sociology*, 1874, advanced an organic theory of society, provided two social morphologies together with his theory of social evolution, it contains a wealth of data about human customs and institutions, but its abiding value lies in the emphasis Spencer placed on the idea of function and his essentially sociological outlook, whereby he pointed to co-existences in social life. Thus, for examples, he focused attention on the co-existence of a high degree of militarism in a society with female subjugation, and on the connection between despotic government and elaborate domestic etiquette.

Spencer's writings were very popular in Britain, even more so in America which he visited in his later years. He was the common man's philosopher of the time. If his works are little read today it is not because he posed problems and failed to solve them, but because so few of his problems are those of modern sociologists.   G.D.M.

statics and dynamics. It was Auguste Comte who introduced the distinction between *social statics* and *social dynamics*. Social statics represented the endeavour to arrive at laws of co-existence, whilst social dynamics endeavoured to arrive at the laws of historical change. The former attempt depended on the discernment of the conditions of existence, which in turn depends upon an understanding of the necessary relations between the parts of a social whole. Radcliffe-Brown, who was much influenced by Comtean sociology, argued that it is the first task of social statics to make some attempt at classification of forms of social life. He believed that such a classification must be typological in character, but that such an attempt had been held up because of the general propensity to study society by means of an historical method.

Social dynamics in Comte's view depended on an analysis of historical data with a view to determining the laws of historical change. This led to naturalistic forms of historicism, to use Sir K. R. Popper's terminology. (See his *Poverty of Historicism*, 1957.) It is, perhaps, worth pointing out that the terms *statics* and *dynamics* have been borrowed from the physical sciences, but that their connotation has altered. The type of system which the physicist calls dynamic, e.g. the solar system, is precisely the kind of system which the Comtean sociologist calls static. In the developing science of group dynamics, however, there is no misnomer, for there the study of the interrelationships between the parts of a social system is properly called group dynamics. But this is not the study of a group over a period of time to discern the changes in its structure. Thus the general propositions about the processes in a social group are of a quite different methodological status from those about the history of mankind, such as Comte's Law of the Three Stages. See GROUP DYNAMICS. G.D.M.

status, status symbol See SOCIAL STATUS.

stem family. One of the three or four fundamental types of family (the others being the Patriarchal, the Unstable and the Particularist) distinguished by Frédéric Le Play (1806–1882) on the basis of his field studies of family organization, published as a series of monographs, *Les ouvriers des deux mondes,* between 1830 and 1880.

The *stem family* Le Play found to predominate among complex and prosperous families in Central Europe, Scandinavia and Spain, averaging about six or seven members and typically engaged in free labour or as farm tenants. The family's place on the land or in a particular occupation was unfailingly handed down from generation to generation. Individual sons and daughters might emigrate to the cities for work, but they retained permanent contact with their family, often sending them money and making personal sacrifices for them and paying visits from time to time.

For Le Play, the stem family was in many ways the ideal family form, combining as it did a high degree of family stability and loyalty with a greater degree of freedom for its individual members than the stricter Patriarchal family, of which the stem family was a modification, permitted. M.H.

stereotype. There are two uses of the term *stereotype*, one sociological and the other psychological, but they are related.

The term may refer to a tendency for a belief to be widespread in any social group or society. Thus there may be a tendency for people to believe that Jews are clever or that Americans are wealthy. Such stereotypes can be determined by means of attitude research.

The term may be used to denote the over-simplification of a belief in regard to its content together with a tendency for the belief to be resistant to factual evidence to the contrary. Thus the belief that Jews are clever might persist despite any evidence that was adduced to show that they were no more so than others, or the belief that Americans are wealthy might prove to be resistant to the evidence that many Americans are very poor. All beliefs tend to be subject to the laws of levelling and sharpening, and so all beliefs may be regarded as stereotypes, but this is merely to say that all beliefs which are subject to such psychological processes are more likely than not to gain widespread acceptance, and so we see a relationship between the psychological concept and the sociological one. One of the main sociological problems is to examine the nature of stereotypes and to discern the factors which enable them to persist; in other words to ask: what is their function? See D. Krech and R. S. Crutchfield, *Theory and Problems of Social Psychology*, 1948, ch. 5. See ATTITUDE RESEARCH.   G.D.M.

Stouffer, Samuel Andrew (1900–1960). American social scientist, he was educated at Harvard, Chicago and London and held teaching posts in the Universities of Wisconsin, Chicago, and Harvard where he was Director of the Laboratory of Social Relations. His early interest was in demography but he is better known for his work on Attitude and Opinion measurement and especially for his major war-time contribution: the four volumes of *Studies in Social Psychology in World War II*, the first two volumes of which are better known as *The American Soldier*. He was noted for his attempts to advance mensuration in sociology without losing sight of the importance of having clear and sensible hypotheses to test. His last volume of papers *Social Research to Test Ideas*, 1962, presents a good sample of his work.   G.D.M.

stratification. See SOCIAL STRATIFICATION.

stratified sampling. See SAMPLING.

structural-functionalism. See FUNCTION, SOCIAL STRUCTURE, SOCIAL SYSTEM.

structuralism. In the common parlance of English language sociology and social anthropology in the year 1978 the term 'structuralism' is usually taken to refer to the body of theory and practice developed by the French social anthropologist Claude Lévi-Strauss in a wide variety of publications from 1945 onwards. A selection of key essays have been reprinted in Lévi-Strauss, *Anthropologie Structurale*, Paris: Librairie Plon, 1958, translated *Structural Anthropology*, 1968, and *Anthropologie Structurale Deux*, Paris: Librairie Plon, 1973, translated *Structural Anthropology Vol. II*, 1977. The present article is mainly concerned with structuralism in this sense but the reader needs to appreciate that the term has wider connotations. Among British social anthropologists in the early 1950s the term was sometimes used to distinguish the special style of social analysis developed by the followers of A. R. Radcliffe-Brown at Oxford, but in recent years, following French usage, *structuralism* has served as a vaguely defined label for the common characteristics of work by a variety of authors coming from many different academic disciplines. Thus Jean Piaget, *Le Structuralisme*, Paris, 1968, translated *Structuralism*, 1971, claims to demonstrate a common thread running through ideas which appear in mathematics, physics, biology, psychology, linguistics, philosophy and the social sciences and there are now a variety of structuralist 'readers' which adopt an equally catholic approach. For example *The Structuralists: from Marx to Lévi-Strauss*, edited R. T. and F. M. De George, New York, 1972, includes items by Marx, Freud, de Saussure, Jakobson, Lévi-Strauss, Barthes, Althusser, Foucault and Lacan.

Actually the five contemporary Frenchmen whose names conclude this list all vigorously reject their common association but all of them are unquestionably indebted to the special insights which originated with the other four. In particular F. de Saussure, *Cours de Linguistique Générale*, Paris, 1916, edited posthumously by two of Saussure's pupils, translated *Course in General Linguistics*, 1958, is a key work which is ancestral to all subsequent exercises in structuralist style either in linguistics, literary criticism, psycho-analysis, social anthropology, marxist theory or social history. The present article makes no attempt to establish the multifarious interconnections within this body of writing; instead it indicates some of the stylistic peculiarities which distinguish the social anthropology of Lévi-Strauss.

In structuralist doctrine the crucial feature which distinguishes human beings (Man in culture) from animals of the species *Homo* (Man in nature) is the possession of language which is both *natural*, in that our ability to speak is a genetic endowment, and *cultural*, in that any particular language serves to distinguish members of one culture from members of another. Language, as uttered in words either verbally or in writing, is a projection into the external world of conceptual patterns in the mind of the speaker. And by analogy this is true also of all other cultural manifestations; our tools, our clothes, our houses, the way we arrange our settlements, the way we prepare our food, our 'manners and customs' in all their aspects, are all human products generated by human minds. Consequently the interrelations which are discernible objectively in such manifest features of culture must correspond in some way to relational characteristics of the minds which produced them in the first place. For example, among speakers of the English language, utterance of the word *son* carries significance for both speaker and listener because of a patterned structure of relationships with a number of other words belonging to the same set such as: *father*, *mother*, *husband*, *wife*, *daughter*, *brother*, *sister*. The word *son* does not mean anything by itself; we credit it with meaning because, unconsciously, we are able to contrast it with other terms and then, again subconsciously, compare and contrast such relationships as mother-son, sister-brother; father-son, brother-brother; mother-son, mother-daughter; husband-wife, brother-sister, mother's brother (uncle) – sister's son (nephew), and so on. The total cultural significance of the single word *son* is embedded in the structure of this total complex of contrasted relationships which Lévi-Strauss refers to as 'the atom of kinship'.

A very similar kind of analysis can also be applied to non-verbal features of customary behaviour. For example the roast turkey which appears on several million English dinner tables on Christmas Day carries meaningful significance not simply because of what it is but because of its relation to a great variety of things which it is not, for example, it is cooked not raw, roast not boiled or smoked, meat not vegetable or fish, a whole bird not cut up meat or offal, a large, unusual, domesticated bird not small or common or wild; accompanied by paradoxical foods such as mince pies which contain no mince and plum pudding which contains no plums, cut up at table by a parent and not beforehand, eaten by all members of the household and not only by adults, and so forth. To evaluate the significance of such binary oppositions we should need to investigate the total pattern of eating habits and food preparation customs in the households concerned for there are other occasions when these same people eat food which is raw not cooked, fish not meat, offal not fine meat, in isolation not together, etc. The structuralist thesis is that all such customary behaviours, which the participant actors take entirely for granted, in fact reflect patterned permutations among a range of limited possibilities and that such patterned operations, if considered collectively as sets rather than one at a time, will be seen to be structured in positive and negative instances, rather like a morse code, and that the pattern as a whole will tell us significant facts about the workings of the human mind. Such an objective may well seem over-ambitious but nevertheless a structuralist analysis of the prototypical English Christmas dinner on the lines indicated above will reveal quite a number of cultural assertions concerning conventional English values relating to social class, the hierarchy of social occasions and the sanctity of the domestic family. It will not tell us why many people prefer goose to turkey! The point here is that what the coded 'messages' of cultural performance are all about is something quite other than the manifest content of that performance. Whatever it is that the word *son* may mean it has nothing to do with the phonetic sequence s-o-n.

Another closely related structuralist principle is that of *transformation*. Patterns of behaviour which are generated as manifest cultural products in the real objective world are generated by 'deep' unconscious structures in human minds or perhaps even by a universal collectivity 'the human mind', which is a shared natural characteristic of all human beings. If the reductionist argument is carried that far, then it must follow that the varieties of cultural product which are generated in the real world must all be transformations of each other since all of them derive from the same ultimate structured source in the human unconscious. At this level there are close parallels between the theories of the structuralists and those of the Freudian psycho-analysts but Lévi-Strauss has gone much further than Freud in that he claims to be able to decipher the transformation rules which will convert the modalities of one culture into the modalities of another, e.g. which will transform the rules of kinship and marriage prevalent among the Australian Aborigines into those prevailing among the North Burma Kachins or alternatively, within the framework of a single culture, will convert the modalities of, say, table manners into the modalities of house construction.

Lévi-Strauss's programme is a good deal more ambitious than his achievement. In practice his main applications of structuralist method have been devoted to wide ranging cross-cultural comparisons in very restricted areas of cultural activity. *Les Structures élémentaires de la Parenté*, Paris 1949; revised edition 1967; translated, *The Elementary Structures of Kinship*, 1969, is concerned with the permutations of formal rules of marriage, residence and descent in relation to the terminology of kinship in parts of Oceania and Eastern Asia. The much more influential *Mythologiques*, 4 vols., Paris 1964–1971, examines the permutations of mythology among Indian tribes over a vast area of North and South America. Both these works are astonishing intellectual achievements though just what they can tell us about such an elusive entity as 'the human mind' is very much of a moot point. There have been numerous attempts to give relatively brief accounts of the bare essentials of Lévi-Straussian structuralism. Lévi-Strauss's own *La Pensée sauvage*, Paris: Librarie Plon, 1962, translated *The Savage Mind*, 1966, is tough going. *Lévi-Strauss*, 1970 (Fontana Modern Masters Series) is a short, greatly oversimplified presentation by the author of the present article.   E.I.

structure. See SOCIAL STRUCTURE.

suburb, suburbia. As city development has taken the form of an outward movement of population to the surrounding areas to form new settlements, often taking the form of housing estates both publicly and privately financed, so the term suburb has grown in use and the kind of life lived by the inhabitants (suburbanites) has given rise to the term suburbia. Between 1950 and 1960 there was a particular interest in this phenomenon, not unconnected with the problems of urban redevelopment following on the war in Europe. Sociological studies focusing on the suburb and suburban values were carried out in Britain, France, the Netherlands and Germany, but there were similar developments in the U.S.A. and Canada. See D. C. Thorns, *Suburbia*, 1972.   G.D.M.

succession. In a broad sense this refers to the transmission of rights in general; in a more narrow sense, to the transmission of rights to office.

It is used sometimes as a synonym of *inheritance*, i.e. succession is the inheritance of office, or conversely inheritance is the succession to rights over property. Most anthropologists have stuck to the narrow use of the term, and confined it to the transmission of office. (See, for example, A. I. Richards, *Land, Labour and Diet in Northern Rhodesia*, 1939.)

The *locus classicus* is Sir Henry Maine, *Ancient Law*, 1861, and in the same tradition is A. R. Radcliffe-Brown, 'Patrilineal and Matrilineal Succession', in *Structure and Function in Primitive Society*, 1952. For a clear distinction between succession and inheritance see R. Piddington, *An Introduction to Social Anthropology*, Volume I, 1950. See INHERITANCE, KINSHIP.   J.R.F.

Sumner, William Graham (1840–1910). American sociologist and champion of laissez-faire, an exponent of inexorable, irreversible unilinear evolution; he planned a comprehensive system of sociology completed posthumously by A. G. Keller as *The Science of Society*, 1927. *Folkways*, 1906, argues that individual habit and group custom arise gradually and unconsciously as fittest usages survive and become crystallized into recurrent patterns. He distinguishes between *crescive* institutions, formed in this way, and *enacted* institutions, formed consciously. Mores are customs recognized as conducive to societal welfare and exerting a coercion for conformity. He contributed the distinction between 'in-group' and 'out-group', based on conformity to group mores; the 'in-group' is a group with strong ethnocentricity. Sumner is important sociologically for his treatment of norms and for initiating a normative approach to social phenomena.   G.D.M.

superorganic. *Superorganic* is a term used by Herbert Spencer in his *Principles of Sociology*, 1876, to distinguish different levels of the evolutionary process; thus, evolution began in the inorganic realm, proceeded in the organic realm and finally in the superorganic realm. By *superorganic* he meant the social interaction of human beings, and animals, including insects, for whilst such interaction may have emerged from the organic realm this social aspect of life is different in quality and deserves to be specially indicated. Modern sociologists seldom use the term *superorganic*, preferring to use the term *cultural*, or if they use it they do so to qualify the term *culture* indicating thereby that whilst the organic nature of mankind may place a limitation on social life and its development, such social life is not determined by it. See CULTURE.

G.D.M.

symbolic interactionism. The term symbolic interactionism was coined by Herbert Blumer in 1937; it refers both to a set of ontological assumptions concerning the nature of social life and a set of methodological prescriptions which, it is claimed, are consistent with the perspective's ontology. Its roots lie in the work of the American pragmatist philosophers, William James and George Herbert Mead, and also in the early American humanist sociology of W. I. Thomas, Florian Znaniecki, Robert Park and Charles Horton Cooley. The perspective developed largely at the University of Chicago, and it was Blumer, his colleagues and students who evolved its main outline in a series of empirical, theoretical and methodological studies published between 1930 and 1950. Despite its being overshadowed by structural functionalism during the 1950s and early 1960s, the last ten years have seen a major resurgence of this immensely productive variant of interpretative sociology.

The social metaphysics of symbolic interactionism rest on three basic premises which have been outlined by Blumer: first 'that human beings act toward things on the basis of the meanings that the things have for them'; second 'that the meaning of such things is derived from, or arises out of, the social interaction that one has with one's fellows'; third 'that these meanings are handled in, and modified through an interpretative process used by the person in dealing with the things he encounters'. These simple premises provide a view of individuals, of social interaction and of social structure which is wholly distinctive: the social actor is seen as an active agent in the construction and interpretation of social situations and their meanings; social interaction is understood as the dynamic interpenetration of lines of action undertaken by individuals in pursuance of chosen goals, these lines themselves constituting selections from a wide variety of available roles; social structure is portrayed as dynamic processual and emergent so that its description at any single point in time is best understood as a snapshot taken of a constantly changing scene.

Methodologically, symbolic interactionists have tended towards a naturalistic perspective, stressing the necessity for studies of *real* social situations rather than the construction of artificial ones via the use of experimental designs or survey studies. In place of formal methods of data collection and analysis, they have substituted only broad and general methodological injunctions which call for an attitude of 'respect' for the phenomena under investigation. Blumer has claimed that such studies are, or at any rate should be, carried out in two stages. The first is that of 'exploration', in which the investigator's main concern is to gain firsthand acquaintance with the social situations that he wishes to study, and at this stage the aim is to depict that world as it is understood and oriented to by those who live in it. Such descriptions are then likely to be uninformed by sociological theory and largely couched in participants' language. In the second stage, however, that of 'inspection', the researcher concentrates on 'analytic elements' in the setting, which are of course only available through theoretically informed observation, and for most interactionists, this stage has consisted in the identification, description and explanation of basic social processes, e.g. socialization, integration, negotiation. This latter concern has often resulted in a fairly formalistic sociology, although on the part of Blumer and his colleagues there has always existed an attempt to temper this tendency with the reminder that these forms themselves only arise from the activities of human agents in pursuit of pragmatic interests. See Herbert Blumer, *Symbolic Interactionism: Perspective and Method*, 1969.   R.W.

system. See SOCIAL SYSTEM.

T

taboo. The term *taboo* refers to prohibitions on conduct which if enacted would endanger some or all of the relationships constituting the universe in which men live. In many societies the universe of relationships commonly includes physical forces as well as social relations.

The word *tabu* entered English through the narratives of Captain Cook who first encountered the word, in its Tongan form, in 1777. Cognate forms of the word occur in various languages of Polynesia, Micronesia and Melanesia.

Taboos may be regarded as symbolizing the structure of relationships peculiar to a group. Their observance by an individual serves to mark membership of the group, commitment to one's roles and recognition of other roles and forces interdependent with one's own. Thus breaking the taboo is disruptive of the moral system and of one's position in it. Rectification requires an appropriate ritual of reinstatement. See A. R. Radcliffe-Brown, 'Taboo', in his *Structure and Function in Primitive Society*, 1952, and Mary Douglas, *Purity and Danger*, 1966.   H.D.M.

Tarde, Gabriel (1843–1904). French judge, criminologist and sociologist; he made important contributions to early social psychology and provided the basis for a theory of social and cultural change through imitation. His works include *Laws of Limitation*, 1890 (translated 1903), and *Social Laws*, 1898 (translated 1899). The keystone of his system is imitation, which is found throughout the realm of science, together with opposition and adaptation. Imitation accounts for the transmission and constancy of social forms and is subject both to logical and non-logical laws. Society comprises a group of men able to imitate one another. Opposition is of two types – opposition of conflict (war, competition, discussion) and of rhythm (fluctuation of social phenomena). Adaptation, or invention, appears in the establishment of a new equilibrium after opposition; it leads to integration.   G.D.M.

task-orientation. See EXPRESSIVE; EXPRESSIVE ORIENTATION.

Tawney, Richard Henry (1880–1962). English economic historian, social philosopher and moralist. Educated at Balliol College, Oxford, he became a dominant force in the formation of the Workers' Educational Association, of which he was president for sixteen years. His books, pamphlets, lectures and articles influenced many people outside the boundaries of academic life. All his work bore the stamp of his radical principles and it is quite clear that this socialist thinker was energized by his concern for human welfare. His search for causation and meaning, if not overtly sociological, had a Weberian slant because, like Max Weber, Tawney used historical facts to illuminate current problems. In major books such as *The Acquisitive Society*, 1921; *Religion and the Rise of Capitalism*, 1926; and *Equality*, 1931, Tawney is not only a Christian advocate but also a critic of the 'idolatry of wealth' which must spell ruin for the personal ideals and values that he cherished. From 1931 to 1949 he was Professor of Economic History in the University of London. His contribution to the growth of a new and more empirical historiography gives him a place in intellectual history, as Talcott Parsons has said: 'His name will long be remembered among the founders of twentieth-century social thought.'   E.W.M.

teknonymy. A word coined by the English anthropologist Sir Edward Burnett Tylor to denote the custom prevalent among some peoples of naming the parent from the child, the husband not being a member of the wife's family, although he acquires that status at the birth of the first child. Usually, the father is known as 'Father of X', X being the infant's name. Similarly, a mother may be named 'Mother of X'; thus *teknonymy* is a term which covers both cases.

theory; social theory. The term *theory* is one of the most misused and misleading terms in the vocabulary of the social scientist.

It may refer to an abstract conceptual scheme which in itself may be little more than a number of definitions, or it may have a systematic reference so that each abstract term is systematically related to the others, rendering the categories exclusive of each other, but pointing to their articulation. If, from such a categorical system, laws may be derived possessing predictive value, then we may say that a *theoretical* system has been evolved. Strictly speaking only this last kind of system is a system of theory, and a law, or generalization derived from it, is properly called a *theory*.

There is a very loose use of the term *theory* to mean that part of the study of a subject which is not practical. In the training of social workers *theory* is often contrasted with *practical work*, but what is meant here is merely the more academic aspects of a course of instruction.

With the prefix *social* the use of the term *theory* has a philosophical connotation derived from political studies. It may be said to have originated in Oxford University with the expression *Theory of the State*, by which is meant discussion of the origins of the modern nation state, together with philosophical justifications for the forms it may take. The expression *social theory* has thus come to denote a range of description and argument concerned with political arrangements, and courses in social theory usually devote a large proportion of the syllabus to the writings of Hobbes, Locke, Rousseau, Hegel, Green and Bosanquet.

There is a range of literature, the contents of which are sometimes referred to as *social theory*, but more often perhaps denoted by the expression *history of ideas*, yet inasmuch as the ideas are those about human relations and human society their discussion may properly be subsumed under this title. Thus, for instance, a work like Carlo Antoni's *From History to Sociology: The Transition in German Historical Thinking*, 1959, might be spoken of as *social theory*, but so also might such works as H. S. Hughes, *Consciousness and*

228

Society: The Reorientation of European Social Thought, 1890–1930, 1958. Such writings border on the discussion of *sociological theory*, although the latter may be distinguished by its reference to methodological discussion related to social structures and systems of social relationships. See P. S. Cohen, *Modern Social Theory*, 1968; S. Mennell, *Sociological Theory: Uses and Unities*, 1974. See METHODOLOGY, SOCIOLOGY.   G.D.M.

Thomas, William Isaac (1863–1947). American sociologist, he made important contributions to conceptul analysis and in his emphasis upon the need for scientific techniques of enquiry, himself employing control groups; he stressed the importance of studying phenomena in their total cultural context. Major works include *Sex and Society*, 1907; *Source Book for Social Origins*, 1909; *The Polish Peasant in Europe and America*, 1918–20 (with F. Znaniecki); *The Unadjusted Girl*, 1923; *The Child in America*, 1928; and *Primitive Behaviour*, 1937. *The Polish Peasant* employs first-hand case studies and personal documents and the situational approach. It introduces the four wishes – recognition, new experiences, mastery, and security – which cause man to join society; and the three basic personality types – Philistine, Bohemian and Creative personality. Thomas regarded the total situation as composed of three elements: *objective conditions*; *pre-existing attitudes of individuals and groups*; and *definition of the situation*. The latter is a concept introduced by Thomas, as are *social situation*, and *social disorganization*. This and other works emphasize the inter-relationship between culture and personality.   G.D.M.

Tocqueville, Alexis Charles Henri Maurice Clerel de (1805–1859). French politician and political sociologist, famous for his visit (with Gustave Beaumont) in 1831 to America, ostensibly to examine the penal system and American prison-reform measures, but in reality to study extensively American institutions, customs and practices. His analysis of the institutionalization of equality was published as *Democratie en Amerique*, 1835. His *L'Ancien régime et la révolution* appeared in 1856 and was the first and only completed volume of a large work on the French Revolution he planned. It reflects his mature views on the causes and course of the events leading up to it. The theme of his work stands in contrast to that of Marx with whom he is often compared as a student of both revolution and a modern social system. The English translation of *Democracy in America* first appeared in 1838; a new translation edited by J. P. Mayer and Max Lerner was published in 1966.   G.D.M.

Tönnies, Ferdinand (1855–1936). German sociologist; his important contributions lie in the twin concepts of *Gemeinschaft* and *Gesellschaft* and in his sociographic works. *Gemeinschaft und Gesellschaft* (translated *Fundamental Concepts of Sociology*, 1940, and *Community and Association*, 1955), argues that society and social relationships are the products of will, of which natural or essential will, and rational or arbitrary will are the two types. A complex of relationships produced by essential will is termed a community; one produced by rational will an association. Tönnies distinguishes between a circle (plurality of persons willing to be in a definite

229

relationship), a collective (plurality forming a unit by virtue of common characteristics), and a corporation (functionally differentiated organization). Also he presents an original classification of social norms. Tönnies applied these concepts in various analyses, e.g. the incidence of suicide in Schleswig-Holstein.   G.D.M.

total institution. An organization of people of a particular kind enabling some to control closely the behaviour of others. The term was introduced by Erving Goffman in *Asylums*, 1961, where he describes the manner in which patients are inducted or 'institutionalized'. In his words total institutions are 'forcing-houses for changing persons: each is a natural experiment on what can be done to the self'. Other examples are military or naval units, boarding schools, prisons and reformatories, convents and monasteries.   G.D.M.

totem; totemism. A *totem* is a species of animal or plant; or part of an animal or plant; or a natural object or phenomenon or the symbol of any of these which signifies distinguishing features of a human group *vis-à-vis* other groups, similarly represented, in the same society. Totemism refers to the occurrence and social usage of this mode of representing social classification.

The word *totem* derives from an Algonquin (Amerindian) dialectical form (NED). Although totem and totemism were both introduced into English in 1791 by J. Long in *Voyages and Travels of an Indian Interpreter*, an anthropological exposition was not forthcoming until J. F. McLennan's papers appeared in 1867 ('Totemism', in *Chambers's Encyclopaedia*) and in 1869–70 (a series of essays on totemism in the *Fortnightly Review*).

The study of totemism throughout the ensuing century has been marked by the formulation of different problems and by few successes in their solution. Why are human groups linked in thought with natural species? The earliest writers (J. G. Frazer, Baldwin Spencer, W. H. R. Rivers, *et al.*) attempted historical explanations, but as A. Lang observed, 'Of the origin of these beliefs ... we can only form ... guesses ...' ('Totemism', *Encyclopaedia Britannica*, 11th edition, 1911).

Totemism appeared to be important in those societies in which it was identified by observers. Why was this? Although it seemed to be associated with the rule of exogamy between totemic groups, with taboos on killing or eating the group's totem, with the use of totemic emblems, with religious attitudes towards the totem, with belief in descent from the totem, it had to be admitted that none of these traits were invariable features of totemic societies. (See A. A. Goldenweiser, 'Totemism: An Analytical Study', *Journal of American Folklore*, 1910.) Thus the question, What is totemism? became a prime problem. Numerous unsuccessful attempts were made to define totemism as an autonomous institution having certain intrinsic characteristics. By the middle 1920s the study was chaotic. (See Goldenweiser, *History, Psychology and Culture*, 1933 for a survey of the literature.)

A. R. Radcliffe-Brown in his papers of 1929 ('The Sociological Theory of Totemism', *Proceedings of the Fourth Pacific Science Congress*, Java, reprinted in A. R. Radcliffe-Brown, *Structure and Function in Primitive Society*, 1952) and of 1951 ('The Comparative Method in Social

Anthropology', *Journal of the Royal Anthropological Institute*, 81, 1951, reprinted in A. R. Radcliffe-Brown, *Method in Social Anthropology*, 1958) shifted attention from the question 'What is totemism?' to the question 'What is the significance of this mental association between natural species and human groups for the *structure* of society?' In the course of developing his theme, particularly in the 1951 paper, he shows, *inter alia*, how in animal tales in various societies 'the world of animal life is represented in terms of social relations similar to those of human society'. Through the use of these animal symbols presented in socially relevant connections thought is directed at the same time to relations between animals and to relations between human groups. C. Lévi-Strauss had developed this view. We are confronted, he says, with a system of thought which does far more than discriminate between human groups. It is a logically constructed system referring to *all* categories of social phenomena, to values and events, on both diachronic and synchronic axes. Its symbols may be drawn from the lexical treasury of the natural universe but the secret of its code lies not in those natural elements which are selected for notational use (and which early thinkers mistakenly sought to reify) but in the principles whereby the elements are classified and in the relations between the categories however represented. Thus totemism as an integrated reality in the classical sense is an illusion. Those totemic representations are absorbed into the breadth and depth of the societal thought-system of which they were for many, and for long, observable but incomprehensible, features. For Lévi-Strauss the problem of totemism is the problem of the structure of human thought. See R. Piddington, *An Introduction to Social Anthropology*, vol. 1, 1952; C. Lévi-Strauss, *Totemism* (translated by R. Needham), 1963; Lévi-Strauss, *The Savage Mind* (translated by S. Wolfram), 1966; E. Leach, *Lévi-Strauss*, 1970.   H.D.M.

town planning. *Town planning*, although very ancient in the sense of the design and layout of towns, is of relatively recent origin when seen as a form of central control over and co-ordination of the use of land. In most rapidly urbanized countries of the world in the nineteenth century it was felt that any government restrictions on the development of land, and the building of factories and houses was an encroachment on personal liberty. The lack of overall control, however, led to such congestion and urban sprawl that some form of central direction came to be realized. In Britain the first legislation was the Housing, Town Planning, etc. Act of 1909 which gave local authorities the right to prepare development schemes. But even up to 1939 most town planning was permissive and only with the war did compulsory planning on a national basis come to be developed and extended to include the building of New Towns. W. Ashworth, *The Genesis of Modern British Town Planning*, 1954. See CONURBATION, NEIGHBOURHOOD, URBAN SOCIOLOGY, ZONING.   P.H.M.

transhumance. The movement of a people from one territory to another in a customarily organized manner. It differs from nomadism in that the cycle is an annual and seasonal one rather than a longer period migration lasting several years. Examples of people who are transhumant are the Nuer and other peoples of the Upper Nile, some Lapps, and other pastoral peoples, especially in India and Pakistan who move their herds to the mountains in summer and back in the winter. See NOMADS; NOMADISM.　　　G.D.M.

tribe. A *tribe* is a socially cohesive unit associated with a territory, the members of which regard themselves as politically autonomous. Sometimes tribes are split up into sections, especially where the territory is large in relation to the size of population. Very often a tribe will possess a distinctive dialect. Many African peoples, especially in Central and Southern Africa, are tribalized, although the characteristics of tribalism are being corroded by migration and urban life.

Troeltsch, Ernst (1865–1923). German theologian, social historian and sociologist of religion. His *magnum opus*, *Die Sozial Lehrer der christlischen Kirchen und Gruppen*, 1911, was translated *The Social Teaching of the Christian Churches* in 1931.

Turgot, Anne Robert Jacques, Marquis (1727–1781). French administrator and Contrôleur Général des Finances to Louis XVI. As a young man he wrote *Deux discours sur l'histoire universelle*, a courteous but radical answer to Bossuet's famous work on universal history. It contains a theory of social progress and of human development. See *Turgot on Progress, Sociology and Economics*, 1973, translated and edited by R. L. Meek.

Tylor, Sir Edward Burnett (1832–1917). English anthropologist; his most important contribution lies in his treatment of culture, which he defined as 'that complex whole which includes knowledge, belief, art, morals, law, custom and any other capabilities and habits acquired by man as a member of society'. *Primitive Culture*, 1871, presents his doctrine of survivals – the view that curious, non-realistic, non-functional customs and beliefs in modern societies are relics of the cultural past, and his theory of animism. Animism, 'the general doctrine of souls and other spiritual beings', forms the basis of the theory of the development and origins of primitive religion. For Tylor, the principal criteria of cultural growth are development of industrial arts, extent of scientific knowledge, type of religion, extent of social and political organization. He originated the method of adhesions based on probability, and he helped to establish comparative religion. Other works include *Anahuac*, 1861; *Researches into Early History of Mankind*, 1865; and *Anthropology*, 1896.　　　G.D.M.

type; typology. A *type* or class is an abstract category having empirical reference. Thus there is a type of stratified society known as a caste society, where members are also members of a social category known as a caste and such membership is related *inter alia* to both occupation and ritual pollution. Such a stratified society may be distinguished from another known as a class society. Or again, there is a type of social group known as a dyadic group, consisting of two and only two members. Individual examples may be found for such types which wholly fit. An *ideal type* is a concept of a special kind and examples may only approximate to the type. See IDEAL TYPE.

A *typology* is no more than a classification. A classification may be an *ad hoc* one such as flesh, fish and fowl, where the categories are neither exhaustive nor mutually exclusive. On the other hand it may be a more useful attempt to provide for complete distribution of the elements so that none is left over and no doubt remains as to which category an element belongs to. Such a typology may be useful, but it does not constitute a theory and by itself cannot produce a theory. Typologies should, therefore, be related to one or more hypotheses which it is desired to test, and accordingly a typology to be useful must be dependent upon the general aims of the study, the nature of the hypothesis which is being entertained, and the techniques relevant and available for testing it. It follows that there is nothing sacrosanct about a typology; it is either useful or not, and there may be many possible typologies relevant to the analysis of the same lot of data. G.D.M.

U

understanding. See HERMENEUTICS.

unilineal. See DESCENT.

urbanization. A term which is used in two senses, demographically and sociologically. The demographic use with its statistical orientation refers to the proportion of a total population living in places of given size. It will be appreciated that there are many definitions of what constitutes an urban population as distinct from a rural one. Such definitions are variously determined by political, administrative, historical and cultural factors. The sociological use of the term is broader, encompassing the notion of a social process which at once is the cause and the consequence of a change in man's way of life, and in which conscious and deliberate planning assumes a greater and greater role. An influential contribution to the discussion is Louis Wirth's 'Urbanism as a Way of Life' (see P. K. Hatt and A. J. Reiss Jr., eds., *Cities and Society: The Revised Reader in Urban Sociology*, 1957) in which he argues that the city, characterized by size, density and heterogeneity is the main determinant of various kinds of social behaviour. In the urban areas we find increasing secondary-group relationships, voluntary associations, a plurality of norms and vagueness with respect to their definition, increasing secularization and segmentary roles.

See P. M. Hauser and L. F. Schnore (eds.), *The Study of Urbanization*, 1965, especially ch. 5 by G. Sjoberg, 'Theory and Research in Urban Sociology'. See URBAN SOCIOLOGY.   G.D.M.

urban sociology. A branch of sociological studies focusing primarily on urban aspects of man's social life and thus related to most other branches of the subject without always very clear distinctions. It ranges from studies of city life, ancient, medieval and modern, often comparative studies, to small scale studies of human interaction in urban communities, suburbs, neighbourhoods and the like. The former is represented by some of the classics of sociology such as *La Cité Antique* by N. D. Fustel de Coulanges, 1864, translated *The Ancient City*, 1874; *Medieval Cities* by Henri Pirenne, 1925; and Max Weber's *The City* (translated 1958) originally part of his *Wirtschaft und Gesellschaft*. More modern studies include G. Sjoberg's *The Pre-Industrial City*, 1960, and R. E. Dickinson's *The West European City*, 2nd edition, 1961. Variously these have a religious, economic or geographical slant as well as being sociological. The latter is represented by a host of inquiries carried out in the 1950s such as *Living in Towns*, 1953, by L. Kuper; *Family and Neighbourhood*, 1956, by J. M. Mogey; *Neighbourhood and*

Community, 1951, by G. D. Mitchell *et al.*; *Changing Attitudes through Social Contact* by L. Festinger and H. H. Kelley, 1951.

Many important urban sociological writings were the product of the Chicago School in the 1920s, such as *The City*, 1925, by R. Park and E. Burgess, Louis Wirth's *The Ghetto*, 1928, and H. Zorbaugh's *The Gold Coast and the Slum*, 1929. Wirth also advanced a theory of urbanism which has proved a powerful contribution to studies of urban development. Although many of the Chicago publications were descriptive there was a strong tendency to adopt a theoretical approach from biology for Park and Burgess made much of the concept of social ecology. Their concentric ring theory of development whilst being reasonable when applied to Chicago is nevertheless very limiting. Generally, since Max Weber's time, the study of cities has tended to be too nationalistic and insufficiently comparative. Some interesting developments have occurred in studies of the political life of cities and here Scott Greer's work in America is of interest, see his *The Urbane View*, 1972. There are also studies of Third World cities in Africa and Latin America. Another development has been in the relationship of sociological studies to urban planning, either substantively as in studies of New Towns, e.g. H. Orlans's *Stevenage: a sociological study of a new town*, 1952, or in relation to public participation; e.g. N. Dennis's *Public Participation and Planners Blight*, 1972. For a general view of urban sociological inquiries see P. K. Hatt and A. J. Reiss, *Cities and Society*, 1951, and P. Mann's *An Approach to Urban Sociology*, 1965. See URBANIZATION.   G.D.M.

utilitarianism. This is a philosophical outlook usually associated with the name of Jeremy Bentham (1748–1832) in whose thought ethics and psychology rest on the fundamental fact that pleasure is better than pain. This principle is, or should be, the guide to life, but unfortunately prejudice and ignorance prevent people from making decisions in accordance with this view. *Utility* is the greatest happiness of the greatest number. The maximization of utility is the proper end of humankind. Thus, he argued, good motives are those leading to a harmony of the individual's interest with those of others. Utilitarianism then is a moral theory with social implications which holds that nothing is desired for its own sake, only for the pleasure it provides. Moreover, as no one kind of pleasure is superior in itself to any other kind the purpose of moral rules is, or ought to be, to encourage behaviour which will increase pleasure and reduce pain, alternatively to discourage behaviour which deprives people of pleasure. The application of this view to economics, administration and law was Bentham's chief activity. Thus the basic principle for testing the adequacy of any law or act of administration is a calculus of pain and pleasure. Early English sociology was much influenced by utilitarianism, especially is this seen in the case of Spencer; it came under severe criticism from Durkheim. It remains a powerful element in modern economic thought.   G.D.M.

utopia. The *Utopia* of Sir Thomas More was printed in Louvain in 1516. It is one of the long series of works of social criticism and exemplification through the creation of an imaginary state and society which stretches from the myth of Atlantis in Plato's *Timaeus* to modern science fiction. It has given its name

235

to the genre. The device of a *Utopia* has many advantages: it permits the conduct of free 'thought experiments' in sociology; it allows an author to escape censure under the cloak of fiction and yet be critical of his own society; it enables the writer to hold constant in his mind certain features of society and, carrying others to their logical extremes, to examine their consequences. It is, in fact, a kind of creative political and sociological play. Most Utopias are deliberately placed in social isolation so that extraneous forces do not work on their social structures. They are to be found, therefore, on remote islands or other planets, in the forgotten past or the unrealized future.

The adjective *utopian* is employed as one of dismissal or abuse. Utopia is nowhere; therefore it is nothing; proposals one dislikes can therefore be condemned by association with such vain fancies through the use of the adjective. *Utopian socialism* is a term by which Marx abused those writers with whom he disagreed.

Karl Mannheim divided *ideology* (*q.v.*) into two species. Ideology proper, which is directed to the stability of the present or the restoration of the past, and Utopia, which is the ideology of revolt, of religious and political aspiration, of apocalyptic and messianic dreams, of the future. This usage has not been widely adopted, but the distinction is of real importance both for political sociology and the sociology of knowledge. It is also helpful in the examination and distinction of different forms of class consciousness in polar opposition to each other. See IDEOLOGY.   D.G.M.

V

value. The term *value* is of importance to economics, sociology and philosophy. In economics the *theory of value* is usually co-terminous with the *theory of price*, but in Marxist economics this is not completely the case for value there is implicated in a theory of the distribution of the goods and services produced in a given economic order and in an assessment of the justice of this distribution. To the sociologist, values are constituent facts of social structure. The sociologist does not try to assess their intrinsic worth, but he treats them as scarce objects of socially conditioned desire, unevenly distributed and differentially ranked. In the Durkheimian sense of *social fact* they are given data for each individual, and constrain social behaviour towards them. This approach is often found emotionally cold and repulsive by social reformers, but values treated sociologically as structural elements largely derived from social interaction are essential constituents of social theory and their study an essential object of sociological research.

The philosophical treatment of values is part of ethics, political philosophy and aesthetics. The problems raised have reached no agreed solution and the answers offered range from the timeless metaphysical status awarded value by Platonism to the dismissal of questions of value as meaningless and indiscussable. This is not to dismiss philosophical analysis. Nihilism and relativism about values are *de facto* untenable. At the least philosophy has disposed of many plausible and slippery errors about value. Perhaps a philosophy which engaged itself directly with the data of sociology, anthropology and psychology can do more. In all these disciplines philosophical as well as factual questions about values are found to be inescapable and fundamental. D.G.M.

variable. In the most general usage a variable is any quantity that varies. More precisely, it may be defined as a measurable characteristic which can assume different values in successive individual cases. The sociological usage reflects the more general meaning and the term is often used inter-changeably with 'phenomenon', 'measure', 'scale', 'indicator' or even 'concept'. Mathematical usage is more clearly defined and different types of variables possessing different properties are recognized. The simplest is the *nominal* measure, a variable (such as sex or religion) composed of two or more categories. More complex is the *ordinal* variable (such as educational level with categories such as 'O' level, 'A' level and 'Honours Degree') where the categories can be considered as a scale. Finally there are *interval* and *ratio* variables (such as age and income) in which distances and ratios within a scale are meaningful.

Much empirical sociology takes the form of *variable analysis*, i.e. investigating the relationship between different variables; such for example as religion and suicide. It is usual, when this sort of association is made between two variables, to term one the *independent variable* and the other the *dependent variable*. This implies that for the purposes of investigation it is assumed that a change in the former brings about a change in the latter. The great problem in this context is to know to what extent it is legitimate to infer that such a relationship is causal.

Another issue of similar concern is that relating to the adequacy of representation of the complexity and diversity of the social world in terms of simple unitary variables and their relationships. Critics argue that human action is meaningful and interpretative and therefore cannot be treated as a variable. It follows that it cannot be measured in the same way as objects in the natural world. These issues are discussed by H. Blumer in 'Sociological Analysis and the Variable', *American Sociological Review*, vol. 21, 1956.

B.H.A.R.

variate. A *variate* or random variable is a quantity which may take one of the values of a specified set with a specified frequency or probability. 'It is defined not just by a set of permissible values, like an ordinary mathematical variable, but by an associated frequency (probability) function expressing how often these values appear in the situation under discussion.' (See M. G. Kendall and W. R. Buckland, *A Dictionary of Statistical Terms*, 1957.)

Veblen, Thorstein Bunde (1857–1929). American economist and sociologist; an exponent of technologically-determined evolutionary theory. In his works is to be found much of modern social-action theory. He founded the 'institutional school'. *The Theory of Leisure Class*, 1899, presents a critique of social life in contemporary America, it attacks the view that true success consists in becoming one of the leisure class. Veblen himself, in the belief that man develops in so far as he is efficient, favoured a technocratic society in which the instinct of workmanship is valued; the leisure class, sheltered from direct contact with the environment, is less ready to adapt to changing conditions, and thus it retards development. Veblen's other works advance this theory and analyse the diverse aspects of capitalism; they include *Theory of Business Enterprise*, 1904; *The Instinct of Workmanship*, 1914; *The Engineers and the Price System*, 1921; and *Absentee Ownership and Business Enterprise in Recent Times*, 1923.

G.D.M.

verstehen. See INTERPRETATIVE SOCIOLOGY.

Vico, Giovanni Battista (1668–1744). Italian jurist, philosopher and sociologist. Professor of Rhetoric at Naples University. His main work was *Principii di una scienza nuova d'intorno alla natura comune delle nazione*, 1725, popularly known as *The New Science*, which attempted a philosophy of history. Vico expounded his views on particular societies and races in which he argued that social institutions such as religion, marriage and sepulture were common to mankind. He held a cyclical view of social change but allowed for social development in which he saw certain principles to be operative. The first stage of social life was characterized by explanations of society in religious categories, and feelings took precedence over reason;

society was theocratic. The second stage was characterized by a belief in heroic action and appropriate values; society was aristocratic. The third stage was humanistic and more rational; society was monarchical or republican. But at each cycle social life was elevated to a new level basing achievements on the successes of previous epochs. He understood the difference between the study of nature and history, the latter depending *inter alia* on a subjective understanding of human motives, values and originations. In this he anticipated the ideas of Dilthey and Weber.   G.D.M.

Vierkandt, Alfred (1867–1953). German ethnologist and sociologist; he elaborated the phenomenological method and applied it. He argued that the chief task of sociology is the systematization of social phenomena; the latter are to be reduced to their ultimate *a priori* forms by the phenomenological method of ideational abstraction. This involves inner contemplation of instances of social life in order to clarify the forms behind them. The method also allows of an understanding of man's mental life. Vierkandt treats societies as systematic wholes with a life and superior spirit of their own, independent of the individuals bound together by mutual dependence who comprise them, and as showing varying degrees of solidarity. He employed Tönnies's twin concepts of *Gemeinschaft* and *Gesellschaft*. His main work was *Gesellschaftslehre*, 1923, revised edition, 1928.   G.D.M.

W

Ward, Lester Frank (1841–1913). American palaeobotanist and sociologist, his systematic sociology hardly influenced American thought on the subject, although subsequently he has been venerated as one of its founding fathers. He was more interested in studying the functioning of society than its structure. Borrowing his ideas both from Comte and Spencer, he asserted that the four stages of evolution were cosmogeny, biogeny, anthropogeny and sociogeny. Like Comte, he distinguished between social statics and social dynamics; the former deals with the formation of structures and with equilibration, the latter with social processes. Besides 'pure' sociology, he described 'applied' sociology which is concerned with what he called *social telesis*, or purposive action by man designed to influence his condition. *Synergy* is a major factor in the formation, equilibration and development of structures; a creative synthesis, it moulds antithetical social forces into new forms. The three basic principles of social dynamics are differences of social potential, innovation and conation. He was interested in sociological laws such as the law of least effort, which is measured in terms of pain and pleasure. He favoured the comparative method, but his anti-individualistic outlook failed to commend itself to American public opinion, especially as he believed in state action to reform society based on the sociologically informed will of the electorate. His ideas were very Comtean. Ward's main works were: *Dynamic Sociology*, 1883; *Psychic Factors of Civilisation*, 1893; *Outlines of Sociology*, 1898; *Pure Sociology*, 1903; and *Applied Sociology*, 1906.   G.D.M.

Warner, William Lloyd (1898–1970). American anthropologist, author of a large study of social stratification in a New England town published as *The Yankee City Series*.

Webb, Sidney (1859–1947) **and Beatrice** (1858–1943) (**Lord and Lady Passfield**). English socialists and reformers; they founded the London School of Economics in 1895; had great influence on the Labour Movement and on the theory of trade unionism. Their works (joint unless stated) include *The Co-operative Movement in Great Britain*, 1891, by Beatrice Webb; *History of Trade Unionism*, 1894; *Industrial Democracy*, 1897; *The Decay of Capitalist Civilisation*, 1923; *Soviet Communism, a new Civilisation?* 1935; *My Apprenticeship*, 1926, by Beatrice Webb; *Our Partnership*, 1948, by Beatrice Webb; and *Methods of Social Study*, 1932, by Beatrice Webb. Sidney Webb contributed to the *Fabian Essays*, 1889, and served on the London County Council from 1892 to 1910; he was a member of the Royal Commission on Trade Union Law (1906) and a Member of Parliament (1922), serving on the

Labour Party Executive from 1915–25. Beatrice Webb (née Potter) collaborated with Charles Booth on his survey; served on the Royal Commission on the Poor Law – both being responsible for the Minority Report. Her *Methods of Social Study* draws attention to then little-used research techniques and sums up her experience of social research. See FABIANS. G.D.M.

Weber, Alfred (1868–1958). Much influenced by his elder brother Max Weber, he developed a view of sociology that sought to focus attention on the nature of modern civilization. His approach was historical and comparative. In his later work he emphasized the crisis of modern western society. Thus at the close of his *Einführung in die Soziologie*, 1955, he writes: 'Die Soziologie ist ein Tochter der Krise, der grössten Krise, die das Abendland bisher durchgemacht hat.' His cultural sociology is an attempt to answer the questions such an analysis suggests. Civilizations have their own individuality, their own pattern of development, and their rise and fall, or (cf. Oswald Spengler) their passage through stages of a seasonal kind.

Weber distinguished between *civilization* and *culture*: the former consists of the whole of positive knowledge, technology and science, and is universally valid and communicable; the latter expresses the soul of a people, it is unique, it develops in fits and starts, it is uncommunicable. His main work is *Kulturgeschichte als Kultursoziologie*, 1935. G.D.M.

Weber, Max (1864–1920). Max Weber was born in Erfurt, Thuringia, and lived most of his early life in Berlin. His initial studies were in the fields of law and legal history, but they developed to include many other aspects of the arts and social sciences. He held chairs in Freiburg, Heidelberg and Munich.

Three ideas constitute the essence of Weber's contribution to the methodology of the social sciences; firstly, the paradigm of reducibility of sociological concepts to actions of individuals; the paradigm of reducibility amounts to the practice of explaining the meaning of words denoting social conditions and positions in terms of the actions of individuals. Formulating his paradigm, Weber simply erected into a methodological canon what always was the practice of all sound thinkers; but it was an important step forward because it makes a great difference whether a procedure is intuitive or reasoned out.

The requirement of 'wertfreiheit', which has been translated as value-freedom or ethical neutrality, or the paradigm of non-valuation, has often been interpreted as enjoining upon the sociologist an indifference to the ills of mankind. However, it can best be regarded as a methodological and semantic rule for classifying propositions. Naturally, in view of the emotional loading of all the words which describe human relations, the strict adherence to this ideal is impossible, but the same is true of ideals such as logical consistency or clarity, which are universally upheld, though only intermittently attained. The validity of a methodological precept is not a matter of truth, but of heuristic utility, and by definition a precept cannot be neutral.

The concept of *ideal type* has been discussed elsewhere in the dictionary. Weber's supremacy is due to his unsurpassed ability for making or suggesting inductive generalizations. He compared social structures and their functioning, noting differences as carefully as resemblances, and trying to relate isolated features to their structural contexts. When information on the structure of the society in which he was interested was lacking, he made truly herculean efforts to extract it from the sources. In spite of many serious errors, his works on China, India and Israel still stand unrivalled as functionalist analyses of these societies, revealing their inner springs, and showing the mutual dependence of culture and society. Weber's *Agrarverhältnisse in Altertum* (1901) also remains unique. For it is neither an economic history, nor a social history (as it is commonly understood), nor a political nor a military, but a truly structural history, which shows how economic changes influenced religion, how innovations in tactics brought about transformations of social stratification, how distribution of political power impeded the growth of capitalism and so on. All the time he tries to trace dynamic relations between various aspects of social life.

Max Weber studied history mainly in order to make comparisons. His case studies are strewn with references to other situations, and with generalizations or hints at possible generalizations. He was not the first to resort to comparisons in order to arrive at generalizations, but he has shown better than any other writer that the knowledge of other societies and the consequent ability to compare, aids enormously the analysis of any given society, and particularly the discovery of causal relationships. His greatness can be measured by the profusion of extremely interesting hypotheses which can be found in his works, each of which could be a subject for a book if it were examined in the light of comparative data available today.

Weber's works are focused on the problem of the conditions which permitted the rise of capitalism. This preoccupation stems directly from Marx, and was shared by many scholars, particularly in Germany. The originality of Weber's approach consisted in something very simple. In order to discover the causes of the rise of capitalism, other scholars studied in great detail the process of its growth, thus confining their attention to western Europe. He, on the other hand, conceived the brilliant idea of throwing light on this problem by concentrating on cases where capitalism failed to develop. Coupled with masterly execution this approach gave to his works a stamp of uniqueness. The comparative point of view, moreover, saved him from pitfalls into which many others fell: he knew that neither the desire for pecuniary gain, nor vast accumulations of liquid wealth were in any way peculiar to the countries where capitalism developed, and could not, therefore, be regarded as crucial factors.

Nothing contributed more to Weber's fame than his essay on Protestant ethics and the rise of capitalism, although it contains no structural analysis, so characteristic of the bulk of his works. However, he nowhere claimed that the Calvinist ethic was the sole cause of the rise of capitalism. Even if in some cases Weber over-estimated the efficacity of religious beliefs in directly determining behaviour in economic matters, he considers both directions of influence: he explains the stultification and decay of capitalism in the ancient world in terms of structures of power, without bringing in the 'economic ethics' as an independent factor.

As he died before completing his final synthesis many of his statements can be misunderstood unless considered in the light of his other works. See R.

Bendix, *Max Weber: An Intellectual Portrait*, 1960, for an appraisal of his principal works, and also S. L. Andreski, 'Method and Substantive Theory in Max Weber' in *British Journal of Sociology*, XV, 1, 1964 (reprinted in *Elements of Comparative Sociology*, 1964, chs. 5 and 13); J. Freund, *The Sociology of Max Weber*, 1968.   S.L.A.

Westermarck, Edward Alexander (1862–1939). Finnish philosopher and sociologist who taught in the Abo Academy as well as at the University of Helsinki. He also held a chair of sociology in the University of London. He carried out fieldwork in Morocco which resulted in *Ritual and Belief in Morocco* (2 vols.), 1926. He was the author of *The History of Human Marriage*, 1889, the fifth edition appearing in 1921 to be followed in 1926 by his more popular work, *A Short History of Marriage*. Westermarck's interest in the sociology of moral ideas came to fruition in his large work *The Origin and Development of the Moral Ideas* (2 vols.), 1906 and 1908.   G.D.M.

Witchcraft. See MAGIC.

Worms, René (1867–1926). French sociologist who advanced the organismic view of human society in *Organisme et société*, 1896, but progressively limited the application of this concept and in *Sociologie, sa nature, son contenu, ses attaches*, 1926, he put forward a view that the State has a life of its own and that society is subject to laws of natural development. He founded the *Revue internationale de Sociologie* in 1893, in opposition to *L'Année Sociologique*.   G.D.M.

243

Z

Zeitgeist A German word referring to the thought or feeling characteristic of a generation or a people in a period of time.

Znaniecki, Florian (1882–1958). Polish sociologist who was resident in U.S.A.; his important contributions lie in his work on systems and in his studies of social groups and specific social roles. *The Polish Peasant in Europe and America*, 1918–20, written with W. I. Thomas, studies changes in personality and social structure of Polish communities after migration, and analyses these changes, together with activity, situation, character, etc. in terms of attitudes and values. *The Social Role of the Man of Knowledge*, 1940, discusses this role in the belief that therein lies a useful approach to the sociology of knowledge. Znaniecki's ideas about the closed system are elaborated and developed in *Laws of Social Psychology*, 1925; *The Methodology of Sociology*, 1934; and *Cultural Sciences: Their Origin and Development*, 1952. He argued that the task of the sociologist is to determine the limits and elements of the system under investigation, and to discover causal relationships and functional dependencies.   G.D.M.

zone; zoning. A *zone* is an area of a city characterized by some particular physical or social feature or features. Thus a city may be divided into one or more business, commercial, manufacturing and residential zones according to the use to which buildings are put. Sociologically, the zones distinguished may reflect differential degrees of wealth or poverty, crime or social amenities. The practice of *zoning*, however, is a matter of official policy regarding the treatment of city areas so that differing treatment is related to planned development. Thus certain building restrictions may operate to guide the development of, say for example, a commercial and shopping zone so that it does not spread in an undesirable direction. Zoning was first practised in Germany but introduced into Britain through the Town Planning Act of 1909, and was shortly afterwards practised in many large American cities.
                                                    G.D.M.